CONTEMPORARY ECONOMIC ISSUES IN DEVELOPING COUNTRIES

CONTEMPORARY ECONOMIC ISSUES IN DEVELOPING COUNTRIES

John Baffoe-Bonnie and Mohammed Khayum

PRAEGER

Westport, Connecticut
London

Library of Congress Cataloging-in-Publication Data

Baffoe-Bonnie, John.
Contemporary economic issues in developing countries / John Baffoe-Bonnie and Mohammed Khayum.
p. cm.
Includes bibliographical references and index.
ISBN 0–275–97454–5 (alk. paper)
1. Developing countries—Economic conditions—20th century. I. Khayum, Mohammed F. II. Title.
HC59.7.B237 2003
330.9172'4—dc21 2002021575

British Library Cataloguing in Publication Data is available.

Library of Congress Catalog Card Number: 2002021575
ISBN: 0-275-97454-5

First published in 2003

Praeger Publishers, 88 Post Road West, Westport, CT 06881
An imprint of Greenwood Publishing Group, Inc.
www.praeger.com

Printed in the United States of America

The paper used in this book complies with the Permanent Paper Standard issued by the National Information Standards Organization (Z39.48-1984).

10 9 8 7 6 5 4 3 2 1

Contents

Illustrations

FIGURES

TABLES

Preface

In spite of the proliferation of writing and research under the rubric of the economics of developing countries, there are critical unresolved issues about the process and effectiveness of alternative strategies for economic development. Most of these issues have centered on the economic problems of developing countries. However, development strategies are often based on the experiences of modern advanced economies, which typically involve differences in internal circumstances and in the global economic environment within which they experienced economic development. The deepening economic crises within a sizable number of developing countries, despite decades of implementation of seemingly appropriate macroeconomic policies, have generated a search for a new paradigm of development that reflects the intrinsic national differences in institutions, time preferences, technical parameters, basic motivation, and values.

The purpose of this book is to shed light on some of the existing and new issues that are emerging with increased globalization, the advent of the "information age," and changes in the global economic structure that have occurred in the past decade. Although some of these issues are well noted in the development literature, the authors in this book present variant views. The composition of the book therefore reflects many diverse areas and ideas. The book, which is composed of contributions by experienced economists with different views, is designed to evaluate both the theoretical and the empirical frameworks of a number of contemporary issues and provide related policy perspectives where necessary.

The book is also a combination of technical and nontechnical expositions of the issues, which are discussed in undergraduate development and macroeconomics courses. The topics in the book will undoubtedly serve as a supplementary reading to graduate students in development economics classes. The book is therefore primarily aimed at undergraduate and graduate students in economic development and macroeconomics courses, but it is equally targeted at a wide range of readers, both those who have some background in development issues and those who are new in the field.

Acknowledgments

A project such as this book is always a collective effort of many people. However, one colleague, Professor John Terrell at Pennsylvania State University, is most instrumental in this project. He read through all the chapters and made valuable corrections and suggestions. A note of thanks to Professor Adam Sorkin for reviewing early proposals for this book. We are also indebted to Professor David Shapiro of Pennsylvania State University for his active encouragement and enthusiasm when the idea of writing a book was discussed with him. The hard work of one of his students, Sean Bresnan, on this project is highly appreciated.

We thank all the contributors for their commitment and enthusiasm in making this book a reality, providing excellent chapters that address pertinent and contemporary issues in developing economies.

Finally, we dedicate this book to our dear wives, Dr. Agnes B. Baffoe-Bonnie and Desiree Khayum. They have been consistent with their encouragement and support throughout the course of this project.

1

Introduction

John Baffoe-Bonnie and Mohammed Khayum

The world economy experienced tremendous change over the course of the previous century. Real per capita gross domestic product of the world grew at a faster rate than preceding centuries,[1] and profound changes occurred in science, technology,[2] the international financial system,[3] and the well-being of individuals across countries.[4] A basic indicator such as life expectancy is highly illustrative of the extent of these changes. In the century prior to 1900 there was minimal improvement in the average lifespan of people in Asia, Africa, and Latin America. However, in the twentieth century, life expectancy in developing countries increased from twenty-six years in 1900 to sixty-four years by the late 1990s while in developed countries the corresponding figures were forty-six years and seventy-eight years over the same time period. Amidst these indications of human progress in the preceding century, there is also evidence that it was a century of considerable unevenness in economic performance across countries and over time (Maddison, 2001). It is the latter evidence that frames much of the contemporary discussion of the nature and sources of economic development especially with regard to developing countries.

Indeed, as Lucas (1988, p. 3) argued, the problem of economic development is that of "accounting for the observed pattern, across countries and across time, in levels and rates of growth of per capita income." Based on accumulated evidence, key features of the observed pattern—often described as development facts—are: considerable disparity in per capita output across countries and regions, with differences as high as a factor of 20 between the poorest and richest regions of the world (Parente and Prescott, 1991); a rise in world income inequality, indicated by an increase in the Gini coefficient[5] from 0.40 to 0.48 between 1900 and 2000 (IMF, 2000); high persistence in the position of countries at the upper and lower tails of the distribution of per capita output, indicated by roughly the same group of countries comprising the highest and lowest income quartiles at both the beginning and end of the twentieth century (Maddison, 1995); less persistence in the position of countries in the two middle quartiles of the distribution of per capita output between 1900 and 2000 (IMF, 2000); and, an upward shift in the distribution of per capita output, indicative of increased income growth across countries over time.[6]

Within the related literature on theories of economic development, individual models fail to account for all of the development facts (Schmitz, 1993). Moreover, research efforts spanning several decades have resulted in an increasingly multidimensional approach when attempting to account for the long-term performance of developing countries. This approach invariably involves aspects of economic theory, econometric methods, social, political, demographic, and cultural issues (Ray, 2000). Nonetheless, a number of distinct emphases can be identified in contemporary theorizing about the development process. For instance, the neoclassical theory of growth,[7] among the earliest to tackle the stylized development facts, relies on differences in physical capital per person across countries as the explanation for observed patterns. Models of the capital accumulation process and the role played by saving, investment, and population dynamics have been key contributions of this theory. Yet, doubts about the consistency of the conclusions of the neoclassical growth theory with differences in per capita income and physical capital across nations paved the way for newer theories of growth.

The more recent models of economic growth, characterized as endogenous growth models, stress differences in human capital, or education, across countries, to explain the diversity in international per capita incomes (Lucas, 1988; Mankiw, Romer, and Weil, 1992). The key idea is that lower levels of physical capital and output per person in poorer countries arise because other inputs are scarce, particularly, capital inputs complementary to physical capital. According to many of the endogenous growth models, the missing capital in many developing countries is human capital.

Accordingly, physical capital does not gravitate to developing countries where it is scarce because of the absence of a skilled workforce. Doubts about whether human capital is indeed the driving force behind economic growth have resulted in alternative hypotheses about the missing capital in developing countries. Parente and Prescott (1991), for example, identify firm-specific or business capital as the missing capital in developing countries. They contend that in developing countries, the limited opportunities to invest physical capital created by entrepreneurs act as deterrents to the movement of physical capital in these countries. Thus, it is the differences across countries in the incentives provided to entrepreneurs to create businesses and adopt technologies that account for the differences in growth rates. One implication of this approach is that policies of deregulation and privatization often recommended by the International Monetary Fund (IMF) and World Bank represent important steps in creating the missing business or firm-specific capital. Another implication of this approach is that because development facts are only consistent with a model in which technology differs across countries, identifying the barriers to technology adoption is an important first step in addressing the issue of slow economic growth.

One barrier to the adoption of new technology lies in the nature of social arrangements. This idea is further developed in the framework that stresses the importance of social capability in promoting economic development. According to this approach, social factors and arrangements such as the legal and institutional framework of a country have an important impact on a country's ability to experience sustained increases in productivity. Temple and Johnson (1998) show that rates of total factor productivity growth are related to a country's initial level of social development and that social development helps to explain polarization in world incomes. Empirical results based on the social capability model suggest that socially traditional countries are unlikely to catch up to others and are likely to fall further behind. In contrast, results indicate that there are opportunities for changing the relative position of developing countries that are socially advanced. The relative importance of investments in physical capital and schooling appears to vary with the extent of social development. In particular, schooling is important at low levels of social development, but physical capital becomes more important at higher levels. The appropriateness of policies suggested by the neoclassical and endogenous growth models, therefore, depends on the level of social development within developing countries.

Within the growth theory framework, attempts to decompose growth into component parts have typically attributed no more than 50 percent of growth in output to growth in labor and capital inputs, taking into account changes in the quality of these inputs. Thus, about half of the growth in output of both developed and developing countries would be explained by technological and other factors, such as institutional change. Empirical studies within this framework show that there are some key determinants of the growth rate of real GDP per capita. These include a positive relationship for the initial quantity of human capital in the form of educational attainment and health, a negative relationship with the ratio of government consumption to GDP as well as for measures of distortions of markets and political instability.

Globalization phenomena and its implications for integration and interdependence among economies also serve to highlight the key challenge of coping with poverty and inequality. At the same time, this process of integration raises new challenges in areas related to international public goods and externalities such as creating a stable international monetary system and reducing environmental degradation.

This book provides insights on these challenges by examining a range of issues that currently face developing countries. The book is divided into fourteen chapters covering an overview of development patterns, debt problems, demographic issues, the linkage between the environment and economic development, stabilization policies, corruption, rent-seeking, and empirical issues related to consumers' behavior and the impact of government behavior on economic growth. In this chapter, we present a synopsis of each of the topics discussed in this book.

One of the current concerns of the governments of both developing and developed countries is the ongoing developing countries' debt crisis. The urgency of the debt problem is self-evident. For almost every developing country, the financial upheaval of the 1980s has set back economic development by a decade or more. Widespread poverty has intensified as countries struggle under enormous debt burdens, and for most of these countries repayment of the debt is nowhere in sight.

The debt crisis is not without internal and external financial problems. The inability of the debtor countries to service their debt has created global financial instability. The recent financial crisis in Japan, Mexico, Brazil, and other emerging-market countries is partly due to the widespread defaults on the foreign debts of the developing countries.

In chapter 2, John Loxley presents a comprehensive discussion of lessons that should be learned from the financial disturbances, and argues that unless these lessons are confronted seriously and the debt crisis managed effectively, the debt crisis is likely to persist. In particular, he points out that the asymmetry in managing the debt crisis, where the interests of the creditor countries are given paramountcy over the debtor countries, needs to be addressed. He concludes by stressing that the inability of debtor countries to be autonomous in economic development policies is due to the IMF, the World Bank, and other international financial institutions' loan conditionality and policy control in the debtor countries.

Rapid population growth continues to be a development problem. The cost of such rapid growth in relation to food balance was first noted by Malthus's (1798) thesis. Although food production has consistently grown faster than population since 1945, there is still a growing concern by some development economists as to whether this pattern will continue in the future, especially in sub-Saharan Africa, where the population growth has outstripped the rate of growth in food production since the early 1970s. Henry Rempel and Kazi N. Islam in chapter 3 examine food production in the context of changing population in sub-Saharan Africa and suggest policies that might increase Africa's ability to feed its population.

Demographic transition theory currently puts developing countries at the beginning of stage III that is characterized by declining fertility. In this stage, birth rates fall rapidly due to more aggressive family planning programs, improvement in human capital, urbanization, and positive economic development. Indeed, there is enough evidence to indicate that family planning programs and policies that are geared toward economic development have substantial monotonic decreasing impact on the fertility rates of both developed and developing countries.

Sub-Saharan Africa, which had the highest death rate in the early 1980s, has for the past decade experienced slow but declining fertility rates that are attributed to increasing public and private expenditures in the educational sector. This fertility decline, which is more profound in the urban areas than in the rural areas, is projected to continue.

In chapter 4, David Shapiro and B. Oleko Tambashe delve into the fertility transition in sub-Saharan Africa with reference to urbanization. Using data from forty-five demographic and health surveys (DHS) that have been carried out in twenty-six different countries, the authors examine fertility levels, changes in age-specific fertility, and trends in urban and rural areas. The analyses show that residents of urban areas play an important role in the process of fertility transition that is presently unfolding in sub-Saharan Africa. In countries where demographic and health surveys have been carried out, Shapiro and Tambashe analysis suggests a three-stage transition pattern, with fertility initially declining in urban areas but remaining stable in rural areas, then fertility falling in both settings but more rapidly in urban places, and finally fertility declining more in rural than urban areas.

The concept of poverty is common to all societies. In the United States, the emergence of poverty as a national issue occurred as a reaction to the characterization of America as a privately affluent society. In some societies, the term *poverty* is synonymous with the level of development. For many years, poverty has become a standard part of economic and political dialogue in developing countries. It is estimated that almost 70 percent of people living in the developing world are poor. The major conceptual issues associated with poverty are the definition of poverty and how to measure it. These are important issues because they have policy implications.

In chapter 5, John Gafar details some of these conceptual problems and provides poverty estimates using different poverty measures for some countries in the Caribbean. In his discussion of diverse poverty reduction policies, Gafar emphasizes that although economic growth remains the key to poverty reduction, "savage capitalism needs to be supplemented with safety nets for the benefit of the poor and the miserable." He concludes the chapter by outlining the ethnic conflicts and ethnic poverty that are generating a chasm and impending national disintegration in the Caribbean country of Guyana.

Environmental problems associated with economic development have increasingly become a major concern to many governments. As a result, several international summits have been held in order to deal with some of the problems. These include the Rio Earth in Brazil in 1994, and the Rio follow-up summit in New York City in 1997. Proposals have been made to enter into environmental treaties modeled after U.S. international trade treaties and to reform and strengthen the United Nations' powers as regards the environment.

In chapter 6, Fidel Ezeala-Harrison models relationships between economic growth and the environment and concludes that the strategy of first promoting economic growth and subsequently tackling the issue of environmental quality is shortsighted and myopic. The author proposes that developing countries simultaneously address both issues, but that success would hinge on support from developed countries that would assist in defraying the opportunity costs of environmental preservation.

Ezeala-Harrison develops his framework within the context of three categories of environmental factors that can constrain the process of economic growth in countries. One category is natural environmental conditions (such as climate) that can influence a population's health and ultimately human resource development. Another set of factors is the negative externalities associated with economic growth (such as pollution) that often result in regulations, or policies that increase production costs and thereby influence the amount of output produced. The third category includes issues of resource depletion and environmental degradation that impact the sustainability of long-term economic growth. Based on these considerations, two types of environmental stress factors are identified from the literature on the relationship between environmental quality and economic growth: depletion stress and pollution stress.

Utilizing the concepts of depletion stress and pollution stress, the author develops an environmental quality trajectory model that addresses the policy choices facing developing countries. In particular, policy makers can use the model to set an environmental quality target as well as a GDP target based on the relationship between the stress factors and gross domestic product (GDP). At the same time, the model is capable of identifying possible levels of environmental degradation (and environmental quality intensity) at each level of GDP. Thus, policy makers can identify growth paths that show how environmental quality changes as GDP changes.

With this model, Ezeala-Harrison suggests that it is possible for developing countries to achieve higher levels of growth without compromising their environmental quality. This would require the implementation of measures that would mitigate the impacts of the three categories of environmental factors on the process of economic growth. He also contends that because the environment is a global public good, the developed countries have a responsibility to provide resources to developing countries for funding plans that can lead to a reduction in environmental degradation.

In chapter 7, John Mukum Mbaku and Mwangi S. Kimenyi examine how government intervention in economic activities creates opportunities for individuals and groups to engage in unproductive activities. Specifically, the focus is on the ways in which governments are influenced to create transfers from certain individuals or groups to other individuals or groups within societies. This process, known as rent-seeking, is suggested to have adverse effects on economic growth through a number of channels. First, the appeal of rent-seeking is directly related to the scope and extent of government intervention in markets. With higher levels of government intervention, there is increased potential for market incentives to be distorted and for resource allocation to be inefficient. Second, rent-seeking permits inefficient firms to remain in operation indefinitely because political allocation replaces economic or market allocation. Third, rent-seeking involves resource use that is socially wasteful because the resources are not used to produce anything. The overall thesis is that rent-seeking activities retard economic growth and wealth creation.

A comparison of rent-seeking behavior between democratic and nondemocratic political systems reveals important differences in the way rent-seeking occurs and how the rents are allocated. In particular, rent-seeking activities in many developing countries reflect a more pervasive role by the state in economic activity. An additional issue identified by the authors is the detrimental effects of rent-seeking on entrepreneurship within developing countries as talented individuals gravitate toward unproductive rent-seeking activities. The authors assemble evidence to support their thesis from previous research as well as from their examination of the experiences of India and Ghana. In addition, it is noted that many of the developing countries that have witnessed economic growth in recent years are those that have instituted economic reforms that emphasized a reduced role for the government in economic activity.

John Mukum Mbaku's article is critical of traditional development models for disregarding the role of laws and institution in the process of economic development. He finds this neglect to be especially problematic in the analysis of corruption and its impact on the process of economic development. In particular, amidst research findings of the severe negative effects of corruption on economic growth as well as social and political development within developing countries, Mbaku contends that public policies have proved incapable of controlling corruption. He suggests that the policy limitations of traditional development models with regard to corruption can be remedied by incorporating insights from the theory of public choice in the design and implementation of relevant policies. These insights include the negotiation and introduction of new rules, institutional reforms, incentive structures, and enforcement mechanisms to reduce the profitability of opportunistic behavior, and thereby, to control corruption.

In his review of the related literature dealing with the causes of corruption within developing countries, Mbaku questions the significance of the explanations provided. Using insights from public choice theory, he suggests that in the absence of adequate laws and their enforcement, opportunistic behavior of politicians and bureaucrats unsurprisingly leads to corruption. Yet, the usual measures for controlling corruption in developing countries are based on the assumption that the agencies or institutions responsible for their implementation and enforcement are reliable, efficient, independent, and devoid of corruption. Mbaku points out, however, that in most developing countries the corruption-controlling institutions are not well constrained by existing law, do not have much independence, and are pervaded by high levels of corruption. Accordingly, a precondition for controlling corruption is the establishment of new constitutional rules and arrangements.

Key factors in the establishment and maintenance of new constitutional rules are the decentralization of political power and the promotion of competition in the economic and political spheres. According to Mbaku this would require a federal governmental system with many autonomous political jurisdictions that accommodate the ethnic diversity and pluralism that exist in many developing countries. Moreover, a constitutionally guaranteed right to migrate freely across political jurisdictions is essential for the maintenance of a viable political system. Overall, success in controlling corruption in developing countries depends on efforts that go far beyond coercive and policing activities associated with traditional strategies. These include an emphasis on new rules and incentive structures to constrain the appeal of opportunistic behavior that is linked to corruption.

The stabilization and economic growth aspects of fiscal and monetary policies in developing economies have long been recognized by economists of different persuasions. However, there is lack of consensus on the suitable fiscal or monetary policy that will effectively promote economic development.

In chapter 9, James C.W. Ahiakpor examines the reasons why modern macroeconomics provides diverse and inconsistent empirical evidence on the macroeconomic effects of fiscal and monetary policies. He emphasizes that there is no consensus on the empirical evidence of inflationary and growth consequences of Keynesian monetary policy as well as the recent supply-side economics that stresses tax cuts, limited government, and privatization. After careful expositions of the classical and Keynesian views on fiscal and monetary policies, he concludes that there is enough empirical evidence for policy makers in both the less developed and the more developed countries to take the classical economists' position seriously. He also suggests a guideline for governments to institute fiscal and monetary policies to promote more efficient economic growth.

In reaction to increasing economic difficulties in developing countries, the International Monetary Fund (IMF) and the World Bank proposed a number of policy measures, termed structural adjustments, aimed at curing the economic ailments of the developing world, especially in Africa. The IMF pressured the governments in the developing countries to liberalize their economic policies as a condition for signing a loan agreement. By 1988, thirty-two African countries had launched structural adjustment operations or borrowed from the IMF to support reform policies. In 1986, the IMF approved its Structural Adjustment Facility (SAF) to assist low-income countries, which had protracted balance-of-payment problems, in adopting medium-term economic policies in an effort to correct what it termed past distortions. This was followed in 1987 by the Enhanced Structural Adjustment Facility (ESAF). Countries wishing to draw from the SAF or ESAF must develop a policy framework proposal in collaboration with the IMF and the World Bank, which broadly outlined a three-year program.

As the economic crisis has worsened, despite over two decades of implementation of the IMF/World Bank programs and policies, a vehement and, at times, bitter debate about the success and failure of the Structural Adjustment Programs (SAP) has erupted. Whereas the IMF and the World Bank claim that the policies worked in countries where the reforms were implemented, citing countries such as Ghana, Egypt, and Tanzania that experienced growth with adjustment, the critics of the SAP contend that the SAP have failed miserably in Africa. For many critics, the IMF/World Bank SAP have deepened the socioeconomic crisis in Africa because they were designed without consideration of the basic features of the African economies: the predominance of subsistence activities, the dependence on external factors of production, the weak institutions, narrow production base combined with inappropriate technology, the neglected informal sector, and the degraded environment. They stress that the SAP will be ineffective in Africa as long as the policies ignore the need for transforming the basic nature of the African economies.

In chapter 10, George B.N. Ayittey provides a comprehensive and commonsense discussion of why the structural adjustment policies failed in Africa. He overwhelmingly attributes the failure to the IMF/World Bank and the African governments. He accuses the IMF/World Bank of designing programs without understanding the institutional framework of most African countries; relying mostly on foreign consultants who at times were inept management consultants; and embarking on poor and overpriced research that had no practical applications to Africa. Through a series of illustrations, he argues that the activities of African governments undermine the effectiveness of the SAP. Ayittey concludes by emphasizing that the reforms did not yield any meaningful benefits to the African countries, partly because "African despots have not been interested in reforming their abominable political and economic system as that would entail a diminution of their power and the erosion of the patronage system they employ to keep their political base."

Chapter 11 provides an overview of recent research on the linkage between economic openness and the economic performance of developing countries. Richard E. Mshomba identifies several methodological problems in recent studies and provides recommendations for future research. He identifies two interrelated difficulties in the literature that explore the role of economic openness in promoting economic development. First, there is the unresolved question of causality. Does economic openness lead to economic development or does economic development cause economic openness to occur? Mshomba contends that studies that are often used to support policies aimed at promoting economic openness do not provide definitive answers. According to Mshomba, this arises because of questionable assumptions—particularly that of homogeneity among countries in terms of the basket of goods and services consumed and, more fundamentally, the assumption that purchasing power parity holds. These assumptions, Mshomba argues, lead to biased results and show up as anomalies and outliers in recent studies.

The second issue is the lack of consensus about appropriate measures of openness. This raises serious questions about the usefulness of empirical tests of the relationship between economic openness and economic development. Mshomba shows that in some widely cited studies it is often assumed that trade orientation and openness are viewed as interchangeable, leading to trade ratios being used as proxies for openness. Moreover, even when more appropriate measures such as the effective rate of protection are used, they are not adjusted for qualitative factors such as infant industry protection and national security considerations that impinge on policies promoting economic openness.

Based on these considerations, Mshomba suggests that researchers and policy makers take into account country heterogeneity and the influence of qualitative factors in economic interaction among countries, and focus more on the microeconomic impact of openness as well as the dynamics of policies promoting openness.

The final three chapters of the book are devoted to empirical analysis of some important issues in developing economies: government expenditure on human capital and its dynamic impact on economic growth; consumers' planning horizon in relation to the level of development; and how defense spending stimulates or retards growth.

There is a general consensus among development economists that government spending and human capital are germane in a country's growth process. Recent endogenous growth models demonstrate that government activities affect the long-run growth rates. In models that include government spending in the production function, any change in government spending shifts the production function and the steady-state level of per capita growth rates. Because government spending is usually financed by taxes, which have a negative impact on output, the total effect of government spending on the long-run growth rates cannot be determined a priori. However, at low rates of taxes, government spending in total output has a positive effect on growth rates, whereas at higher rates of taxes, the taxation effect dominates, and the growth rate of output declines. Human capital accumulation has been characterized as an engine for sustained growth. The basic idea of the proponents of human capital theory in relation to growth is that a nation's growth is primarily determined by the accumulation of human capital. Growth rates differ across countries due to differences in the rates at which countries accumulate human capital over time.

This is precisely what John Baffoe-Bonnie in chapter 12 attempts to demonstrate empirically. Applying an endogenous growth model, Baffoe-Bonnie investigates the dynamic relationship among the growth rates of output, government spending, private investment, and expenditures on education (proxy for human capital) for developing countries at different levels of human development. The general conclusion is that government spending and human capital have only a small effect on the long-run growth rates of developing countries in the study. He also finds that the long-run growth rates of countries that spend more on education do not differ from those that spend less on education.

The two approaches that have been featured prominently in recent work on modeling consumption behavior are the error correction (EC) model based on the work of Davidson et al. (1978) and the random walk (RW) model of consumption developed by Hall (1978). The basic RW model builds on the idea that forward-looking consumers prefer a smooth consumption stream to an uneven one and that under certain conditions they are able to maintain a stable path of consumption. Under the assumption of rational expectations, this outcome forms the basis for the conclusion that current consumption would be the best predictor of future consumption. If any change in consumption was to occur, it would be because of unexpected changes in income, and as an extension, consumption would not track the path of current income very well. There are strong a priori reasons to question the validity of several aspects of the RW model for developing countries. There are factors, however, that make it extremely difficult for most consumers in developing economies to maintain a stable path of consumption. In many developing countries, there is a high degree of uncertainty about income security, due in part to the openness of these economies. In light of these criticisms, Winder (1988) provides a third approach that reconciles the intertemporal utility maximization process underlying the RW model approach with the dynamic specification of consumption obtained from the EC approach. Winder alters the assumption that the planning horizon for forward-looking consumers is the same as their expected lifetime, and arguing that consumers are more likely to make consumption decisions for a much shorter time frame in the future than their expected lifetime, he generates a model of moving planning horizons (MPH) over the consumer's lifetime.

In chapter 13, John Baffoe-Bonnie and Mohammed Khayum apply this MPH model to a group of developing countries that exhibit differences in the level of economic development. They found that consumers in developing countries are more likely to make consumption decisions for a much shorter time frame than their expected lifetime. The average length of a planning period for consumers in a sample of developing countries is about 1.4 years. The results also indicate that the length of planning horizon is positively related to the level of economic development.

Most developing countries allocate a substantial portion of their gross domestic product to defense, in spite of heavy debt burden, poor infrastructure, and a high incidence of poverty associated with developing economies. Economic theory does not tell us the exact direction and magnitude of the economic effects of defense spending on growth. An increase in defense spending may reduce resources in the more productive sectors of the economy, thwart investment and consumption, and thus exert a negative impact on growth. On the other hand, high defense spending may stimulate aggregate demand, which has a positive impact on growth.

Wimal Rankaduwa, in chapter 14, analyzes the impact of defense spending on economic growth in Sri Lanka using a model developed within the framework of an aggregate production function. The model incorporates both direct and indirect effects of defense and nondefense spending on economic growth along with possible structural breaks due to political regime changes and the "militarization of ethnic conflict." The empirical results indicate that the direct and indirect effects of defense spending have been negative and positive, respectively, on Sri Lanka's economic growth with the negative effect dominating. Although nondefense spending was not a significant factor in determining growth in Sri Lanka from 1961 to 1983, it has since been a major determining factor in influencing economic growth in this country. The author observes that the increase in defense spending that has occurred in the last four decades in Sri Lanka has been significantly costly to the country's economic growth.

NOTES

1. Maddison (1995) estimates that average global per capita output growth was 0.8 percent between 1820 and 1870 and 1.2 percent between 1870 and 1900. Recent estimates from the World Economic Outlook (IMF), May 2000—Chapter 5: The World Economy in the Twentieth Century, show that between 1900 and 2000 world GDP at constant prices increased about nineteen-fold, corresponding to an average annual rate of growth of 3 percent.

2. The twentieth century witnessed the widespread use and commercialization of many nineteenth-century inventions as well as the introduction of innovations in aeronautics, nuclear energy, and electronics.

3. At the beginning of the twentieth century the classical gold standard prevailed, but by the end of the century the international monetary system was characterized by an exchange rate system that allowed for adjustment in the event of fundamental equilibrium, capital mobility, and the existence of an international organization—the International Monetary Fund (IMF)—that focuses on issues of international monetary cooperation.

4. While GDP per capita indicates limited convergence between the wealthiest and poorest regions or countries over the course of the twentieth century, the Human Development Index (HDI) developed by the United Nations Development Program (UNDP) as a measure of a country's well-being shows considerable convergence between countries and a general pattern of reduced poverty. See Chapter 5: The World Economy in the Twentieth Century in the 2000 World Economic Outlook (IMF).

5. This represents a measure of inequality, which ranges from 0 (perfect equality) to 1 (complete inequality).

6. Per capita income of the poorest quarter of the world's population, for example, increased just less than threefold over the course of the twentieth century (IMF, 2000).

7. Given a neoclassical production function such as:

$$Q = AL^{\alpha} K^{\beta} \tag{1}$$

where Q is output, L is labor, K is capital, and A is a shift parameter reflecting technological change or factors that influence productivity and efficiency in the use of labor and capital. A time derivative version of equation 1 permits equation 1 to be rewritten as:

$$q = a + \alpha l + \beta k \tag{2}$$

Equation 2 represents an economy's growth rate as a composite of the weighted sum of the growth rates of the two (or more) factors of production and the growth of the technological and other factors captured by a.

REFERENCES

International Monetary Fund (IMF). 2000. *World Economic Outlook: Asset Prices and Business Cycles*, (May): 149–80.

Lucas, R.E., Jr. 1988. "On the Mechanics of Economic Development." *Journal of Monetary Economics* 22 (July): 3–42.

Maddison, A. 1995. *Monitoring the World Economy 1820–1992*. Paris: Organization for Economic Cooperation and Development.

———. 2001. *The World Economy: A Millennial Perspective*. Paris: Organization for Economic Cooperation and Development.

Malthus, T.R. 1798. *Essay on the Principle of Population.*

Mankiw, N.G., D. Romer, and D.N. Weil. 1992. "A Contribution to the Empirics of Economic Growth." *Quarterly Journal of Economics* 107 (May): 407–37.

Parente, S.L., and E.C. Prescott. 1991. "Technology Adoption and Growth." *Research Department Staff Report* 136. Federal Reserve Bank of Minneapolis.

Ray, D. 2000. "What's New in Development Economics?" *American Economist* 44 (Fall): 3–16.

Schmitz, J.A., Jr. 1993. "Early Progress on the 'Problem of Economic Development.'" *Federal Reserve Bank of Minneapolis Quarterly Review* 17 (Spring): 16–29.

Temple, J., and P. Johnson. 1998. "Social Capability and Economic Growth." *Quarterly Journal of Economics* 13(3): 965–990.

2

International Debt: Ten Lessons for the New Millennium

John Loxley

INTRODUCTION

The last twenty years of the twentieth century were marked by several major international financial crises in which debt problems played a crucial role. The debt crisis of the early 1980s was initially a crisis of the international banking system that threatened to topple the global capitalist economy. For a number of years the preoccupation of governments of industrial nations and the international financial institutions charged with managing this systemic crisis overshadowed what should have been a central concern from the outset: that the debt crisis was a human crisis of major proportions for debtor countries themselves, culminating in what has become known as the "lost decade" for the major debtors of Latin America and elsewhere.

Concern over the debt problems of the larger debtors also overshadowed a growing inability of poorer countries to maintain their debt loads. These debts did not pose any significant systemic risks to the international financial system because the absolute amounts involved were relatively small and the creditors were largely public agencies. But the relative burdens of debt and debt servicing had become so large that, in many cases, they greatly exceeded those of the large debtor countries and the political, social, and economic ramifications of attempting to service these debts were becoming unbearable in the mid-1980s. Managing the debts of poorer countries has continued to preoccupy both debtors and creditors into the new millennium.

The last ten years have witnessed financial crises in Mexico (1994–1995), Asia (1997), Russia and Brazil (1998–1999), Turkey and Argentina (2000). International debt played an important role in each of these. By far the most important of these, the Asian crisis, appeared to threaten international financial stability in much the same way as the debt crisis of the 1980s and resulted in sharp falls in living standards in several countries.

This chapter seeks to draw ten lessons from these financial upheavals as a guideline to formulating policy in both developing countries and the international financial institutions (IFIs), the IMF and the World Bank, in the early years of the new millennium.

LESSON 1—THE INTERNATIONAL CREDIT MARKET CONTINUES TO OPERATE INEFFICIENTLY

It is now widely accepted that international financial markets were characterized by a number of glaring inefficiencies prior to and during the 1980s debt crisis (Loxley, 1997). Lenders were organized oligopolistically, and competition was driven by a desire to increase market share. Lead banks suffered from myopic profit maximizing and a reluctance or inability to take systemic risk into account. High levels of global liquidity made it possible to lend huge sums to developing countries, regarded as the "customer of last resort," which have an insatiable demand for foreign exchange (Palma, 1998). Although borrowing from abroad was initially associated with improved growth and efficiency in the handful of countries qualifying for bank loans, this was not the case after 1978, when "irrational exuberance" seems to have set in among both borrowers and lenders. Bank lending increasingly financed capital flight and unproductive investment or luxury consumption. There was a mismatching of maturities, with relatively short-term debt being used to purchase longer-term assets, exposing borrowers to potential liquidity and/or repayment problems. The price mechanism failed; spreads did not reflect individual country risk, nor did they serve to restrict total lending as the limits of systemic prudence were reached. On the contrary, spreads actually fell as the debt crisis approached. "Herd instinct" drove movement into the market and, much later after concerted lending had been abandoned, it equally drove movement out of the market.

Banks behaved in a very similar fashion in Asia in the 1990s. "Market indicators, such as interest rate spreads . . . were clearly ineffective in predicting the Asian financial crisis" (Basel Committee on Banking Supervision, 1999, p. 56). Once again, spreads actually fell even as evidence mounted of excessive borrowing and deterioration in the real economy—for example, falling profit margins (Palma, 1998, p. 791). In conditions of "bountiful global liquidity," maturities also lengthened and "loan covenants weakened" (Goldstein, 1998).

Herd instinct was again apparent in the Asian crisis with net private capital inflows doubling to over $60 billion per annum in 1995 and 1996, relative to average 1991–1994 levels, but then becoming negative for the rest of the 1990s. The fall in net flows between 1996 and 1997 was $85 billion (IMF, *Outlook*, May 2000, p. 44).

Mismatching of maturities was very evident in Asia too, with over 60 percent of the debt falling due in one year or less, and a half of this in ninety days or less (Palma, 1998, p. 792). These short-term debts were in excess of foreign reserves in Thailand and greatly so in Indonesia and Korea (Culpeper, 1998).

There were also indications of deteriorating investment quality in Asia. Capital output ratios rose strongly in some countries in the mid-1990s, suggesting falling returns. There was evidence of overproduction in some key sectors—cars and semiconductors, for example—large speculative investments in real estate and the stock markets, and overambitious infrastructure investments by the public sector (Goldstein, 1998). None of this curtailed the capital inflows. Thus, even though the credit flows to Asia were essentially private flows to private borrowers, in contrast to the 1980s crisis in which private credit flowed to public or publicly guaranteed borrowers, they were characterized by essentially the same irrationality and market imperfections. Roughly the same can be said of Mexico, where foreign capital supported both luxury consumption and highly speculative investments (Palma, 1998, p. 799) and where collapse, when it came, was sudden and largely unexpected.

LESSON 2—COUNTRY RISK ANALYSIS AND EARLY WARNING INDICATORS ARE OF LIMITED USE

After the debt crisis of the 1980s, there was a belief that better country risk analysis and the development of early warning indicators might have averted the disaster. More resources were devoted to these tasks, and an international organization was created by banks specifically to assist this initiative (Loxley, 1986, p. 80). At the same time, considerable attention was paid to tightening up the regulation of financial institutions and international financial flows, through the Basle Accord and other agreements. This clarified responsibility for different types of foreign institutions, laid down reserve requirements, and attempted to create uniformity in the approach to financial management.

It is evident, in hindsight, that whatever else was accomplished by these developments, they did not prevent the major crises under review. Neither Moody's nor Standard and Poor's (S&P) downgraded the credit ratings of any of the countries centrally involved in the Asian crisis before it broke. In fact, both upgraded the Philippines early in 1997, S&P upgraded both China and Hong Kong in May 1997 (Bank for International Settlements, 1998, p. 127), and the rest remained unchanged for eighteen months before the crisis. Once the crisis happened, the credit ratings of several countries went into free fall, from BBB to B− in five months for Indonesia, from AA− to B+ in two months for Korea, and from A to BBB− in four months for Thailand, all on the S&P basis (ibid). But this was after the event, not before it. As the IMF (September 1998) has admitted, "The entire sovereign credit rating industry . . . was taken by surprise when the crisis broke."

There are sound reasons for the failure of country risk analysis. Indicators of deterioration in risk may be ignored by irrationally exuberant lenders propelled by competition for market share. The risks of lending to an individual country can also shift dramatically with systemic shifts in the economic and political environment. Sudden changes in commodity prices or world interest rates may be all that is needed to reverse capital flows. Financial panic need not be rational; herd instinct and contagion develop rapidly, and by the time deterioration in specific country indicators is apparent, the damage is done. Sometimes critical data, such as the extent of short-term debt exposure and of foreign reserves, is not available or is inaccurate. This was the case with some Asian countries and with Mexico, Russia, and Brazil.

Academic analysis of early warning indicators has produced mixed results. The most positive results, by Kaminsky (1998) are that, based on historical data on "fundamentals" (problems in current and capital account, growth, credit and financial institutions) of 100 financial crises in twenty countries, all but the Indonesian crisis could have been predicted. Generally, however, while *"market variables ... do not do well in predicting currency crises"* (Kaminsky, Lizando, and Reinhart, 1998, p. 13), the "signals" approach to predicting crises generally does not perform well either (IMF, September, 1998). The real problem with this type of analysis is that it tends to predict more crises than actually occur.

LESSON 3—MORAL HAZARD REMAINS IMPORTANT

Irrational exuberance and over-lending were driven, in all cases, by a belief that local governments would stand ready, explicitly or implicitly, to guarantee foreign debts, whether these be to public or private borrowers, or to bail out local banks that had borrowed heavily abroad. In addition, the United States, other industrialized countries, and the IFIs could always be relied upon to shore up debtor economies with large emergency capital infusions, providing yet another level of security. Excessive lending is, therefore, partly the result of the moral hazard flowing from these "guarantees."

Moral hazard certainly seems to have played a role in the crises under review. The bailing out of troubled banks by governments characterized Latin America in the early 1980s, Indonesia in 1992 (with World Bank money), and Thailand in 1996 (Palma, 1998, p. 795). Banks were recapitalized by the state in Indonesia, Korea, Malaysia, Thailand, and China during the Asian crisis (IMF, 1999, p. 5). For larger debtors, the sums of money advanced by the IFIs have increased steadily, in both absolute and relative terms, with each successive crisis, partly because of the increasing needs that capital account liberalization has brought and partly because of the systemic risk that their crises carried. The IMF offered Mexico $17.8 billion in 1995; the Asian bailout amounted to almost $60 billion from the IFIs, the IMF alone providing $35 billion. Recent rescue packages for Brazil, Argentina, and Turkey, all beset by crisis in the last two years, totaled $32.4 billion. To put this in perspective, the amount the IMF loaned Brazil alone in late 1998, $13 billion, was over four times the total advanced by the IMF under its Poverty Reduction and Growth Facility (PRGF) and equivalent arrangements for all borrowers, thirty-seven in total, between 1998 and 2001.

These huge sums were often accompanied by even larger bilateral bailouts. Massive infusions of emergency capital were provided in all cases, with the

United States taking the lead in the 1980s and, even more prominently, in the case of Mexico where it provided $20 billion in loans and guarantees (Lustig, 1997). In the Asian rescue package, bilateral donors provided over half of the more than $120 billion (Culpeper, 1998), with the IMF pledging $35 billion (double its contribution to Mexico in 1995). These public infusions of capital enabled private lenders to withdraw their capital, either immediately or over time, and minimized private risk. They, in effect, socialized the debt of private lenders.

This is not to argue that bankrupt local institutions were always bailed out, or that moral hazard is as centrally important in explaining crisis as the orthodoxy claims. Taylor (1998) argues that Korea allowed three large *chaebols* to go under between 1990 and 1997. He also argues that in the Asian crisis the sharp outflow of funds, equal to 10 percent of GDP, occurred before the bailout, making the rescue "a self-fulfilling prophecy" (p. 673). There is also no question that some foreign creditors, particularly those holding equities or longer-term bonds, did suffer losses in Asia, just as some banks eventually incurred losses in the 1980s crisis. Nonetheless, there is a broad consensus that bank credit inflows, in particular, are driven by implied guarantees of bailouts and the fact of their repatriation without help from emergency inflows in Asia does not undermine the argument that moral hazard encouraged excessive inflows in the first place.

In the Asian and Mexican case, international assistance is best seen as an alternative to capital controls or the compulsory bailing in of private creditors with a much greater risk of capital loss. A consensus is now developing that rescue packages must involve private creditors too (Griffith-Jones, 1998). A senior representative of the IMF has gone further, arguing that "the only thing that will deter their excessive risk taking is a nontrivial probability of incurring a significant loss, which in turn requires that they occasionally actually do suffer a loss" (Goldstein, 1998, p. 40). Though well intentioned, this view overlooks the political economy of international debt and, in particular, the role of the state, in both debtor and creditor countries, in underwriting capital. Nowhere was this more apparent than in the Mexican crisis of 1994–1995. Much of the Mexican debt took the form of *tesobonos* bonds, which were denominated in pesos but exchange rate indexed and held by U.S. mutual funds. In return for its assistance, the U.S. government forced Mexico to denominate and bail out the bonds in U.S. dollars, leaving Mexico with a huge increase in its foreign debt (Palma, 1998, p. 798). The real problem with international moral hazard is that it shifts problems of crisis and adjustment disproportionately onto the people of debtor countries and lets international creditors off the hook. We return to this later.

LESSON 4—CAPITAL ACCOUNT LIBERALIZATION HEIGHTENS INTERNATIONAL FRAGILITY

The crises of the 1990s took place in a context of market liberalization and, especially, of pressure from the IFIs for developing countries to liberalize the capital accounts of their balance of payments. Indeed, just prior to the Asian meltdown, the IMF was on the verge of amending its Articles of Agreement "to make the promotion of capital account liberalization a specific purpose of the Fund and to give the Fund appropriate jurisdiction over capital movements" (IMF, 1997, p. 39; see also IMF, 1998, pp. 74–77). In effect this would have formally acknowledged what the Fund had been informally doing for the best part of a decade. This proposal has since been quietly abandoned. The Fund is more cautious now about the speed of liberalization, if not less messianic about the objective itself, precisely because of the widespread view that such liberalization played a key role in the Asian and subsequent crises.

What made the liberalization of the capital account such a dubious proposition in Asia was the fact that savings and investment rates were among the highest in the world and certainly large enough to sustain very high rates of real GDP growth on the basis of any reasonable assumptions about the productivity of capital. There was, therefore, a strong association between large capital inflows and the growth of speculative investment and rising capital output ratios. Capital account liberalization was not only disastrous, it was entirely unnecessary.

This, however, is not the lesson the IMF has taken from the crisis. Rather, it seems to have concluded that the problem was not liberalization per se, but rather its pace and the lack of preparedness of local governments and financial institutions to cope properly with large capital inflows. In particular, it views inconsistent monetary and exchange rate policies and poor risk management as being the main causes of crisis (IMF, 1999, p. 46). At the same time, it conceded that even countries not suffering from these deficiencies were negatively affected by the withdrawal of international capital subsequent to the crisis, although they were "better able to handle" it (ibid.).

Capital inflows are naively assumed to be an unqualified virtue because of the higher growth rates they supposedly permit. But if one were to calculate the indirect costs of large inflows, the costs of sudden capital flight and the economic pain this causes, both immediately and over the years it takes to pay off emergency assistance, one's assessment of the merits of these flows must surely be less positive. The large capital inflows into Mexico in the seven years between liberalization and crisis were associated with an appreciating peso, which steadily undermined exports and which stimulated large increases in consumer imports, with a consequent deterioration of the current account. When the crash came, the capital outflow was equivalent to 40 percent of exports or 10 percent of GDP. In 1995 alone, GDP fell by 7 percent—the largest fall since the Great Depression—unemployment doubled, and real wages fell by 22 percent (Lustig, 1997, p. 60)

LESSON 5—ADJUSTMENT TO CRISIS REMAINS ASYMMETRICAL

Although the stories of crisis vary in their detail, the common thread is that the burden of adjustment falls squarely on the people of the debtor countries, not on the creditors. This asymmetry has long been a major shortcoming in the architecture of international finance, implicitly viewing disequilibrium from one side only. Balance-of-payments surpluses and "strong" currencies are considered virtuous, whereas deficits and weak currencies are considered the cause of global instability. Because one cannot exist without the other, this subjective view of economic reality is fundamentally flawed.

Added to this has been an unwillingness of the major powers, especially the United States, which also control the IFIs, to allow domestic creditors to feel the full impact of financial crises. In the debt crisis of the 1980s, major banks were allowed almost seven years to make adjustments to their balance sheets, showing increased profits from Third World debt in many of the intervening years. While this was partly because the debt instrument was not securitized, so that it had no overt market value that could be written down the moment a crisis hit, shifting some of the burden of adjustment to creditors, this was not the only or perhaps even the main reason. The Mexican crisis of 1994–1995 shows that securitization does not automatically enhance risks for creditors. U.S. intervention guaranteed the redemption price for *tesobonos*, even though the common perception at that time was that "the severity of the market's reaction following the December 1994 devaluation was totally disproportionate" (Lustig, 1997, p. 61). The fear once again was that the crisis might spread globally, and, especially given U.S. commitment to Mexico through NAFTA, the United States felt that massive intervention would be in the interest of U.S. capital generally. Even though a global meltdown of markets was avoided and U.S. intervention considered a success, Mexico paid the price in a huge fall in living standards, repaying all its emergency funding within two years.

Dealing with international asymmetry requires action on a number of fronts. First of all, much tougher sanctions need to be applied to surplus countries than currently exist. If IFIs are to implement policy conditionality, then it should apply equally to all countries in disequilibrium, whether they be running balance-of-payments surpluses or deficits. This will require changing the current rules of the game. Surcharges could be levied by the IMF on reserves held by surplus countries, as originally envisaged by Keynes (Loxley, 1986, p. 106). But these would have to be very high to promote changes in economic policy, so it would mean developing a system that would require surplus countries to adjust. One could envisage the IMF developing a series of indicators of economic performance that, once they reach a predetermined level, would trigger the requirement to adjust monetary or fiscal policy. These could be based on trends in the balance of payments, real effective exchange rates, levels of foreign reserves or other assets, and the like. The difficulty would be in persuading the major powers to expose themselves automatically to the kind of IMF policy intervention they so freely impose on others. The problem would be to find the levers that would require them to adjust should they choose not to. Without a willingness on the part of surplus countries to voluntarily opt into such a scheme, IMF policy conditionality, through which adjustments to crises are carried out, will, as Keynes put it, continue to "throw the burden on the countries least able to support it, making the poor poorer" (quoted in Dell, 1981).

The inequity in global adjustment mechanisms is all the more apparent when the oversimplification of "rich countries run surpluses, poor countries run deficits" is dropped. In reality, the savings of some Third World countries are actually financing the external deficits of some of the wealthiest countries in the world, the United States and the United Kingdom. At the start of the new millennium, according to the IMF (May, 2001, pp. 226–231), Third World countries as a whole were actually running balance-of-payments surpluses, equal to 1.8 percent of GDP. Within this group, even Africa had a positive resource balance of 0.5 percent GDP (the first positive balance for years), the Asian NICs had a positive balance of 4.0 percent GDP, and the Middle East 9.8 percent GDP. Latin America and the Caribbean had a modest deficit, while countries relying heavily on official finance were running a negative resource balance of 2.5 percent GDP, but this was down significantly from its 1995 level of 7.7 percent GDP. The United States, however, was running a deficit of 3.7 percent of GDP, while the EU and Japan were running surpluses (0.5 percent and 1.5 percent respectively).

LESSON 6—POLICY CONDITIONALITY IS EXERCISED THROUGH DEBT DEPENDENCY

It has become readily apparent over the past twenty years that the main entrée of the IFIs in shaping the economic policy of developing countries has been through the management of debt. Every major initiative dealing with the debt of larger debtors, from bridge financing, debt rescheduling through the London Club, the Baker Plan, to the Brady debt write-down plan, has required the preexistence of stabilization and structural adjustment programs under the auspices of the IFIs. For poor country debtors, Paris Club rescheduling and the many subsequent steps taken to reduce debt servicing burdens, up to and including the Highly Indebted Poor Country Initiative (HIPC), introduced in 1996, have all similarly required IFI policy conditionality. This has meant a steady diet of external policy direction for the best part of a generation for many debtor countries. As of 2001, no fewer than sixty countries were borrowing from the IMF (IMF Survey, May 21, 2001). Of these, eighteen were borrowers in 1980 and thirty in 1990 (IMF, *Annual Report*, 1980, 1990), and some sixteen did not exist in the earlier periods. Several countries, such as former Zaire, Liberia, Sierra Leone, and Somalia are war torn, but would otherwise be under IMF tutelage, as they were in 1980 and 1990. Several poor countries that are not currently borrowing from the Fund are, or will be, conditioned by it nevertheless, through the HIPC program (Uganda, Guinea, and Ghana). Debt dependence has meant, therefore, a growing state of heteronomy, or the control of the economy by external forces.

The HIPC initiative was particularly demanding from this point of view. Until 1999, applicants had to undertake structural adjustment programs for six years before debt would be written down. What made this requirement particularly demanding was that HIPC countries are often countries that have been conditioned by the IMF/World Bank for several years already before applying for HIPC relief. Between 1980 and 1991, HIPC countries on average undertook six such adjustment programs, lasting 6.4 years. They accounted for about 80 percent of all Structural Adjustment Facility and Enhanced Structural Adjustment Facility programs to 1994 (Serieux, 2000). The persistence of policy conditionality did little to alleviate their debt problems. HIPC then required them to adjust, up front, for six years before financing relief would kick in. What this approach implicitly denies is that up-front financing can alleviate adjustment pressures and speed transition from one economic regime to another. There are not only real trade-offs between finance and adjustment but also important complementarities. But the IMF, in particular, has always put the priority on adjustment, and especially so for debtors, like the poorest, whose economic problems do not carry systemic threats.

The HIPC emphasis on adjustment-first is yet another example of asymmetries in global management of economic imbalances. It puts all the responsibility for debt problems on the people of the poorest countries, effectively absolving bilateral and multilateral lenders from any responsibility for the problems, at least until the requisite adjustment period is up. After much pressure from the Third World and from nongovernmental organizations (ngos), in 1999 the IMF introduced the possibility of reduced adjustment periods before HIPC countries qualified for debt write-downs, to somewhere between three and six years. It also went some way toward meeting the criticism that its eligibility requirements were too harsh for poor debtors, but these still remain very demanding, and progress in countries qualifying for and receiving write-downs, though improving since 1999, still remains very slow (ibid).

Because the debt of poorer countries is not much more than $200 billion, about 30 percent of which is multilateral, it poses no threat to global stability and, as the churches' Jubilee 2000 campaign argued, could easily be written off in its entirety. Under the restrictive access conditions of HIPC, only about $130 billion of debt would be covered and, in the most optimistic of circumstances, would be reduced to $40 billion, a 70 percent write-down. Even after forgiveness, debt/export ratios would average 150 percent (Development Committee, 2001, p. 5). Because debtors already pay only about 40 percent of the debt servicing that is due, nominal debt relief is much less than actual debt relief—that is, much relief simply writes off debt that was not being serviced anyway. Thus, for the twenty-two HIPC countries reaching their decision points in 2000, debt servicing will fall from about $2.7 billion a year in 1998–1999, to $1.9 billion p.a. in 2001–2003 (ibid, p. 9). Even the Enhanced HIPC will continue to ensure, therefore, that many of the world's poorest countries will continue to be conditioned by the IFIs for many years to come.

The nature of that conditionality has remained essentially unchanged for years and is designed to ensure the payment of international debts, the closer integration of debtors into the world economy, greater use of market mechanisms, and the promotion of the private sector at the expense of the state. Critics have argued for years that much conditionality, if not all except repayment of balance-of-payments assistance, should be dropped, that it is in some respects theoretically suspect, and that the track record of success is at best mixed. The implications of adjustment programs for long-term growth and for social spending, especially in the context of a large debt overhang, have also been questioned. There has also been much critical discussion about the impacts of these programs on income distribution, gender, and the environment (Loxley, 1998). In partial recognition of possible shortcomings, in 1999 the IMF replaced its ESAFs with a PRGF and replaced the Policy Framework Papers it required of borrowers, which underpinned the conditionality of ESAFs, with Poverty Reduction Strategy Papers (PRSPs) (IMF, *Annual Report*, 2000, p. 52). These seek to give greater emphasis in adjustment programs to distributional impact and the social dimensions of public spending. They also call for popular participation in the drawing up of PRSPs. Although conceptually these developments must be acknowledged as representing progress, relatively few countries have been successful in putting together PRSPs, the vehicles of popular input are often not readily available, and there is ambiguity as to what would happen if poverty alleviation strategies were felt to conflict with the IFIs' views on appropriate stabilization or adjustment policies.

The theoretical and practical short comings of IMF/IBRD conditionality, about which scholars and officials in Latin America, Africa, and low-income Asia have complained for years, came to the fore dramatically during the crisis in the richer, Asian miracle countries. Suddenly, a model of development that had been the envy of the rest of the developing world, delivering unprecedented growth rates and economic and social transformation for more than a generation (Bienefeld, 1994), ground to a halt. The international community suddenly began to portray these systems as suffering from crony capitalism, excessive state intervention, and serious structural weakness.

It is important to recognize that, given the asymmetric nature of global adjustment policies, there would be no policy conditionality without debt dependence. Countries incurring large debts in the face of massive capital flight pay the price in terms of policy conditionality. Countries with long-standing debt problems have been conditioned by the IFIs for many years now and have effectively lost control of their economic policy. Many of these countries are also aid dependent, and donors have made IFI conditionality a prerequisite for their assistance, reinforcing the pressures from debt dependence.

Under persistent structural adjustment, the size of government is reduced significantly. Its capability to intervene in the economy in redistributive ways is restricted. Furthermore, the structure and focus of government changes, with disproportionate amounts of scarce skills and time being devoted to renegotiations of debt and adjustment programs. Nef (1995, p. 78) describes these states as "receiver states" in which financial decision making has become paramount. "The world over, ministries of Finance, Treasury Boards, Central Banks and the like have become the heart of governance, subordinating other functions, ministries and agencies to the implementation of structural adjustment agendas of fiscal management. It is these globalized agendas, not national priorities or popular demands which determine government policies."

LESSON 7—THERE IS A ROLE FOR CAPITAL CONTROLS IN REDUCING VOLATILITY

The Asian crisis not only forced the IMF to backtrack on the issue of capital account liberalization, it also caused it to look more seriously at capital controls, their various possible forms and effectiveness. There were clear differences of opinion on the IMF Board about the usefulness of controls and a recognition that they "may provide a breathing space for corrective action" (IMF, *Annual Report*, 2000, p. 44), a far cry from two years earlier when the Fund led the charge against the use of exchange controls by Malaysia to stem its capital outflow.

Nonetheless, in spite of the evidence of capital account liberalization being a factor in the Asian crisis, the IMF remains committed to it as a means of reducing future volatility. It squares this circle by arguing that it was not capital account liberalization per se that helped cause the Asian crisis but liberalization without appropriate accompanying prudential regulation of financial institutions and other financial institution reform. It acknowledges that "Malaysia's decision to impose controls on capital outflows—and support for the idea among some academics—raises the question of whether such controls will once again become widespread" (Fischer, 1998). It stresses, however, that its "position has long been that capital account liberalization should proceed in an orderly way: countries should lift controls on outflows only gradually as the balance of payments strengthens; liberalization of inflows should start at the long end and move to the short end only as banking and financial systems are strengthened" (ibid). Korea's liberalization, promoted in part by heavy pressure from the United States and the OECD, has been roundly criticized, however, precisely for being precipitous, too comprehensive and too heavily biased in terms of promoting short-term capital inflows (Chang, Park, and Yoo, 1998).

Capital account liberalization per se, however, is not held responsible by the IMF for instability although it acknowledges that "the margins for error in macroeconomic, debt management, and financial policy more generally are extremely tight in the face of open capital markets" (Boorman, 1999, p. 65). But it is precisely the risk of hyper-reaction to what capital holders might perceive as "policy errors," which others might even see as "sound policy," that underlies the argument for some form of capital control.

Most of the emphasis in the literature about how to minimize fragility and reduce the risk of crisis focuses on borrowing countries taking the initiative. It also stresses reducing certain capital inflows rather than introducing controls on capital outflows. Wade and Veneroso (1998) are typical in this respect, arguing the case for semipermanent controls on inflows to most of Asia on the grounds that Asia's high rates of domestic savings reduce the need for inflows; that unrestrained short-term inflows create speculative bubbles and that they make otherwise relatively stable economies "vulnerable to the whims and stampedes of portfolio and hedge fund managers" (p. 31).

The kind of controls they have in mind are similar to those of Chile and Colombia, requiring the deposit, without interest, of a proportion of the inflow with the central bank for a stipulated period of time. This serves to penalize short-term flows relative to longer-term ones. The IMF, it should be noted, claims not to oppose these "market-based measures," "but they must be considered case-by-case" (Fischer, 1998).

There are other possible forms of controls on the recipient end of capital flows. Higher reserve or capital requirements could be imposed on banks either for all their borrowing abroad or for that portion borrowed abroad on a short-term basis. To deal with the possibility of nonbanks borrowing abroad short term, regulations might require prior approval of the central bank, which in turn might demand certain guarantees or deposits.

Yet another approach could be the differential tax treatment of short-versus long-term foreign borrowing to skew transactions away from the short term. Alternatively, banks and others could be required to cover open positions in currency forward or future markets or to close open positions by matching the currency composition of foreign assets and liabilities. The latter measures might not reduce overall risk but would at least shift risk away from financial institutions to customers, perhaps reducing systemic risk in the process (Eichengreen, 1998, p. 338).

Paul Krugman is one of a relatively small number of prominent commentators calling for exchange controls on capital outflows in Asia. His reasoning is that this is the only way in which real interest rates can be reduced—a sine qua non for economic recovery—without causing further capital outflow and further large exchange rate depreciations (Krugman, 1998).

Given the relative stability of India and China throughout the Asian crisis, it seems reasonable to argue that countries that have exchange controls already in place would be well advised to think carefully before removing them. A number of writers have argued persuasively that the management of volatile capital flows cannot reasonably be left entirely to recipient, usually emergent market, countries. Often, however, they are extremely vague about what, concretely, can be done by source countries to reduce volatility. Thus, Michael Mussa of the IMF has argued that the contraction in gross capital flows to emergent markets between mid-1997 and mid-August 1998—of some $400 billion on an annual basis—was so massive that "No country ... no matter how soundly managed its economic policies, no matter how solid its banking system, can maintain an open attitude toward international capital flows in the face of that type of system disturbance" (Mussa, 1998, p. 340). He concludes that the international community must take some responsibility, without saying precisely how.

One possibility is for creditor nations and the IFIs to institute arrangements whereby when a crisis hits, lenders would be subject to credit standstills and orderly workouts (Griffith-Jones, 1998). This would force creditors to share in the responsibility for crisis and would reduce the need for huge IMF loan inflows and for massive increases in domestic interest rates. Only in this way is moral hazard likely to be minimized and "adjustment with growth" policies, as advocated earlier, made feasible. Senior staff of the IMF have shown some sympathy for using the Fund's legal powers to protect debtors against actions of creditors that might undermine adjustment efforts to deal with crisis (Boorman, 1999, p. 72).

Others put great emphasis (and some, such as David Felix, 1998, *sole* emphasis) on the introduction of a Tobin tax on international transactions as a means of controlling the outward movement of short-term capital. Such a measure would significantly reduce returns to very short-term speculative movements of capital, thereby also helping stabilize exchange rates, and it might also raise significant sources of revenue that could be put to creative and equity-enhancing uses on a global scale. It would not, however, prevent massive speculative attacks or large capital flight based on a loss of confidence where the risk of capital gain or loss greatly outweigh the cost of the tax, usually suggested at no more than 0.25 percent and often much lower. Neither would such a level of tax necessarily discourage short-term lending in the three- to twelve-month range if foreign interest rates were sufficiently in excess of those that might be earned at home.

Other measures that might be introduced by source governments include requiring lending institutions to hold different levels of provisions for countries deemed to offer different degrees of risk in terms of the state of their banking system and other considerations such as level of reserves relative to short-term debt, but at this time there is no mechanism for administering such a scheme. Also, as argued previously, risk assessment by agencies currently undertaking that task leaves much to be desired. Imposing differential levels of taxation on earnings from overseas investments with different maturities would be more practical but less sensitive to differential country risk. It should be noted that the Basle Committee regulations currently give a lower weight to short-term foreign lending for capital adequacy purposes than they do to loans of over one year (20 percent versus 100 percent). This bias increases the profitability of short-term lending and requires reconsideration. This will undoubtedly be reviewed in the development of a new Basel Capital Accord, which is now under way (Basel Committee on Banking Supervision, 2001).

The G-7 have been quite cautious in accepting reform of the international financial system, arguing that "sweeping institutional changes are not needed" (IMF, *Survey*, March 8, 1999, pp. 69–71). Instead, under the so-called Tietmeyer Proposal (named after the president of the Bundesbank), a Financial Stability Forum has been convened. The responsibilities of this forum are to facilitate cooperation between existing institutions on issues of surveillance and early warnings, to identify the need for regulating nonregulated agencies, and to encourage the development and application of best practices in different areas of international finance. Given the scale of the Asian crisis and the damage it has done worldwide, this seems to be a wholly inadequate level of response. Future similar upheavals are unlikely to be avoided by streamlining procedures and adopting common rules of bookkeeping and best practice.

LESSON 8—FINANCIAL CRISES ARE ENDEMIC TO CAPITALISM: DEBT CRISES WILL RECUR

Hyman Minsky (1985) has argued that "the normal functioning of our economy leads to financial trauma and crises, inflation, currency depreciations, unemployment, and poverty in the midst of what could be virtually universal affluence—in short ... financially complex capitalism is inherently flawed" (p. 287). He then goes on to argue that "there is no possibility that we can ever set things right once and for all: instability put to rest by one set of reforms will, after time, emerge in a new guise" (p. 333). Ito and Portes (1999) reach similar conclusions from a different theoretical viewpoint, arguing that "all crises are 'crises of success,'" involving debt default, foreign exchange shocks and failure of banking systems and that "we should not expect or even wish to prevent them all" (p. 3).

Given the inherent tendency of private banks and related financial institutions to be overexuberant, to be speculative, and to participate in ponzi lending (Minsky, 1985), both nationally and internationally, and the tendency of the finance sector to reflect and exaggerate the inevitable fluctuations in the real economies of capitalist societies, financial crises will inevitably recur, whatever the regulatory system.

At the present time, a number of Third World countries continue to be heavily exposed to international debt and may be inherently more crisis prone than others. Disconcertingly, among them would appear to be a number of larger debtors in Latin America that figured prominently in the debt crisis of the 1980s. According to the IMF (*Outlook*, 2001, p. 220), "Western Hemisphere" countries, Latin America and the Caribbean, owe about $780 billion, over a third of total developing country debt, 70 percent of which is owed to the private sector. This debt is the equivalent of over 211 percent of export earnings, higher than that of any other regional grouping, including Africa. Annual debt servicing amounts to about $150 billion or over 40 percent of export earnings, again the highest by country group. Although there has been some marked improvement in the aggregate debt/exports and debt service/export ratios in the past couple of years, much of this has been the result of strong export growth, which may not persist given the global slowdown in growth in 2001 and, in any event, Mexico alone was responsible for two thirds of it (ECLAC, 2001, p. 96). Countries that appear to be most at risk—with the debt/export (2000) and debt servicing/export ratio (1999) in parentheses—are Argentina (473 percent, 72 percent), Brazil (366 percent, 106 percent), Colombia (228 percent, 43 percent), and Peru (320 percent, 32 percent) (ECLAC, 2001, p. 107 for debt/export ratio and World Bank, 2001, pp. 145–47 for debt servicing ratio). Between them they accounted for $446 billion or about 60 percent of total debt outstanding in the region in 2000 (ECLAC, 2001, p. 102). With the exception of Peru, absolute debt more than doubled in the 1990s, and debt burdens (debt/export ratios) are higher now than a decade ago. Six other Latin American countries have debt to export ratios at or well above 150 percent.

In Asia, no major debtors are as heavily debt dependent as Brazil or Argentina. Indonesia's relative debt and debt servicing burdens, at 247 percent and 29 percent respectively, are close to Colombia's, while Thailand's, at 131 percent and 22 percent, are much lower, in the region of Mexico's and Venezuela's (ibid). Other middle income countries that might be prone to further debt servicing problems in the near future are Turkey, Algeria, Morocco, and Hungary.

It is the countries of Latin America, however, that would seem to pose the biggest threat of instability in the near future, given their high debt and debt servicing burdens and the uncertainties surrounding the global economy.

In addition, the HIPC countries continue to have massively high debt burdens. The twenty-two countries approved for HPIC relief have average debt/export burdens of over 340 percent, and any downturn in the global economy may prevent them qualifying for promised debt relief. Furthermore, there are thirteen countries that have not yet obtained HIPC approval (Development Committee, IMF, 2001, p. 4). Some of these are war-torn economies that have debt/export ratios that defy belief: Sudan, 2,254 percent; Sierra Leone, 1,629 percent; Burundi, 1,421 percent (World Bank, 2001). Others, such as the Central Africa Republic (579 percent), Togo (278 percent), Myanmar (336 percent), Côte d'Ivoire (250 percent) and Chad (329 percent) have difficulty qualifying because of erratic economic performance, though this is not unconnected with the huge debt management problems they struggle with. Thus, while the Enhanced HIPC marks progress, the debt problems of the poor countries are far from over and are still sensitive to global economic performance. Though they do not threaten the stability of the international financial system, as do the debtors of Latin America, failure to deal quickly with their debt problems could lead to other types of global systemic risk, such as uncontrolled population flows, widespread disease or social disorder, and disruption of normal flows of trade or payments.

LESSON 9—REDUCING DEBT DEPENDENCE IS NECESSARY BUT DIFFICULT

Foreign debt is clearly a double-edged sword. It is attractive because it is accompanied, automatically, with foreign exchange that might not otherwise be available. It serves to relieve, therefore, the foreign exchange bottleneck in economies that are highly import dependent. In many cases it is, initially at least, cheaper than borrowing locally, although that can soon change if the exchange rate depreciates. It permits local investment to be free, to some extent, from the domestic savings constraint and may allow governments to undertake projects that otherwise would fall victim to the domestic revenue constraint. It may be accompanied by needed foreign technology or technical assistance. For all these reasons, foreign borrowing is attractive, in theory raising GDP and possibly exports to permit the servicing of debt from higher incomes and foreign exchange earnings in future years.

In practice a clear majority of developing countries have had difficulty managing external debt. Several middle-income countries and most poor countries have never recovered from the debt crisis of the 1980s. With the onset of recession in the early 1980s, debt and debt servicing burdens were seen to be unsustainable and since then debtor countries have been struggling with the implications of meeting debt obligations. A significant portion of foreign earnings and local tax receipts have been automatically required for debt servicing, building inflexibility into economic management and the ability to deliver social programs. The debt overhang has had a clear disincentive effect on local and foreign investment and has depressed the value of existing capital assets. Financial fragility has made local equity markets quite volatile and, in Latin America since 1998, very depressed. Above all, debt dependence has led to loss of economic policy independence.

It is clear, in retrospect, that re-entry into international credit markets by larger debtors in the early 1990s was premature. But such is the irrationality of those markets that availability of credit was not a problem from the early 1990s to the onset of the Asian crisis. After the crisis there is evidence that private creditors shifted their lending from Asia to Latin America and even to sub-Saharan Africa (IMF, *Outlook*, May, 2001, pp. 213–14) and, most surprisingly, to the HIPCs (ibid., p. 216).

High-debt countries do not appear, therefore, to be particularly anxious to reduce borrowing. Private creditors appear to be happy to continue lending to them, despite the apparent risks, perhaps because in previous crises, in the 1920s and 1980s, for example, lending was quite profitable, in spite of defaults and service interruptions (Ito and Portes, 1999).

For countries anxious to regain control over economic policy, however, reducing debt dependence is absolutely necessary. There is, indeed, a "debt trap" constraining economic independence, the ability to set priorities, and the flexibility to adjust to changing domestic and international contexts. This is not the result of conspiracy between private lenders and the IMF, as Cheryl Payer (1974) argued some years ago, but rather the outcome of structural problems facing debtors that drive them to borrow, imperfections of the international capital market that drive creditors to lend excessively, and asymmetrical approaches to adjustment built into the architecture of the international financial system.

For those governments wishing to reduce debt dependence there are no easy solutions. Raising the productivity of investment is a need in most regions of the developing world. The implied average capital-output ratio in the 1990s ranges from 7.7 in the Middle East and North Africa to 3.9 in South Asia (author's calculations from data in World Bank, 2000, pp. 295–96 and 298–99). Most regions had a c/o ratio in excess of 5, including East Asia and the Pacific, which, in that case, was offset by investment rates in excess of 30 percent to give large average growth rates, just under 6 percent p.a. Latin America and the Caribbean had similar investment productivity, but investment rates of only 20 percent, resulting in much lower growth rates of 3.4 percent p.a. Sub-Saharan Africa combined relatively low investment rates of about 16 percent p.a. with relatively high capital-output ratios of 6.7, to yield growth rates of only 2.4 percent p.a.

The starting point for reducing debt dependence has to be greater self-discipline by governments in the rate of investment and in the selection of investment projects. Reduced military spending is essential in this regard. According to data released recently by the IMF, such spending now accounts for over 2 percent of the GDP of all developing countries and for over 10 percent of all government spending. In poorer countries eligible for IMF Poverty Reduction and Growth Facilities, military spending is even higher, at 3.3 percent of GDP and almost 12 percent of government spending (IMF, *Survey*, June 4, 2001, p. 195). Much of this spending is debt financed and directly (where it is not) or indirectly (in debt servicing) reduces resources available for more productive or socially useful purposes. Militarization, conflict, and civil unrest are, therefore, inextricably linked with the need to borrow abroad, and peace and conflict resolution are essential for raising local resources to reduce debt dependence.

More generally, governments need to ensure that local savings rates are increased, preferably at the expense of luxury consumption, and that the productivity of investment is improved. Restructuring state spending is necessary but insufficient. Because the private sector is becoming more influential in developing countries, taxation and regulation policies must be designed both to limit volatile inflows of funds that often fuel speculative investment, luxury consumption, or even capital flight and to encourage their use in longer-term productive investment. This will require a greater degree of state involvement in capital markets than the IFIs might desire.

High capital-output ratios may suggest critical foreign exchange bottlenecks and, if this is the case, should direct public policy toward the more efficient use of foreign exchange and the encouragement of nontraditional exports. From this perspective, food security will assume a high priority as food shortages lead to unplanned demands on scarce foreign exchange and are also a common cause of borrowing abroad. All of this will entail shifting scarce skilled people from dealing with finance and debt into addressing broader issues of developing policy for and helping manage the real sectors of the economy.

As far as possible poorer countries should borrow on concessional terms only. All countries should attempt to set upper limits on their debt and debt servicing in ways that recognize the vulnerability of their economies to large fluctuations in export earnings, income, and government revenue. This would mean setting maximum ratios at very conservative levels and having the discipline to keep them there or lower. Countries with debt servicing problems or facing vulnerability on the debt front should not undertake new debts, however attractive they might appear to be. For many countries this essentially would mean withdrawing from any new borrowing, whether it be from private or public sources. This is the logic of withdrawing from debt dependence.

LESSON 10—ABOLISHING DEBT DEPENDENCE IS NECESSARY FOR THE REBIRTH OF DEVELOPMENT ECONOMICS

Debt dependence led to the widespread adoption of IMF/IBRD policy conditionality and in the process greatly narrowed the discourse of development economics. The collapse of the Soviet Union and the Eastern bloc and the subsequent Asian crisis not only extended the reach of the IFIs in terms of their conditionality, but further served to limit the parameters of dialogue around both alternative notions and strategies of development. Over the past twenty years, development theory has been reduced to structural adjustment theory, and the terms of the debate have been set disproportionately by the IFIs with their seemingly unlimited budgets for academic and propagandistic dissemination, which are difficult to distinguish. This is not to say there has not been debate; there has. Nor is it to say that the IFI view of the world has gone uncontested; it has been challenged, and critics can point to some notable victories in the design of adjustment programs (length of adjustment programs, phasing in of measures, attention to poverty and distribution, supply-side concerns, etc.). The point is that the IFIs have set the agenda for the debate and, in acting as gatekeepers for financial assistance and debt relief, have had complete control over how that debate has played itself out in policy formulation on the ground.

The debate has always been a limited one developed at a very macro level and, of necessity therefore, abstracting from the messy reality of differences in economic structure, social systems, and politics that inevitably exist on the ground. Not that IMF staff ever stay around long enough in borrowing countries to detect these important differences. Their view of the world does not require this, and their budget would not permit it anyway. The appeal of structural adjustment programs, and ultimately their Achilles' heel, lies in their very simplicity.

For the foreseeable future, debt dependence and heteronomy are a fact of life for most of the developing world. In this situation, the scope for open debate about the nature of development and a frank discussion of alternative strategies of development will inevitably be circumscribed.

CONCLUSION

There is a disturbing recurrence of themes when examining the recent history of international debt. Successive major financial crises that have affected Third World countries in the last twenty years have underscored the fact that the international financial system continues to be characterized by irrationality, myopia, and turbulence. In managing the crises, the major powers and the IFIs have ensured that the interests of the global capitalist system have been given paramountcy over those of the people of the Third World debtor countries, their states, and their domestic capitalist classes. This asymmetry in crisis management was particularly evident in both the debt crisis of the 1980s and the recent Asian financial crisis. Crisis intervention took the form of imposing harsh austerity measures on borrowing countries while minimizing the impact on creditors. Many private debts were, in the process, socialized by both debtor governments and the IFIs. The price of assistance was essentially the loss of policy autonomy of debtor states to the IFIs, which now condition directly over half of the nations of the world while holding great sway over policy in many of the other countries. In the process, a hegemony of ideas has developed as to what properly constitute the major goals, problems, and acceptable strategies of development. Though the implications of debt dependence are likely to last long into the future, as policy conditionality limits both the scope of democratic decision-making in much of the world and, possibly, the substantive approach to social and economic development strategies, this monopoly of ideas and thought may well prove, tragically, to be the most important legacy of excessive dependence on international debt.

REFERENCES

Bank for International Settlements. 1998. *68th Annual Report 1st April, 1997–31st March, 1998*. Basel.

Basel Committee on Banking Supervision. 1999. "Supervisory Lessons to Be Drawn from the Asian Crisis." *Working Paper No. 2*, Bank for International Settlements, Geneva.

———. 2001 (January). *Consultative Document: Overview of the New Basel Capital Accord*. Bank for International Settlements, Geneva.

Bienefeld, M. 1994. "The New World Order: Echoes of a New Imperialism." *Third World Quarterly* 15 (1).

Boorman, J.T. 1999. "Recovery from Financial Crisis: Macroeconomic Policy Alternatives for Equitable Growth." In *Recovery from Crisis: Policy Alternatives for Equitable Development*. Ottawa: The North-South Institute.

Chang, H.J., H.J. Park, and C.G. Yoo. 1998. "Interpreting the Korean Crisis: Financial Liberalization, Industrial Policy and Corporate Governance." *Cambridge Journal of Economics* 22, no. 6 (November).

Culpeper, R. 1998 "Systemic Instability or Global Growing Pains? Implications of the Asian Financial Crisis." *Briefing B-41*, North-South Institute, Ottawa.

Dell, S. 1981. *On Being Grandmotherly: The Evolution of IMF Conditionality*. Princeton Essays in International Finance, No. 144, Princeton University, New Jersey.

Development Committee. 2001 (April 19). *Heavily Indebted Poor Countries (HIPC): Progress Report*. International Monetary Fund. Washington, D.C.

ECLAC (Economic Commission for Latin America and the Caribbean). 2001. *Preliminary Overview of the Economies of Latin America and the Caribbean, 2000*. United Nations, Santiago, Chile.

Eichengreen, B. 1998. *IMF Survey* 27, no. 20 (November).

Felix, D. 1988. "Asia and the Crisis of Financial Globalization." In *Globalization and Progressive Economic Policy*, edited by D. Baker, G. Epstein, and R. Pollin. Cambridge: Cambridge University Press.

Fischer, Stanley. 1998. "Reforming World Finance: Lessons from Crisis." *The Economist* (October 3–9).

Goldstein, Morris. 1998 (December). "The Asian Financial Crisis: Origins, Policy Prescriptions and Lessons." African Economic Research Consortium, Nairobi.
Griffith-Jones, Stephany. 1998. "The East Asian Financial Crisis: Its Causes, Consequences, Policy and Research Implications." IDS discussion paper draft, Sussex.
IMF. 1980, 1990,1997, 2000. *Annual Report*. Washington, D.C.
IMF. 1998. *International Capital Markets*. Washington, D.C. September. Annex III.
IMF. 1999, 2001. *Survey*. Washington, D.C.
IMF. 2000. *World Economic Outlook*. Washington, D.C. May and October.
IMF. 2001. *World Economic Outlook*. Washington, D.C. May.
Ito, T., and R. Portes. 1999. "Crisis Management." *European Economic Perspectives* (17). London: Centre for Economic Policy Research.
Kaminsky, G.L. 1998. "Currency and Banking Crisis: The Early Warnings of Distress." Paper presented at the conference, Asia: An Analysis of Financial Crisis, Chicago, October 8–10, 1988. 8–10. Proceedings published by the Federal Reserve Bank of Chicago, 1999.
Kaminsky, G., S. Lizando, and C. Reinhart. 1998. "Leading Indicators of Currency Crises." *IMF Staff Papers*, 45 (1, March).
Krugman, P. 1998. "Saving Asia: It's Time to Get Radical." *Fortune*, September 7.
Loxley, J. 1986. *Debt and Disorder: International Finance for Development*. Boulder, Colorado: North-South Institute, Ottawa and Westview Press.
———. 1997. "International Capital Markets, the Debt Crisis and Development." In *Global Development Fifty Years After Bretton Woods*, edited by R. Culpeper, A. Berry, and F. Stewart. London and North-South Institute, Ottawa: Macmillan Press.
———. 1998. *Interdependence, Disequilibrium and Growth: Reflections on the Political Economy of North-South Relations at the Turn of the Century*. New York and the International Development Research Centre, Ottawa. London: Macmillan Press; London: St Martin's Press.
Lustig, N. 1997. "The United States to the Rescue: Assistance to Mexico in 1982 and 1995." *CEPAL Review* 61 (April)
Minsky, H.P. 1985. "The Financial Instability Hypothesis: A Restatement." In *Post Keynesian Economic Theory: A Challenge to Neo-Classical Economic*, edited by P. Arestis and T. Skouras. Sussex: Wheatsheaf Books.
Mussa, M. 1998. Quoted in *IMF Survey* 27 (no. 20) (November).
Nef, J. 1995. *Human Security and Mutual Vulnerability: An Exploration into the Global Political Economy of Development and Underdevelopment*. International Development Research Centre, Ottawa.
Palma, G. 1998. "Three and a Half Cycles of 'Mania, Panic, and [Asymmetric] Crash': East Asia and Latin America Compared." *Cambridge Journal of Economics* 22(6): 789–808.
Payer, C. 1974. *The Debt Trap*. New York: Monthly Review Press.
Serieux, J. 2000. "Reducing the Debt of the Poorest: Challenges and Opportunities." Mimeo. North-South Institute, Ottawa.
Taylor, L. 1998. "Capital Market Crises: Liberalization, Fixed Exchange Rates and Market-Driven Destabilization." *Cambridge Journal of Economics* 22, no. 6 (November).
Wade, R., and F. Veneroso. 1998. "The Gathering World Slump and the Battle over Capital Controls." *New Left Review* 231 (September/October).
World Bank. 2000. *World Development Report*. Washington, D.C.
World Bank. 2001. *Global Development Finance*. Washington, D.C.

3

Population Dynamics and Food Production in Sub-Saharan Africa

Henry Rempel and Kazi Nazrul Islam

INTRODUCTION

An important theme in the literature on sub-Saharan Africa is that there will be a growing food insecurity problem in many parts of that continent. For example, Alexandratos (1995: 49–50) reports that estimates of the incidence of chronic malnutrition "have been increasing rapidly, both in absolute terms and as a proportion of the region's total population." Karen Gellen (1994: 5) cites a 1993 World Bank study that projects a food shortfall of 80 million tons by 2020 if population growth and food production trends continue. In his critique of this conclusion in the literature, George Abalu (1995: 121) poses the question: "Why does the Malthusian specter continue to emerge from these projections?"

In addition, Awudu Abdulai and Christopher Delgado (1995: 1) report that the agriculture sector in sub-Saharan Africa accounts for 42 percent of the gross domestic product in low-income countries and 27 percent in middle-income countries. In a majority of the countries cash crops account for at least 60 percent of export earnings, and between 65 and 80 percent of the labor force is employed primarily in agriculture.

These projections and statistics point to the importance of a productive use of the available arable land as a primary means to both increase food availability and economic development. Associated with increased land productivity will be a demographic transition where the proportion of the population dependent on agriculture as a primary source of livelihood declines from more than two thirds to less than one third.

In this study we combine new estimates on the arable land base and the sustainable use of such land with population projections for the first two decades of this century to analyze the potential food base at the country and regional levels. The ability to produce food is then related to changes in employment prospects that are required to enable the productivity increases that can reduce the widespread rural poverty evident in many parts of sub-Saharan Africa. These projections are based on regression analysis of data from 1970 to 1996, which seeks to explain the determinants of food production across countries and over time.

The intent of this analysis is not to predict what will happen. Rather, it seeks to highlight what is possible. The chapter concludes with a brief discussion of policy issues that can shape Africa's potential to feed its population with means that are economically feasible and environmentally sustainable.

AN OVERVIEW OF FOOD SUPPLY

In their survey of the prospects for global food security Pinstrup-Andersen, Pandya-Lorch, and Rosegrant (1997: 8–14) project for sub-Saharan Africa that by 2020:

- population size will double;
- there will be positive but low growth in per capita income;
- child malnutrition could reach 40 million, an increase of 45 percent from 1993;
- every third person is likely to be food insecure;
- the average daily calorie availability will be 2,300 per person, deemed to be marginally above minimal requirements;
- land area under cereals will increase by some 25 million hectares; and
- net cereal imports will increase by 150 percent.

In what seems like a fairly pessimistic prognosis for the future, the authors arrive at an interesting conclusion:

> Thomas Malthus's basic argument was that the world's natural resources could not assure expansions in food supply that would match population growth. Region after region has disproved his prediction, but in Sub-Saharan Africa the population growth rate has exceeded the rate of growth in food production since the early 1970s and the gap is widening, resulting in declining per capita food production. . . . Simple extrapolations of the trends in population and food production growth since 1961 show a further increase in the gap between population and food production. This is exactly the gap predicted by Malthus. However, several recent developments suggest that Malthus's shadow over Sub-Saharan Africa could finally be waning. (1997: 21)

As a starting point for understanding the prospect for a better future, Table 3.1 provides Food and Agriculture Organization (FAO) data on average levels of calories per capita available for 1995 to 1997. In addition, we observe the relative importance of cereals, other vegetables, and animal products as sources of these calories. Estimates of recommended daily calories per capita are drawn from the United Nations Development Programme's *Human Development Report* for 1994.

Table 3.1
Level of Calories Consumed and Primary Source of Calories (by country/region/total)

	Calories/Capita/Day		Source of Calories (percent)		
	Average 1995-97	Percent of Recommended Levels	Cereals	Other Vegetable	Animal Products
Sudano Sahel	**1936**	**92**	**60**	**25**	**15**
Burkina Faso	1601	72	72	23	5
Chad	2298	132	60	33	7
Gambia	2252	98	67	28	5
Mali	2178	96	74	15	11
Mauritania	1987	81	48	21	31
Niger	1709	76	67	22	11
Senegal	2338	101	58	34	8
Somalia	1750	94	46	14	40
Sudan	1887	92	54	30	17
West Africa	**2287**	**103**	**43**	**54**	**3**
Benin	1930	81	40	56	4
Côte d'Ivoire	2127	83	26	69	5
Ghana	2015	94	24	71	5
Guinea	2213	99	41	56	2
Guinea-Bissau	1924	86	51	41	8
Liberia	2195	97	41	55	4
Nigeria	2391	109	47	50	2
Sierra Leone	1826	96	46	51	4
Togo	2330	103	32	65	3
Central Africa	**2191**	**102**	**18**	**78**	**4**
Cameroon	2125	96	43	53	4
Central African Republic	2237	121	17	79	3
Congo, Dem. Rep.	2214	104	12	84	4
Congo, Republic of	2169	94	7	87	5
Gabon	1967	81	13	76	11
East Africa	**1997**	**101**	**50**	**41**	**9**
Burundi	2064	106	14	84	2
Ethiopia	1849	109	68	23	9
Kenya	2131	103	56	33	11
Madagascar	2330	108	58	30	12
Mauritius	2387	82	55	38	7
Rwanda	1892	99	22	76	2
Tanzania	1796	82	37	55	8
Uganda	2303	106	24	69	6
Southern Africa	**2274**	**93**	**54**	**35**	**11**
Angola	1903	101	34	61	6
Botswana	2020	89	56	26	18
Lesotho	1992	94	79	14	7
Malawi	2049	100	68	29	3
Mozambique	1951	108	34	63	3
Namibia	2163	110	37	45	19
South Africa	2678	86	55	29	16
Swaziland	2228	85	55	30	15
Zambia	2093	104	71	24	6
Zimbabwe	2073	92	68	23	10
Total	**2142**	**99**	**46**	**46**	**8**

Sources: FAO, 2000; UNDP, 1994.

We observe first that the recommended per capita calorie intake is slightly lower than the 2,300 used by Pinstrup-Andersen, Pandya-Lorch, and Rosegrant (1997: 9). Given that the ratio of children to adult population will be lower in 2020 than during the 1990s, this increase is warranted. As of 1996, the total area provides 99 percent of the average calories provided.[1] The two notable exceptions are the Sudano Sahel region and Southern Africa. The latter primarily reflects significantly higher recommended calorie levels for South Africa and to a lesser extent for Zimbabwe, Botswana, Lesotho, and Swaziland. No explanation for these higher recommended levels is provided. They likely reflect a more varied diet that is associated with higher per capita incomes for significant numbers within the respective populations. Several countries have calorie availability that is more than 10 percent below recommended levels: Burkina Faso, Mauritania, Niger, Benin, Côte d'Ivoire, Guinea-Bissau, Gabon, and Tanzania.[2]

Second, we observe considerable variation among regions in the sources of calories available. For the total area, cereals and other vegetable crops (roots and tubers, to a lesser extent pulses) are of equal importance, whereas animal products are relatively insignificant. The Sudano Sahel, Southern Africa, and East Africa rely relatively more on cereals, wheareas roots and tubers feature prominently in Central Africa and, to a lesser extent, in West Africa. Animal products are important in a few countries dominated by pastoral groups, especially Somalia and Mauritania, and to a lesser extent in Sudan, Botswana, Namibia, South Africa, and Swaziland.

The question can be raised whether average calorie availability is an appropriate measure for nutrition and health. First, it is only one element of a diet that contains the range of nutrients required for good health. Second, it does not allow for differences in the human condition that affect a body's capacity to absorb and utilize the nutrient intake. Third, average values do not provide information on the distribution of the calories available. Widespread malnutrition may reflect primarily differential access to the available food.

Peter Svedberg (1993) examines this issue in detail. He observes that average calorie availability reported in FAO data correlates fairly well with other indicators of health and nutrition drawn both from national and survey data. He concludes, if anything, that the FAO data have tended to overstate the extent of malnutrition in sub-Saharan Africa. For most children, food intake has normally been adequate.

The widespread malnutrition that is observed from time to time is shaped significantly by the primary reliance on rain-fed agriculture. Periodically rains fail for several rainy seasons in a row creating serious malnutrition within selected countries. In other cases a significant portion of the rural population may experience some malnutrition in the month leading up to a new harvest. Both can create vivid images of hunger and starvation in particular locales, which need not be indicative of food availability more generally in each of these regions in sub-Saharan Africa.

An indicator of food insecurity cited frequently is the growth in cereal imports from 1970 onwards. Table 3.2 provides regional data for every fifth year for the period 1970 to 1997 on cereal production and the trade in cereals. To limit the possible bias of exceptional conditions in a particular year, a three-year average is used for each of these six data points. All regional totals represent a sum of the data for the countries in that region. Hence the trade flows reported include exports and imports within a region as well as among regions in Africa. The last column provides the average annual rate of growth from 1970 to 1996.

Table 3.2
Average Regional Production and Trade of Cereal Grains (Metric Tons), 1970–1997

Region/Commodity	1969-71	1974-76	1979-81	1984-86	1989-91	1995-97	Average Annual Rate of Growth(%)
Sudano Sahel							
Cereal Production	7,241,698	8,093,104	8,660,841	9,849,397	10,965,199	13,591,293	2.5
Cereal Exports	84,955	135,508	288,316	44,321	152,665	187,247	3.1
Cereal Imports	758,367	1,050,481	1,469,714	2,708,237	2,435,614	2,005,702	3.8
Net Cereal Imports	673,412	914,974	1,181,398	2,663,916	2,282,949	1,818,456	2.3
West Africa							
Cereal Production	11,967,322	12,224,774	11,289,244	16,987,917	23,131,449	28,103,025	3.3
Cereal Exports	1,896	22,589	9,558	46,280	65,211	52,329	13.6
Cereal Imports	791,999	993,619	3,040,318	2,878,071	2,356,065	3,351,300	5.7
Net Cereal Imports	790,103	971,030	3,030,761	2,831,791	2,290,854	3,298,971	5.6
Central Africa							
Cereal Production	1,544,897	1,814,024	1,894,454	2,150,236	2,510,160	3,012,565	2.6
Cereal Exports	246	877	4,926	10,124	69,556	296	0.7
Cereal Imports	339,361	504,664	660,653	672,221	858,337	750,445	3.1
Net Cereal Imports	339,115	503,787	655,727	662,097	788,781	750,149	3.1
East Africa							
Cereal Production	12,293,180	13,106,253	14,870,163	14,987,974	17,660,753	20,648,338	2.0
Cereal Exports	223,944	121,763	86,102	123,482	185,813	288,910	1.0
Cereal Imports	409,187	735,561	1,155,266	1,644,349	1,403,136	2,303,723	6.9
Net Cereal Imports	185,243	613,798	1,069,164	1,520,867	1,217,322	2,014,813	9.6
Southern Africa							
Cereal Production	14,357,208	18,678,959	20,212,486	16,895,443	19,537,577	18,789,276	1.0
Cereal Exports	1,720,100	3,464,777	3,833,380	1,210,878	2,848,861	2,429,880	1.3
Cereal Imports	984,783	746,178	1,640,975	3,098,565	2,454,991	3,974,920	5.5
Net Cereal Imports	-735,317	-2,718,600	-2,192,405	-1,887,687	-393,870	1,545,039	4.5
TOTAL							
Cereal Production	47,404,305	53,917,114	56,927,188	60,870,966	73,805,137	84,144,498	2.2
Cereal Exports	2,031,141	3,745,514	4,222,281	1,435,085	3,322,106	2,958,662	1.5
Cereal Imports	3,283,697	4,030,503	7,966,926	11,001,442	9,508,143	12,386,090	5.2
Net Cereal Imports	1,252,556	284,989	3,744,645	9,566,358	6,186,037	9,427,429	8.1

Source: FAO, 2000.

We observe first that the average rate of growth in cereal production for the total area was 2.2 percent, below the average rate of population growth for this period. The main exception is Southern Africa, a primary source of cereals, with levels produced remaining fairly constant over time. To make up for the shortfall, cereal imports grew at an average annual rate in excess of 5 percent. This rate of growth is highest in East Africa and lowest in Central Africa, where roots and tubers are much more important.

Several countries, especially South Africa and Zimbabwe, and to a lesser extent Kenya, export cereals, especially white maize. Therefore, net imports (imports minus exports) of cereals are somewhat lower than cereal imports in Southern and Eastern Africa. Nigeria dominates West Africa, and to some extent all of sub-Saharan Africa, as a major importer of cereals.

Table 3.3
Average Regional Net Exports of Agricultural Production ($1,000) and Proportion of Total Cereal Imports That Are Wheat and Rice (percent)

Region/Commodity	1969-71	1974-76	1979-81	1984-86	1989-91	1995-97	Average Annual Rate of Growth(%)
Sudano Sahel							
Net Exports	1,010,427	1,224,107	734,858	-102,503	63,474	-123,744	-8.5
Wheat and Rice	81	66	82	81	91	97	
West Africa							
Net Exports	2,291,672	3,155,502	547,205	3,751,901	2,737,732	3,147,181	1.2
Wheat and Rice	94	94	91	95	98	97	
Central Africa							
Net Exports	530,800	803,970	1,128,215	864,279	148,991	188,200	-3.9
Wheat and Rice	78	62	68	85	92	93	
East Africa							
Net Exports	2,115,472	4,001,687	5,437,568	5,291,728	3,915,700	5,292,238	3.6
Wheat and Rice	81	75	75	75	96	66	
Southern Africa							
Net Exports	2,416,363	5,416,462	6,055,054	1,746,576	3,651,859	2,718,116	0.5
Wheat and Rice	56	79	62	46	63	62	
TOTAL							
Net Exports	8,364,734	14,601,728	13,902,900	11,551,981	10,517,756	11,221,991	1.1
Wheat and Rice	76	75	79	73	86	79	

Source: FAO, 2000.

Table 3.3 augments the information given above with data on the role of wheat and rice as cereal imports and the role of net agricultural exports as a means of paying for cereal imports. As agricultural exports and imports cover a range of products, the net exports are expressed in value rather than quantity terms.

We observe first that wheat and rice account for at least three quarters of all cereals imported. This has generally been the case, with the mid-1970s somewhat of an exception, in all regions except Southern Africa. There the internal movement of white maize among countries in the region offsets the extent of wheat and rice imports. East Africa shows a marked increase in the role of wheat and rice at the beginning of the 1990s, but this does not appear to represent a new trend over time. This temporary increase occurred primarily in Kenya and Tanzania. The latter then had a marked decrease in wheat and rice imports in the latter half of the 1990s.

At the aggregate level, the importation of food is paid for with agricultural exports. Net agricultural exports have exceeded the $10 billion level in all years shown in Table 3.3 except 1970. At the regional level, the one exception to this general pattern is Sudano Sahel, which became a net importer of agricultural goods in both the mid-1980s and the mid-1990s. These data indicate that sub-Saharan Africa's "dependence" on food imports is more of a choice in land use—that is, produce export crops as a means to access imported food, among other goods and services.

Table 3.4
The Determinants of the Value of Food Produced Annually per Capita (constant international U.S. dollars)

Variable	Equation 1	Equation 2	Equation 3	Equation 4
Constant term	3,112 174 0.00	1,983 853 0.03	1,890 896 0.05	-4,696 2,085 0.04
Sustainable land area (hectares/capita)	15.69 1.12 0.00	11.24 1.92 0.00	11.35 1.95 0.00	
Female agricultural labor force as a per cent of female labor force				2.54 0.57 0.00
Real GDP per capita		0.057 0.020 0.01	0.056 0.020 0.01	0.059 0.020 0.01
Fertilizer use (kilograms per hectare of cultivated land)		0.134 0.681 0.85	0.133 0.699 0.85	-0.052 0.617 0.93
Foreign exchange: export revenue plus net foreign transfers as a per cent of GDP			0.085 0.188 0.66	
Index of farm gate price for primary food crop/index of farm gate price for primary agricultural export, lagged one year (1989 – 1991 = 100)	-0.06 0.02 0.02	-0.034 0.027 0.23	-0.036 0.028 0.22	
Index of farm gate price for primary food crop/index of price for food imported, lagged one year (1989-91=100)				0.072 0.037 0.07
Dummy variable: 1 if agricultural exports > 50% of value of total exports; 0 otherwise	102.98 65.03 0.13	125.54 43.71 0.01	127.92 45.57 0.01	111.39 50.26 0.04
Dummy variable for drought: 1 if drought year; 0 otherwise	-66.05 73.46 0.38	-129.82 58.41 0.04	-129.14 61.38 0.05	-149.75 63.35 0.03
AR(1)		0.248 0.191 0.21	0.225 0.200 0.28	0.126 0.225 0.58
Adjusted R-squared	0.902	0.941	0.938	0.930
F-Statistic	56.262 0.00	53.727 0.00	44.655 0.00	44.474 0.00
Durbin-Watson statistic	1.376	2.056	2.112	2.053

Results reported for each variable are the coefficient, standard error, and probability of significance.

PRIMARY DETERMINANTS OF FOOD PRODUCTION

Having observed some of the trends in food production and the trade in cereals, we now consider some of the determinants of food production among countries and over time. The regression results reported in Table 3.4 are based on a combination of cross-section (forty-one countries) and times series (1970 to 1996) data.

The dependent variable is the value of food produced, expressed in constant international U.S. dollars. This represents the most consistent indicator over time for the production of food in these countries. The selection of independent variables was shaped significantly by data available rather than a preferred specification of a food production model. Further, several preferred variables trend together creating multicollinearity problems. This was the case especially for measures of land availability and the agricultural labor supply. Therefore, some variables had to be dropped to overcome this problem. In equations 2 to 4, the AR1 variable represents a correction for first order auto-correlation within the data.

For the production of food, the natural inputs are land, labor, and capital. The land variable used is the sustainable land area available per capita where sustainable land area is based on the estimates made jointly by the International Institute for Applied Systems Analysis and the Food and Agriculture Organization (FAO) (1993). The arable land area is based on seven categories according to soil and climate conditions. In each of the seven categories the cropping intensity that is deemed sustainable is indicated. From this total is then subtracted the land area covered by habitation and the land area set aside as protected areas. It is possible, but unlikely, that the sustainable level of multiple cropping is sufficiently high that this measure generates an arable land area that exceeds the total land area of a country.

The coefficient for sustainable land area per capita is consistently significant with a positive sign, which indicates an increase in the value of food produced where more land per capita is available. At the mean value for the two variables, the elasticity of food supply with respect to land available is 0.31. This shows that there is a land constraint to food production, but the overall effect is inelastic.

The labor input variable was the female agricultural labor supply per hectare of land under cultivation. The female agricultural labor supply was chosen given the emphasis in the literature that women take a primary role in producing the food supply (e.g., FAO, 1987; Quisumbing et al., 1995; Whitehead, 1993: 429–34). Given that this variable was highly correlated with the sustainable land area per capita, an alternative variation was attempted: the female agricultural labor force expressed as a percent of the total female labor force. The hypothesis would be that the lower this percentage, the more developed the agriculture sector as less labor is required. This variable was highly correlated with the land variable, so it was entered only as an alternative to the land variable in equation 4.[3]

Contrary to our expectation, the coefficient has a positive sign. At the mean value, the food supply elasticity with respect to the labor variable is 1.36. This is somewhat higher than that for land, suggesting that a labor constraint is stronger than the land constraint. The positive coefficient partly reflects that this variable also measures the effect of the land variable as an input. Further, it implies that the technology available to the small farmers is such that the availability of women as an agriculture labor force does have a significant, direct effect on the value of food produced.

Of interest is that substituting the labor variable for the land variable plus the use of an alternative measure for the effect of farm gate prices on production causes the constant term to be negative in equation 4, whereas it was positive in the other equations. There is no obvious explanation for this reversal in the sign of this coefficient.

As there was no appropriate measure for capital used in the production of food, the quantity of fertilizer per hectare was entered as a proxy variable. The expectation was that the use of chemical fertilizer was an indicator of agricultural technology, where the use of fertilizer was assumed to be associated directly with the intensity of capital employed in agriculture. The data show that fertilizer use was not a significant determinant of the value of food produced. In part this reflects the unimportance of chemical fertilizer: The average level was low, 18 kilograms/hectare, and was likely applied primarily for the production of export crops.

Given that much of agriculture in sub-Saharan Africa is rain fed, a dummy variable was entered for drought. The variable was measured with the same method used by William Jaeger (1992: 1637), where a country was deemed to be experiencing a drought in any year where the value of food production was significantly below the trend line for the country. This variable is significant, with a negative sign, in equations 2 to 4, which provides consistent support for the claim that the rainfall variability has an important bearing on the quantity of food produced (Benneh, 1996: 6).

Policy from the mid-1980s onward was driven by the presumption of the International Monetary Fund, the World Bank, and various donors that a primary reason for poor performance in the food production subsector was "low" prices obtained by farmers. This policy was tested with two variations: (1) an index of the farm gate price of a country's staple food divided by an index of the farm gate price of the country's primary export crop; and (2) the index of farm gate prices for the staple food crop divided by an index of prices for all food imports. Both variables were lagged a year where last year's prices were deemed to influence food production in the current year.

The first of these two variables is significant, with a negative sign, only in equation 1. The second is significant with the postulated positive sign, based on a one-tail test for significance (see equation 4). These results are consistent with the literature that argues that farm gate prices for food are not particularly important given significant farm input supply constraints, especially technology appropriate for use by small farmers (Benneh, 1996; Bryceson, 1993; de Alcántara, 1993; Krueger, Schiff, and Valdés, 1992; and Platteau, 1993: 282, 297). The positive role of the second price variable is consistent with the conclusion by

John Mellor and Raisuddin Ahmed (1988), who argue that price levels more generally govern the behavior of farmers rather than the price for one particular crop.

An attempt was made to analyze whether there was an effective foreign exchange constraint to increased food production. The evidence here is mixed with no clear indication of an effective foreign exchange constraint. The direct variable employed to test this hypothesis was the rate of export revenue plus net foreign transfers of funds as a percent of Gross Domestic Product (GDP). The coefficient for this variable is not significant (see equation 3).

Given the importance of agricultural exports as a means of funding imports, a dummy variable was entered with a value of 1 for each year for a country where the value of agricultural exports was more than half the value of total exports and 0 otherwise.[4] This variable is significant, with a positive sign, in equations 2 to 4. These results are consistent with the subset of the literature that argues that export crop production can complement food production (Kennedy and Cogill, 1988; Maxwell and Fernando, 1989: 1693–94; von Braun and Kennedy, 1987; and Whitehead, 1993: 434–35) Where competition exists, it is more likely to be a conflict between large-scale production of cash crops for export and the small-scale farming that characterizes much of food production in sub-Saharan Africa.

Finally, it is to be expected that the capacity to produce food is correlated positively with the overall standard of living as measured by GDP per capita. The regression results confirm that this is the case. Even though the coefficient has a positive sign and is statistically significant, the effect on the value of food production is quite small with a supply elasticity, at mean values, of 0.27.

The overall explanatory power of the model is good with adjusted R-squares in excess of 0.9. The set of explanatory variables are statistically significant at the 1 percent level (F-Statistic) and the Durbin-Watson statistic is within an acceptable range.

THE LAND BASE FOR SUSTAINABLE AGRICULTURE

Sustainable land area available per capita was shown in the previous section to be one of the determinants of the value of food produced. Given that the land area does not change much over time, the growth in population has adverse effects on the land area available.

A weakness of a direct use of the arable land variable provided in the FAO data set is that it does not take into account whether it needs to remain fallow periodically or rainfall and irrigation conditions are such that it can be cropped on a sustainable basis more than once in a year. As a result, we use the International Institute for Applied Systems Analysis and the Food and Agriculture Organization (IIASA/FAO, 1993) measure of sustainable land area as defined for Table 3.4.

In Figure 3.1 this sustainable land area is assumed to remain constant. Population and agricultural labor force estimates are then utilized for each decade from 1970 to 2020 to show the declining sustainable land base over time. At the

Figure 3.1
Estimates of Changes in Sustainable Land Area per Capita of the Agricultural Labor Force, 1970–2020

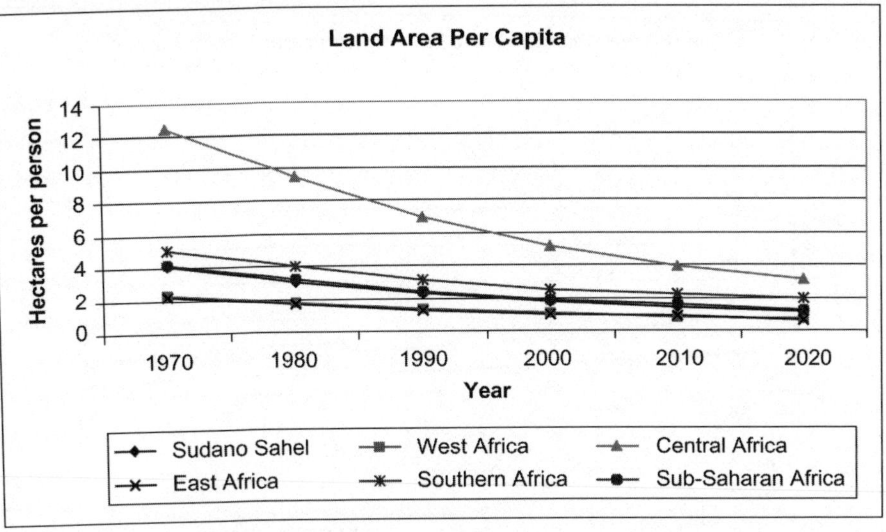

aggregate level the per capita land base declines from 4.2 hectares to 1.3 hectares. A rapid decline is especially evident in Central Africa. Land available per capita is below average for West and East Africa. At the country level, three have estimated land available per capita below 0.1 hectare by 2020: Mauritius, Rwanda, and Somalia. Burundi has only slightly more, 0.12 hectares

The decline in sustainable land area per member of the agricultural labor force (Figure 3.2) is not quite as dramatic because this segment of the labor force is growing slower than the total population. At the aggregate level the decline is from 11.5 hectares per member to 4.2 hectares. Even in East Africa the estimated sustainable land area per member of the agricultural labor force remains in excess of a hectare (1.4). This still exceeds the global average land utilization level of 1.2 hectares per person (Wood, Sebastian, and Scherr, 2000: 34).

These estimates show that population is indeed increasing the pressure on the land, but on average there is still the prospect by 2020 of 4 hectares available for each member of the agricultural labor force. To achieve this potential, there will need to be full utilization of all arable land available, a proper use of water resources, and specific action to maintain soil fertility.

THE POTENTIAL TO MEET STAPLE FOOD REQUIREMENTS

As a means of estimating the land area to maintain food supplies for a growing population, it was assumed that the quantity of cereals, pulses, and roots and tubers per capita would be the same in 2020 as during the 1990s. For each of

Figure 3.2
Estimates of Changes in Sustainable Land Area per Member of the Agricultural Labor Force, 1970–2020

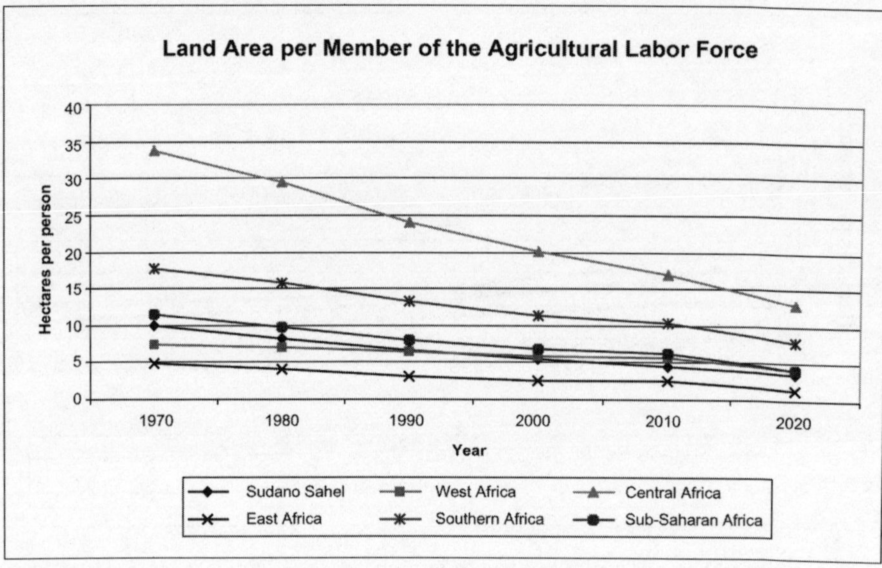

these three types of crops, the maximum produced in any one year during the 1990s was entered as the base amount. For the cereals, the quantity of cereals imported was added to the production total. These base quantities were seen as an estimate of food available for the best year during the 1990s. For each country this base quantity for each of these three types of crops was increased by the average annual rate of population growth from 1996 to 2020. These three values were then used as an estimate of the food required in 2020.

Table 3.5
Estimates of Land Requirements to Maintain Food Levels for the 1990s for the Population Size Estimates for 2020

Region	Land Required to Grow Projected Food Crops for 2020 (1000 ha)		Change in Yield Required to Maintain Current Area for Arable Land Plus Permanent Crops		Land Required as a Percent of Sustainable Land Base with No Decrease in Forest Area	
	Based on 1996 Yields	Based on a 20% Yield Increase	Change 1996 to 2020 (%)	Average Annual Rate of Increase 1996 – 2020	1996 Yields	20% Yield Increase
Sudano Sahel	49,122	40,935	65	2.1	54	45
West Africa	66,342	55,285	35	1.3	43	36
Central Africa	16,809	14,007	-5	-0.2	10	8
East Africa	44,848	37,373	30	1.1	32	27
Southern Africa	44,218	36,848	36	1.3	21	18
TOTAL	231,494	192,912	41	1.4	30	25

Source: FAO (2000).

In Table 3.5, columns 2 and 3 estimate the land area required to produce the three types of crops as estimated for 2020. Column 2 assumes the same yields per hectare for each of the three crop types that were observed in 1996 (an average yield for 1995 to 1997). Column 3 estimates the land area required to produce the 2020 required food if the yields for each of the three crop types increased by 20 percent.

For columns 4 and 5 it is assumed that the land area to produce the crop levels in 2020 remains the same as the arable land plus permanent crops in 1996. The increases in yields are then estimated for each region as well as the average annual rate of growth in yields between 1996 and 2020.

At the aggregate level, yields would need to increase by 41 percent. This represents an annual increase in yields of 1.4 percent. Central Africa as a region would not need to increase crop yields. The region that will either need to increase land area or yields by a substantial amount is the Sudano Sahel. If land area is maintained at 1996 levels, yields will need to increase by 65 percent, which is a 2.1 percent annual increase in yields from 1996 to 2020.

A limitation of the IIASA/FAO (1993) sustainable land area estimates is that land remaining in forest cover is limited to land not suited for crops. Therefore, for each country the difference in land area designated as forest in the FAO (2000) data set and the forest area in the IIASA/FAO data set is subtracted from the total estimate of sustainable land area available for crops. In column 6, the estimated land area required to grow the estimated crop levels for 2020, using 1996 yields, is shown as a percent of this reduced estimate of sustainable land area available made by IIASA/FAO. In column 7, we show the same estimate but assume a 20 percent increase in yields.

We observe that there is no obvious land constraint in any of the regions, even if yields for these three types of crops are merely maintained at 1996 levels. These estimates are consistent with Partha Dasgupta's (1995: 1882) conclusion that population growth is not a primary cause of observed deterioration in living standards. What holds at the regional level, though, does not hold necessarily for each country within these regions. The country level data identify the following problem areas:

- Burkina Faso would need to reduce its 1996 forest area by 12 percent if 1996 yields are maintained; by 3 percent if yields increase by 20 percent.
- Mauritania would need to reduce its 1996 forest area by 26 percent at current yields; by 20 percent if yields increase.
- Niger would need to use all of its forest area. There is an anomaly here in that the FAO data lists forest area below that given in the IIASA/FAO estimates.
- Kenya would need to reduce the 1996 forest area by 6 percent at current yields; by 0.5 percent if yields increase.
- Rwanda would use all of its forest area if yields are maintained; 94 percent of its forest area if yields increase by 20 percent. Again, there is somewhat of an anomaly here as the IIASA/FAO estimate of forest area is larger than that shown by the FAO (2000).

It needs to be emphasized that the estimates in columns 6 and 7 of Table 3.5 merely indicate the potential for increased use of available land. In practice, the concentration in land ownership, the limited infrastructure development in some countries, and the presence of such diseases as malaria, river blindness, and sleeping sickness in some of the potentially productive land areas are all shaping how population pressure is causing both the use and misuse of the arable land available. The problems identified in the projections for 2020 made by Pinstrup-Andersen, Pandya-Lorch, and Rosegrant (1997: 38–44) are indicative of problems that will need to be addressed if the potential of sub-Saharan Africa's sustainable land base is to be realized.

THE ROLE OF INCREASED LABOR PRODUCTIVITY

Merely having sufficient land to grow adequate supplies of food does not necessarily solve the problems of famine and malnutrition. The people need to have access to such supplies of food. In sub-Saharan Africa, poverty is a basic cause of malnutrition (Eicher, 1982: 151). This poverty is located primarily in the rural areas (Benneh, 1996; Mellor and Ahmed, 1988: 285; Pinstrup-Andersen, Pandya-Lorch, and Babu, 1997: 23). Therefore, the productive employment of rural labor is an important means to addressing the endemic malnutrition (Desai, 1992: 162; Mellor and Ahmed, 1988; Radwan, 1995: 23; and Wangwe, 1993: 289).

The productive employment of rural labor includes both increased productivity for labor engaged in farming and remunerative forms of nonagricultural employment. The latter can be located in the rural areas and in the smaller towns as well as in the major urban centers. In general, all countries in the world that have increased productivity of rural labor have also achieved development that reduces the proportion of the population that relies on agriculture as the primary source of income from two thirds to less than one third.

To analyze what this might mean for the countries under study, we have imposed the condition that one third of the estimated population for 2020 will be agriculture based and two thirds will draw their primary source of income from nonagricultural activities. Table 3.6 reports the population that derives its primary source of income from agriculture as of 2000 and what the estimate of this number would be for 2020 with one third of the total population deemed to be agriculture. The FAO (2000) data set projects agriculture population and the number economically active (labor force) in agriculture for 2010. This ratio of agriculture labor force to agriculture population in 2010 is applied to the 2020 estimated agriculture population to arrive at the estimate for agriculture labor force in 2020 as shown in Table 3.6. The last two columns in Table 3.6 then utilize the estimated land area required to grow food, as reported in Table 3.5, to estimate the changes in land area utilized per member of the agricultural labor force.

We observe first that the transition out of agriculture projected for 2020 reduces the absolute size of the agriculture population, but not the absolute size of the agricultural labor force. At the regional levels, there are some variations

Table 3.6
The Impact on Land Labor Ratios of Shifting Agricultural Labor Out of Agriculture

	Population and Labor Force (1000)				Land Area Per Person (ha.)		
	Agriculture Population		Agriculture Labor Force		Agriculture Labor Force		
	2000	2020 (33%)	2000	2020	2000	2020	2020 (+20%)
Sudano Sahel	**69,553**	**49,472**	**31,476**	**24,785**	**0.78**	**0.99**	**0.83**
Burkina Faso	10,968	6,694	5,412	3,276	0.66	0.78	0.65
Chad	5,714	4,007	2,766	1,868	0.73	1.04	0.87
Gambia	1,025	638	518	309	0.26	0.62	0.52
Mali	8,985	5,951	4,383	3,487	0.57	0.58	0.48
Mauritania	1,383	1,387	639	628	0.74	1.77	1.47
Niger	9,400	6,209	4,415	3,049	2.05	2.38	1.98
Senegal	6,938	4,858	3,105	2,265	0.53	0.96	0.80
Somalia	7,187	5,931	3,075	2,913	0.49	0.59	0.49
Sudan	17,901	13,798	7,143	6,022	1.27	1.67	1.39
West Africa	**72,605**	**85,687**	**30,335**	**43,302**	**1.22**	**1.49**	**1.24**
Benin	3,266	3,192	1,472	1,603	0.84	1.11	0.92
Côte d'Ivoire	7,224	6,874	2,889	3,093	0.89	1.38	1.15
Ghana	11,308	10,507	5,436	5,420	0.46	0.57	0.48
Guinea	6,221	3,741	2,946	1,986	0.32	0.44	0.36
Guinea-Bissau	995	564	467	267	0.33	0.50	0.42
Liberia	2,114	1,859	853	741	0.25	0.47	0.39
Nigeria	37,005	54,156	14,670	27,228	1.88	2.32	1.93
Sierra Leone	3,003	2,375	1,118	932	0.54	0.85	0.71
Togo	2,744	2,418	1,134	1,075	0.82	1.05	0.88
Central Africa	**44,537**	**40,768**	**18,936**	**19,096**	**0.42**	**0.57**	**0.47**
Cameroon	7,882	7,470	3,624	4,062	0.46	0.66	0.55
Central African Republic	2,603	1,653	1,257	852	0.35	0.44	0.37
Congo, Dem Rep	32,408	29,456	13,357	12,853	0.41	0.52	0.44
Congo, Rep	1,191	1,611	491	707	0.33	0.95	0.79
Gabon	459	577	209	273	0.44	1.18	0.98
East Africa	**144,619**	**90,922**	**69,806**	**60,838**	**0.36**	**0.34**	**0.28**
Burundi	6,003	3,373	3,274	2,056	0.25	0.25	0.21
Ethiopia	54,286	34,632	23,491	17,222	0.41	0.45	0.38
Kenya	22,552	12,338	11,627	8,048	0.28	0.32	0.27
Madagascar	11,763	8,370	5,547	4,701	0.36	0.39	0.32
Mauritius	133	423	58	199	0.06	1.19	0.99
Rwanda	6,926	3,641	3,752	2,136	0.26	0.29	0.24
Tanzania	25,961	16,214	13,730	11,012	0.45	0.51	0.42
Uganda	16,983	11,931	8,438	6,948	0.46	0.52	0.43
Southern Africa	**52,680**	**46,979**	**24,297**	**27,834**	**1.10**	**1.24**	**1.03**
Angola	9,180	7,135	4,213	3,424	0.43	0.72	0.60
Botswana	706	657	314	340	1.17	3.29	2.74
Lesotho	813	1,005	335	492	0.87	1.54	1.28
Malawi	8,396	5,528	4,313	4,101	0.61	0.67	0.56
Mozambique	14,881	8,916	8,172	7,071	0.40	0.51	0.43
Namibia	839	669	290	249	1.34	2.59	2.16
South Africa	5,813	13,826	1,532	7,167	4.43	5.74	4.78
Swaziland	339	510	124	198	0.79	1.30	1.08
Zambia	6,302	4,384	2,678	2,094	0.47	0.55	0.45
Zimbabwe	7,257	4,349	3,349	2,620	0.79	0.81	0.67
Sub-Saharan Africa	**381,566**	**313,828**	**173,622**	**180,746**	**0.72**	**0.82**	**0.68**

to this pattern: In Sudano Sahel and in East Africa, the absolute size of the agricultural labor force declines; in West Africa, the absolute size of the agriculture population increases. Two countries, South Africa and Mauritius, are already to the stage of development where less than one third of the population is deemed agriculture.

This transition in the employment of the rural people opens up new possibilities for increased productivity of the agricultural labor force. If yields remain at the 1996 levels and land area is either expanded or utilized more intensively, the agricultural labor force will have more land to work with in 2020 than in 2000. For the total area, the land area increases from 0.72 to 0.82 hectares. The one exception is East Africa, where land area per person declines from 0.36 to 0.34 hectares. In Sudano Sahel, West and Central Africa the remaining agricultural labor force will have more land to work with in 2020 than 2000 even if land productivity increases by 20 percent. In East Africa and Southern Africa, the increase in yield will be offset slightly by less land being cultivated or land being cultivated less intensively.

In nineteen of the forty-one countries, agricultural labor could enjoy the double benefit of increased land area per person plus productivity increase. For all countries in East and Southern Africa, the increased yields would be offset partially by a decline in land area.

Table 3.7 then considers the implications for nonagricultural activities if the assumption is imposed that two thirds of the estimated population for 2020 will draw their primary source of livelihood from nonagricultural activities. The first two columns indicate the population totals and the next two provide estimates of the labor force. The last column shows the annual rate of growth in nonagricultural employment that would need to occur between 2000 and 2020 to make the fourth column numbers possible. To place these estimates in perspective, the second-last column shows the annual rate of growth in nonagricultural employment from 1970 to 2000.

At the aggregate level, the annual rate of employment creation would need to be 25 percent higher in the next twenty years than the rate observed during the past thirty years (5.6 versus 4.5 percent). The need for an increased rate of nonagricultural employment creation would be especially pronounced in East Africa (9.8 versus 4.8 percent) and secondarily in Sudano Sahel (7.7 versus 4.7 percent). In both cases, the relative size of the agricultural labor force is higher in 2000 than in the other regions in sub-Saharan Africa. In West Africa, this rate of growth in employment could decline, and in Southern Africa it could remain constant. Burkina Faso, Mali, Niger, Guinea, Burundi, Ethiopia, and Rwanda face especially daunting challenges in their respective struggles to increase the productivity of rural labor.

POTENTIAL FOR ADEQUATE NUTRITION AND SUSTAINABLE AGRICULTURE

Achieving food security for all within a sustainable agricultural system is a major challenge. Various authors have identified a litany of issues that would need to be addressed. One summary statement on the subject is that of George Benneh (1996):

> Several factors account for the poor performance of the food sector of Sub-Saharan African agriculture. They include the constraints of the physical environment and

Table 3.7
Nonagricultural Employment Implications of Addressing Rural Poverty

	Number in Non-agricultural Activities (1000)				Annual Rate of Growth	
	Population		Labor Force		Non-agricultural Labor Force	
	2000	2020 (67%)	2000	2020	1970 - 2000	2000 – 2020
Sudano Sahel	24,506	98,944	10,615	46,486	4.7	7.7
Burkina Faso	927	13,387	457	6,559	2.0	14.3
Chad	1,885	8,013	913	3,735	6.4	7.3
Gambia	273	1,277	138	616	5.0	7.8
Mali	2,108	11,901	1,028	6,968	5.4	10.0
Mauritania	1,272	2,774	588	1,258	6.2	3.9
Niger	1,291	12,417	607	6,105	4.7	12.2
Senegal	2,480	9,716	1,109	4,531	4.0	7.3
Somalia	2,910	11,862	1,245	5,824	4.6	8.0
Sudan	11,412	27,596	4,553	12,045	4.9	5.0
West Africa	100,441	171,374	40,641	83,294	5.0	3.7
Benin	2,782	6,385	1,254	3,208	5.3	4.8
Côte d'Ivoire	7,439	13,748	2,977	6,185	5.7	3.7
Ghana	8,822	21,014	4,123	10,368	3.2	4.7
Guinea	1,197	7,482	567	3,975	4.3	10.2
Guinea-Bissau	207	1,128	97	530	4.1	8.9
Liberia	1,016	3,719	410	1,486	4.3	6.7
Nigeria	74,026	108,313	29,346	54,457	5.4	3.1
Sierra Leone	1,826	4,750	680	1,864	3.2	5.2
Togo	1,851	4,836	766	2,151	4.1	5.3
Central Africa	29,417	81,535	11,778	34,925	4.5	5.6
Cameroon	7,090	14,941	2,474	5,860	5.8	4.4
Central African Republic	979	3,307	472	1,701	4.9	6.6
Congo, Dem Rep	18,853	58,911	7,769	25,709	4.1	6.2
Congo, Rep	1,732	3,223	715	1,412	4.6	3.5
Gabon	757	1,154	345	548	6.2	2.3
East Africa	37,365	181,843	17,428	112,778	4.8	9.8
Burundi	647	6,747	352	4,105	3.5	13.1
Ethiopia	11,784	69,264	5,114	34,599	4.6	10.0
Kenya	7,354	24,675	3,791	16,094	5.3	7.5
Madagascar	4,078	16,740	1,923	9,400	4.3	8.3
Mauritius	1,015	846	437	396	3.3	-0.5
Rwanda	739	7,281	401	4,262	3.9	12.5
Tanzania	7,249	32,429	3,338	16,615	5.2	8.4
Uganda	4,511	23,861	2,092	12,007	4.7	9.1
Southern Africa	57,793	93,959	24,476	48,440	3.5	3.5
Angola	3,596	14,271	1,649	6,853	3.3	7.4
Botswana	908	1,314	403	679	7.0	2.6
Lesotho	1,331	2,011	549	984	2.4	3.0
Malawi	2,430	11,057	889	4,379	5.1	8.3
Mozambique	4,680	17,831	1,970	8,467	3.4	7.6
Namibia	873	1,338	415	747	3.9	3.0
South Africa	34,359	27,652	14,408	16,201	3.1	0.6
Swaziland	663	1,019	243	397	5.1	2.5
Zambia	2,781	8,768	1,182	4,188	3.7	6.5
Zimbabwe	4,326	8,698	1,997	5,240	4.3	4.9
Sub-Saharan Africa	251,950	627,655	105,879	317,487	4.5	5.6

deteriorating natural resource base, inefficient agricultural technology, inadequate land tenure arrangements, gender bias in policy formulation and implementation, rapid population growth, increasing incidence of rural poverty, poor socioeconomic infrastructure, the neglect of agriculture—especially the food sector—by governments and researchers, political instability, the noninvolvement of local communities in the design and implementation of agricultural programs and projects, and researchers' disregard of indigenous technical knowledge in their search for solutions to agricultural problems.

The relative importance of each of these factors may vary from one country to another. (p. 5)

Others are more direct in locating blame for the food crisis. For example, Jean Philippe Platteau (1993: 294) refers to "extortion on the part of the state" in the form of taxation and agriculture pricing policies that has "pumped the economic surplus out of agriculture." Meghnad Desai (1992: 65) adds to this the destabilizing effects of civil war in a number of countries. In addition, he is inclined to locate the source of the widespread rural poverty with international policies: structural adjustment and international debt (Desai, 1992: 64). We limit ourselves to the two issues that flow from the preceding analysis: the productive use of rural labor and sustainable use of the available land. There is some overlap with the issues identified by Benneh, Platteau, and Desai in that the development of markets for agricultural output is an important element, especially for the productive use of rural labor.

The focus for the productive use of labor must be the small farmers who "account for 70 percent of total employment, 40 percent of total merchandise exports, 33 percent of GDP" (Delgado, 1997: 147). Stein Hansen (1992) argues that the most effective way to reduce their poverty is to make use of their most abundant resource, their labor. "Policies that are effective in this contest are those that do not discriminate against smallholder agriculture and the informal sector. At the same time the productivity of their time can be greatly enhanced if they are provided better access to markets and social services (schools, extension services and health centers)" (p. 162).

A prominent theme in discussions on increasing smallholder production is the absence of markets or the imperfect nature of markets (Muller, 1997: 1; USDA, 1986: 5). Others emphasize the high cost of marketing, especially storage and transport. According to Benneh (1996: 24), agricultural marketing margins are typically twice those observed in Asian countries.

A contributing factor to high marketing costs is the combination of agricultural pricing policy and inaccessibility of markets to all farmers. There is evidence that such policies played an important role in nation-building where governments seek to integrate all people into an economy (Bryceson, 1993: 84). Estimates now indicate that at least partial liberalization could reduce significantly the marketing costs of a staple crop such as maize (Argwings-Kodhek, Mukumbu, and Monke, 1993: 346).

The policy prescription of market liberalization and allowing market prices to establish agricultural prices has not met with the expected success (de Alcántara, 1993). In part this reflects the limited development of national markets and hence the lack of effective competition in many markets within a country. In large part, though, market liberalization has failed to deliver expected results, at least in the short term, because supply constraints faced by small farmers exceed any motivating effects price levels provide (Platteau, 1993: 297; Wangwe, 1993: 285). The prescriptions proposed include stabilizing prices (Mellor and Ahmed, 1988: 166), advancing technology that is appropriate for the small farmers involved (Gellen, 1994; Pinstrup-Andersen, Pandya-Lorch, and Rosegrant, 1997; Platteau, 1993), and reducing transport and storage cost through infrastructure development (Collier and Gunning, 1998: 9–10; Delgado, 1997: 166–67; Idachaba, 1993: 199–200). Especially in the area of technology, the definition of "appropriate" needs to factor in the place of women within the larger systems that govern food production (Whitehead, 1993).

The development of alternative employment opportunities needs to occur concurrently with these other measures. To some extent, they exist already. Several authors note the role of off-farm employment, especially during the off-season in farming activity, as a means of supplementing household income and to minimize risk through diversification of income sources (Delgado, 1997: 153–57; Moris, 1989: 220–21; Wangwe, 1993: 289–91).

To enable the more enterprising small farmers to apply appropriate technology and raise farm productivity, alternative employment opportunities need to be generated for the growing rural labor force (Eicher, 1992: 87; Rahmato, 1987: 281; von Braun, de Haen and Blanken, 1991: 109–10; and Stewart, Lall, and Wangwe, 1992: 14). The beneficial effects are evident in the countries that have made the most progress in developing nonagricultural employment opportunities in that they were better able to maintain food security in the face of the devastating employment effects and adverse economic growth effects of structural adjustment programs (Rempel, 1998: 12–17).

Even if such employment options are developed during the next twenty years, there is still a major issue of sustainable approaches to providing food security. Traditional approaches to social organization and land use are breaking down (Desai, 1992: 141: Ghai, 1992). Two important contributing factors are large-scale commercialization of farming and refugee movements caused by civil strife. In other areas, marginal farmers try to extend the technology they know on to land where rainfall is too low and irregular, causing the soil to erode and to lose its limited fertility.

The extent of the problem is severe (Harsch, 1995; Pinstrup-Andersen, Pandya-Lorch, and Babu, 1997: 38–40). These authors estimate that 30 percent of the agricultural land and forest area is degraded and another 35 percent of the agricultural land has some degradation of the soil. Deforestation is occurring in many areas and several countries are deemed to have water stress.

In part, these problems are occurring because the potential agricultural land is not distributed evenly as approximately two thirds of the land area is too arid for rain-fed crop production (Platteau, 1993: 316). Pinstup-Andersen, Pandya-Lorch, and Rosegrant (1997: 24) project that land area under irrigation could be doubled by 2020, but the amount of land involved would still be too small to enable a revolutionary change in agricultural production. A more promising option is building on the traditional methods of the small farmers to extend water harvesting, in the form of contouring soils and building rain catchment systems, to another 50 million hectares (Bryant, 1994: 27).

We conclude with an additional observation. The data provided in the previous sections indicate that food supplies are basically adequate at the regional level. Further, the land well suited for agriculture is limited and distributed unevenly within and among countries. This suggests that a regional, rather than a country-based, approach to food security is warranted. Two studies have analyzed the potential and the means for such a strategy in Southern Africa (Gyekye and Rempel, 1995; Koester, 1986). Provided the political will is there, this approach to building up, maintaining, and distributing strategic food reserves is commended for the various regions in Africa.

NOTES

1. The term "total" is used as several countries were excluded because of a lack of data for some variables or for some of the years under study. The countries omitted are Cape Verde, Comoros, Djibouti, Equitorial Guinea, Réunion, Sao Tome and Principe, Seychelles, and St. Helena. Given their small size, their being omitted will not really affect either the regional totals or the total reported. Also, rather than drop both Ethiopia and Eritrea from the sample, the data for the two countries were combined for the period 1993 to 1997.

2. Mauritius also shows 82 percent but has a much higher recommended calories level similar to that of some of the Southern Africa countries.

3. In general, the ratio of the female agricultural labor force to the total female labor force was trending downward over time in most of the countries in the sample.

4. This could be seen as a competing hypothesis on the foreign exchange constraint issue, especially for the countries where agricultural exports are an important source of foreign exchange. That the coefficient changes very little between equations 2 and 3 suggests that this variable is not capturing directly what is being measured with the foreign exchange variable.

REFERENCES

Abalu, G.I. 1995. "Comments on Part II: Sub-Saharan Africa." In *Population and Food in the Early Twenty-First Century: Meeting Future Food Demand of an Increasing Population,* edited by N. Islam. Washington, D.C.: International Food Policy Research Institute.

Abdulai, A., and C.L. Delgado. 1995. *Re-establishing Agriculture as a Priority for Development Policy in Sub-Saharan Africa*. Washington, D.C.: International Food Policy Research Institute.

Alexandratos, N. 1995. *World Agriculture: Towards 2010—an FAO Study*. Chichester: John Wiley and Sons.

Argwings-Kodhek, M.G. Mukumbu, and E. Monke. 1993. "The Impacts of Maize Market Liberalization in Kenya." *Food Research Institute Studies* 22 (3): 331–47.

Benneh, G. 1996. *Toward Sustainable Smallholder Agriculture in Sub-Saharan Africa.* IFPRI Lecture Series 4, International Food Policy Research Institute, Washington, D.C.

Bryant, E. 1994. "Water: Tapping Africa's Most Basic Resource." *African Farmer* 12 (July): 25–28.

Bryceson, D.F. 1993. "Urban Bias Revisited: Staple Food Pricing in Tanzania." In *Real Markets: Social and Political Issues of Food Policy Reform*, edited by C. Hewitt de Alcántara. London: Frank Cass.

Collier, P., and J.W. Gunning. 1998. *Explaining African Economic Performance*. Working Paper Series WPS/97-22, Institute of Economics and Statistics, University of Oxford, Oxford.

Dasgupta, P. 1995. "The Population Problem: Theory and Evidence." *Journal of Economic Literature* 33 (December): 1879–1901.

de Alcántara, C.H. 1993. "Introduction: Markets in Principle and Practice." In *Real Markets: Social and Political Issues of Food Policy Reform*, edited by C.H. de Alcántara. London: Frank Cass.

Delgado, C.L. 1997. "The Role of Smallholder Income Generation from Agriculture in Sub-Saharan Africa." In *Achieving Food Security in Southern Africa*, edited by Lawrence Haddad. Washington, D.C.: International Food Policy Research Institute.

Desai, M. 1992. "Population and Poverty in Africa." *African Development Review* 4:2 (December): 63–78.

Eicher, C.K. 1982. "Facing Up to Africa's Food Crisis." *Foreign Affairs* 61 (Fall): 151–74.

———. 1992. "African Agricultural Development Strategies." In *Alternative Development Strategies in Sub-Saharan Africa*, edited by F. Stewart, S. Lall, and S. Wangwe. New York: St. Martin's Press, Inc.

Food and Agriculture Organization. 1987. "Women in African Food Production and Food Security." In *Food Policy: Integrating Supply, Distribution, and Consumption*, edited by J.P. Gittinger, J. Leslie, and C. Hoisington. Baltimore: The Johns Hopkins University Press.

Food and Agriculture Organization. 2000. *FAOSTAT Statistical Database*. Rome.

Gellen, K. 1994. "Filling Africa's Granaries: Continent Confronts Challenge of Production." *African Farmer* 12 (July): 2–7, 41.

Ghai, D. 1992. *Conservation, Livelihood and Democracy: Social Dynamics of Environmental Changes in Africa*. Discussion Paper 33, United Nations Research Institute for Social Development, Geneva.

Gyekye, A., and H. Rempel. 1995. "Regional Co-operation as a Means to Food Security in the SADC." *The South African Journal of Economics* 63(2): 272–82.

Hansen, S. 1992. "Population and the Environment." *African Development Review* 4:2 (December): 118–64.

Harsch, E. 1995. "Safeguarding Africa's Environment." *African Farmer* (May–September): 2–7, 40.

Idachaba, F. 1993. "Policy Options for African Agriculture." In *The Political Economy of Hunger*, Vol. 3: *Endemic Hunger*, edited by J. Drèze and A. Sen. Oxford: Clarendon Press.

International Institute for Applied Systems Analysis and Food and Agriculture Organization. 1993. *Potential Cultivable Land: Africa*. Laxenburg and Rome.

Jaeger, W.K. 1992. "The Causes of Africa's Food Crisis." *World Development* 20: 1631–45.

Kennedy, E., and B. Cogill. 1988. "The Commercialization of Agriculture and Household-Level Food Security: The Case of Southwestern Kenya." *World Development* 16(9): 1075–81.

Koester, U. 1986. *Regional Cooperation to Improve Food Security in Southern and Eastern African Countries*. Research Report No. 53, International Food Policy Research Institute, Washington, D.C.

Krueger, A.O., M. Schiff, and A. Valdés. 1992. "Agricultural Incentives in Developing Countries: Measuring the Effect of Sectoral and Economy Wide Policies." In *World Food in the 1990s: Production, Trade, and Aid*, edited by L.B. Fletcher. Boulder: Westview Press.

Maxwell, S., and A. Fernando. 1989. "Cash Crops in Developing Countries: The Issues, the Facts, the Policies." *World Development* 17(11): 1677–1708.

Mellor, J.W., and R. Ahmed. 1988. "Conclusions: Agricultural Price Policy for Accelerating Growth." In *Agricultural Price Policy for Developing Countries*, edited by J.W. Mellor and R. Ahmed. Baltimore: The Johns Hopkins University Press.

Moris, J.R. 1989. "Indigenous versus Introduced Solutions to Food Stress in Africa." In *Seasonal Variability in Third World Agriculture: The Consequences for Food Security*, edited by D.E. Sahn. Baltimore: The Johns Hopkins University Press.

Muller, C. 1997. *The Consequence of Past Agricultural Outputs on the Interacting Nutrition and Health of Autarkic Peasants: Evidence from Rwanda*. Working Paper Series WPS/97-7, Institute of Economics and Statistics, University of Oxford.

Pinstrup-Andersen, P., R. Pandya-Lorch, and S. Babu. 1997. "A 2020 Vision for Food, Agriculture, and the Environment in Southern Africa." In *Achieving Food Security in Southern Africa*, edited by Lawrence Haddad. Washington, D.C.: International Food Policy Research Institute.

Pinstrup-Andersen, P., R. Pandya-Lorch, and M.W. Rosegrant. 1997. *The World Food Situation: Recent Developments, Emerging Issues, and Long-term Prospects*. Washington, D.C.: International Food Policy Research Institute.

Platteau, J.P. 1993. "The Food Crisis in Africa: A Comparative Structural Analysis." In *The Political Economy of Hunger*, Vol. 2: *Famine Prevention*, edited by J. Drèze and A. Sen. Oxford: Clarendon Press.

Quisumbing, A.R., et al. 1995. "Women: The Key to Food Security." Food Policy Statement No. 21, International Food Policy Research Institute, Washington, D.C.

Radwan, S. 1995. "Challenges and Scope for an Employment-Intensive Growth Strategy." In *Employment for Poverty Reduction and Food Security*, edited by J. von Braun. Washington, D.C.: International Food Policy Research Institute.

Rahmato, D. 1987. *Famine and Survival Strategies: A Case Study from Northeast Ethiopia*. Food and Famine Monograph Series No. 1, Institute of Development Research, Addis Ababa University, Addis Ababa.

Rempel, H. 1998. "The Interaction of Non-agricultural Employment, Agricultural Development and Reduced Chronic Food Insecurity: Sub-Saharan Africa, 1970 to 1990." *African Development Review* 10(2): 1–26.

Stewart, F., S. Lall, and S. Wangwe. 1992. "Alternative Development Strategies: An Overview." In *Alternative Development Strategies in Sub-Saharan Africa*, edited by F. Stewart, S. Lall, and S. Wangwe. New York: St. Martin's Press, Inc.

Svedberg, P. 1993. "Undernutrition in sub-Saharan Africa: A Critical Assessment of the Evidence." In *The Political Economy of Hunger*, Vol. 3: *Endemic Hunger*, edited by J. Drèze and A. Sen. Oxford: Clarendon Press.

United Nations Development Programme 1994. *Human Development Report, 1994*. New York: Oxford University Press.

United States Department of Agriculture 1986. Sub-Saharan Africa: Situation and Outlook Report. RS-86-9, Economic Research Service, United States Department of Agriculture, Washington, D.C.

United States Department of Agriculture 1995. *World Agriculture: Trends and Indicators, Sub-Saharan Africa*. Economic Research Service, Washington, D.C.

von Braun, J., H. de Haen, and J. Blanken. 1991. *Commercialization of Agriculture under Population Pressure: Effects on Production, Consumption, and Nutrition in Rwanda*. Research Report 85, International Food Policy Research Institute, Washington, D.C.

von Braun, J., and E. Kennedy. 1987. "Cash Crop versus Subsistence Crops: Income and Nutritional Effects in Developing Countries." In *Food Policy: Integrating Supply, Distribution, and Consumption*, edited by J.P. Gittinger, J. Leslie, and C. Hoisington. Baltimore: The Johns Hopkins University Press.

Wangwe, S. 1993. "The Contribution of Industry to Solving the Food Problem in Africa." In *The Political Economy of Hunger*, Vol. 3: *Endemic Hunger*, edited by J. Drèze and A. Sen. Oxford: Clarendon Press.

Whitehead, A. 1993. "Rural Women and Food Production in Sub-Saharan Africa." In *The Political Economy of Hunger*, Vol. 1: *Entitlement and Well-Being*, edited by J. Drèze and A. Sen. Oxford: Clarendon Press.

Wood, S., K. Sebastian, and S.J. Scherr. 2000. *Pilot Analysis of Global Ecosystems: Agroecosytems*. Washington, D.C.: International Food Policy Research Institute and World Resources Institute.

4

Ongoing Fertility Transition in Sub-Saharan Africa

David Shapiro and Basile Oleko Tambashe

INTRODUCTION

Up until the latter part of the 1980s, sub-Saharan Africa was the only major world region in which fertility transition at the level of national populations had not yet begun (Lesthaeghe, 1989). During the past decade or so, however, this situation has changed considerably. A few countries have shown strong evidence of fertility decline, and a number of other countries appear to be at various early stages of fertility transition (Tabutin, 1997; Shapiro and Tambashe, 2000). This unfolding fertility transition is influenced in part by investments in children's education, and in turn these are two important aspects pertinent to economic growth.

Even prior to the emergence of fertility decline at the national level, however, there were clear signs of fertility decline in urban areas (cf., Jolly and Gribble, 1993), with fertility being especially low in capital cities as compared to other urban and rural areas (Cohen, 1993). From a theoretical or conceptual perspective, the emergence of fertility transition in urban areas is not at all unexpected. Whether one looks at the question from the perspective of the Easterlin synthesis framework (Easterlin, 1975; Easterlin and Crimmins, 1985) or that of Caldwell's wealth-flow theory (Caldwell, 1976, 1982), one can make a good case that the net benefits to parents of having large numbers of children are distinctly lower in urban than in rural places. In rural areas, children typically begin contributing to agricultural production at relatively early ages, whereas this benefit of children to parents is either not present or else substantially diminished in urban places, and especially so in large cities.

Alternatively, this onset of fertility transition in urban areas is integral to innovation-diffusion theories emphasizing urban settings as places of innovation in fertility behavior (Reed et al., 1999). Greater opportunities for schooling in urban places and the corresponding higher school enrollment rates are also a contributing factor raising the net cost of children to urban parents and bringing into play quality-quantity trade-offs. Increased age at marriage, greater contraceptive use, declining infant and child mortality, and economic crisis are additional factors that have been identified in the literature as contributing to changes in reproductive behavior (Tabutin, 1997; Shapiro and Tambashe, 2000; Lesthaeghe, 1993).

This chapter explores the fertility transition in sub-Saharan Africa in some detail, with particular emphasis on differences between urban and rural places in the onset and pace of fertility transition. We provide an overview of reproductive change by examining recent data on overall levels and trends of fertility, and patterns of fertility by age in a number of countries, separately for urban and rural areas. These changes are then discussed in the context of parents' investments in the education and health of their children, and implications for economic growth.

The data used in the paper are from the Demographic and Health Surveys (DHS) that have been carried out since the mid-late 1980s. To date, there are twenty-six countries in sub-Saharan Africa in which at least one DHS survey has been conducted, and in fourteen of these countries there have been at least two DHS surveys. The larger group provides an opportunity to examine levels of the total fertility rate and age-specific fertility rates overall and separately for urban and rural areas, and in a number of these cases data are reported separately for the capital city or region and other urban areas. The subset of countries in which there have been multiple surveys allows one to examine trends in fertility and to determine whether those trends are common to both urban and rural areas, or whether fertility decline is concentrated in urban places.

The following section provides a descriptive overview of levels and trends in fertility, overall and separately for urban and rural places. Patterns of age-specific fertility rates and changes over time are also examined for countries with multiple DHS surveys. The concluding section of the chapter reviews the process of fertility transition in sub-Saharan Africa, with emphasis on the key role being played by urban residents. It also discusses links among this transition, investments in children, and economic growth.

LEVELS AND TRENDS IN URBAN AND RURAL FERTILITY IN SUB-SAHARAN AFRICA

Table 4.1 shows data on total fertility rates, overall and separately for urban and rural places, for the forty-five national DHS surveys that have been carried out in sub-Saharan Africa.[1] The twenty-six countries involved had an estimated total population in 1995 of close to 360 million, or about 61 percent of that of sub-Saharan Africa.[2] In addition, information on total fertility rates of capital cities or regions and of other urban places is also shown in Table 4.1 for those countries where the survey reports provide such detail.

Consider first the overall national levels of fertility. They range from a low of just under 4 for Zimbabwe in 1999 to a high of 7.5 for Niger in 1998, with a

Table 4.1
Total Fertility Rates, Urban and Rural Places

Country (year of survey)	National TFR	Rural	Urban	Capital City/ region	Other Urban
Benin (1996)	6.32	7.02	5.24	---	---
Botswana (1988)	4.9	5.4	3.9	---	---
Burkina Faso (1993)	6.9	7.3	5.0	4.7	5.5
Burkina Faso (1998)	6.8	7.3	4.1	4.1	---
Burundi* (1987)	6.6	6.6	5.2	---	---
Cameroon (1991)	5.82	6.29	5.17	4.41	5.64
Cameroon (1998)	5.2	5.8	3.9	3.1	4.5
Central African Republic (1994/95)	5.07	5.23	4.86	4.66	5.06
Chad (1996/97)	6.6	6.8	6.1	5.8	6.3
Cote d'Ivoire (1994)	5.7	6.4	4.7	4.1	---
Cote d'Ivoire (1998)	5.21	6.03	4.02	3.45	4.89
Eritrea (1995)	6.10	6.99	4.23	---	---
Ghana (1988)	6.41	6.63	5.13	4.54	---
Ghana (1993)	5.50	6.36	3.99	3.56	---
Ghana (1998)	4.55	5.41	2.96	2.66	---
Guinea (1999)	5.5	6.1	4.4	4.0	---
Kenya (1989)	6.7	7.0	4.8	---	---
Kenya (1993)	5.4	5.8	3.44	3.40	---
Kenya (1998)	4.7	5.16	3.12	2.61	---
Liberia (1986)	6.5	6.8	6.1	---	---
Malawi (1992)	6.73	6.88	5.51	---	---
Mali* (1987)	6.73	6.97	6.09	---	---
Mali (1995/96)	6.7	7.3	5.4	4.7	5.9
Mozambique (1997)	5.61	5.75	5.12	---	---
Namibia (1992)	5.4	6.3	4.0	---	---
Niger (1992)	7.37	7.52	6.71	5.86	7.24
Niger (1998)	7.5	7.9	5.9	5.2	6.5
Nigeria (1990)	6.01	6.33	5.03	---	---
Nigeria (1999)	5.15	5.44	4.5	---	---
Rwanda (1992)	6.23	6.33	4.51	---	---
Senegal (1986)	6.6	7.3	5.6	---	---

Table 4.1 (continued)
Total Fertility Rates, Urban and Rural Places

Senegal (1992/93)	6.03	6.74	5.06	---	---
Senegal (1997)	5.67	6.74	4.29	---	---
Tanzania (1991/92)	6.25	6.59	5.14	4.00	5.60
Tanzania (1996)	5.82	6.34	4.11	3.43	4.36
Tanzania (1999)**	5.55	6.48	3.16	—	---
Togo (1988)	6.59	6.98	4.72	4.13	5.66
Togo (1998)	5.40	6.54	3.32	2.91	3.85
Uganda (1988/89)	7.4	7.6	5.7	5.9	---
Uganda (1995)	6.86	7.17	4.97	---	---
Zambia (1992)	6.5	7.1	5.8	5.5	---
Zambia (1996)	6.08	6.86	5.08	4.87	---
Zimbabwe (1988/89)	5.31	6.06	3.86	---	---
Zimbabwe (1994)	4.29	4.85	3.09	---	---
Zimbabwe (1999)	3.96	4.57	2.96	2.98	

Note: *Ages 15–44, **Reproductive and Child Health Survey, — = not available.

mean (unweighted) average of just under 6. For the forty-five surveys, fifteen report a total fertility rate (TFR) of 5.5 or less, sixteen have a TFR of 5.5 to 6.5, and in fourteen cases the TFR exceeds 6.5. Among the twenty-six countries covered by these surveys, examination of the most recent data shows that eleven have a TFR of 5.5 or less compared to another eight with TFRs between 5.5 and 6.5 and seven countries with TFRs above 6.5.

Further, among the fourteen countries that have had multiple surveys, it is apparent that fertility is declining. If one calculates the initial and subsequent TFR for each pair of surveys in the same country, one finds the average initial TFR to be 6.2, while the subsequent TFR (typically about five to six years later) is 5.6. Hence, there is a clear indication in the data that for many countries in sub-Saharan Africa, fertility transition is under way.

The estimated total fertility rates are always lower in urban areas than in rural areas. Among the twenty-six countries, in only seven cases is the difference less than 1.0, and for eleven countries it reaches or exceeds 2.0.[3] The average difference (unweighted) for all of the surveys taken together is 1.8, reflecting an average rural total fertility rate of 6.5 as compared to an average of 4.7 for urban places. If one considers only the most recent survey for each country, the average total fertility rate in rural areas falls slightly to 6.3, that for urban places declines to 4.1, and hence the average urban-rural difference increases to 2.2. These figures thus indicate that on average, urban fertility is 28 percent lower than rural fertility for all surveys taken together, and 35 percent lower when only the most recent survey is taken into consideration.

Further, in those cases where data are given for both the capital city or region and other urban places, the total fertility rate is always lower in the capital city. Among the thirteen surveys for which data are provided for both the capital and other urban areas, the mean difference in total fertility rates between the two is about 1.1 overall (that difference is 1.0 if one looks only at the most recent surveys for each country). In relative terms, the average total fertility rate in the capital city in these countries is about 80 percent of the level of the TFR in other urban areas. More broadly, of the twenty-four surveys that report a TFR for the capital city or region, fertility in the capital is lower than in all urban areas in twenty-two cases (Uganda in 1988–1989 and Zimbabwe in 1999 are the sole exceptions).

These urban-rural and capital-other urban fertility differentials do not appear to exhibit much in the way of any regional pattern. Overall, they are comparable, although the differentials are slightly larger in Western Africa than in Eastern Africa if one focuses on the most recent survey for each country (for example, the urban-rural difference is 2.0 in Western Africa as compared to 1.7 in Eastern Africa). There are also somewhat smaller urban-rural differences among the countries of Middle Africa (the average is only 1.0), but it should be noted that there are only four surveys for countries in Middle Africa.

With respect to colonial heritage, it may be noted that overall, fertility in the Francophone countries is somewhat higher than that in the Anglophone countries, by approximately 0.5 children (this is the differential both for all surveys and for the most recent surveys only).[4] The urban-rural differences are generally about 1.9 for both Anglophone and Francophone countries.

For fourteen of the countries shown in Table 4.1, there are multiple DHS surveys. The duration between surveys among these countries ranges from three to ten years, with an average of a little under six. Here we consider changes over time in fertility, by place of residence, between pairs of surveys for each country.[5] By focusing on successive pairs of surveys, we end up with nineteen observations of changes in fertility for the fourteen countries. Overall, as noted earlier, fertility falls from an average of nearly 6.2 as of the first survey in each pair to an average of 5.6 for the second survey.

With respect to rural total fertility rates, the data show increases (Niger, Mali, Tanzania) or stability (Burkina Faso, Senegal) in five cases.[6] It is noteworthy that three of these countries are among those with especially high fertility, with the national TFR approaching or exceeding 7.[7] In ten cases these rural fertility rates show modest declines ranging from about 0.2 to 0.6. And in the remaining four cases (Kenya, Ghana, Nigeria, and Zimbabwe) there were substantial declines in rural fertility, ranging from 0.9 to 1.2.[8] It is worth noting that these four cases where rural fertility declines are relatively large include the only three countries with relatively low national TFRs (5.5 or less) as of the initial year of the last pair of surveys. Overall, the (unweighted) average rural TFR declines by almost 0.4 between these pairs of DHS surveys, representing 6 percent of the initial level.

For urban areas, by contrast, there are declines in TFRs for all fourteen countries and for all nineteen pairs of observations, and these tend to be relatively large. Except for Kenya and Zimbabwe, which most recently experienced drops in urban fertility of only 0.32 between 1993 and 1998 and only 0.13 between 1994 and 1999, respectively (after having seen urban fertility fall by 1.36 between 1989 and 1993 in Kenya and by 0.77 between 1994 and 1999 in Zimbabwe), the declines in urban fertility between pairs of surveys range from 0.5 to 1.4, and average more than 0.8. This represents a relative drop in urban fertility of 17 percent.

As a consequence of these changes in rural and urban fertility, the urban-rural difference in fertility is greater in the most recent survey than in the preceding survey in fourteen of the nineteen cases. Of the five cases where the urban-rural difference in fertility decreased, three are from Zimbabwe and Kenya, the two countries with the lowest overall fertility levels. Further, in those cases where data are available, it is evident that although fertility is consistently lower in capital cities or regions as compared to other urban areas, the declines in fertility between DHS surveys tend in general to be somewhat smaller in the capital cities than in the other urban places.

Overall, it appears that the magnitudes of the observed declines in fertility between pairs of DHS surveys depend on the initial level of fertility, as may be seen in Table 4.2. For those countries that had a national TFR in excess of 6.5 as of the first survey within a pair, there was, on average, an (unweighted) decline

Table 4.2
Levels and Changes in Fertility Between DHS Surveys, by Initial Level of Fertility and Place of Residence (fourteen countries with multiple DHS surveys)

		Levels						Changes (Declines)					
Initial National TFR		National		Rural		Urban		National		Rural		Urban	
	Countries	TFR_0	TFR_1	TFR_0	TFR_1	TFR_0	TFR_1	Absolute	Relative	Absolute	Relative	Absolute	Relative
>6.5	Burkina Faso, Mali, Niger, Togo, Uganda	6.90	6.39	7.24	6.96	5.52	4.79	.51	7%	.27	4%	.93	17%
5.5-6.5	Cameroon, Cote d'Ivoire, Ghana, Nigeria, Tanzania, Zambia	6.00	5.41	6.53	6.16	4.90	4.00	.59	10%	.37	6%	.90	18%
<5.5	Kenya, Zimbabwe	5.00	4.32	5.57	4.86	3.46	3.06	.68	14%	.71	13%	.41	12%
All pairs of surveys		6.18	5.60	6.64	6.25	4.90	4.07	.58	9%	.39	6%	.83	17%

of just over 0.5, reflecting a modest decline in rural fertility (of less than 0.3) and a substantial decline in the urban TFR (by more than 0.9). For the countries with an initial national TFR between 5.5 and 6.5, by contrast, between pairs of DHS surveys the overall decline approaches 0.6, being primarily the outcome of a modest drop of not quite 0.4 in rural areas and a distinctly larger decline of 0.9 in urban places.[9] Finally, for the two countries with an initial national TFR of less than 5.5, the overall decline approaches 0.7, reflecting a fall in the average rural TFR that was greater than 0.7 and a smaller drop in the average urban TFR of about 0.4.[10]

The figures in the preceding paragraph give the absolute changes for the high-, medium-, and low-fertility groups. It is useful to consider the relative changes as well. Within the high-fertility group, the average overall drop in the TFR was 7 percent, with a decline in the average rural TFR of 4 percent and a fall in the average urban TFR of 17 percent. Among the medium-fertility cases, for which (as indicated note 9) the average duration between surveys was only about three-quarters that of the high-fertility group, the average national decline was 10 percent: The average rural TFR was reduced by 6 percent while the average urban TFR diminished by 18 percent. And lastly, the low-fertility group saw the largest overall decline, 14 percent: The average rural TFR fell by 13 percent, compared to a decline in the average urban TFR of 12 percent.

These results are suggestive of a three-stage transition pattern in which overall fertility decline begins slowly and then accelerates. In the initial stage, with overall fertility quite high, rural fertility is more or less stable while urban fertility declines. Subsequently, both urban and rural fertility decline, with the decreases in the former being clearly larger than those in the latter. And finally, when a generally low overall level of fertility has been reached, the pace of continued fertility decline appears to be as great or greater in rural than in urban areas. Given the relatively small number of countries under consideration here, we do not wish to push this three-stage scenario too hard; however, we believe that the results are quite suggestive.

Age-specific fertility rates from the two most recent surveys are shown in Figure 4.1 and Figure 4.2 for urban and rural areas in five of the countries that have had multiple DHS surveys. The five countries—Mali, Côte d'Ivoire, Cameroon, Kenya, and Zimbabwe—were chosen in order to represent a variety of demographic situations as well as different parts of the continent. In particular, Mali has continuing high fertility and, as noted previously, actually had an increase in rural fertility between the two DHS surveys, while urban fertility declined, but by a relatively modest amount. Côte d'Ivoire and Cameroon, in the medium-fertility group, have experienced recent declines in fertility in both rural and urban places, with the declines in Côte d'Ivoire being close to or slightly smaller than the averages for the fourteen countries with multiple DHS surveys and those in Cameroon being somewhat larger. Finally, Kenya and Zimbabwe have the lowest levels of fertility observed in sub-Saharan Africa apart

Figure 4.1
Urban and Rural Age-Specific Fertility Rates

(Two Most Recent DHS Surveys, Selected Countries)

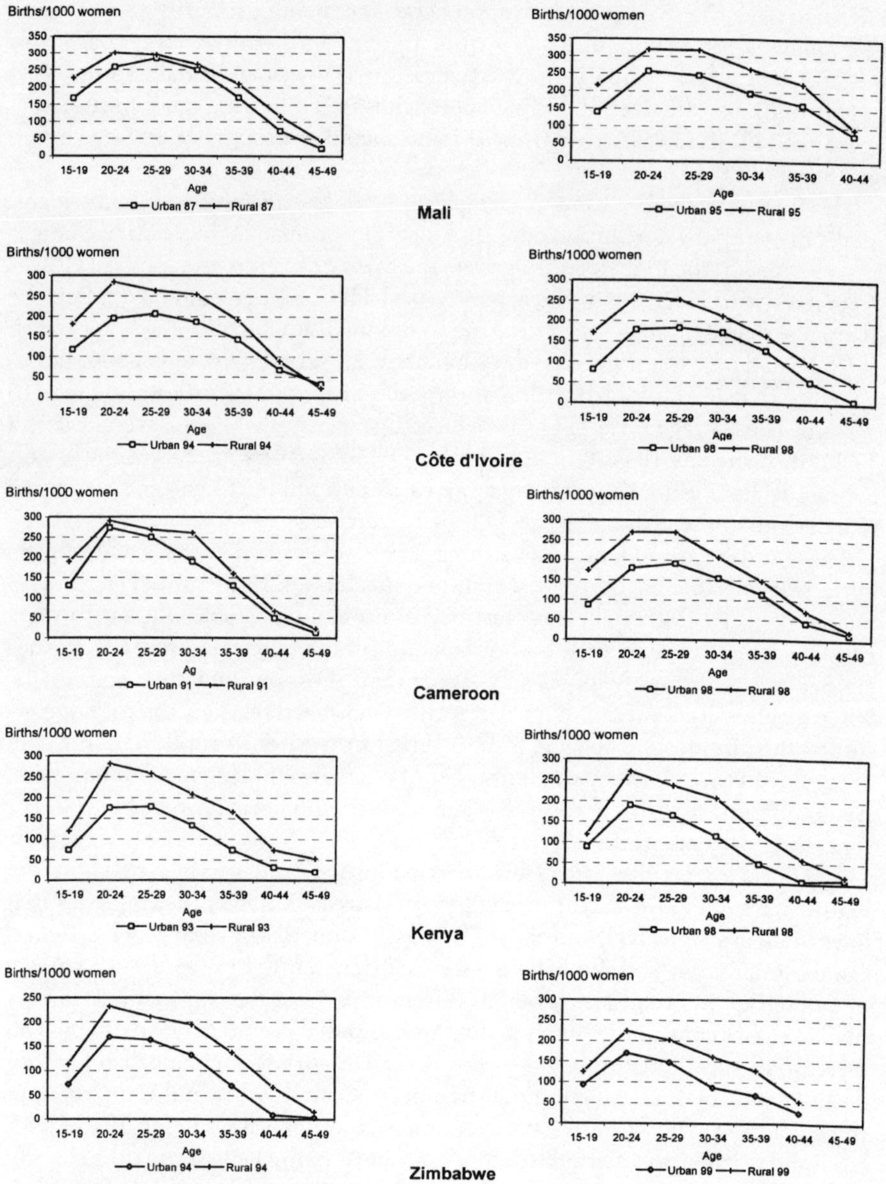

Age-specific fertility rates for women 45-49 in the 1999 DHS were no reported, since the rates are based on less than 125 woman-years o exposure (Zimbabwe DHS Report, 1999, p. 39).

Figure 4.2
Trends in Urban and Rural Age-Specific Fertility Rates

(Two Most Recent DHS Surveys, Selected Countries)

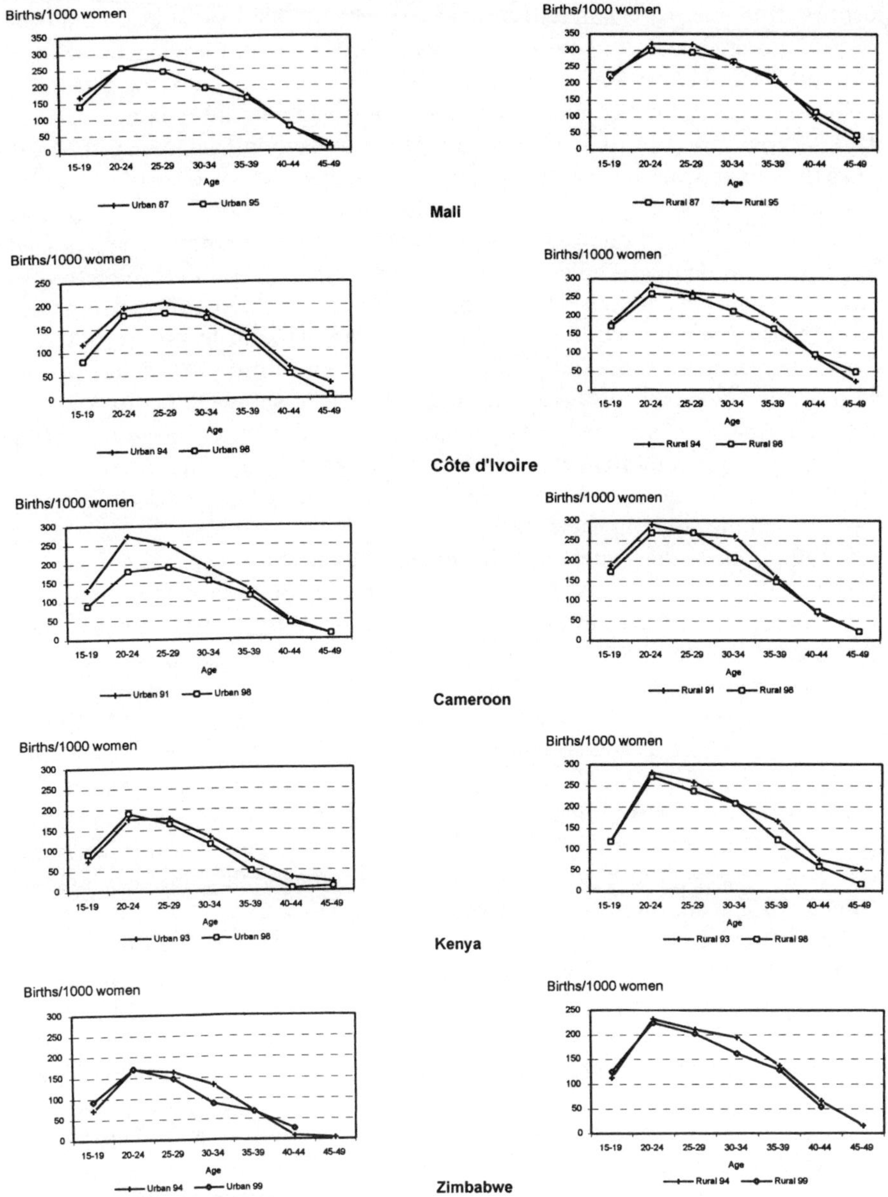

Age-specific fertility rates for women 45-49 in the 1999 DHS were not reported, since the rates are based on less than 125 woman-years of exposure (Zimbabwe DHS Report, 1999, p. 39).

from South Africa,[11] and as already noted the recent declines in fertility there have been larger in rural areas than in urban areas.

Examination of Figure 4.1 shows a distinct widening over time of urban-rural fertility differences in Mali, reflecting increased rural fertility at the same time that urban fertility declined. The widening is most evident among those aged 20 to 39. From Figure 4.2, it is clear that the urban fertility decline in Mali is greatest at ages 25 to 34, and there is also a noticeable decline among those in the 15–19 age group. In rural areas, fertility increased among women aged 20–29, more than offsetting the declines among women aged 40–49. Côte d'Ivoire also experienced a widening of urban-rural differences in fertility, but it is modest overall and uneven (there was a narrowing of differences among women aged 30–39). This widening is evident for two of the three age groups under age 30 and for both groups in their 40s. Among the younger women, this widening occurs because urban fertility fell by somewhat more than the decline in rural fertility, whereas among the older women it reflects declining urban fertility in conjunction with stable or increasing rural fertility. As shown in Figure 4.2, fertility in urban areas declined in all age groups, with the largest declines among the very youngest and the very oldest women. In rural areas there was greater variability of changes across age groups, and the largest fertility declines were apparent among those in their 30s.

In Cameroon, urban-rural fertility differences widened most among those aged 20–29, and also increased noticeably among 15- to 19-year-old women. In urban areas, Figure 4.2 shows that the largest fertility drop was among those in their 20s, with distinct declines as well among 15- to 19- and 30- to 34-year-olds. In rural Cameroon, there was a substantial drop in fertility among those in their early 30s and rather modest declines among women aged 15–24 and 35–39.

In Kenya, there was a narrowing of urban-rural fertility differences evident among those aged 15–24, 35–39, and 45–49. Among urban women, Figure 4.2 reveals modest declines in fertility for those aged 25–49 and increases in fertility among younger women (ages 15–24). In rural areas, by contrast, declines were largest among those aged 35–39 and 45–49 and negligible among younger women (15–24) and those aged 30–34.

For Zimbabwe, changes in urban-rural fertility differences between the two most recent surveys are rather modest. There is a small narrowing of these differences for women under age 25, a modest narrowing among women aged 35–39, and a much larger narrowing among women aged 40–44 (data on age-specific fertility rates by place of residence were not provided for those aged 45–49 in 1999). Partially offsetting this narrowing is a slight widening of the urban-rural differences for women aged 25–34. As may be seen in Figure 4.2, fertility declines in urban areas are concentrated in the 25–34 age group; for the 15–19 and 40–44 age groups urban fertility actually increased. By contrast, whereas fertility of rural women aged 15–19 also increased, in all other age groups for which data were reported rural fertility declined, and most notably among women aged 30–34.

This detailed examination of changes over time in urban and rural fertility by age group does reveal some similarities of experience across countries if one separates out the two low-fertility countries. That is, the three countries with high or medium fertility all show widening of urban-rural differences among those aged 25–29 and declines (usually substantial) in fertility of urban women aged 25–34. The two low-fertility countries experienced a narrowing of urban-rural differences among women aged 15–24 and a widening of these differences among women aged 30–34. In addition, fertility of adolescents tended to rise somewhat in both urban and rural places (except for rural Kenya, where there was no change). At the same time, however, there is substantial diversity of experience across countries. Even within a broad fertility range (i.e., comparing the two medium-fertility countries or the two low-fertility countries), there are distinct differences in age-specific changes over time.

Elsewhere (Shapiro and Tambashe, 2000) we have carried out multivariate analyses of the age-specific fertility rates of urban and rural women, using the most recent survey data available for each country covered by a DHS survey. Those analyses find that women's education, marriage patterns, and contraceptive use all help to account for fertility differences between urban and rural women. Education levels and use of modern contraception are substantially higher in urban than in rural areas, and women in urban places delay marriage relative to their rural counterparts. These factors, which typically tend to be relevant to fertility in specific age ranges, thus work to contribute to the lower fertility in urban places. Infant and child mortality also is a significant (positively related) influence on fertility, and hence the fact that these mortality levels are typically lower in urban places than in rural areas also contributes to lower urban fertility.

Overall, average rural and urban age-specific fertility rates across all countries are depicted in Figure 4.2. This shows that urban fertility is lower than rural fertility for all age groups. In addition, peak fertility among rural women occurs at ages 20–24, whereas the peak among urban women is at 25–29, reflecting in part the effect of delayed entry into marital life. As a consequence, the largest difference is at ages 20–24. Overall, these age-specific fertility rates imply a rural total fertility rate of 6.47 and an urban TFR of 4.65. That is, on average, rural fertility is 39 percent higher than urban fertility.

FERTILITY TRANSITION, QUALITY OF CHILDREN, AND ECONOMIC GROWTH

There is clear evidence from the overview of data on urban and rural fertility that although urban-rural differences in total fertility rates are pervasive, there is considerable diversity across countries in terms of urban-rural differences in age-specific fertility rates and in the pace and character of fertility change. Though we do not find much evidence of regional patterns to the differences by place of residence, we do note a tendency for fertility to be somewhat higher on average for Francophone countries as compared to Anglophone countries.

Further, it appears, at least broadly, that there are some systematic differences in trends according to where a country is situated with respect to fertility transition. In particular, those countries in which overall fertility is rather high (e.g., TFR of 6.5 or greater) frequently experience little change in rural fertility over time, while showing some declines in urban fertility. Countries with medium fertility levels (e.g., TFRs below 6.5 but above 5.5) tend to experience declines in both rural and urban fertility, with the changes being larger in the urban places. And finally, the small number of countries with low overall fertility (TFRs below 5.5) show larger declines in rural fertility than in urban fertility. At the national level, there appears to be an acceleration of fertility transition as a country moves from high to medium to relatively low levels of fertility.

More generally, we believe that fertility transition is well under way in urban areas of sub-Saharan Africa, and for many countries this transition has extended to rural areas as well. We anticipate continuation of this process as time goes by, fueled by continued increases in women's educational attainment and in the age at first marriage, increasing proportions of women practicing modern contraception, and by growth in the extent of urbanization. Conversely, to the extent that economic crisis may have contributed to increases in infant and child mortality in some countries in sub-Saharan Africa in recent years (as suggested by data from several of the recent DHS surveys—cf., Barrère et al., 1999), there may be countervailing tendencies slowing the fertility decline.

How far fertility will decline remains to be seen. However, in four countries (Ghana, Kenya, Togo, and Zimbabwe) the most recently observed TFR in the capital city/region has fallen below 3, and in three others (Cameroon, Côte d'Ivoire, and Tanzania) the corresponding figures are less than 3.5.

We believe that the fertility transition that is taking place in sub-Saharan Africa is intimately tied to growing parental investments in the education and health of their children. With increasing investments in the human capital of children, parents confront the so-called "quality-quantity trade-off" (Becker and Lewis, 1973; Becker, 1991). Parental aspirations for relatively high levels of education for their children (high child quality) contribute to desires to limit overall fertility, so as not to dilute available resources across larger numbers of children (cf., Parish and Willis, 1993). Further, the fact that parental aspirations for their children's education are positively related to the parents' own education means that the long-term trend toward increased education in sub-Saharan Africa (Schultz, 1993) will create additional momentum toward lower fertility and higher levels of educational attainment.

Lowering of fertility will also slow population growth and hence will mean less pressure on governments to provide school places for a burgeoning population. More resources can be used to enhance the quality of education if there is less pressure to increase the quantity. Greater educational levels, in turn, are a key element contributing to economic growth (Mankiw et al., 1992).

In sum, then, growing parental investments in the education and health of their children are associated with the slowdown in fertility both as causes and consequences. The mutually reinforcing effects of lower fertility and greater investments in human capital are key to the economic future of sub-Saharan Africa.

NOTES

This research was partially supported by the William and Flora Hewlett Foundation grant in International Demography to the Population Research Institute at Pennsylvania State University. We are indebted to Tesfayi Gebreselassie for outstanding research assistance, and to the organizers of the 1999 Chaire Quetelet Symposium in Demography at the Catholic University of Louvain, Louvain-la-Neuve, Belgium, for encouraging us to pursue this topic and for helpful comments on an earlier version of the paper. Responsibility for the contents of this paper rests solely with the authors.

1. We have limited our analyses to those countries on the continent. Hence, the Comoro Islands and Madagascar are not included in the analyses here. Further, we have ignored two early DHS surveys that covered only subnational populations: Northern Sudan and Ondo State in Nigeria.

2. Four countries not covered by the DHS surveys—Ethiopia, the Democratic Republic of Congo (DRC), South Africa, and the Sudan—account for nearly 30 percent of the population of sub-Saharan Africa. South Africa is a unique case, in which fertility transition among the African-origin population has been taking place over the course of the past thirty years. For an excellent overview, see Moultrie and Timaeus (2001). Coverage of the DHS surveys varies considerably by region within Africa: whereas 95 percent of the population of Western Africa is included in the DHS surveys, the figure falls to 63 percent for Eastern Africa, and in Middle and Southern Africa the corresponding numbers are 28 and 6 percent, respectively. The absence of the DRC and South Africa is largely responsible for the low coverage in the latter two regions.

3. The seven countries in which the urban-rural difference was less than 1 were the Central African Republic (1994–1995), Chad (1996–1997), Liberia (1986), Mali (1987), Mozambique (1997), Niger (1992), and Nigeria (1999). Note that both Mali and Niger had subsequent DHS surveys in which the urban-rural gap in fertility had widened substantially.

4. It has been shown that although contraceptive use remains generally low in sub-Saharan Africa, it is much lower in Francophone countries than in Anglophone countries (National Research Council, 1993).

5. Nine countries had two surveys, five others had three. Those countries with three surveys each provide two opportunities to observe changes over time in fertility—namely, between the first and second surveys and between the second and third surveys. We have "double counted" these cases (i.e., used both pairs of surveys) so as to have the maximum number of observations of changes over time in fertility. However, it is worth noting that the conclusions here are unaffected by this double counting—indeed, in some ways differences would be more dramatic if we simply looked at the most recent pair of observations from each country.

6. In two of these countries, there were three surveys and hence two pairs of surveys across which comparisons may be made. Tanzania experienced a drop in rural fertility between the first two surveys and then a smaller increase between the latter two surveys. There was a decline in rural fertility of 0.56 in Senegal between the first and second surveys, but then no further change between the second and third surveys.

7. Four of the fourteen countries had TFRs as of the last DHS survey that were in excess of 6.5: Burkina Faso (6.8), Mali (6.7), Niger (7.5), and Uganda (6.86).

8. In three of these countries there were three surveys. Kenya experienced a drop of 1.2 in the rural TFR between 1989 and 1993; from 1993 to 1998 there was a further decline of more than 0.6. Between 1993 and 1998, Ghana's rural TFR fell by 0.95, compared to a smaller decrease of 0.27 between 1988 and 1993. Similarly, Zimbabwe saw a rural fertility decline of 1.21 between 1988 and 1994, and then a smaller drop of 0.28 between 1994 and 1999.

9. It should be noted that the average duration between surveys in this latter group was only 5.1 years, compared to an average of 6.6 years for the observations in the high-fertility group. Hence, although the overall absolute declines in urban fertility of countries in the two groups are comparable, it is clear that the pace of urban fertility decline is distinctly more rapid in the group with lower fertility. More specifically, the average decline per year in the urban TFR in the medium-fertility group is 0.177, more than 25 percent greater than the comparable figure of 0.139 for the high-fertility group.

10. Changes in the national TFR in any country reflect not only the changes in the urban and rural TFRs but also population redistribution, which typically is from higher-fertility rural areas to lower-fertility urban places.

11. As indicated in note 2, South Africa is a unique case. Fertility decline has been taking place there during the past thirty years, and fertility is lower there than in any other country in sub-Saharan Africa (Moultrie and Timaeus, 2001).

REFERENCES

Barrère, B., M. Goram, and A. Mohammed. 1999. *Enquêtes Démographiques et de Santé en Afrique de l'Ouest: résultats des Enquêtes Démographiques et de Santé réalisées au Burkina Faso (1998–99), au Cameroun (1998), en Côte d'Ivoire (1998–99) et au Togo. (1998)*. Calverton, Maryland: Macro International Inc.

Becker, G.S. 1991. *A Treatise on the Family*, enlarged edition. Cambridge, MA: Harvard University Press.

Becker, G.S., and H.G. Lewis. 1973. "On the Interaction between the Quantity and Quality of Children." *Journal of Political Economy* 81 (2, pt. 2): S279–S288.

Caldwell, J.C. 1976. "Toward a Restatement of Demographic Transition Theory." *Population and Development Review* 2 (3 and 4): 321–66.

———. 1982. *Theory of Fertility Decline*. London: Academic Press.

Cohen, B. 1993. "Fertility Levels, Differentials, and Trends." In *Demographic Change in Sub-Saharan Africa*, edited by K.A. Foote, K.H. Hill, and L.G. Martin. Washington, DC: National Academy Press.

Easterlin, R.A. 1975. "An Economic Framework for Fertility Analysis." *Studies in Family Planning* 6: 54–63.

Easterlin, R.A., and E.M. Crimmins. 1985. *The Fertility Revolution: A Supply-Demand Analysis*. Chicago: University of Chicago Press.

Jolly, C.L., and J.N. Gribble. 1993. "The Proximate Determinants of Fertility." In *Demographic Change in Sub-Saharan Africa*, edited by K.A. Foote, K.H. Hill, and L.G. Martin. Washington, DC: National Academy Press.

Lesthaeghe, R.J. 1989. *Reproduction and Social Organization in Sub-Saharan Africa.* Berkeley: University of California Press.

———. 1993. "Are There Crisis-led Fertility Transitions?" Paper presented at the 1993 Annual Meeting of the Population Association of America, Cincinnati, OH.

Mankiw, N.G., D. Romer, and D.N. Weil. 1992. "A Contribution to the Empirics of Economic Growth." *Quarterly Journal of Economics* 107: 407–21.

Moultrie, T.A., and I.M. Timaeus. 2001. "Apartheid's Children: The South African Fertility Decline, 1960–1998." Paper presented at the 2001 Annual Meeting of the Population Association of America, Washington, D.C.

National Research Council, Working Group on Factors Affecting Contraceptive Use. 1993. *Factors Affecting Contraceptive Use in Sub-Saharan Africa.* Washington, D.C.: National Academy Press.

Parish, W.L., and R.J. Willis. 1993. "Daughters, Education, and Family Budgets: Taiwan Experiences." *Journal of Human Resources* 28 (4): 863–98.

Reed, H., R. Briere, and J. Casterline. 1999. "The Role of Diffusion Processes in Fertility Change in Developing Countries: Report of a Workshop." Committee on Population, National Research Council. Washington, D.C.: National Academy Press.

Schultz, T.P. 1993. "Investments in the Schooling and Health of Women and Men: Quantities and Returns." *Journal of Human Resources* 28 (4): 694–734.

Shapiro, D., and B.O. Tambashe. 2000. "Fertility Transition in Urban and Rural Areas of Sub-Saharan Africa." In *Reproductive Change in Sub-Saharan Africa,* edited by P.M. Eloundou-Enyegue and J.F. Phillips. Oxford: Clarendon Press.

Tabutin, Dominique. 1997. "Les Transitions Démographiques en Afrique sub-Saharienne: Spécificités, changements ... et incertitudes." In *International Population Conference, Beijing 1997,* Vol. 1, pp. 219–247. Liège, Belgium: International Union for the Scientific Study of Population.

5

Poverty Estimates and Poverty-Reducing Strategies for the Developing Economy

John Gafar

INTRODUCTION

Adam Smith (1776) in the *Wealth of Nations* wrote:

> No society can surely be flourishing and happy, of which by far the greater part of the numbers are poor and miserable. (quoted in Todaro 1997: 137)

Two centuries later, notwithstanding the phenomenal economic and scientific progress in the world, the poor still constitute a large part of society. Sen (1976) has argued that the construction of theoretically sound indexes to measure welfare and poverty must satisfy well-defined theoretical properties and that any aggregation rule must be transitive and complete, Pareto compatible, and independent. This chapter provides a brief discussion of how poverty is measured and examines the distinction between absolute and relative poverty. Next, the chapter surveys the empirical evidence of the depth and magnitude of human poverty worldwide, focusing on the distinction between the Human Development Index (HDI) and the Human Poverty Index (HPI). Finally, the paper discusses poverty strategies applicable to developing countries with particular reference to the Caribbean region. Some concluding observations are made about the issues of ethnic conflict (e.g., the conflicts ravaging Europe, the African continent, and elsewhere) and ethnic poverty that pose serious challenges for the development of poverty reduction strategies.

MEASUREMENT OF POVERTY

The measurement of poverty goes back to more than 100 years. Atkinson (1987) and *Human Development Report 1990* (UNDP, Technical Notes) provide a useful survey of the attempts to measure poverty, and from which this chapter borrows quite liberally. The earliest studies on poverty were undertaken in the eighteenth century in England because the King had to provide estimates of the number of paupers. Sir F.M. Eden (1797) provides materials on family budgets. Booth (1892) provides firsthand observations of his attempts to measure the extent of poverty in London. Using the street as his unit of analysis, Booth was able to capture and construct his celebrated poverty maps of London.

Bowley (1913) used survey methods and sampling techniques to study poverty. Bowley used a one-in-twenty random sample of working-class households in Reading to study poverty.[1] In the case of the United States, Atkinson notes that the first attempt at defining a poverty line was in 1904, when attempts were made to measure "the minimum comfort" based on budgets for New York City. But it was not until the 1960s that the issue and measurement of poverty dominated the policy agenda in the United States. Harrington's (1962) *The Other America* and Galbraith's (1958) *The Affluent Society* emphasized the need to deal with the issues of fairness, equity, and poverty; just as Myrdal's (1944) *An American Dilemma* did with its focus on the disadvantaged position of Afro-Americans. Myrdal's (1968) monumental study, *Asian Drama: An Inquiry into the Poverty of Nations*, provided a more global perspective to these issues.

A central methodological issue in poverty studies is whether poverty should be expressed and discussed in absolute or relative terms.[2] An absolute measure of poverty is generally expressed to reflect some biological or physiological needs, but this is invariably difficult if not impractical to measure. Absolute poverty is generally based on some level of basic needs. A relative measure of poverty depends on circumstances, such as the disparities between the rich and poor in that society or community. In essence, poverty is concerned with the absolute standard of living of that part of society, to wit, the poor, and their ability to attain some minimal standard of living and well-being.

ABSOLUTE POVERTY

Estimates of poverty need to be specified in absolute terms if it is to be fixed across time and space. [*HDR, 1990*, p. 106] This absolutist measure of poverty is based on the notion of subsistence, a concept that is fraught with measurement problems. In the empirical literature, in order to arrive at some measure of subsistence, a minimum calorie intake is specified. Once the level of calories is specified, it is then converted into a consumption basket, which should be culture specific. After the consumption basket is obtained, it is then priced, at market prices, in order to establish the poverty line. In the 1960s the Indian Planning Commission used 2,250 calories as the minimum, while the Anglophone Caribbean countries, using epidemiological studies, have established a benchmark of 2,400 calories.[3] In studies done by ECLAC for Latin America, the commodity basket has been adjusted to satisfy the calorie intake (by age, sex, activity, and health status). This specification is an improvement over delineating a common threshold minimum calorie intake. The consumption basket omits nonfood items needed for subsistence; hence, an adjustment must be made for nonfood items. The standard approach is to multiply the amount of money needed to buy the food basket by the Engel coefficient. The Engel coefficient is taken as the reciprocal of the ratio of food expenditure to total expenditure. By Engel's law, the food ratio is higher for the poor than that of the nonpoor. If the reciprocal of the food ratio of the poorest is taken as the Engel law, this would tend to lower the poverty line, and thus the percentage of the poor.

Any poverty line, once established, has to be adjusted for changes in time and inflation. A crude method is to index the poverty line to the consumer price index or to the price index of food. There are three problems associated with this approach. First, there is the assumption of a common, constant calorie intake, which may be unrelated to an individual's personal circumstances over time. Second, any poverty line recalculated over time for price changes should allow for substitution between foodstuffs as relative prices and tastes change over time, hence, necessitating recomputing the Engel coefficient. And, finally, the assumption of a common calorie intake leads to the well-known aggregation problem. In many poor countries, and in some cultures (and I am familiar with the East Indians in Guyana), it is not uncommon for women to ensure that the males are well-fed (most East Indian women in the rural areas would only eat after the males finished). This is to ensure that the males have the energy to work on the farms. Because of scarcities, the consumption levels and health of poor women and girls tend to be below the minimum calorie intake. In short, there are intrahousehold inequalities in consumption and health care.

RELATIVE POVERTY

The relativist approach to poverty defines requirements not merely in terms of subsistence, but what is needed to satisfy a full life—for example, education, long life, full employment, and the like (see *HDR 1990*, p. 107). Poverty, in this context, is viewed in terms of inequality. One method of defining poverty is to take the poverty threshold as some measure of the median income. *Human Development Report 1998* (*HDR 1998*) arbitrarily took 50 percent of the median income in the industrial countries as the poverty benchmark for the industrial countries. In arriving at the poverty line in developing countries, consumption expenditures, rather than incomes, are used for the following reasons:[4] (1) There are problems relating to income estimation—particularly the incomes of the informal sector and the self-employed. Then there are problems with valuation of nontraded goods and estimating transfers or income remittances from abroad. Many Caribbean economies are "barrel economies": They depend heavily on the supplies and gifts shipped by relatives abroad, particularly from the United States. (2) Consumption, as a measure of welfare, is more robust than incomes, because respondents are more likely to provide reliable estimates of expenditures; income is always subject to under-reporting. (3) Consumption is a better measure of long-run welfare because people can dissave or borrow to maintain consumption levels—that is, consumption expenditures are less "noisy" than income estimates.

STATISTICAL MEASURES OF POVERTY

Though there are various measures of poverty, the one most frequently used is the head-count index or ratio, which is simply a fraction of the population below the poverty line.[5] One problem with the head-count index is that it fails to capture the extent to which individual incomes (expenditures) fall below the poverty line, and it is insensitive to transfers of incomes within the poverty population. Any measure of poverty must be sensitive to the depth and intensity of poverty, and it should indicate an increase of poverty if there is some transfer of income from someone who is very poor to someone who is less poor. The head-count ratio does not capture this if the transfer of incomes from the very poor to the less poor does not push any of the less poor over the poverty line.

Building on the work of Sen (1976), Foster, Greer, and Thorbecke (1984) developed a class of indices that meet these requirements. Referred to in the literature as the FGT class of measures, they are defined as (see Sen and Foster [1997]:

$$P\alpha = \left[\sum_{i=1}^{q} z_i^{\alpha}\right] \Big/ n \tag{1}$$

where

n = number of individuals in the population

q = number of individuals with an income less than the poverty line

k = poverty line

y_i = income of individual i

$Z_i = (k-y_i)/k$ is the normalized variable

α = degree of poverty aversion

The FGT is the summation of the percentage gap between the income of each individual and the poverty line, raised to the power that reflects the degree of poverty aversion [see Psacharopoulos et al., 1997].

Case 1: If $\alpha = 0$, this implies no interest in the intensity of poverty, and the index reduces to the head-count index (ratio):

$$P_o = H \tag{2}$$

where H is the head-count ratio. Most studies on poverty concentrate on the head-count ratio because of its ease of computation and simplicity.

Case 2: If $\alpha = 1$, the index reduces to the poverty gap index:

$$P_I = HI \tag{3}$$

where I is the income gap ratio.

The poverty gap measure is an improvement on the head-count index because it is sensitive to the depth of poverty and it is dependent not only on the number of persons below the poverty line but also on how far they are on average below the poverty line. However, the poverty gap measure is still insensitive to transfers within the poverty population (provided that the transfers do not take any individuals out of the poverty population) because such transfers within the poverty population would leave the average income of the poor unchanged (see Sen and Foster, 1997; Psacharopoulos et al., 1997).

Case 3: If $\alpha = 2$ or higher, then P_α will be distributionally sensitive. If $\alpha = 2$, we have

$$P_2 = H[I^2 + (1 - I)^2 C_p^2] \tag{4}$$

where C_p is the coefficient of variation among the poor. Sen and Foster (1997, p. 179, footnote 101) point out that the relationship of P_2 with the coefficient of variation ensures that P_2 satisfies the transfer property axiom. Sen and Foster also point out that the FGT measures satisfy the properties of symmetry, replication invariance, scale invariance, the focus axiom, and also continuity. Sen and Foster (1997, pp. 179–80) noted that all indices with α greater than 1 satisfy the weak and strong forms of the transfer axiom. The P_α indices are also decomposable, because a population comprising n individuals can be divided into m mutually exclusive subgroups (for example, by ethnicity, sex, geographical region, etc.). In view of this property, the overall FGT poverty measure is a weighted average of the various subgroups.[6]

HUMAN DEVELOPMENT INDEX (HDI) AND HUMAN POVERTY INDEX (HPI)

The head-count index is income based. Poverty is manifested in hunger, lack of the basic human rights, abuse by the state, illiteracy, lack of good health, deprivation, exclusion, lack of gainful employment, vulnerability, lack of access to infrastructure and voice, and the like. Human development is concerned with increasing choices needed for a long, healthy, and productive life, a decent standard of living, freedom, well-being, and self respect (see *Human Development Report 1977* [HDR 1977], p. 15). Because of the limitations of income in capturing the pervasiveness of poverty, the United Nations Development Program (UNDP) developed the Human Development Index (HDI). The HDI focuses on three essential elements of well-being: longevity, knowledge, and a decent standard of living. For longevity, life expectancy at birth is a crude approximation because life expectancy reflects improvements in health, sanitation, and nutrition. In the case of knowledge, literacy rates represent access to education. Per capita income is the most readily available proxy for the standard of living. But the presence of nontraded goods and exchange rate distortions make per capita income at nominal prices not particularly useful, hence, UNDP used PPP$US to correct for these distortions. The HDI is the simple average of the life expectancy index, educational attainment index, and the adjusted real per capita income (PPP$US) index.

In 1997 the UNDP developed the Human Poverty Index (HPI) for seventy-eight developing countries (see *HDR 1997*). The HPI concentrates on three essential dimensions in human life, already captured in HDI. The HPI is based on three essentials of deprivation. First, there is the deprivation in longevity, and this is measured by the percentage of people not expected to live to age 40. Second, there is the deprivation in knowledge, and this is measured by the percentage of people who are illiterate. And, third, there is the deprivation of a decent standard of living, and this is a simple average of three variables: the percentage of people without access to water, the percentage of people without access to health services, and the percentage of moderately and severely underweight children. The HPI is an average of the deprivation in longevity, the deprivation in knowledge, and the deprivation of a decent standard of living.

EMPIRICAL ESTIMATES OF POVERTY

In order to obtain poverty estimates that allowed for cross-country comparison, the World Bank, *World Development Report 2000/2001* (WDR, 2001), arbitrarily chose a US$1 per person a day as the poverty line. Purchasing power parity (PPP) indices at 1993 prices were used to convert the US$1 per person per day standard into local currency. Estimates of the population living below US$1 a day in developing countries and transitional economies for 1987, 1990, 1993, 1996, and 1998 are summarized in Table 5.1. The head-count index is the population below the poverty line of US$1 a day per person. The poverty gap index is the average distance below the poverty line (zero to the nonpoor) expressed as a percentage of the poverty line. The data in Table 5.1 may differ from other estimates of poverty. For example, in Latin America, a US$2 per day per person is often used (World Bank, 1996a).

In Europe and Central Asia, other studies use a poverty line of US$4 a day to capture the effects of higher levels of incomes. And China's official poverty line is approximately US$0.60 per person a day. The data in Table 5.1 and other available statistics reveal much.

About 1.2 billion people live on incomes of less than US$1 a day. About one quarter of the world's population live in poverty. The poor in Europe and Central Asia increased from 1.1 million in 1987 to 24 million in 1998. In the case of the Latin American and Caribbean countries, the poor increased from 63.7 million in 1987 to 78.2 million in 1998, or by 20 percent. The world's poor are concentrated in South Asia, East Asia and Pacific, and sub-Saharan Africa.

South Asia has the most people affected by poverty: 522 million. Together, South Asia, East Asia, and Pacific have more than 800 million of the 1.2 billion

Table 5.1
Income Poverty by Region, Selected Years, 1987–1998

	People Living on less than $1 a day (Millions)				
REGION	1987	1990	1993	1996	1998
East Asia and Pacific	417.5	452.4	431.9	265.1	278.3
Excluding China	114.1	92.0	83.5	55.1	65.1
Europe and Central Asia	1.1	7.1	18.3	23.8	24.0
Latin America and the Caribbean	64.7	73.8	70.8	76.0	78.2
Middle East and North Africa	9.3	5.7	5.0	5.0	5.5
South Asia	474.4.	495.1	505.1	531.7	522.0
Sub-Saharan Africa	217.2	242.3	273.3	289.0	290.9
Total	1,183.2	1,276.4	1,304.3	1,190.6	1,198.9
Excluding China	879.8	915.9	955.9	980.5	985.7

	Share of population living on less than $1 a day (Percent)				
REGION	1987	1990	1993	1996	1998
East Asia and Pacific	26.6	27.6	25.2	14.9	15.3
Excluding China	23.9	18.5	15.9	10.0	11.3
Europe and Central Asia	0.2	1.6	4.0	5.1	5.1
Latin America and the Caribbean	15.3	16.8	15.3	15.6	15.6
Middle East and North Africa	4.3	2.4	1.9	1.8	1.9
South Asia	44.9	44.0	42.4	42.3	40.0
Sub-Saharan Africa	46.6	47.7	49.7	48.5	46.3
Total	28.3	29.0	28.1	24.5	24.0
Excluding China	28.5	28.1	27.7	27.0	26.2

Source: World Bank (2001), *World Development Report 2000/2001*; Table 1.1.

people who are poor. More than 44 million Russians, or 30 percent of the population, live below the poverty line at a per capita income of US$32 a month. Poverty in Russia rose from 31 million in 1997 to 44.3 million in September 1998, because of the 9.9 percent contraction of GDP between 1997 and 1998.[7] The evidence shows that poverty in Russia (similar to the experiences in the Third World) is more likely to affect women and those who do not finish high school, and that younger workers between the ages of 18 and 54 are likely to be poor because they have no supplemental income (pensions, disability benefits, and other benefits that are available to employed workers). The statistics also indicate that about 2 million children in Russia lack families—about one third of these children live in orphanages, and the rest live in the street. After leaving orphanages, one in three of these children become alcoholic, and 10 percent commit suicide after one year out on their own. About 10 million Russian school-age children never attend school (*New York Times*, November 19, 1998). The situation in Russia grimly reflects the conditions of many Third World countries ravaged by prolonged economic crises.

The economic meltdown in Asia has resulted in more than 17 million Indonesians falling below the poverty line of US$1 a day per person and 60 million more below US$2 a day. The economic crisis in Indonesia is about affordable food. The financial crisis in Indonesia has also resulted in widespread unemployment, a loss of purchasing power by the poor, and increased poverty.

Recently hurricane Mitch left more than 9,000 dead and 1.5 million homeless in Honduras and Nicaragua and destroyed more than 70 percent of the agricultural production. The poor are mostly engaged in agricultural activities. But it was the working class, particularly the rural poor and the urban poor living in the shanty towns, who bore the brunt of the disaster because of inadequate, if not nonexistent, infrastructures. Many of the poor who had no information of the gravity of the natural disaster remained in their homes instead of going out to investigate conditions; and a number of them who lived on the hillsides got buried alive by the avalanche of mud as they tried to outrun the flow of mud. This demonstrates that without reliable information, markets do not work well, disasters happen, and the poor suffer, because the nonpoor who can afford it will seek the information and avoid the risks. The *World Development Report 1998* (p. 72) makes it very clear that information is the "lifeblood of every economy." It helps to reduce uncertainty and to establish and enforce standards for the benefit of all. And because information is costly to develop but cheap to share, the state should ensure that there is a constant flow of reliable information to enable the poor to make better decisions that will improve their lot.

Sub-Saharan Africa and South Asia have the highest poverty rates, 46 percent and 40 percent respectively. For Latin America and Caribbean countries the poverty rate is around 16 percent (see Table 5.1).

Children are especially vulnerable—they suffer from malnutrition and illnesses. Some 160 million children in the Third World are moderately or severely malnourished (see *HDR 1997*).

Poverty offers a breeding ground for the spread of HIV/AIDS. In Latin America and the Caribbean, the HIV/AIDS cases are concentrated in the urban slums. Over 94 percent of the world's known HIV/AIDS cases are in the developing countries, with sub-Saharan Africa having the greatest concentration. In Botswana, the hardest hit country in sub-Saharan Africa, life expectancy, which was 61 years only five years ago, has dropped to 47 and is expected to drop to 41 between 2000 and 2005. And in Guyana, life expectancy in 1998 was 64 years, which was expected to rise to 68 years (without AIDS) in 2010. However, it is now estimated that the HIV/AIDS pandemic will reduce life expectancy to 50 years in 2010. In 1998 it was estimated that the HIV/AIDS pandemic has increased the child mortality rate by 100 percent in Guyana and Kenya and by 150 percent in Zimbabwe (*HDR 1998*, p. 15). Poverty will rise because the HIV/AIDS-infected workers would be unable to engage in productive activities, and also because Third World health budgets cannot afford the US$15,000 a year for protease inhibitor "cocktails" to prolong the life of an infected AIDS patient. Estimates by the World Bank suggest that the cost of one AIDS dosage is sufficient to keep 400 children in school (*New York Times*, November 15, 1998). The damage that the AIDS epidemic will do to the poor is easy to illustrate. For example, the typical breadwinner in Africa has around ten dependents, and there are (apart from South Africa) no welfare systems. The death of a child (much less that of the breadwinner) is a financial burden because funeral expenses mean that the family may have to sell land or cattle (capital) or take a healthy child out of school (*New York Times*, November 15, 1998). The AIDS epidemic in Africa (similar to the fourteenth-century Black Death) affects the profitability of companies in several ways: absenteeism for funerals, medical and death expenses, and the costs of recruiting and training new workers. A massive safe sex public education campaign and a concerted program of distribution of free condoms are essential prerequisites for dealing with the AIDS crisis. For the poor in the Third World (or for that matter anywhere), if the choice is between the purchase of food to feed the family or the purchase of condoms for safe sex, the choice will be for food.

Nearly one third of the people in Third World countries mostly in sub-Saharan Africa are not expected to survive to age 40, due to the HIV/AIDS pandemic, and this will place more children in poverty because of the early death of their parents (*HDR 1997*).

Nearly 1 billion people are illiterate. Most studies have shown a negative correlation between poverty and the level of education (*HDR 1996*, p. 20). In India half of the country's 1.09 billion people (61 percent of females and 36 percent of males, aged 7 and above) are unable to read and write (The Probe Team, 1999). Less than 30 percent of all adults have completed 8 years of schooling. The average adult in India has little more than 2 years of schooling, compared with 5 years in China, 7 years in Sri Lanka, and over 9 years in South Korea. The average years of schooling for men in India is 2.9 years, compared with 1.8 years for women (The Probe Team, 1999). Literacy rates in the Third World countries are usually lower for the poor.

Women are disproportionately poor. They are burdened by the strains of work, child care, caring for the family, and they tend to suffer from malnutrition, which explains why they die from childbirth. In China, women who are 35 years and over are more likely to be laid off.

As Burns (1998) noted, the status of women in India is even more troubling, relegating women who are widowed to certain poverty. The reason for this is the custom of Hindi brides marrying into their husbands' families and cutting ties with their own family. Indian parents, who view their daughters as a liability or financial burden, arrange childhood marriages. Once a woman is widowed, she is unwanted again and is forced in many cases to become an unpaid servant for her in-laws or is left to work the streets. And even though laws have been enacted in India to protect widows' rights to inheritance, these laws are not enforced. Many of their husbands' families, wanting to keep property intact, often force the widows to remarry back into the family. There are nearly 33 million unwelcomed widows who are driven to poverty. To reduce human misery, there is a strong need throughout the world to reduce the gender inequality that women experience.

Unemployment rates are highest among the poor. In Haiti for the age group 15–24 years, at least 75 percent are unemployed. The poorest 40 percent of households receive less than 15 percent of total incomes. Inequality is pervasive in poor countries, particularly in Latin America (see Gafar, 1998a). In Latin America the top 5 percent of income earners get more than one third of total incomes and control nearly 70 percent of total wealth.

Of the more than 4.4 billion people in developing countries (i.e., approximately 80 percent of the world's population) nearly three fifths lack basic sanitation; one third have no access to clean water; one fourth do not have adequate housing; one fifth have no access to modern health services; and one fifth do not have enough dietary energy and protein (*HDR 1998*, p. 2).

Poverty is highly correlated with landlessness in South Asia, Southern Africa, and Latin America (*World Development Report 1990*). Many of the poor have some access to fragmented and small plots of land, but no ownership rights, which are important prerequisites for risk taking in a market economy. In Brazil the top 2 percent of landowners control 60 percent of the arable land, whereas the bottom 70 percent of rural households are landless or just about so (*HDR 1998*, p. 22).

Households with the lowest incomes tend to be large. The decision by the poor to have many children is not irrational, because mortality rates for children of the poor are high, and there is also the need to have some surviving children take care of the old parents (social assistance for the elderly in developing countries is minimal at best, if not nonexistent).

Poverty is predominantly rural, and most of the poor are engaged in agriculture on small plots of land (*WDR 1990*). In recent years urban poverty and the growth of shanty towns are on the rise. In Brazil in 1985, 75 percent of the poor worked in the informal sector (*WDR 1990*). Many of the urban poor may be full-time beggars, garbage sifters, prostitutes (a source for the AIDS infection), or pickpockets. In China, urban poverty is on the rise due in part to the prevailing financial crisis and the liberalization process.

The situation in China reflects the objective reality for the Third World, as the streets of Calcutta, Bombay, Manila, Mexico City, Caracas, and Lagos will attest. Urban economies in Third World countries cannot absorb all the rural poor—urban infrastructures are inadequate. Cairo, Egypt, built for a population of 2 million, now has over 10 million. All Third World cities are too crowded. In Latin America and the Caribbean, 22 percent of the people in Panama City were poor in 1983, 64 percent of the people in Guatemala City in 1983, 45 percent of the people of Santiago, Chile, in 1985 (see *HDR* 1998, p. 86) and 46 percent in Jamaica (Gafar, 1998c).

Concomitant with the rise in urban poverty is the widespread growth of urban violence in the ghettos, as anyone familiar with Kingston, Jamaica, would know.

Crime, prostitution, violence, and illegal drugs are all part of the urban subculture that the poor have to confront daily.

Nearly 60 to 70 percent of the expenditures of the poor go for food, compared to around 10 percent in the advanced countries (*WDR 1990*).

Poverty is correlated with race and ethnicity. Indigenous peoples in Guyana (Gafar 1998a), Bolivia, Ecuador, Australia, Guatemala, Mexico, and Peru are disproportionately poor (*WDR 1990*). In the United States, the overall poverty rate in 1996 was 13.3 percent, for African-Americans 28.4 percent, and for Hispanic Americans 27.1 percent.[8]

The *Human Development Report 1998* states that globally, the 20 percent of the world population in the industrial countries account for nearly 86 percent of the world's incomes. This glaring inequality in the distribution of the world's incomes is also manifested in other forms. For example, the richest fifth in the industrial world consume 45 percent of all meat and fish; the poorest fifth, 5 percent; and the richest fifth consume 58 percent of total energy, the poorest fifth, less than 5 percent. To highlight the inequality of incomes, a fundamental question in any discussion of poverty issues is the status of the ultrarich. According to *Human Development Report 1998*, the world's 225 richest people have a combined wealth of over US$1 trillion, equal to the annual income of 47 percent of the world's people (i.e., 2.5 billion people). The three richest people have assets that exceed the combined GDP of the forty-eight least developed countries. The wealth of the thirty-two richest people exceeds the total GDP of South Asia. The assets of the eighty-four richest exceed the GDP of China, the most populous country, with 1.2 billion people. It is against this background, notwithstanding the increases in Third World countries' incomes and food supplies due to the Green Revolution, the gains in life expectancy, and the near eradication of yellow fever, that there a is need to improve the welfare of the poor. Solutions to the financial crisis ravaging the Third World economies should not be aimed exclusively at improving the health of international banks (indeed there are moral hazard questions involved), while ignoring the human pain of the poor, the downtrodden, the faceless and the voiceless, the hungry, the orphaned child, the old and the destitute, the miserable and the politically unrepresented.

ESTIMATES OF THE HUMAN POVERTY INDEX

Estimates of the Human Poverty Index (HPI) were computed by UNDP for seventy-eight developing countries that have adequate data (*HDR 1997*, p. 20). The HPI, as noted before, deals with deprivation in three essential elements: longevity, knowledge, and a decent standard of living. The HPI rankings for some countries are summarized in Table 5.2. The HDI shows how far a country has to go to attain an average life expectancy of 85 years, universal education, and minimal standards of living. The maximum possible HDI value is 1, and the difference between 1 and the reported HDI value shows a country's shortfall in HDI. In 1994 the average HDI value for high human development countries was

Table 5.2
HDI and HPI for Some Developing Countries

COUNTRIES	DEVELOPMENT INDEX (HDI) 1994	POVERTY INDEX (HPI) (%)	HPI RANK	RANK MINUS HDI RANK	MINUS 1$-a-day POVERTY RANK
Trinidad & Tobago	0.880	4.1	1	-4	n.a
Cuba	0.723	5.1	2	-18	n.a
Costa Rica	0.889	6.6	5	2	-15
Mexico	0.853	10.9	7	-1	- 9
Jamaica	0.736	12.1	12	-6	1
China	0.626	17.5	18	-11	-12
Dominican Rep.	0.718	18.3	20	-1	- 5
Kenya	0.463	26.1	32	-14	-13
Algeria	0.737	28.6	37	20	21
Egypt	0.614	34.8	44	14	15
India	0.446	36.8	47	-2	n.a.
Nigeria	0.393	41.6	54	3	9
Haiti	0.338	46.2	61	-3	n.a.
Pakistan	0.445	46.8	64	14	11
Sierra Leone	0.176	59.2	77	-1	n.a.
Niger	0.193	66.0	78	2	3

Note: n.a. = not available. The maximum value for HDI is 1. HDI and $1-a-day poverty ranks were calculated for the seventy-eight developing countries that the HPI was calculated for. A negative number indicates that the HPI rank is better than the other, a positive the opposite.

Source: UNDP, *Human Development Report 1997*, p. 21.

0.907, 0.667 for medium human development countries, and 0.403 for low human development countries.

The data in Table 5.2 show that Trinidad and Tobago and Cuba have an HPI value of less than 10 percent. This means that these countries have reduced human poverty where it affects less than 10 percent of the population; whereas Haiti has an HPI of 46.2 percent.

What is the difference between HDI and HPI? According to the *Human Development Report 1998* (p. 25), the HDI measures progress in a country as a whole; HPI measures the extent of deprivation, the proportion of the society that is left out of progress. *Human Development Report 1998* (p. 26) also noted that although Egypt and Pakistan have reduced their income poverty to less than 15 percent, the HPI in these countries is much higher, 34.8 percent and 46.8 percent, respectively. The HPI also shows progress that may not be revealed in the head-count ratio of poverty because head-count ratio is based only on income.

POVERTY IN THE CARIBBEAN

I now briefly outline the poverty rates for the Caribbean region. Table 5.3 summarizes the details. The head-count poverty index varies from a low of 8 percent in Barbados to a high of 65 percent in Haiti. Why is the poverty rate in Guyana higher than that of the other English-speaking Caribbean countries?

Table 5.3
Poverty Estimates for Selected Caribbean Countries

COUNTRY	YEAR	HEAD COUNT INDEX (P_0)	POVERTY GAP INDEX (P_1)	POVERTY SEVERITY(P_2)	DAILY PER CAPITA EQUIVAENT US$ POVERTY LINE
Barbados	1995	8.0	-	-	-
Dominican Republic	1994	20.6	-	-	$1.24
Guyana	1993	43.2	16.2	8.2	$1.04
Haiti	1987	65.0	-	-	-
Jamaica	1992	34.2	10.6	4.4	$1.76
Trinidad & Tobago	1992	21.2	7.3	3.7	$1.54
Caribbean Average		**27.0**	-		

Source: World Bank, Caribbean Countries: Poverty Reduction and Human Resource Development in the Caribbean, May 1996, Table 1.2.

One reason is bad governance, which resulted in economic decline, inflation, and wage erosion. There was also a production crisis because incentives were distorted, and property rights were not secured owing to the nationalization process. Property rights are the lifeblood of a market economy. Another explanation is that the political system in Guyana was undemocratic; elections were fraudulent, corruption and discrimination were institutionalized, and there was no effective way to throw the government out of office. Between 1980 and 1990 real per capita GDP in Guyana fell at an annual average rate of 3 percent. According to the World Bank (1994), had per-capita GDP in Guyana increased at an annual rate of 2 percent, poverty in Guyana would have fallen from 26 percent in 1980 to 14 percent in 1990. Economic growth is obviously poverty reducing.

STRATEGIES FOR POVERTY ALLEVIATION IN THE CARIBBEAN

I now outline some strategies to deal with poverty based on my experience with some of the Caribbean countries. A popular view in the 1960s and 1970s in the Caribbean and elsewhere (particularly among the dependency school and the black power movement), was the clamor for structural changes, implying that state-run development was needed to alleviate poverty. Fidel Castro's authoritarian Marxist model was championed by the political left (Michael Manley in Jamaica; Cheddi Jagan and Forbes Burnham in Guyana; Maurice Bishop in Grenada; and academics at the regional universities) as the way forward, notwithstanding the obvious inefficiencies, economic decline and human repression, and the massive Cuban exodus that was/is associated with Castro's rule.

In Guyana, the Forbes Burnham government proclaimed the attainment of the socialist revolution when it nationalized the key sectors of the economy, decreed a socialist constitution proclaiming that "[t]here shall be no exploitation of man by man," that land shall go to the tillers, and instituted "socialist" (bureaucratic) planning and controls. In pursuit of its socialist objectives, the Burnham government made the judiciary, civil service, and other organs of the state subservient to its political will. There were human rights violations and censorship, and the leading newspaper was state controlled. Elections were rigged, and the government silenced some of its critics by force. The socialist constitution mandated which labor (party) union would represent public employees, and a labor law was passed in the 1980s reducing wages to 1978 levels (which was later held to be unconstitutional). The state control of the economy and the nondemocratic nature of the government meant economic collapse, financial bankruptcy, inflation, fiscal and trade deficits, increasing foreign debt, exodus of skilled people, and an increase in the head-count index of poverty from 26 percent in 1980 to 43 percent in 1990 (Gafar, 1998a). One of the sad and damaging consequences of the exclusionary policies of the Burnham regime is that nearly a whole generation of Guyanese children were pulled out of school and are semi-illiterate. Indo-Guyanese parents pulled their sons from school to be engaged in petty trades to supplement the families' incomes, simply because educated Indo-Guyanese were predominantly discriminated against by the Burnham regime in securing public sector employment. With a collapsing economy, the minority government had nowhere else to turn, and at the urging of the IMF and World Bank, Guyana in 1988 implemented liberalization policies and free elections in 1992. These changes have resulted in openness, more freedom, and economic growth (Gafar, 1996).

Michael Manley in Jamaica pursued a policy of democratic socialism (economic populism) involving state controls and some state ownership. These policies were perceived by many Jamaicans (most vocally by the middle class) to threaten the democratic process and the Jamaican way of life. Economic decline resulted, investment contracted, unemployment soared, capital flight ensued, and skilled people emigrated (Gafar, 1988). There is substantial anecdotal evidence to suggest that human misery and poverty increased under this period of democratic socialism. The Manley government was thrown out of office in 1980, and its socialist experiment abandoned in favor of market policies, liberalization, and deregulation. Since then, there has been some economic growth, increased employment but in the low-productivity informal sectors, and a reduction in poverty rates (Gafar, 1998c).

The tendency of Caribbean governments, in response to economic crisis, is to resort to controlling activities, licensing, price controls, tariffs and quotas, and overvalued exchange rates. These policies are urban biased and pro-industry; they encourage inefficiencies, rent-seeking, and corruption; and they stifle growth and employment and worsen poverty. Price controls on domestically produced foodstuffs is a tax on the rural farmer and a subsidy to the urban population; price controls on foodstuffs reduce agricultural production, exacerbate rural poverty, and encourage the rural-urban migration. There is considerable scholarly evidence to demonstrate that the African food famines are the result of price distortions, suppression of incentives, and high rates of taxation. According to the World Bank (1998, p. 48)

The combination of high explicit taxes and overvalued currencies contributed to alarming declines in Sub-Saharan Africa's agricultural growth rates: from an annual of 2.2 % in 1965–73 to 1.0 % in 1974–80 and 0.6 % in 1981–85.

The data summarized by Gafar (1998b) indicate that the maximum implicit tax, as a result of distortions in the exchange rate in Guyana, averaged around 66 percent between 1981 and 1990, and this entirely accounted for the reduction of agricultural output and exports.

Bhagwati (1993, p. 50) pointed out for India, the rush to bureaucratic control arises from two factors: "firstly, the inability of policy makers to trust markets, and its resulting distribution, when scarcities are acute; and secondly, the failure of policy makers to understand that markets will do a better job in resource allocation than central planning." Bardhan (1990) noted that markets impose discipline and encourage learning and cost- and quality-consciousness. The failed interventionist economic policies and poor economic management by the Burnham and Manley regimes have seriously hurt the poor and made it difficult to have any faith in left-of-center administrations and their programs. In contrast to Guyana and Jamaica, Barbados with fewer resources, but with a respect for democratic rule, market-oriented policies, openness, an independent judiciary and civil service, fiscal discipline, free and fair elections, freedom of the press, and a less threatening economic policy, has the highest per capita GDP in the Caribbean, life expectancy of 76 years, an adult literacy rate of 97.4 percent, and an HDI value of 0.909 in 1995. (For comparison purposes, in the case of the United States, life expectancy at birth is 76.4 years, the adult literacy rate is 99 percent and the HDI is 0.943 [see *HDR 1998*].)

These three Caribbean experiences confirm Sen's (1990) analysis and underline the importance of good governance, sound macroeconomic policies, the rule of law, political moderation, free and fair elections, a free press, and free markets in achieving economic growth and improvements in human welfare. The poverty-reducing strategy outlined in the *World Development Report 1990* is still relevant today.

This strategy consists of three basic elements: broad-based economic growth, developing human capital of the poor, and the provision of social safety nets for the vulnerable groups (World Bank, 1996a). The evidence in the literature (Morley, 1994; Bruno et al., 1996) suggests that the elasticity of poverty (head-count ratio) with respect to growth in mean incomes is around −2, which clearly supports the proposition that growth is poverty reducing. Gender equality is essential for empowering women and reducing poverty. Women need equal rights and access to land, credit, and job opportunities. The evidence shows that poverty and unemployment are directly related (Gafar, 1998a) and that there is a positive correlation between unemployment and violence (Gafar, 1988). The rates of urban violence, particularly in Kingston, Jamaica, affect the poor in terms of health costs and loss of property, life, and employment opportunities. Unemployment rates among Caribbean youths are extremely high, and this partly explains the increasing gang warfare, violence, and youth poverty.

Macroeconomic policies in the Caribbean should not only be market oriented, but they need to be credible, consistent, and transparent; property rights need to be secured to enable risk taking (no more nationalizations); and the state should not indulge in activities that the private sector can do more efficiently. Macroeconomic policies should also aim at keeping inflation low and budget deficits manageable, because protracted budget deficits, financed by monetary accommodation, are just inflationary, invariably leading to dollarization of the economy and capital flight. In essence, inflation is antigrowth. But reductions in fiscal deficits in the Caribbean come with the reality of slashing public employment and social expenditures, and this creates more poverty, and in the case of Guyana, ethnic tensions and a national chasm. Overvalued exchange rates in the Caribbean favor the import-substituting industries and city dwellers at the expense of the labor-intensive agricultural industry, and it is a tax on labor; hence, exchange rates need to be competitive. Openness and trade liberalization would force competition, innovation, and quality improvements and would allow for resources to be allocated more efficiently, favoring the use of the abundant resource (i.e., labor). But there is a problem here. If the export sector is the user of a specific factor (land for cultivation or minerals—e.g., bauxite), the increase in income arising from liberalization will accrue as rents, and the welfare gains will depend on who owns the specific factor. Because the sugar estates in the Caribbean are more or less owned by the wealthy (the poor have small land holdings), then the wealthy stand to benefit substantially (a tax-subsidy program can be implemented). For many Caribbean countries exporting primary goods, the depressed state of world commodity prices is not encouraging news.

Any strategy of poverty reduction must provide Caribbean countries more open and equitable access to markets in the industrial countries, adequate prices for primary products (extension of Lome IV is important for the sugar and banana economies), and debt relief. External debt burden is a major development constraint for Guyana, Jamaica, and many African countries. Debt payments contribute to increased poverty, because scarce foreign exchange is diverted from improving health, education, and the physical infrastructure. There is need to increase the flow of aid to poor countries, especially since the United Nations (1998) pointed out that official development assistance (ODA) has fallen to 0.25 percent of gross domestic product, the lowest level since foreign aid was institutionized with the Marshall Plan. An integrated rural development program in the Caribbean is essential to ameliorate poverty (because most of the poor are in rural areas); rural infrastructure needs improvement; land reforms are essential; and agricultural prices need liberalization because farmers are responsive to price (John Gafar [1997] summarizes the econometric evidence of the supply of agriculture for the Caribbean).

Although economic growth remains the key to poverty reduction, attention must also be placed on safety nets for the benefit of the poor. Throughout the Caribbean the poor lack adequate access to employment, good education, health care, and proper sanitation. And, if the poor manage to see a doctor at the ill-equipped public health clinics, they cannot afford to pay for medicines (which are imported). The related literature shows that increasing the human capital of the poor (good education and better health) is important for growth. Early childhood development (for example, nutrition programs) can have lasting effects. The governments of the Caribbean countries need to provide quality primary education because the private rates of return on education at the primary level are high. Education is important for giving voice to the poor, because as people learn, they become aware of their circumstances (*World Development Report 1998*, p. 118).

Although state control of the economy in the Caribbean region and elsewhere has not eradicated poverty, the gospel of reliance on unfettered markets alone is not the solution either, because of imperfect information, incomplete markets, externalities, and the lack of public goods. Without reliable information, markets (for example, the labor market) do not work efficiently. Therefore, the state should be engaged in producing and sharing information. Caribbean governments need to provide more social safety nets for the sick, the old, the disabled, and those in the poorest regions. Short-term public works (e.g., building roads, canals, school repair), which provide employment opportunities, are recommended to deal with the high levels of unemployment. In formulating and designing safety nets and poverty programs to benefit the poor, Margaret Grosh (1995) underscored the fact that these programs must be evaluated in terms of administrative feasibility, political feasibility, collateral effects, targeting, and tailoring the solution to the problem.

Any poverty program must satisfy some minimum level of administrative efficiency to make it workable. For example, consider food price subsidy programs, foodstuffs distribution programs, food stamps, and school meal programs. In the case of food price subsidies, this can be achieved easily, the price of foodstuffs can be regulated leaving the implicit tax to be borne by the producers of foodstuffs, but this would result in loss production and a flight from agriculture. Food stamp programs require the selection of the beneficiaries, the distribution and the collection of the food stamps. The choice of the beneficiaries can be costly, time-consuming, or open to nepotism and corruption; and some recipients can simply sell the food stamps, thereby negating the objective of nutritional improvements. School meal programs are well targeted and easy to implement. Food commodity distribution programs at health clinics aimed at meeting the needs of pregnant and lactating women and the needs of young children are administratively manageable because it is easy to identify the beneficiaries.

A living standards survey of households in Jamaica provides useful information about two programs designed to benefit the poor: subsidies for basic foods and food stamps for low-income households. Health clinics are used to identify food stamp recipients. The survey revealed that the middle- and upper-income families were the main beneficiaries of food subsidies (as the poor did not have the ability to purchase the food). The survey also found that food stamps targeted to the poor were effective in reaching the poor, and, moreover, because clinics were used, health problems were treated (see *World Development Report 1998*, p. 119).

But here is the policy dilemma: Although the provision of large basic needs and properly targeted safety net programs are poverty ameliorating, all Caribbean governments do not have adequate resources to fund these programs for a sufficiently long period to reduce poverty significantly. Governments of the Caribbean region have implored their fellow countrymen living in North America to continue to send remittances and barrels of supplies to keep the local economy afloat and thus help to alleviate human suffering. A majority of the skilled and talented people from the region have emigrated, thus making it difficult to manage the Caribbean economies. The Bhagwati tax proposal on the human drain needs some form of implementation, as the emigration of skilled, technical and professional personnel, and entrepreneurial skills from the Caribbean countries is increasingly making it difficult, if not impossible, for these countries to transform and grow their economies and improve the lot of their people.

CONCLUSION

In conclusion I want to discuss an issue on which policy makers need some articulation and guidance. It concerns the problems of ethnic conflicts and ethnic poverty. For example, in a recent opinion poll, the Guyanese people (22 percent) ranked racial tension as the number one problem, followed by poor governance (16 percent), corruption (14 percent), poverty (13 percent), crime (13 percent), illegal drugs (13 percent), and other problems and no response (10 percent).[9] Guyana's population consists largely of two ethnic groups. Fifty-one percent of the population is of East Indian descent (who largely support the PPP party), and 42 percent of the population is of African descent (who largely support the PNC party). Voting in Guyana is racially entrenched, and the PPP (given that the population growth of East Indians exceeds that of Afro-Guyanese) will likely win any free and fair elections, but as the ethnic violence after the December 15, 1997, free and fair elections suggests, the PPP will not be able to govern effectively. The state organizations (army, civil service, etc.) are all predominantly staffed by Afro-Guyanese. The army is more than 80 percent Afro-Guyanese, and for every 1 Indo-Guyanese in the public sector (civil service, nursing, teaching, etc.) there are 2.8 Afro-Guyanese. However, poverty rates for Afro-Guyanese are higher than that of Indo-Guyanese (Gafar, 1998a). There are discussions in Guyana to implement some form of ethnic balancing in the army, police, and public sector, and some affirmative action program to address the problem of ethnic poverty and ethnic tension in Guyana. The experiences from Malaysia and India are worth noting in this regard.

In Malaysia, as in Indonesia, the ethnic Chinese minority controls most of the private wealth, and the poor masses are concentrated among the majority Muslims. To ease ethnic tensions, Malaysia ten years ago ordered that any Chinese entrepreneur must give a 30 percent stake in the company to native Malay, known as *bumiputera,* as the price for obtaining government contracts. This policy has led to deals and bribes, and as Bardhan (1996) points out, these deals are referred to as Ali-Baba combinations, Ali being the Muslim *bumiputera* front man in the business contract, and Baba the Chinese businessman. Ethnic Chinese in Malaysia and Indonesia have been targeted and made the scapegoats for the economic crisis, and many had to flee these two countries, even though they were born there.

India's Constitution of 1950 tried to erase lines of caste prejudice by expanding a system of "reservations" that guaranteed the untouchables 15 percent of all seats in Parliament, university places, civil service, and so on. This policy has led to the creation of a multiplicity of castes and the permanent institutionalization of caste prejudices (see Bearak, 1998). This would happen to Guyana if it attempts this ethnic balancing with quotas. Moreover, quotas once given to any ethnic group would open the floodgates for other minorities (based on religion or otherwise) to demand the same. Indeed, the only immediate economic benefit that any race-based policy would produce would be the growth of DNA industries trying to count ethnic characteristics! Enforced ethnic balancing in the civil service and security forces is an affront and an assault to incentives, professionalism, productivity, and efficiency and is nothing more than an incestuous child of the race myth. The problem is how ethnic balancing would be implemented: more bureaucracy, more intervention, and controls. This is nothing more than institutionalizing the Burundi and Rwanda Hutu-Tutsi tribalism conflicts, which Howard French (1998) aptly titled "Rwanda's Disease." Race-based policies (similar to the infant industry argument used to justify the failed import substitution strategy) would lead to labor market distortions (stifling economic growth), dependency, resentment, red tape, and corruption, might well reduce the chances of the protected for upward mobility, and might well exacerbate poverty.

Research has shown that ethnic tensions and conflicts are both a cause and a consequence of poor economic performance, and civil conflicts can lead to the collapse of the state, thereby hurting the poor (World Bank, 2001). Pro-growth policies, a political philosophy aimed at the median voter (moderation and pragmatism), political stability, empowerment, inclusion, and voice; free and fair elections and acceptance of the will of the people, adherence to the rule of law, a vigorous opposition and a free press; an open, competitive, merit-based public sector employment policy; zero tolerance for corruption; independence of the judiciary; and policies that reward effort and promote savings and foreign investment are necessary conditions to create the environment conducive for growth and creating the framework to ease ethnic tensions and ethnic poverty—but whether they are sufficient is another issue.

NOTES

I wish to thank Dr. Udayan Roy for the many conversations we had on this topic, and Dean Paul Sherwin for his encouragement and financial support. All errors and interpretations are my responsibility.

1. The estimates obtained from a properly drawn sample can be robust, and they are much more cost-effective to produce compared to census taking.

2. The discussion between absolute and relative poverty is based on the various Technical Notes in the *Human Development Report 1990*.

3. For the Caribbean data, see World Bank (1996b).

4. These arguments are contained in Gafar (1998a) and World Bank (1994).

5. This section is based on the exposition in Sen and Foster (1997) and Psacharopoulos et al. (1997).

6. Head-count ratios for Caribbean countries are contained in World Bank (1996b) and Gafar (1998c). Detailed head-count ratios for Guyana are in Gafar (1998a) and World Bank (1994).

7. *New York Times*, Tuesday, October 20, 1998, p. A8.

8. A family of four in the United States was classified as poor if it had cash income of less than $16,400 in 1997. The threshold for a family of three was $12,802. Income, as officially defined, does not include capital gains, health insurance, or government benefits like food stamps, Medicaid, etc. (See Robert Pear, "Black and Hispanic Poverty Falls, Reducing Overall Rate for Nations," *New York Times*, September 25, 1998 p. A25).

9. See *Caribbean Daylight* (New York), March 9, 2001, p. 36.

REFERENCES

Atkinson, A.B. 1987. "Poverty." In *The New Palgrave: A Dictionary of Economics*, edited by J. Eatwell, M. Milgate, and P. Newman. New York: Macmillan Press.

Bardhan, P. 1990. "Symposium on the State of Economic Development." *Journal of Economic Perspectives* 4 (3): 3–7.

Bardhan, P. 1996. "Efficiency, Equity and Poverty Alleviation: Policy Issues in Less Developed Countries." *The Economic Journal* 106 (September): 1344–56.

Bearak, B. 1998. "Caste Hate, and Murder Outlast Indian Reforms." *New York Times*, September 19, p. A.3.

Bhagwati, J. 1993. *India in Transition: Free the Economy*. New York: Oxford University Press.

Booth, C. 1892. *Life and Labour of the People of London*. 9 Vols. London: Macmillan.

Bowley, A.L. 1913. "Working Class Households in Reading." *Journal of the American Statistical Society* 76(June): 672–701.

Bruno, M., M. Ravallion, and L. Squire. 1996. "Equity and Growth in Developing Countries, Old and New Perspective on the Policy Issues." *Policy Working Papers 1563*. The World Bank: Washington, D.C.

Burns, J. 1998. "Once Widowed in India, Twice Scorned." *New York Times*, March 29, p. A-1.

Eden, Sir F.M. 1797. *The State of the Poor*. London: Frank Cass.

Foster, J., J. Greer, and E. Thorbecke. 1984. "A Class of Decomposable Poverty Measures." *Econometrica* 52: 761–65.

French, H. 1998. "Congo Catches Rwanda's Disease." *New York Times*, August 9, p. A. 3.

Gafar, J. 1988. "Economic Growth and Economic Policy: Employment and Unemployment in Jamaica, 1972–1984." *The Journal of Developing Areas* 23: 63–84.

———. 1996. "Guyana: From Cooperative Socialism to Economic Liberalization and Growth: 1976–1994." *The Journal of Developing Areas* 31: 41–74.

———. 1997. "The Supply Response of Aggregate Agricultural Output in Jamaica." *Agricultural Economics* 16: 205–17.

———. 1998a. "Growth, Inequality and Poverty in Selected Latin American Countries with Emphasis on Guyana." *Journal of Latin American Studies* 30: 591–617.

———. 1998b. "Economic Policy and Growth: Agricultural Performance and the Rice Industry of Guyana." *Canadian Journal of Development Studies* 19 (1): 153–74.

———. 1998c "Poverty, Income Growth, and Inequality in Some Caribbean Countries." *Journal of Developing Areas* 32: 467–90.

Galbraith, J.K. 1958. *The Affluent Society*. Boston: Houghton Mifflin.

Grosh, M. 1995. "Five Criteria for Choosing among Poverty Programs." In *Coping with Austerity, Poverty and Inequality in Latin America*, edited by N. Lustig. Washington, D.C.: The Brookings Institution.

Harrington, M. 1962 *The Other America*. New York: Macmillan.

Morley, S. 1994. *Poverty and Inequality in Latin America: Past Evidence, Future Prospects*. Overseas Development Council, Washington, D.C.

Myrdal, G. 1944. *An American Dilemma*. New York: Harper (paperback ed. 1964).

———. 1968. *Asian Drama: An Inquiry into the Poverty of Nations*. New York: Twentieth Century Fund.

Pear, R. 1998. "Black and Hispanic Poverty Falls, Reducing Overall Rate for Nation." *New York Times*, September 25, p. A.1.

Probe Team, The. 1999. *Public Report on Basic Education in India*. New Delhi: Oxford University Press.

Psacharopoulos, G., S. Morley, A. Fiszbein, H. Lee, and B. Wood. 1997. "Poverty and Income Distribution in Latin America. The Story of the 1980's." *World Bank Technical Paper No. 351*. Washington, D.C.: The World Bank.

Sen, A.K. 1976. "Poverty: An Ordinal Approach to Measurement." *Econometrica* 46: 437–446.

Sen, A. 1990. "Individual Freedom as a Social Commitment." *The New York Review of Books* (June 14): 49–53.

Sen, A.K., and J. Foster. 1997. *On Economic Inequality*. New York: Oxford University Press.

Todaro, M. 1997 *Economic Development*, 6th ed. New York: Longman.

United Nations. 1998. *The Changing Face of Poverty 1998*. New York: United Nations Department of Public Information Newsletter, October.

United Nations Development Program (UNDP). 1990. *Human Development Report 1990*. New York: Oxford University Press, and various issues.

World Bank. 1990. *World Development Report 1990*. New York: Oxford University. Press.

———. 1994. *Guyana. Strategies for Reducing Poverty*. Report No. 12861-GUA. Washington, D.C.: World Bank.

———. 1996a. *Poverty Reduction and the World Bank. Progress and Challenges in the 1990s*. Washington, D.C.: The World Bank.

———. 1996b. Caribbean Countries Poverty Reduction and Human Resource Development in the Caribbean. Report No. 15342-LAC. Washington, D.C.: The World Bank.

———. 1998. *World Development Report 1998*. New York: Oxford University Press and Various Issues.

———. 2001. *World Development Report 2000/2001: Attacking Poverty*. New York: Oxford University Press.

6

Environmental Issues in Economic Growth: Application of an EQT Model for Developing Countries

Fidel Ezeala-Harrison

INTRODUCTION

An environmental quality trajectory (EQT) model is developed and applied in this chapter to determine effective methods for growth-enhancing environmental quality management for developing countries. That a nation's environmental situation has significant bearing on its economic growth and development has become well recognized by economists and policy makers. For developing countries, the environmental degradation problem is compounded by their use as pollution havens.

Environmental degradation retards economic growth both in the short run and in the long run. However, in the face of rising poverty levels, many developing countries appear to have adopted an environmental attitude of grow first and clean up later. Thus, as pollution havens, the pace of environmental degradation in the developing countries tends to be far ahead of the situation in the rich developed countries. The EQT model is applied in this study to evaluate this environmental attitude and explore policy options for alternative approaches for reduction of environmental degradation with a view toward wider potential global benefits.

Ordinarily it is thought that a poverty-stricken developing country is primarily concerned with ways and means to achieve greater economic growth. Therefore, such a country must be less concerned with environmental preservation. But this view neglects the fact that ultimately any level of environmental degradation, resulting from economic growth, tends to inhibit the pace of economic growth itself. The pollution-haven hypothesis (Field and Olewiler, 1994) maintains that developing countries tend to function as pollution havens when developed countries can easily relocate their operations without complying with stringent environmental standards and regulations that apply in their home countries. This premise is based on two assumptions: (1) Tough environmental control measures in the developed countries cause firms there to seek relocation in developing countries where such controls are either lax or nonexistent; and (2) many developing countries, in their desperate bids to attract industries from developed countries, have encouraged or even actively invited firms with promises of minimal or outright waiver of any environmental standards.

Sachs (1997) offered some enlightening quantitative measures of shortfalls (in terms of percentage national income growth) that some countries in certain regions of the world suffer as a result of their peculiar natural and geographical (that is, environmental) factors. Africa, for example, suffers a shortfall in growth of an estimated 2.3 percentage points per year due to "poor geography" and natural health hazards. Among other things, bad climates, poor soils, physical isolation, infectious tropical diseases and the consequent poor human and animal health are likely to hinder growth in spite of good policy.

Thomas and Belt (1997) considered the potential impacts of economic growth on environmental quality. They observed that the achievement of high growth and poverty reduction in the newly industrializing countries (NICs) of East Asia and China have been at the expense of severe environmental losses. The writers cited several environmental facts as evidence of the severe environmental threat that growth has brought to the East Asia region.[1] For example, it was noted that nine of the world's fifteen cities having the highest levels of particulate air pollution are in this region. Also, close to 20 percent of vegetation-covered land in the region suffered from soil degradation through erosion, waterlogging, and overgrazing beyond world averages. Furthermore, the region had undergone some of the highest rates of deforestation in the world, and about 50 to 75 percent of its coastlines and marine-protected areas were classified as areas of highly threatened biodiversity. The study suggested that the challenges of growth and the environment must be addressed simultaneously as a matter of high priority.[2]

The present study extends these contributions by offering a theoretical analysis of the role of environmental issues and how they impact growth and development in general, and for developing countries in particular. The next section outlines the major aspects of contemporary environmental constraints to economic growth and highlights the main issues that need to be addressed. This is followed by the presentation of the EQT model, which is developed in a first-principles format and applied to analysis of the role of environmental issues in the economic growth of developing countries. The policy conclusions of the study are offered in the final section.

ENVIRONMENTAL CONSTRAINTS ON GROWTH AND DEVELOPMENT

The economic activities of production and consumption place heavy physical demands on the environment. Construction of industries, agricultural development, housing, construction and operation of machinery, mining, forestry, and construction and use of infrastructure, all bring about environmental deterioration. For example, industrialization processes bring with them air and water pollution, as well as pollution of the earth surface in areas where industrial solid wastes were discarded. These are problems that are often taken lightly until their effects begin to manifest themselves in severe negative impacts on human health, production costs, and resource availability.

The impact of negative environmental conditions on a country's growth relate to both the direct and indirect costs that these conditions impose, as well as the costs involved in environmental quality control (usually to combat their effects or eliminate or reduce their sources). These include such measures as air-quality control, water-quality control, hazardous waste disposal, solid waste management, and management of toxic substances from industrial production. Some examples are the imposition of emission standards on industries and automobiles, installing water purification facilities, and imposing vigorous conservation measures on natural resources use (such as fish stocks, minerals, and trees). There is no question that these environmental enhancement measures result in higher short-run production costs in firms and industries within the country.

Negative environmental impacts (NEIs) on growth and development are measures of the most direct effects of a country's impaired economic performance by environmental factors. These can be classified under the following categories:

1. Problem of sustainability
2. By-products of society's economic and social life
3. Constraints of natural environmental conditions

We examine each of these in turn, with a view to providing the background for the EQT model.

PROBLEM OF SUSTAINABILITY AND GROWTH

One of the most pressing environmental issues of economic growth is that of the sustainability of the society's environmental (including human and material) resources. This is the problem of using environmental resources for current economic activity for the benefit of the present generation, while preserving these resources for future economic activity for the benefit of future generations.

Regarding human resources, the problem centers mainly on the population. A situation of either overpopulation or underpopulation will negatively affect productivity of resources. Overpopulation will result in undue pressure and overuse of the environment, thus jeopardizing productivity of resources. Underpopulation will result in relative scarcity of labor, higher labor costs, and overall relatively higher production costs in the country.

Of course, there is a need to avoid the extinction of natural resources. The country must adopt the most efficient rate of harvesting of, say, fish, or trees, or even crude petroleum, to ensure that (1) while the rate of utilization sufficiently meets the economic developmental goals of the current generation, the stock does not get depleted; and (2) the resource use and the processes involved in its harvesting and utilization neither harm the environment nor pose major health risks to present and future generations.

There is currently a great fascination with the principle of sustainable development in most societies.[3] Ordinarily, by definition, the sustainable development objective could hardly be met as far as depletable environmental resources are concerned. This is because every unit of depletable resource used by the current generation is a unit that is unavailable for the use of future generations, indicating that the future generation will probably be worse off than the current generation.

A country's broad economic policy goals should include a sustainable yield policy for natural resource use. The sustainable yield in the harvesting of replenishable natural resources is the harvesting rate that equals the natural rate of growth of the resource biomass. At this rate of resource use, the resource stockpile would remain undiminished from period to period, thereby safeguarding the society from the ever-present fear of extinction of the resource. Of course, the question of whether or not this rate is consistent with the country's target goals of economic growth and full employment is ever present.

IMPACT OF ECONOMIC BY-PRODUCTS ON GROWTH AND DEVELOPMENT

The necessary social and economic activities of life in a country involve by-products that result from such activities. All of these activities involve the processes of either production or consumption—the two main activities that shape the state of economic performance. The environmental by-products of human life on earth generally include: the toxic contamination of the atmosphere, the earth, and the waters; deforestation; endangered animal species; acid rain, global warming, ozone layer thinning, and solid waste disposal. There is also the "eyesore" effect of environmental use—some members of society are denied their "psychic" benefits from an unspoiled environment.

The production (supply-side) and consumption (demand-side) economic activities of society each have their necessary by-products, namely, gaseous, liquid, and solid wastes generated in the course of these economic activities. These wastes that are discharged into the environment are often harmful to the environment and its occupants. This then, in turn, impairs the human activities of production and consumption, resulting in lower economic activity.

The by-products of production, from the supply side of economic activities, affect the quality of air, water, earth, and eventually, the food supply. The by-products resulting from consumption activities, the demand side of the economy, are closely associated with the population level of the country. Often, a high population level brings about high waves of rural-urban migration and their attendant explosive growth of urban communities. Urban slums erupt, where the poor living conditions give rise to congestion, squalor, and unsanitary conditions, with their resulting social problems such as crime and insecurity. Such an environment becomes prone to the spread of diseases and epidemics, all of which are detrimental to economic growth and development.

In many countries with significant levels of industrial expansion as well as large-scale applications of chemicals to agricultural production and mining, rivers and lakes have often been used as a means of disposing toxic waste products and heavy metals. These rivers and other groundwater have also been contaminated by seepage of hazardous materials from industrial sites and solid waste dumps. This presents serious environmental hazards to the society. Poor environmental situations such as pollution impair human health and also impair the productivity of labor. Higher medical costs would often result in higher production costs as firms pay higher health-care expenses for their labor force.

Many countries face increasing environmental problems of deforestation, global warming, and species extinction. The rapid depletion of forests, which act to absorb atmospheric carbon dioxide, results in reduced sinkage effect, meaning that the increased concentration of carbon dioxide gas in the atmosphere results in atmospheric warming. This greenhouse effect worsens the already unsuitable high-temperature problems in many developing countries.

NATURAL ENVIRONMENTAL CONSTRAINTS TO ECONOMIC GROWTH

Environmental issues in the context of economic growth and development present themselves very differently to the developed and less developed countries. In developed countries, environmental problems are mainly human-made (such as those previously discussed regarding the problems of sustainability and environmental by-products). In marked contrast to this, in less developed countries, most of the environmental problems are natural.

Many less developed countries in the areas of Asia, Africa, the Middle East, and Latin America and the Caribbean, must deal with very serious natural environmental problems. These regions occupy the least environmentally favorable parts of the world. Apart from those arising from the problems of high rates of urbanization and congestion in unhygienic ghetto dwellings, as well as some problems of industrial pollution in certain areas of Latin America, most of the developing countries' environmental problems arise from natural causes. In water pollution, for example, parts of Africa and South Asia suffer from waterborne parasites that infect humans and animals due to pollution from natural sources rather than pollution from industrial waste products.

Another example is climatic conditions. The developing regions are all tropical and semitropical, with unconducive weather and climatic conditions for human, animal, and plant growth and development. Most of these areas have arid or semiarid climates, associated with very harsh environmental living conditions.

The climates of these tropical areas range in extreme temperatures from lows of 15°C to highs of 42°C all year round, with very infertile soils and little or no rainfall.

Geographically, the bulk of the areas occupied by the developing countries lie within a span of about 2,500 kilometers on either side of the equator, with their tropical effects extending much wider than this range. Three types of tropical climates are found in these regions: the wet equatorial tropical climate, characterized by high humidity and constant (equatorial) rains of about 190 to 300 centimeters per year; the monsoon tropical climate, characterized by a mix of alternate wet and dry seasons; and the arid tropics, characterized by little or no rainfall.[4]

The environmental adversities presented by the tropical conditions of many countries have tended to grossly impede their overall economic production and growth. The natural environmental constraints impede education and human resource development, agriculture, infrastructural construction, and industrialization. The severe dehydrating effects of the tropical heat are restrictive of the application of human mental and physical efforts in production. It requires constant food and nourishment during the course of every production activity involving labor, thereby tending to not only raise the labor costs of production, but also to render labor relatively less productive than capital (resulting in the desire for employers to prefer capital to labor, that is, relative unemployment of the labor force).

The tropical environment, with its attendant extreme heat, high humidity, and absence of frost, is conducive to the growth of destructive bacteria, parasites, insects, pests, and several species of tropical diseases that constantly inhibit plant and animal life. Tropical storms are incessant and can be extremely destructive. The unpredictable torrential rains simply wash away the soil with their ferocious erosions, often sweeping away agricultural crops and leaving behind lands that are largely unsuitable for habitation.

Arguably, some potentially fertile areas exist in the tropics. Much has been written of the volcanic soil of the East African highlands and parts of Asia and the Pacific regions, as well as the clay soil of the alluvial plains of Africa and South America. These are all areas of the tropical zones that may be particularly suitable for agricultural development. Other than these, however, the bulk of the soil found in much of the tropics is formed from old acid parent rock, poor in calcium and other plant nutrients. Most parts of West and Central Africa, South Asia, and South America are rain forest regions. Agricultural land tenure involves the removal of the forest, and as this is done, the proportion of iron and aluminium hydroxides in the soil tends to increase, resulting in the formation of laterite soil, which becomes intractably hard and uncultivable. Agricultural output is, therefore, always very limited relative to the amount of investment made; this is a major constraining factor in economic growth and development.

DUAL-STRESS FACTOR AND THE EQT MODEL[5]

Society's economic needs of supply (production of goods and services) and demand (consumption of goods and services) are met by a constant reliance upon the environment to provide the necessary resources. These resources include the material resources that are taken from the environment's natural estate and the spatial resources into which the by-products of production and consumption are released and deposited.

On the supply side, massive production of society's goods and services impose a depletion stress (d-stress) on the environment; and on the demand (consumption) side, a combination of direct use of environmental resources and the release and deposit of consumption by-products impose a pollution stress (p-stress) on the environment. These stress factors are negative externalities. Together, they amount to a dual-stress factor that human demands impose on the environment.

The reality of the dual-stress factor can be conceptualized by positing the total demand that society imposes on the environment as a whole entity. We can denote this entity as the index, s, of environmental stress, which can be written as:

$$s = u + v,$$

where:

u = p-stress (pollution effect), and
v = d-stress (depletion effect)

Thus, total environmental stress can be depicted as an index whose value ranges from 0 (possible lower limit) to 1 (possible upper limit):

$$1 \geq s \geq 0.$$

$s = 0$ suggests a scenario in which the environment is free from stress—a case of environmental utopia, where humankind can live off the earth without any environmental consequences whatsoever. $s = 1$ implies a case scenario of environmental saturation, where the environment has reached its assimilative capacity limit of human exploitation. This scenario suggests the so-called doomsday in which society has run out of environmental support—the environment is unable to support human life on planet earth.

Environmental degradation over time is a function of the intensity of the stress being imposed on the environment. The higher the intensity of stress, the greater the amount of degradation, and vice versa. It is the amount of environmental degradation that gives rise to the level of NEIs, which determines the state of environmental quality of the society.

THE RUTTAN-KUZNETS MODEL

Chapman (1999) presents an analysis applying the theories of Simon Kuznets and Vernon Ruttan in depicting the relationship between environmental degradation and per capita income.[6] The Kuznets model and the Ruttan model propose separate and opposite relationships between environmental degradation and per capita income.

The Ruttan model suggests that high levels of environmental degradation are consistent with low per capita income; but as per capita income increases, the level of environmental degradation falls steadily. The nature of causality implied by this proposal is not clearly stated until we examine the Kuznets case. In the Kuznets model, environmental degradation is positively correlated with low levels of per capita income up to a maximum level, and then becomes negatively correlated with per capita income thereafter. The level of per capita income corresponding to the maximum level of environmental degradation can be said to represent an individual's environmental quality income threshold, y^*.[7] Thus, for all per capita income levels below y^*, a positive causal relationship can be said to exist between per capita income and environmental degradation.

These theories are based on the idea that the demand for environmental quality depends on people's income levels. If, as supposed, "pollution levels and forest degradation increase as incomes grow," during the phase of economic development when per capita income lies around US$4,000 to US$5,000, then it means that at lower income levels, p-stress and d-stress are greater relative to higher income levels. It is supposed that beyond y^* (the environmental quality income threshold) greater demand for environmental quality tends to bring about decreases in the intensities of *d*-stress and *p*-stress. Thus, as stated by Chapman (1999, p. 29), the Ruttan-Kuznets model proposes that income levels and living standards are major factors that influence the desire (demand) for greater environmental quality in society.

Denoting the intensity of environmental degradation as φ, and given the functional relationship between degradation and stress:

$$\varphi = f(s), f'(s) > 0, \tag{1}$$

the Ruttan-Kuznets relationship can be formally stated in terms of these environmental parameters, population level, and GDP.

Following Ehrlich, Ehrlich, and Holdren (1970) and Chapman (1999), a relationship linking the size of a society's population, per capita income, and pollution per unit of consumption imposed by that income, may be specified.[8] The relationship depicts total environmental degradation intensity (φ) as the product of the size of population (N), the level of per capita income (y), and the level of stress intensity (s) per unit of goods/services produced and consumed in the economy:

$$\varphi = N.y.s = N.y.(u + v).$$

Given that $y = Y/N$ (where Y = GDP) and substituting, we have

$$\varphi = Y(u + v) \tag{2}$$

Equation (2) may be termed the *Ruttan-Kuznets equation*. It formalizes the Ruttan-Kuznets theories linking environmental degradation with income. It suggests that the intensity level of environmental degradation at any given time period is a fraction (or proportionate amount represented by the level of stress intensity) of the society's GDP level.[9]

ENVIRONMENTAL QUALITY TRAJECTORY

The level of pollution intensity (represented by the parameter u in equation [2]) can be expressed as:

$$u = \varphi/Y - v$$

This shows that pollution is a positive function of environmental degradation, and a negative function of GDP (Ruttan theory) and depletion stress. But our concern is with environmental quality, which is the negative of environmental pollution. The level of environmental quality intensity, σ, is deduced from this relationship as:

$$\sigma = -u = v - \varphi/Y \qquad (3)$$

Environmental quality is given as a positive function of the d-stress parameter and GDP level, and a negative function of environmental degradation intensity.

The ratio φ/Y in equation (3)—the ratio of environmental degradation intensity to GDP—gives the measure of environmental degradation index (EDI) for any given country. It indicates an index for determining the environmental health of a country. Its values, both cross-sectional and time series, can be determined and used to assess the state of environmental performance across countries or trend performance within a given country.[10]

The dual-quadrant graphical model depicted in Figure 6.1 is used to illustrate the trajectory of environmental quality and GDP that is equation (3). The vertical axis measures the level (intensity) of environmental quality (σ). The leftward horizontal axis measures the level of EDI (φ/Y), and the rightward horizontal axis measures the time path of GDP level (Y_t). The right-hand quadrant shows the *environmental quality trajectory* (EQT) curves, with horizontal intercepts at $Y = \varphi/v$. The EQT curve is such that at the upper limit of σ, which is 1, the curve assumes a horizontal path—indicating that for all possible levels of GDP, environmental quality remains optimal at its maximum intensity level. The OT curve illustrates the optimal trajectory of environmental quality. However, the ability of a country to attain this OT at any given GDP level (Y_t^*) and time period (t) is the crucial environmental policy objective facing any country. But a country can be on any EQT (other than the OT) such as EQT_1 or EQT_2, according to its level of economic development and state of environmental health. As a country's environmental health improves, it is able to shift its EQT upward toward OT; but the poorer its environmental health, the more its EQT shifts downward away from OT. A country's position on its given level of EQT yields a corresponding point on the EQ curve shown on the leftward quadrant, with the corresponding level of EDI.

The EQT is a long-run model that can be applied toward long-term planning and projection of a country's environmental targets. For example, a country may project its environmental quality target at some future date and corresponding

Figure 6.1
Environmental Quality Trajectory

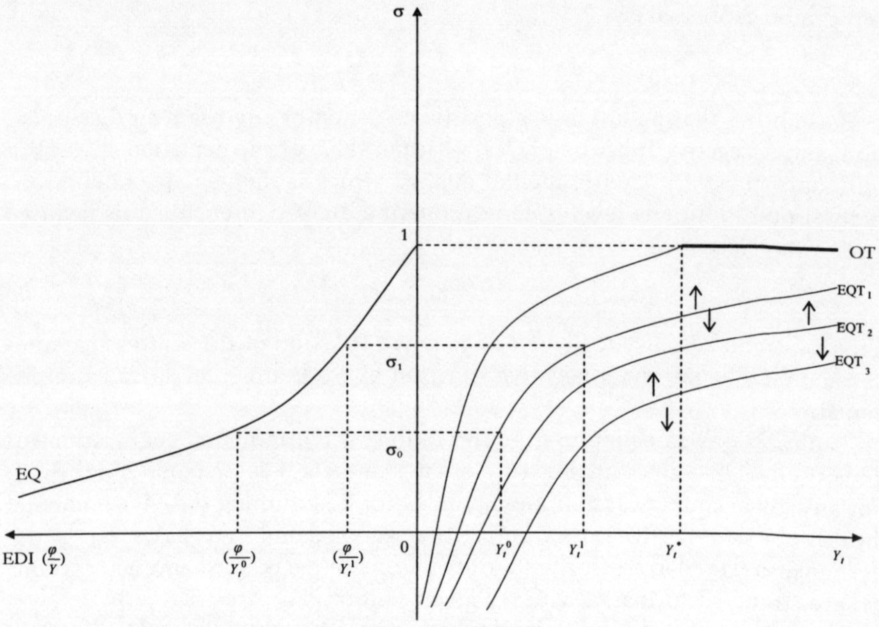

level of GDP. Under the *Kyoto Protocol,* various countries undertook to achieve some set levels of reduced emissions (pollution) over a certain time period.[11] In this case a given country would be setting choices for its process of shifting its EQT curves upward while operating along the curve at the given combinations of levels of environmental quality intensity, GDP, and EDI. The country could then determine how fast it wishes to attain these set levels by reducing the levels of environmental degradation.

POLICY APPLICATION FOR DEVELOPING COUNTRIES

The EQT model yields some growth-oriented environmental policies for developing countries that need to be adopted to pursue corrective measures to address the inevitable violation of the environment's sustainable development resulting from the course of economic activities. The model has shown that it is possible for a developing country to maintain steady long-term economic growth together with environmental sustainability along an environmental quality trajectory.

With an effective sustainable development policy program, a developing country could even operate along its optimal trajectory path. This would offer a strong long-term incentive for economic growth for a developing country that is least able to afford the disrputive and distortionary effects that environmental degradation has on economic growth. The question then is what specific policy actions need to be implemented in the developing country to enable it to achieve and operate along an optimal environmental quality trajectory.

Environmental problems are more detrimental to economic development in the developing countries than in the developed countries. Developing countries tend to be relatively more dependent on agriculture and therefore more vulnerable to climatic changes. Moreover, the implication of being a pollution-haven is that the country's environment suffers permanent damages that could limit the potential for economic growth.

Apart from the pollution side of the environmental problem in developing countries, there also is the more serious aspect relating to unsuitable environmental conditions that confront these countries. This presents the most challenging environmental constraint to economic growth. To help mitigate the impact of this condition, of central importance is the need to encourage the choice of rural dwelling among the population through aggressive programs of rural and agricultural development. These programs are to be combined with programs of education, urban planning, and infrastructure construction. With the improved level of development that these measures can provide, notably, increases in the per capita income, the country is able to attain higher EQT curves.

High poverty levels in developing countries are behind the high levels of environmental degradation. Conservation and sustainability measures would have little importance in a society lacking basic needs of food and housing. Increasing economic well-being contributes an important solution to environmental degradation; as per capita income increases, there is a reduced tendency for slum living, overgrazing, or pollution tolerance. But it appears that standards of living are not increasing in the developing countries. Thus, the forests continue to be depleted by slash-and-burn farming methods, and trees are depleted by loggers who ignore environmental costs as they pursue their immediate means of sustenance.

Environmental protection need not be sacrificed for the convenience of short-term growth. This is to say, the so-called policy of grow first and clean up later that many developing countries seem to choose in their bids for quick achievement of growth, will prove to be a very costly and unwise strategy in economic, social, and ecological terms. A high level of environmental degradation brings immediate economic and social costs that impair the economy's short-term growth performance. Health problems, asset and property depreciation, and high production costs are only few of the most obvious negative externalities. The long-term problems of resource depletion and atmospheric alteration add to the overall high cost of the grow-first-and-clean-up-later policy that make it an unwise policy.

As for the pollution havens, it should be noted that both the polluter and the polluted countries are ultimately hurt by this policy. The environment is a global public good whose potential benefits and costs ultimately extend to all societies irrespective of jurisdiction. For example, rain forests in developing countries support much of the world's species that possess overwhelming ecological, biological, and medicinal values. Rain forests also act as carbon sinks—as they contain new and growing plants that absorb carbon from the atmosphere—thereby reducing atmospheric warming. Creating pollution havens reduces these potentials and denies both the polluting and polluted countries those environmental benefits.

Because the environment is a global public good, the world as a whole has an important stake in environmental preservation efforts in developing countries. This is more so because of the constraints that growing poverty levels place on the abilities of the developing countries to attain optimal environmental trajectories themselves. This calls for policy responses on the part of the rich countries designed to help developing countries attain their optimal EQT levels. Rather than exploit them as pollution havens, the rich countries need to provide assistance in the form of compensational support to developing countries to help them defray the opportunity costs of environmental preservation. And this effort should go beyond mere allocations of foreign aid as commonly practiced. As Schelling (1992, p. 13) noted, a developing-world carbon-abatement effort should be directed to protecting our "same global common."

NOTES

1. The study specifically covered the southeast Asian countries of Malaysia, Singapore, Indonesia, and Thailand. Apparently, similar situations have occurred in other Asian countries such as Japan, South Korea, Hong Kong, and Taiwan where rapid economic growth and development have taken place during the twentieth century.

2. It must be pointed out that these environmental problems are not solely caused by rapid economic growth and development. In fact, they could equally be the results of growing poverty and underdevelopment. Experiences of many countries in Africa, South and Central America, and parts of East Asia indicate that slow-growing or negative-growing economies could equally suffer from severe environmental deterioration brought about by the fact of their economic deprivation and underdevelopment. Pressures of overpopulation and mass poverty cause severe deforestation, overgrazing, and growth of urban slums and squalor in the bid to eke out a basic existence.

3. Sustainable development is a rule of maintaining an optimal rate of resource and environmental exploitation that would neither result in making future generations worse off nor leave the needs of the present generation unsatisfied. Thus, environmental resource allocation rates that either enrich the current generation but might impoverish future generations or that impoverish the current generation in order to enrich future ones defeat the sustainable development objective.

4. In recent years, the effects of the types of severe drought that are characteristic of these areas have been seen in the world by the famines of Ethiopia (1985 and be-

yond), Somalia (1993 and beyond), Mozambique, and more recently in Sudan, all in Africa. They have also been evident in the Philippines, Bangladesh, and North Korea, in Asia.

5. This section is based on Ezeala-Harrison (2001).

6. The idea of *Environmental Kuznets Curve* depicting a positive relationship between environmental degradation and income at low income levels, and a negative relationship between these at high income levels, has been applied by some researchers such as Suri and Chapman (1998) and Selden and Song (1994). The Ruttan theory is based on Ruttan's (1971) proposal that the demand for environmental quality increases with the level of income as well as the rate of increase in income.

7. Studies based on U.S. data indicate that y^* range around US$4,000 to US$5,000 (see Chapman 1999, p. 29).

8. Chapman (1999, pp. 182–83) reformulated this Ehrlich-Holdren relationship in an economic context by redefining and stressing the impact of population growth on total pollution (environmental degradation) as a one-to-one effect (that is, a unitary population-elasticity of pollution), and by suggesting that the relationship can be made a "more realistic economic relationship" by specifying it as: *Pollution per Unit of Consumption = Environmental Policy and Practice times Pollution Intensity per Unit of Consumption.* Without delving into the complex theories of demographic transition, the simple Ehrlich-Holdren relationship seems to adequately capture the level of environmental degradation in terms of the total stress imposed by the population on the environment. This relationship can be applied to model a Ruttan-Kuznets environmental degradation theory.

9. A slight difference here is that this model relates environmental degradation to level of GDP rather than per capita GDP. This difference should not alter the theoretical underpinning that makes this model analogous to the Ruttan-Kuznets theory. Also, equation (2) represents an explicit version of the implicit relationship that is equation (1), expressing the total intensity of environmental degradation as a positive function of environmental stress intensity (and GDP).

10. Applying known values of GDY (Y), the values of EDI (φ/Y) would depend on the value of the environmental degradation intensity (φ). This can be proxied by monetary costs of NEIs, such as cost of treating environment-related illnesses (say, air and water pollution ailments), contingent valuation of eyesore costs, cost of suburban-inner city commuting, and the like.

11. Under the *Kyoto Protocol,* various countries committed to a voluntary systematic reduction of their levels of greenhouse-gas emissions. For example, Canada has committed to cutting its greenhouse gasses by 6 percent from its 1990 levels by the year 2010. In November 2000, a follow-up environmental conference in The Hague was slated to further these commitments and more negotiations on global climate change.

REFERENCES

Abler, D.G. 1993. "NAFTA, Agriculture, and the Environment in Mexico." *American Journal of Agricultural Economics,* 75.

Alpay, S. 2001. "Measuring the Impact of Economic Growth and Trade Liberalization on Environmental Policy Performance: Comparison of Developed and Developing Countries." Paper presented at the 35th Annual Meeting of the Canadian Economics Association, Montreal, June.

Barrows, R., and M. Roth. 1990. "Land Tenure and Investment in African Agriculture." *Journal of Modern African Studies* 28(2): 265–98.

Bhagwati, J.N. 1977. *The New International Economic Order: The North-South Debate*. Cambridge: Cambridge University Press.

Carriere, J. 1991. "The Crisis in Costa Rica: An Ecological Perspective." In Environment and Development in Latin America, edited by D. Goodman and M. Redclift. New York: Manchester University Press.

Chapman, D. 1999. *Environmental Economics: Theory, Application and Policy*. Don Mills, Ontario: Addison Wesley.

Dasgupta, P. 1995. "The Population Problem: Theory and Evidence." *Journal of Economic Literature* 33(4): 1879–1902.

Deardoff, A.V. 1984. "Testing Trade Theories and Predicting Trade Flows." In *Handbook of International Economics*, edited by R.W. Jones and P.B. Kenen. New York: North-Holland.

Ehrlich, P.R., A.H. Ehrlich, and J.P. Holdren. 1970. *Ecoscience: Population, Resources, Environment*. San Francisco: Freeman Press.

Ezeala-Harrison, F. 2001. "EQIP Approaches toward Environmental Stress Abatement." Paper pesented at the 35th Annual Meeting of the Canadian Economics Association, Montreal, June.

———. 1996. *Economic Development: Theory and Policy Applications*. Westport, CT: Praeger.

Field, B.C., and N.D. Olewiler, 1994. *Environmental Economics*, 1st Canadian ed. Toronto: McGraw-Hill Ryerson.

Goldstein, E.S. 1995. *Economics and the Environment*. Englewood Cliffs, N.J.: Prentice-Hall.

Khalafalla, K. 2001. "Trade, Economic Growth, and the Environment: A Survey." Paper presented at the 35th Annual Meeting of the Canadian Economics Association, Montreal, June.

Pearson, Peter J. 1994. *Energy, Externalities and Environmental Quality: Will Development Cure the Ills It Creates?* Guildford, U.K.: Surrey Energy Economics Centre, University of Surrey.

Ruttan, V.W. 1971. "Technology and the Environment." *American Journal of Agricultural Economics* 53(5): 707–17.

Sachs, J. 1997. "Nature, Nurture, and Growth." *The Economist*, June 14.

Schelling, T.C. 1992. "Some Economics of Global Warming." *American Economic Review* 82(1): 1–14.

Selden, T.M., and D. Song. 1994. "Environmental Quality and Development: Is There a Kuznets Curve for Air Pollution Emissions?" *Journal of Environmental Economics and Management* 27(2): 147–62.

Steer, A. 1996. "Ten Principles of the New Environment." *Finance and Development* 33(4): 4–7.

Suri, V., and D. Chapman. 1998. "Economics Growth, Trade and Energy: Implications for the Environmental Kuznets Curve." *Ecological Economics* 25(2): 195–208.

Thomas, V., and T. Belt. 1997. "Growth and the Environment: Allies or Foes?" *Finance and Development* 34(2): 22–24.

World Bank. 1986–1996. *World Development Report*. Various Issues. New York: Oxford University Press.

———. 1992. *World Development Report: Development and the Environment*. New York: Oxford University Press.

World Resources Institute. 1998. *World Resources 1997–98*. New York: Oxford University Press.

7

Rent-seeking and Economic Growth in Developing Countries

John Mukum Mbaku and Mwangi S. Kimenyi

INTRODUCTION

Economists usually define *economic rent* as a payment to a production input above and beyond its opportunity cost. In a purely competitive market, firms may be able to earn economic rents in the short run. However, the existence of such rents attracts the entry of other firms who compete them away as supply increases and price falls. Pure competition assumes that the market is characterized by free entry and exit such that when incumbent firms earn excess profits (i.e., above normal rates of return on investment), others enter. On the other hand, firms that earn economic loss in the long run exit from the market. In many countries, government policies often create barriers to entry, enhancing the ability of incumbent firms to earn economic profits in the long run. Protection from competition, however, is not without cost to the protected firms and to society in general. Firms, in order to secure such protection, may invest significant amounts of resources in lobbying and other activities to influence the government. The investment of resources to capture artificially created transfers is called rent-seeking (Tollison, 1982).

Although the term rent-seeking was coined by Anne O. Krueger (1974), the concept was developed by Gordon Tullock (1967). Rent-seeking refers to the expending of resources to have the government create transfers and to capture them. It is the process through which firms and organized interests manipulate the political process in order to earn economic returns above and beyond their opportunity costs. Because the scarce resources expended in the process of rent-seeking do not create any value, they are considered a social waste (Buchanan, Tollison, and Tullock, 1980).

The productive search for rents (profit-seeking) must not be confused with socially wasteful rent-seeking. Business owners regularly seek ways to increase the amount of economic rent that accrues to their enterprises. In order to achieve this important objective, they innovate and adopt more efficient ways to produce goods and services—in other words, they make an effort to meet their customers' demand more efficiently. Through such efficient production and delivery of goods and services, they can operate at lower per unit costs and, as a consequence, put themselves in a position to earn economic rents. For example, an entrepreneur who invests in research and develops a new and less expensive cure for malaria and obtains a patent for the new drug would be able to earn significant economic rents. Such investment of resources in productive processes is called profit-seeking and involves the creation of value. In such a scenario, two important things happen: (1) The firm that created the new product is better off; and (2) the welfare of society increases. It is obvious, then, that profit-seeking is socially beneficial.

When, on the other hand, firms expend resources to influence policy makers so that the latter can create barriers to entry into the economy, this is called wasteful rent-seeking. If, for example, the government of a country, at the behest of a favored firm, creates monopoly rights in the production of nails and assigns these rights to the favored firm, the latter can earn a rate of return that is above and beyond opportunity cost. The rents that accrue to the holder of the monopoly rights in nail production are considered transfers from nail consumers to the nail monopolist. The monopolist, on the other hand, expends resources to (1) have the government create the artificial scarcity (i.e., the nail monopoly) and (2) capture it. To the extent that the firm spends real resources in such activities as lobbying, campaign contributions, and bribery in order to influence the political system and secure access to the monopoly rights, these expenditures create no value from the point of view of society (Tollison, 1982, p. 577). Rent-seeking, as we have mentioned, involves efforts by individuals and groups to have the artificial rents created and also to compete for their capture. Because government intervention in the economies of developing countries is quite pervasive, the main source of rent-seeking in many of these countries has been government-created monopoly power (Buchanan, 1980a, 1980b).

In democratic political systems, lobbying, bribery, and campaign contributions are the main rent-seeking behaviors. In such societies, individuals and groups who invest in the creation of rents expect that once the rents are created by legislation, they would accrue to those whose activities created them. According to Browning (1974), however, after rents are created, they usually become "a type of collective consumption good" to be competed for by all members of society, including those who did not contribute to or invest in their creation. As a consequence, a free-rider problem arises, constraining but not eliminating investment in the creation of rents (i.e., artificial scarcities). As argued by Flowers (1987), the willingness of individuals within a society to invest in rent-creation depends on how much of the resulting rents they expect to receive. If market participants must devote additional resources to compete for capture of the rents once they are created, then they are less inclined to invest in rent-creation.

In dictatorial political systems, the incumbent ruler usually has a monopoly on the supply of legislation and governs primarily by decree. If there is a legislature in such a country, it would serve at the pleasure of the dictator and legislation passed usually represents the will and interests of the incumbent ruler. After rents are created, the ruler will have significant input into their allocation. Because the bulk of rents in such economies is created through decrees and not by legislation, the majority of rent-seekers usually do not lobby lawmakers (if they exist) or the dictator. The latter devotes most of the rents to regime security (e.g., through subsidies to military leaders). The poorly organized and politically marginalized rural agricultural sector has served as the main supplier of the rents (see, e.g., Bates, 1981, 1987).

Rent-seekers in nondemocratic societies invest primarily in the capture of the apparatus of government. Of course, rent-seekers in democratic countries also invest in capture of the government. However, there are major differences in the process of regime change in the two societies. In a democratic country, regime changes take place according to rules and procedures entrenched in the constitution. In nondemocratic countries, however, constitutional methods for regime change either do not exist or function poorly. Thus, individuals seeking to capture the government must resort to extraconstitutional means—usually violence. As a consequence, rent-seeking in nondemocratic countries often involves significant levels of violence as individuals and groups seek ways to capture the rent-creating apparatus of government and employ the latter's redistributive powers to enrich themselves at the expense of the rest of the people (Mbaku, 1997; Kimenyi, 1989).

AN OVERVIEW OF THE THEORY OF RENT-SEEKING

To illustrate the social costs associated with rent-seeking, we refer to a situation in which the government is helping protect the monopoly position of a producer. For many years, economists knew that such government protection of monopoly rights was associated with social costs. However, these costs were consistently underestimated. Figure 7.1 shows the demand for a monopolized good. The competitive price and output and the monopoly price and output are respectively, *Pc*, *Qc* and *Pm*, *Qm*. If the firm were to charge consumers the competitive price, consumer surplus would be *FAPm*. The rectangle *PmABPc* represents the monopoly rents or the transfer of income from the consumers to the monopoly supplier. The triangle *ABC* represents consumer surplus that is lost as a result of the higher price by the monopolist and the subsequent reduction in the output from *Qc* to *Qm*. Traditionally, economists have not considered the monopoly rents represented by the rectangle *PmABPc* a social cost, but rather a transfer of income from consumers to the producers. Only the area represented by the triangle *ABC* was traditionally considered a social welfare loss due to monopolization—it has generally been referred to as deadweight loss. Employing this approach, several economists have estimated the social costs of monopoly to be relatively small (Harberger, 1954).

Figure 7.1
The Social Costs of Monopoly with Rent-seeking

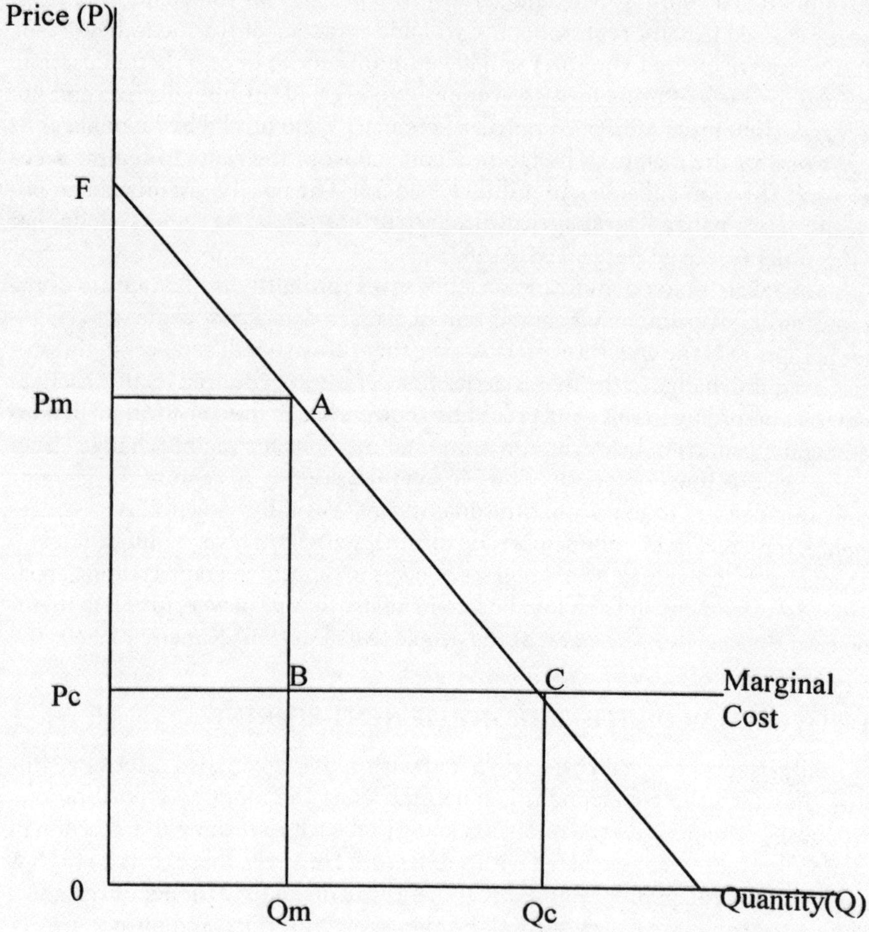

Tullock (1967) pointed out a major error in the determination of the social costs of government intervention in private exchange. To understand Tullock's insight, let us assume that the monopoly position is created and protected by the government. Entrepreneurs will invest heavily in lobbying and other ways to influence the government in order to improve their chances of capturing or being awarded the monopoly rights just created. If firms compete for the monopoly rents—competitive rent-seeking—then the entire area of the rectangle *PmABPc* would be competed away in essentially nonproductive or wasteful activities as firms seek ways to influence the government and capture the monopoly rights. Tullock's insight showed that the resources that firms invest in the capture of the rents are also a social cost of monopolization. He suggested that both rectangles and triangles are critical in the determination of the social costs of government intervention in private exchange.

Government intervention in the international trade sector and the regulation of domestic business are good examples of activities that grant some entrepreneurs privileged or monopoly positions in the economy and, thus, lead to rent-seeking. Most international trade restrictions take the form of import tariffs and quantity restrictions (e.g., quotas). These two forms of intervention create rents and encourage firm owners to undertake nonproductive investment of resources in efforts to capture the rents created (see, e.g., Kimenyi and Tollison, 1999).

Based on the preceding discussion, one may be tempted to conclude that only producers/sellers engage in rent-seeking activities. On the contrary, those who expect to lose from the monopolization of an economic activity do invest resources either to prevent those losses or minimize them. Thus, we expect consumers, who stand to suffer substantial reductions in consumer surplus as a result of the monopolization of a market, to invest resources in lobbying to prevent any supply restrictions. Peltzman (1976) extended the model developed by Stigler (1971) and incorporated consumers and producers as active participants in the rent-seeking game. According to Peltzman's model, politicians who serve as suppliers of legislation, attempt to maximize their chances of re-election (i.e., they maximize votes). The number of votes received by a politician in an election is a function of the utilities of both the consumers and producers of the regulated product. As mentioned earlier, the higher the regulated price, the greater is the monopoly rent generated. This results in more support for the politicians by producers of the good. Such a higher price, however, is bound to elicit significant opposition from consumers who stand to suffer a fall in consumer surplus. Thus, the higher regulated price results in less support for the candidate by consumers. To maximize votes obtained by the politician, the latter sets the regulated price so that the marginal gain in support from producers for an increase in monopoly rent is just offset by the loss in votes from consumers. This suggests that the price that regulators set is dependent on which group has the greater ability to influence public policy outcomes. For an individual consumer, the gain for opposing a regulated price is relatively small compared to the gain that accrues to the individual producer (see Kimenyi and Tollison, 1999, p. 204). Additionally, because there are usually many consumers, the cost of organizing consumers is higher than that of bringing together producers, and as a result, the main beneficiaries of regulation are most likely to be the regulated firms. Although both consumers and producers are engaged in the rent-seeking game, it is usually the well-organized producers who are able to influence the political system and, consequently, public policy outcomes.

The cornerstone of Tullock's rent-seeking insight is that government intervention in private exchange creates rents resulting in wasteful expenditure by firms seeking ways to capture those rents. This insight has been critical in our understanding of the full cost of government intervention in economic activities. Although Tullock's concept is now generally accepted, it is still not clear how much is expended to capture any given amount of rent. It has not yet been established whether rents are exactly, under-, or overdissipated

THE COSTS OF RENT-SEEKING

The discussion up to this point has dealt primarily with the direct use of resources by individuals and groups to have the government create transfers, as well as the resources involved in competing for the capture of these transfers. The preceding discussion, however, has not exhausted the social costs of government intervention in the economy. For example, we need to discuss the waste of resources associated with activities as the avoidance of regulations by exiting into the underground economy. Controls imposed on the foreign exchange market by the government usually result in shortages, creating opportunities for individuals to profit from buying and selling foreign exchange in the informal sector. The larger the discrepancy between the official (formal sector) rate and the informal (so-called black market) sector rate, the larger the number of transactions being undertaken illegally. In other words, the higher the demand for foreign exchange in a regulated formal sector, the higher the informal (black market) rate. The existence of a discrepancy between the legal and illegal rates implies that as a result of the risk associated with transacting illegally, there are real resource costs involved in engaging in such dealings. In addition, where government regulations are considered to be ruinous or represent an important burden on entrepreneurial effort, individuals may engage in smuggling (Blomqvist and Mohammad, 1986). Several studies have documented activities that emerge in many countries as a result of the imposition on those economies of quotas and other restraints on export. For example, in a study of Indonesia in 1996, Bohman, Jarvis, and Barichello determined that the imposition of export quotas on coffee resulted in illicit trading and bureaucratic corruption. All these activities involve real resource waste.

Krueger (1974) examines rent-seeking costs associated with the competition for import licenses in a trade regime of quantity restrictions. The most important rent-seeking activities in such a regime include: (1) the tendency of importers to invest in excess capacity in an effort to enhance the probability that they would be awarded the permit to import; (2) excessive market expansion through the entry of firms resulting in less than optimal sized firms; (3) paying of bribes to regulators (i.e., bureaucrats at the trade ministry) in order to enhance one's chances of being awarded the import license; and (4) the tendency not to base hiring decisions on merit, with the result that most firms hire relatives who are often less productive. These activities do not create value and therefore must be considered socially wasteful. Although a bribe can be considered a simple transfer and therefore not a social waste, Krueger (1974) argues that if bribes become part of the civil servant's overall compensation package, then there will be increased competition for government jobs, leading to the wasteful employment of scarce resources.

Several researchers have examined the process through which individuals and groups expend scarce resources to have the government create artificial scarcities and then compete to capture them (see, e.g., Tullock, 1993; Tollison, 1982). Kimenyi and Tollison (1999, p. 209) provide a typology of the common forms of government regulations that create opportunities for individuals and groups to capture rents. In these cases, intervention by the government in private exchange results in the misallocation of resources by (1) reducing market efficiency; (2) distorting market incentives; and (3) increasing the amount of resources that entrepreneurs must devote to seeking favors from the government and trying to minimize the impact of government regulations on their businesses (see Table 7.1).

Several studies provide empirical evidence of the social costs of rent-seeking in both developed and developing countries (see, e.g., Krueger, 1974; Mohammad and Whalley, 1984; Ampofo-Tuffuor, DeLorme, and Kamerschen, 1991).

Table 7.1
Government-Created Opportunities for Entrepreneurs to Capture Rents

Opportunity	*Activity*	*Waste/Transfer*
Tariffs	Lobbying	Both
	Enforcement	Waste
	Smuggling	Both
	Misallocation	Waste
Domestic monopoly	Lobbying	Both
	Enforcement	Waste
	Cheating	Both
	Misallocation	Waste
Credit rationing	Lobbying	Both
	Enforcement	Waste
	Black market	Waste
	Misallocation	Waste
Foreign exchange rationing	Lobbying	Both
	Capital flight	Waste
	Misallocation	Waste
Government allocation	Lobbying	Both
	Misallocation	Waste
Domestic monopsony	Misallocation	Waste
	Smuggling	Both

Source: Kimenyi, M. S. and Tollison, R. D. (1999), "Rent-seeking, Institutions, and Economic Growth," in Kimenyi, M. S. and Mbaku, J. M. (eds.), *Institutions and Collective Choice in Developing Countries: Applications of the Theory of Public Choice* (Aldershot, UK and Brookfield, VT: Ashgate), p. 209.

Though the results from all these studies differ depending on the methodology employed, they all show very convincingly that government intervention in private exchange comes with a very high cost. The results also indicate that the costs of rent-seeking are significantly higher in the developing than in the developed countries.

Krueger's 1974 study determined the value of rents created by government regulation of various economic activities in India and Turkey. She determined that losses from rent-seeking in the 1960s might have accounted for as much as 7.3 percent of India's national income. In Turkey, she determined that rents generated through import licenses might have represented as much as 15 percent of the gross national product. In a study of Kenya, Ross (1984) determined that trade-related rent-seeking activities accounted for up to 38 percent of the gross domestic product. In a more recent study of India, Mohammad and Whalley (1984) produce rent-seeking estimates for the period 1980–1981 that are significantly higher than those reported by Krueger. They determined that rent-seeking activities in India during that period accounted for between 30 and 45 percent of the GNP per year. In a study of the nature, significance, and cost of rent-seeking in Ghana, Ampofo-Tuffuor, DeLorme, and Kamerschen (1991) determined that as much as 18 to 21 percent (1981) and 22 to 25 percent (1984) of the gross domestic product was wasted on rent-seeking activities.

Although these studies represent an important effort to determine the costs of government intervention on the society, it is important to note that there are many costs associated with government regulations that have not been specifically subjected to empirical estimation. This is particularly true in developing countries where government intervention is usually quite pervasive. Although it is currently quite difficult to estimate some of these rent-seeking costs empirically, it is nevertheless important to recognize their existence and the fact that they constitute a significant drain on, or a diversion of, critical resources from the economy. Many activities such as smuggling, illegal dealings in foreign exchange, and bribery involve a waste of resources. All these wasteful activities are related to government intervention in economic activities. In the remainder of this section, we examine government regulatory activities in selected developing countries. A more thorough examination of the costs of rent-seeking in these countries can be found in Kimenyi (1991).

INDIA

The Indian economy presents an excellent case study of how government regulatory activities can result in relatively large social costs associated with rent-seeking and other forms of opportunism such as rent-avoidance. Several studies have been done to document the impact of these controls and the costs associated with them. From 1956 to 1970, the Indian economy went through four major import regimes (Bhagwati and Srinivasan, 1975). The first phase lasted from 1956 to 1962 and was marked by severe quantity restrictions in imports, which, along with an industrial licensing scheme, constituted the government's response to balance-of-payments problems encountered in 1957. The government of India designed both policies to enhance its ability to undertake selective industrialization. As a consequence, during the period, resource allocation in the foreign trade sector was totally politicized. The second phase began in 1962 and ended in 1966 and was characterized, like the previous period, by quantity restrictions in imports and industrial licensing. It should be noted, however, that the government did attempt to undertake partial liberalization. Phase 3 lasted from 1966 until 1968 and saw a significant effort at liberalization of the international trade sector, including the devaluation of the country's currency and the abandonment of export subsidies. However, many of the liberalization programs were soon reversed as the government entered the fourth phase (1968–1970) by reversing many of the earlier liberal programs. Premiums on imports were raised significantly to their preliberalization levels, averaging between 30 and 50 percent, export subsidies were reinstated, and automatic protection resulting from quantity restrictions was brought back.

In general, then, India's import regime between 1956 and 1970 was characterized primarily by severe import controls and industrial licensing that offered significant protection to the country's export sector. To ensure the functioning of the import regime, the government put in place a highly complicated and tedious licensing program involving three license-issuing agencies: (1) the Chief Controller of Imports and Exports; (2) the Development Officer, Tools, Development Wing of the Ministry of Commerce; and (3) the Iron and Steel Controller. In the processing of all applications for import licenses, the government followed two major criteria: (1) the principle of essentiality; and (2) the principle of indigenous nonavailability. The issuance of licenses was not based on economic considerations but was left to the discretion of civil servants in the various licensing agencies. This approach created many opportunities for rent-seeking. Strict controls of import licenses for the importation of goods resulted in significant wasteful spending as entrepreneurs fought each other to secure the lucrative licenses. Bhagwati and Srinivasan (1975) argue that in addition to creating many opportunities for rent-seeking, the government's licensing scheme also generated widespread corruption, public malfeasance, and general illegality. Quite often, the latter included bogus claims to import license entitlement under the existing rules, corruption, and bribery. In addition, tight government controls resulted in lucrative underground market transactions, all of which were not subject to taxation by the government. Because all the licensing bureaus were located only in the major industrial areas—primarily in Delhi—traffic from the rural areas to Delhi increased significantly as prospective importers continued to flow into town to seek permits. To those who made them, such trips involved two important costs—the actual expenditure incurred in traveling from one's hometown to Delhi, including lodging and incidentals, as well as the opportunity cost of travel (i.e., lost production due to the absence from one's place of business). These activities represented real resource costs.

GHANA

Shortly after it gained independence from Britain in 1957, Ghana's leaders initiated an economic development program that involved significant government control and regulation of economic activities, creating many opportunities for rent-seeking and corruption. The country's economic policies from the late 1950s to the mid-1980s were characterized by heavy government intervention in private exchange. Many of these regulations were imposed to help the government carry out an import substitution industrialization program. To reduce what was considered excessive demand for foreign goods, the government introduced an import licensing scheme. However, by 1963, the scheme had been overwhelmed by high levels of corruption (see, e.g., Leith, 1974; Werlin, 1972, 1973; LeVine, 1975). The government changed the rules often and without enough notice to allow entrepreneurs to adjust. After the military overthrow of the Kwame Nkrumah government in 1966, there was partial liberalization involving the reduction in the number of items requiring import permits. However, beginning in 1970, the country went back to severe restrictions on international trade.

Excessive government intervention in economic activities created opportunities for rent-seeking and for civil servants to extort bribes from entrepreneurs seeking government favors or ways to minimize the burden of such regulations on their enterprises. Especially susceptible to corruption was the licensing scheme designed during the early years of independence to meet the needs of the import substitution industrialization program. Bureaucrats at the trade ministry regularly used the system to extract additional compensation for themselves. Corruption and other forms of opportunism eventually thwarted the government's development program as presented to the Ghanaian people shortly after independence. One other consequence of heavy government intervention in the Ghanaian economy through exchange rate controls, as well as quantity restrictions in imports, was the emergence of a lucrative parallel market. Severe foreign exchange controls led to illegal exporting and underinvoicing. Within a few years after these controls were put in place, a large underground market for cocoa, Ghana's main foreign exchange earner, emerged. Table 7.2 indicates the extent of cocoa smuggling in the country between 1960 and 1979.

Restrictive foreign trade policies in Ghana also created opportunities for enterprising individuals to benefit from foreign currency trading in the underground economy. As a result of the severe controls on the foreign exchange market, as well as the relatively high demand for foreign exchange, there existed a significantly high premium between the official or formal market foreign exchange rate and the "black" (or informal) market one. Such a high premium encouraged arbitraging activities between the two markets (see Table 7.3).

Government intervention in the economies of many developing countries remains pervasive, even during this post–Cold War period with global emphasis on liberalization and greater reliance on markets for the allocation of resources. Unfortunately, many of these countries are still unable to recognize the damage that excessive government intervention in economic activities and the accompanying rent-seeking inflict on the society. This wastage of resources has a negative impact on economic growth and thus represents an important constraint to development in these societies.

Table 7.2
Cocoa Production and Smuggling in Ghana, 1960–1979 (Thousands of Metric Tons)

Year	*Production*	*Smuggled Cocoa*	*Percent of Production Smuggled*
1960/1961	430	10	2.3%
1961/1962	409	8	1.9%
1962/1963	413	14	3.3%
1963/1964	428	11	2.5%
1964/1965	538	14	2.6%
1965/1966	401	17	4.2%
1966/1967	368	17	4.6%
1967/1968	415	21	5.1%
1968/1969	323	17	5.2%
1969/1970	403	25	6.2%
1970/1971	413	31	7.5%
1971/1972	454	37	8.1%
1972/1973	407	42	10.3%
1973/1974	340	34	10.0%
1974/1975	376	30	7.9%
1975/1976	396	38	9.5%
1976/1977	320	40	12.5%
1977/1978	271	45	16.6%
1978/1979	265	50	18.8%

Source: May, E. (1983).

Table 7.3
Official and "Black" Market U.S. Dollar Exchange Rates in Ghana (End of Year–Nation's Currency per U.S. Dollar)

Year	*Official Rate*	*"Black" Market Rate*	*"Black" Market Rate/Official Rate*
1974	1.116	1.54	1.370
1975	1.116	1.92	1.720
1976	1.116	4.35	3.897
1977	2.750	7.69	2.790
1978	2.750	10.00	3.630
1979	2.750	14.29	5.196
1980	2.750	11.11	4.036
1981	2.750	50.00	18.180
1982	2.750	120.00	43.630
1983	30.000	97.00	3.230

Sources: (1) IMF (1990), *International Financial Statistics, 1990*, IMF: Washington, D.C.
(2) IMF (1990), *Currency Yearbook, 1990*, IMF: Washington, D.C.

RENT-SEEKING AND ECONOMIC GROWTH

According to the preceding discussion, rent-seeking activities retard economic growth and wealth creation. First, rent-seeking is related to the scope and extent of government intervention in markets. Such intervention distorts market incentives and severely impedes the efficient allocation of resources. In markets with distorted incentives, resources or factors of production cannot flow to where their opportunity cost is highest or where they are likely to earn the highest return. Resource misallocation usually forces the economy to operate below its potential, implying that output is less than that indicated by the country's production possibilities. Second, through rent-seeking, inefficient firms can remain in operation indefinitely. Quite often, production rights are awarded to the most efficient rent seeker and not necessarily to the entrepreneur who is efficient at production and/or servicing the market well. Through rent-seeking, political allocation replaces economic or market allocation, and as a consequence, many inefficient firms are able to remain in the market (i.e., they remain operational) indefinitely not because they have the comparative advantage in meeting consumer demand, but because they are very efficient at lobbying or bribing regulators and, as a consequence, are protected or shielded from competition by the government. Finally, rent-seeking involves real resource costs—resources devoted to rent-seeking activities do not produce any value and from a social point of view are considered a waste. Activities such as smuggling, bribery, illegal trade in foreign exchange, and the like, involve real resources and therefore are a waste of those resources. The negative impact on economic growth is quite significant.

There is a lot of evidence to support the assertion that excessive government intervention stunts economic growth. In the case of Ghana just discussed, government intervention is primarily responsible for most of the economic problems from which the country has suffered during most of its existence as a sovereign nation. In 1970 Ghana had a per capita income of U.S.$250 (World Bank, 1991, p. 2), but by 1999 (forty-two years after independence), the country's gross national product per capita had risen only to U.S.$390 (World Bank, 2000, p. 274). Most of the country's poor economic performance can be traced to pervasive corruption made possible by excessive government intervention in private exchange (see, e.g., LeVine, 1975; Werlin, 1973; Mbaku, 1998). Recent research has uncovered evidence that shows that the rapid economic growth encountered by the so-called East Asian Tigers has been due primarily to the fact that entrepreneurs in these economies have enjoyed more economic freedom than their counterparts in other developing regions (Gwartney and Lawson, 2000; Stepanek, 1999). That is, unlike other developing regions of the world, the East Asian countries, during the last several decades, have not experienced excessive government intervention in private exchange. Lower levels of government intervention imply that resource allocation is more dependent on market forces, resulting in less distorted incentives and, as a consequence, more efficient utilization of resources. Of course, less government intervention implies fewer opportunities for rent-seeking and for civil servants to engage in corruption and other opportunistic activities that contribute to poor economic performance. Where there are fewer opportunities for rent-seeking and the profitability of firms is based primarily on managerial expertise and efficiency (not on how efficient a business owner is at rent-seeking), entrepreneurs are most likely to devote their resources, including their time, to productive activities.

Murphy, Schleifer, and Vishny (1991) made an interesting connection between rent-seeking and economic growth. In the model that they used, the most skilled and talented individuals prefer those professions or occupations that offer or are characterized by increasing returns to talent. The implication of their model for rent-seeking is that rent-seeking activities, because they have the weakest diminishing returns to scale, attract the brightest and most talented individuals. As a consequence, if the most talented individuals in society choose rent-seeking activities (e.g., lobbying/lawyering) instead of undertaking entrepreneurial activities, we can expect lower levels of national income. In economies characterized by high levels of government intervention, the most talented people are likely to prefer to earn their living through engagement in rent-seeking, resulting in lower levels of income for the society. It is important to recognize here that as larger and larger numbers of talented people move into rent-seeking activities, the part of the economy that is left to create wealth continues to be weakened. In other words, the mass exodus of talented people into rent-seeking pursuits would weaken the entrepreneurial sector and, hence, wealth creation in the country. Of course, as the less talented are left to occupy positions in the entrepreneurial sector, the economy is most likely to suffer from less invention, less innovation, and thus less economic growth.

Since Tullock's (1967) insight on rent-seeking, a large literature has developed that points to the negative impact that rent-seeking has on economic growth. Because most rent-seeking activities are associated with government intervention in private exchange, the degree, scope, and magnitude of rent-seeking and other socially wasteful activities are related to the scope of government intervention in the economy. Rents, as a percentage of the gross domestic product, tend to rise with the size of government. According to Buchanan (1980a), rent-seeking activities are directly related to the scope and extent of government activities in the economy. In addition, as the evidence from many countries has shown (see, e.g., Mbaku, 2000, 1997, 1998; Gould, 1980; LeVine, 1975), corruption, bribery, smuggling, and other illegal transactions are related to the degree of government intervention in economic activities.

It is important to note here that most of the gains made by many developing countries in terms of economic growth during the last several years have come about as a result of economic reforms that have reduced the role of the state in the economy. These reforms basically include privatization and deregulation, both of which have resulted in the transfer of more economic activities to the market (i.e., the private sector). Both privatization and deregulation, however, entail substantial losses to politicians, bureaucrats, and rent-seeking special interest groups. Consequently, many incumbent regimes in the developing countries, including those in Africa, have been reluctant to adopt these types of reforms. Thus, it is in fact the case that once a government artificially creates rents, changing arrangements that assure the flow of those rents can be a significant barrier to reforms. The poor economic performance of many developing countries can therefore be attributed to the failure to engage in institutional reforms due to benefits derived through rent-seeking. Rent-seeking is therefore a primary barrier to economic growth in most of the Third World today.

In Africa, another dimension of rent-seeking that impacts negatively on economic and political reforms is ethnicity. Ethnic rent-seeking is a primary feature in all African societies whereby ethnic groups organize to influence wealth transfers. In most cases, this occurs through investment toward the capture of the apparatus of government. This rent-seeking strategy has been shown to result in the establishment of nondemocratic regimes that are best suited to transferring benefits to members of specific ethnic groups (Kimenyi, 1987). Often, such ethnic rent-seeking translates into various forms of conflicts, including military coups, all of which have negative consequences on economic growth.

CONCLUSION

In this chapter, we have focused on rent-seeking and other activities that evolve from excessive government intervention in private exchange. The main objective of our discussion was to show that government intervention in economic activities creates opportunities for individuals and groups to engage in unproductive activities. Government intervention creates rents, encouraging organized interests to expend scarce resources to capture those rents. Such employment of resources does not create any value and, as a result, is considered a waste. In addition to rent-seeking, government intervention in private exchange also forces traders within the economy to engage in defensive activities to avoid being the suppliers of the transfers or to minimize the burden of government regulations on their enterprises. These activities involve real resource costs. This unproductive use of resources affects, in a significant way, economic growth. We have shown that one of the most important reasons why many developing countries have failed to encounter rapid economic growth is because these economies, during the last several decades, have been pervaded by high rates of corruption and rent-seeking, with the latter made possible by excessive government intervention in private exchange.

Tullock's (1967) rent-seeking insight is a significant contribution to the study of the social costs of monopolization and has important implications for the public policy in many of today's poor countries. Although we have dealt primarily with the relationship between rent-seeking and economic growth, it is important to recognize that the positive and normative implications of rent-seeking are numerous. A lot of research still needs to be undertaken to understand the importance of rent-seeking for development in the Third World. Already, several scholars are now investigating how developing countries, through institutional reforms, can alter incentive structures and minimize rent-seeking and other opportunistic activities and in the process, enhance economic growth and development (Kimenyi and Mbaku, 1999; Mbaku, 1999, 1997).

REFERENCES

Ampofo-Tuffuor, E., C.D. DeLorme, Jr., and D.R. Kamerschen. 1991. "The Nature, Significance, and Cost of Rent-seeking in Ghana." *Kyklos* 44(4): 537–59.

Bates, R.H. 1981. *Markets and States in Tropical Africa*. Berkeley, CA: University of California Press.

———. 1987. *Essays on the Political Economy of Rural Africa*. Cambridge: Cambridge University Press.

Bhagwati, J.N., and T.N. Srinivasan. 1975. *India*. New York: National Bureau of Economic Research.

Blomqvist, A., and S. Mohammad. 1986. "Controls, Corruption, and Competitive Rent-seeking in LDCs." *Journal of Development Economics* 21(2): 161–80.

Bohman, M., L. Jarvis, and R. Barichello, 1996. "Rent-Seeking and International Commodity Agreements: The Case of Coffee," *Economic Development and Cultural Change*, 44(2): 379–404.

Browning, E. 1974. "On the Welfare Costs of Transfers." *Kyklos* 27(2): 378–81.

Buchanan, J.M. 1980a. "Rent-seeking and Profit Seeking." In *Toward a Theory of the Rent-Seeking Society*, edited by J.M. Buchanan, R.D. Tollison, and G. Tullock. College Station, TX: Texas A&M University Press.

———. 1980b. "Reform in the Rent-Seeking Society." In *Toward a Theory of the Rent-Seeking Society*, edited by J.M. Buchanan, R.D. Tollison, and G. Tullock. College Station, TX: Texas A&M University Press.

Buchanan, J.M., R.D. Tollison, and G. Tullock. 1980. *Toward a Theory of the Rent-Seeking Society*. College Station, TX: Texas A&M University Press.

Flowers, M.R. 1987. "Rent-seeking and Rent Dissipation: A Critical Review." *Cato Journal* 7(2): 431–40.

Gould, D.J. 1980. *Bureaucratic Corruption and Underdevelopment in the Third World: The Case of Zaire*. New York: Pergamon Press.

Gwartney, J.D., and R. Lawson. 2000. *Economic Freedom of the World: 2000 Annual Report*. Vancouver, BC: The Fraser Institute.

Harberger, A.C. 1954. "Monopoly and Resource Allocation." *American Economic Review* 44(2): 77–87.

Kimenyi, M.S. 1987. "Bureaucratic Rents and Political Institutions." *Journal of Public Finance and Public Choice* 3: 189–99.

———. 1989. "Interest Groups, Transfer Seeking and Democratization." *The American Journal of Economics and Sociology* 48(3): 339–49.

———. 1991. "Barriers to Efficient Functioning of Markets in Developing Countries." *Konjunturpolitik*, Berlin, 37(4): 199–227.

Kimenyi, M.S., and J.M. Mbaku. 1999. *Institutions and Collective Choice in Developing Countries: Applications of the Theory of Public Choice*. Aldershot, UK, and Brookfield VT: Ashgate.

Kimenyi, M.S., and R.D. Tollison. 1999. "Rent-seeking, Institutions and Economic Growth." In *Institutions and Collective Choice in Developing Countries:*

Applications of the Theory of Public Choice, edited by M.S. Kimenyi, and J.M. Mbaku. Aldershot, UK, and Brookfield, VT: Ashgate.

Krueger, A.O. 1974. "The Political Economy of the Rent-Seeking Society." *American Economic Review* 64(3): 1291–1303.

Leith, C.J. 1974. *Ghana*. New York: NBER.

LeVine, V.T. 1975. *Political Corruption: The Ghanaian Case*. Stanford, CA: The Hoover Institution.

May, E. 1983. *Exchange Controls and Parallel Market Economy in sub-Saharan Africa: Focus on Ghana*. The World Bank: Washington, D.C.

Mbaku, J.M. 1997. *Institutions and Reform in Africa: The Public Choice Perspective*. Westport, CT: Praeger.

———. 1998. *Corruption and the Crisis of Institutional Reforms in Africa*. Lewiston, NY: The Edwin Mellen Press.

———. 1999. "Making the State Relevant to African Societies." In *Preparing Africa for the Twenty-First Century: Strategies for Peaceful Coexistence and Sustainable Development*, edited by J.M. Mbaku. Aldershot, UK, and Brookfield, VT: Ashgate.

———. 2000. *Bureaucratic and Political Corruption in Africa: The Public Choice Perspective*. Malabar, FL: Krieger.

Mohammad, S., and J. Whalley. 1984. "Rent-seeking in India: Its Costs and Policy Significance." *Kyklos* 37(3): 387–413.

Murphy, K.M., A. Schleifer, and R.W. Vishny. 1991. "The Allocation of Talent: Implication for Growth." *Quarterly Journal of Economics* 106(2): 503–31.

Peltzman, S. 1976. "Towards a More General Theory of Regulation." *Journal of Law and Economics* 19(2): 211–40.

Ross, V.B. 1984. "Rent-seeking in LDC Import Regimes: The Case of Kenya." Graduate Institute of International Studies, Geneva, Discussion Paper No. 8408.

Stepanek, J.E. 1999. *Wringing Success from Failure in Late-Developing Countries: Lessons from the Field*. Westport, CT: Praeger.

Stigler, G.J. 1971. "The Theory of Economic Regulation." *Bell Journal of Economics and Management Science* 2(1): 3–21.

Tollison, R.D. 1982. "Rent-seeking: A Survey." *Kyklos* 35(4): 575–602.

Tullock, G. 1967. "The Welfare Costs of Tariffs, Monopolies and Theft." *Western Economic Journal* 5(3): 224–32.

———. 1993. *Rent-seeking*. Aldershot, UK: Edward Elgar.

Werlin, H.H. 1972. "The Roots of Corruption—The Ghanaian Enquiry." *The Journal of Modern African Studies* 10(2): 247–66.

———. 1973. "The Consequences of Corruption: The Ghanaian Experience." *Political Science Quarterly* 88(1): 71–85.

World Bank. 1991. *World Tables, 1991*. Baltimore, MD: The Johns Hopkins University Press.

World Bank. 2000. *World Development Report, 2000/2001*. New York: Oxford University Press.

8

Corruption Control in Developing Societies: Lessons from Public Choice

John Mukum Mbaku

THE THEORY OF PUBLIC CHOICE AND ITS RELEVANCE TO THE STUDY OF CORRUPTION

During the last several decades, social scientists have developed an interest in the study of the political dimension of economic growth and development. This new interest can be explained partially by the frustration arising from the inability of traditional constructs to provide policy-relevant development options. Particularly important to many social scientists, including policy analysts, is the fact that the bulk of the traditional development models have failed to emphasize the importance of laws and institutions to economic growth and development. For example, the neoclassical economics model, widely applied in development studies, is concerned only with choice-through-markets. Unfortunately, its policy recommendations are usually implemented through a nonmarket or political process by civil servants whose behavior and activities are not included as arguments in the model. In critiquing the neoclassical economics model, Wiseman (1990, p. 105) remarks that the state is usually treated as the "exogenous, omnicompetent and costless instrument for the implementation of policies promoting 'economic efficiency.'" In the early 1960s, James M. Buchanan and Gordon Tullock (1962) introduced the public choice model as a more effective and intellectually satisfying paradigm for the study of public policy.

The modern theory of public choice evolved out of a general dissatisfaction with orthodox political science's inability to adequately explain the functioning of government, especially the behavior of civil servants. Public choice scholars such as Buchanan and Tullock (1962), Anthony Downs (1967), and W.A. Niskanen (1971) argued that there was an inconsistency between Aristotle's dictum that "man is by nature a political animal" and Adam Smith's conclusion from studying the Scots in the eighteenth century that "man is by nature an economic animal" (also see Mueller, 1989, p. 1). These scholars subsequently developed an economic theory of political behavior in which they argued that an individual cannot be assumed to be self-interested when he makes private choices but benevolent, selfless, and benign when he makes choices in political markets (see, e.g., Buchanan, 1972).

Public choice, which can be viewed as a positive economic theory of collective choice, traces its origins to the works of scholars such as Buchanan and Tullock (1962) on the study of rules, how they are designed, and how they function; Black (1958) on collective choice; and Downs (1957) on the economic study of democracy. In addition, work by Bentley (1908), Truman (1951), Olson (1965), and Becker (1983) has significantly enhanced the development of the subdiscipline. In the 1960s and 1970s, significant insights into the behavior of civil servants were provided by Tullock (1965) and Niskanen (1971), and in the 1980s, Brennan and Buchanan (1980, 1985) made important advances in constitutional political economy. The purpose of this chapter is not to provide the reader with an exhaustive and/or comprehensive review of the literature on public choice theory, but to help the reader appreciate the contributions of public choice to a more enhanced understanding of collective decision making and how the theory can help us deal more effectively with corruption in developing societies (for more in-depth treatment of public choice, see Mueller, 1989; Tullock, 1993, 1998; Buchanan and Tullock, 1962; Brady and Tullock, 1996; Buchanan and Tollison, 1972).

In examining and explaining public policy, public choice theorists apply the voluntary exchange paradigm of economic theory in which the individual is assumed to maximize his own self-interest. The design of rules and how they function is affected by the several individual political actors that exist in the polity. These include (1) lawmakers or legislators; (2) voters; (3) civil servants or bureaucrats; and (4) political coalitions, including interest or pressure groups. Public choice theory emphasizes several things that are critical to the understanding of public policy. First, individuals living in a society usually find it efficient and convenient to accept rules governing their sociopolitical interaction. Second, once elected, politicians should not be expected to radically change their objectives and become passive, obedient, and attentive servants of the median voter. On the other hand, public choice scholars argue that elected politicians are expected to remain egoistic, rational, utility maximizers (Mueller, 1989, p. 2) who seek to maximize their own welfare. Given the fact that bureaucrats and politicians seek to maximize their self-interest the same way they would in private (economic) markets, it is necessary that they be constrained constitutionally in order to minimize their ability to engage in political opportunism (e.g., rent-seeking, bureaucratic corruption, and rent extraction). A proper understanding of how individuals behave in political markets is important so that society can design and adopt institutional arrangements that effectively constrain the individuals whose job it is to serve the public and prevent them from engaging in behaviors that harm or reduce the national welfare. Public choice theory gauges the efficiency of social organizations by the "ability of the citizen to constrain government-as-Leviathan in a context of multi-level choice" (Wiseman, 1990, p. 101). Third, the rules selected form the foundation for the social arrangements within which members of the society will make choices and interact with one another. Put another way, individual as well as collective choices are made in a postconstitutional society within rules chosen in an earlier period. As a consequence, the outcomes that result from social interaction (e.g., market exchange) in the postconstitutional society are determined by the nature of the rules chosen earlier. One must emphasize that the rules that govern the behavior of market participants (be they traders in political or economic markets) are themselves products of choices made in an earlier period.

Although traders in both economic and political markets are motivated by self-interest, they do not face the same set of constraints. As a consequence, they usually behave differently. The theory of public choice seeks to show how these differences in constraints or incentives affect the behavior of participants in political markets and, as a result, outcomes to public policy, as well as bureaucratic efficiency. Additionally, public choice theory also provides specific recommendations on how to minimize political opportunism, including such behaviors as corruption and rent-seeking (Gwartney and Wagner, 1988; Anderson and Hill, 1986; Mbaku, 1997, 1998, 2000). Because most rent-seeking activities are linked to the scope and extent of government intervention in economic activities, constitutionally constraining the exercise of government agency should minimize the ability of legislators to pass fiscally discriminatory laws and of civil servants to engage in opportunism. Poorly constructed, inappropriate, and nonviable institutional arrangements are responsible for much of the opportunism that has characterized the economies of many developing countries during the last several decades. Public choice theory provides specific recommendations on how each developing society can reconstruct their states through proper constitution making to provide themselves with more viable institutional arrangements—those that adequately constrain the state (and thus, minimize corruption and other opportunistic behaviors), enhance entrepreneurship (and improve wealth creation), and advance peaceful coexistence of groups (see, e.g., Mbaku, 1997, 1999).

The renewed interest in the study of laws and institutions and the role they play in economic growth and development has resulted in an increase in investigations devoted to bureaucratic behavior. Most of these studies, however, have dealt primarily with bureaucratic compensation (Mbaku, 1991; Couch, Atkinson and Shughart, 1992) and bureaucratic corruption (Mbaku, 1998, 2000). Bureaucrats or civil servants attempt to maximize their compensation packages through the manipulation of the political system. Compensation paid to the civil servant consists of the salary or wage paid by the state, any income (legal or illegal) derived from participation in outside activities, and the perks of the particular office. A bureaucrat who is able to extract more income from external sources (e.g., from interest groups seeking government favors) than from regular employment may devote more time to meeting the demands of these external groups than to the effective and efficient performance of public duties. If civil service compensation rates are relatively low, then more of the returns to the bureaucratic position may be derived from external activities. Existing laws and institutions within a country have a significant impact on the ability of public employees to seek and secure external compensation, either legally or illegally (Brennan and Buchanan, 1985). In a 1987 article, Mwangi S. Kimenyi showed that civil servants in autocratic political systems are less constrained in their employment of public resources to influence legislators with direct responsibility for determining civil service compensation levels. Civil servants generally attempt to influence the political system (through, for example, lobbying legislators or contributing to the latter's re-election effort) in order to maximize their compensation packages. Such activities, on the part of civil servants, are harder to undertake in democratic countries where rules constraining such behavior are effectively enforced and legislative oversight committees exist to make certain that civil servants do not engage in opportunistic behaviors. In autocratic political systems, such constraints on the behavior of civil servants either do not exist or function poorly.

THE CONCEPT OF CORRUPTION

The literature provides several definitions for corruption, most of which contain two important elements: the performance of a public duty and deviations from the rules that regulate the activities of bureaucrats. Thus, a civil servant can be considered corrupt if in performing his public functions, he sacrifices the interests of the people for his own. Corruption, then, has been described by some scholars as a deviation from the norms or practices of modern bureaucracy (Alam, 1989, p. 442). Most people in the Third World see corruption in more practical terms: theft of state resources by civil servants; illegal taxation; nepotism, including favoring relatives, friends, and other acquaintances in the distribution of public goods and services, and employment in the public sector; embezzlement of public funds; the abuse of one's office to extract income for the office holder and his or her relatives and friends; capricious and selective enforcement of state regulations in an effort to benefit the regulator; and differential treatment of enterprise owners in the expectation of a bribe from the business owner being accorded preferential treatment.

Several scholars (e.g., Bayley, 1966) have argued that corruption is an unavoidable consequence of development and modernization. According to Alam (1989, p. 42), in modern bureaucratic systems, corruption is an attribute of all principal-agent relationships. The people or the principal, usually grant the government (their agent) the power to impose taxes and provide them with public goods and services (e.g., national defense, police protection, health care, education, law and order, etc.). However, in the performance of these duties, the agent may sacrifice the interests of the people for his own. For example, instead of using tax revenues collected to provide public goods, the civil servant (the agent) may illegally appropriate the funds for personal use, denying the principal (the people) the necessary public goods.

In the view of J. van Klaveren (1990, p. 26), a corrupt civil servant views his public office as a business from which he can extract extralegal income. Thus, his total compensation "does not depend on an ethical evaluation of his usefulness for the common good but precisely upon the market situation and his talents for finding the point of maximal gain on the public's demand curve." Usually, the civil servant's compensation is made up of the salary paid by the state and legal or illegal income obtained through participation in outside activities. John Mukum Mbaku (1992, p. 247) argues that if "bureaucrats are able to earn more income from external sources (e.g., from interest groups seeking government transfers or relief from government regulation) than from their regular employment, they may pay more attention to the demands of interest groups than to the needs of society as a whole." Thus, in a highly regulated economy, bureaucrats may spend a significant part of their time and effort to helping business owners evade the rules and thus, minimize the burden of government regulation on their enterprises. In exchange, of course, the bureaucrat is rewarded with extralegal income.

Leff (1964) is one of several scholars who advanced the argument, beginning in the 1960s, that corruption could be used to improve the participation of historically deprived and excluded individuals and communities in political and economic markets. Unfortunately, the evidence has since indicated that corruption has not been able to improve effective participation of these groups in the economic and political systems of their countries. In addition, corruption enhances the ability of inefficient enterprises to remain in business indefinitely. In the last several years, the survival of business enterprises in many developing countries has come to be determined not by competition and managerial expertise, but by how well their owners manipulate the political system through payment of bribes to civil servants and politicians.

CAUSES OF CORRUPTION IN DEVELOPING COUNTRIES: THE VIEW OF THE DEVELOPMENT LITERATURE

The development literature has identified several structural factors that are said to contribute to corruption in developing countries. One of these factors is the "soft state," which, according to some researchers, is characterized by citizens with a "weak or diffuse sense of national interest" and who do not have "a commitment to public service" (Gould and Mukendi, 1989, p. 431). The failure for many developing countries to secure for themselves an efficient and professional civil service with competent, well-trained, and honest civil servants has been cited as an important determinant of corruption in these societies. As the argument goes, most civil servants in the developing countries view service in the public sector as an opportunity to enrich themselves and their families. As a consequence, instead of designing and implementing public policies that enhance the national welfare, they promote perverse economic programs that generate benefits for themselves but impose significant costs on greater society. Thus, the choice of public policies is not based on their potential contribution to national development but on their ability to generate benefits for the ruling coalition and its benefactors. Eventually, government degenerates into an instrument of plunder for the benefit of a few politically dominant individuals and groups. Such an approach to governance is illustrated relatively well by Nigeria's several military governments, Mobutu Sese Seko's reign in Zaire, Ferdinand Marcos's government in the Philippines, to name just a few. In fact, in many developing countries during the last five decades, the public security network—which many citizens believed would be used to enforce laws against theft, illegal capture of public resources, fraud, embezzlement, and other forms of political opportunism—either operates very poorly and capriciously or does not function at all. Since independence in many of these countries, state instruments of coercion have been employed routinely to secure extralegal income for the ruling coalition and its supporters. In the process, many people have been impoverished.

The second determinant of corruption given by the literature is civil service incompetence and inefficiency. It is argued that in order to ensure sustainable economic growth and development, each country requires a competent, efficient, and professional bureaucracy. To enhance innovation and productivity in the economy, the civil service must be responsive to the needs of the entrepreneurial class. Additionally, the bureaucracy should be able to deliver public goods and services efficiently and equitably to the population. Implicit in these arguments is the fact that recruitment into the civil service should be based on merit and not on political considerations. A bureaucracy staffed by poorly trained, incompetent, and severely inefficient workers can seriously undermine a country's growth and development prospects. In many developing countries today, a large number of the individuals in top-level civil service positions are either political appointees with strong connections to the ruling coalition or people who have bribed their way into positions. These people owe their jobs and allegiance to the incumbent government and not to the general public they are supposed to serve. As a consequence, the general population is unable to effectively discipline poorly performing, recalcitrant, and opportunistic bureaucrats.

The third factor identified by the literature as contributing to corruption in developing societies is chronic poverty and deprivation, as well as severe inequalities in the distribution of income and wealth. In many regions of the Third World, especially in Africa and South Asia, poverty and deprivation levels are quite high, especially among rural inhabitants and those of the urban periphery. Among the latter are many low-level civil servants whose wages are usually not enough to provide for them and their families. Although a few top civil servants in many developing countries are paid relatively well, most public workers are poorly paid. For example, in a study conducted by the World Bank in Zaire in 1979, it was determined that nearly 92 percent of state workers were unable to meet their subsistence needs (e.g., food, clothing, and shelter) with their legal salaries. Even taking food subsidies into consideration, many of these people were still unable to feed themselves and their families. Of course, the situation that the World Bank found in Zaire is not unique. Throughout most of the Third World (from Caracas's hillside slums to Cape Town's so-called "informal settlements") there are large populations of "working poor," who hold several jobs in the urban periphery but earn too little to support themselves and their families. Many of these individuals are most likely to participate in corrupt activities in order to secure the additional resources needed to buy food, shelter, and other necessities of life. The few individuals who control governance structures and, by implication, the economy (i.e., top civil servants and other members of the ruling coalition) continue to enjoy a relatively high standard of living, thanks to corruption (also see Mbaku, 2000).

The fourth factor listed by the literature as contributing to corruption in the developing countries is culture. It is argued, for example, that a significant level of corruption in many African countries can be traced to defective cultural norms within many of the continent's societies. According to some of these scholars (see, e.g., Jabbra, 1976; Merton, 1976), corruption arises from the clash between traditional African cultural values and the norms that were imported from abroad with modernization. Viewed from this perspective, corruption is seen as a cost that each developing society, seeking to modernize, must accept.

We can find fault with virtually all four determinants of corruption cited in the existing literature on development. For example, the argument that corruption is due to defective cultural norms is very weak, especially when one considers that many societies outside Africa have either the same or similar norms but do not suffer from equivalent levels of venality. Additionally, one can also question why corruption was not as widespread during colonialism as it is today. Did Africans suddenly discover their cultural norms only after independence? As is made more evident later in this chapter, incentive structures and not cultural norms determine a society's propensity to engage in corrupt activities. Existing incentive structures may create opportunities for corruption and provide an environment in which even honest and highly ethical individuals may be forced to engage in corruption in order to survive. As will be argued later, such perverse incentives can be changed through proper institutional reforms.

CORRUPTION AND DEVELOPMENT IN THE THIRD WORLD

What effect does corruption have on the economies of the developing countries? Does corruption have a positive or negative effect on economic growth and development in the Third World? On the one hand, some economists argue that corruption can enhance growth and development and, on the other, the argument is that corruption is one of the most important constraints to human development in the Third World. According to the former school, corruption can "grease" the wheels of a bureaucracy that is traditionally rigid and unresponsive and make it more responsive to the needs of the private sector, notably that of entrepreneurs whose job it is to create the wealth that these countries need to deal with poverty and deprivation. Bayley (1966), Nye (1967), and Leff (1964) have argued that corruption has both beneficial and harmful effects for economic development. They mention four ways in which corruption is said to provide benefits for society. First, corruption can facilitate economic growth by channeling scarce resources to the most productive and enterprising individuals within society. Second, corruption can improve access to the civil service for individuals who otherwise would be unable to obtain service from the state. Third, corruption can generate revenues that can be used to reduce conflict between politicians and members of the civil service. An improved and less adversarial relationship between lawmakers and the bureaucracy should significantly enhance the design and implementation of national development programs. Finally, corruption can remove critical bottlenecks in the service, producing a more efficient, flexible, and responsible administrative and regulatory system.

Most, if not all, of these propositions have not been supported by research. In a study of Ghana published in 1975 by Victor T. LeVine, he determined that most of the resources derived from corrupt activities were invested outside Ghana, primarily in Western Europe and North America or devoted to the importation of luxury items from these developed countries. Virtually none of the money was invested in domestic activities. In the rare instances in which the proceeds of corruption were invested locally, the investments were usually opportunistic projects designed to enhance the ability of the bureaucrat to plunder the economy further and derive additional benefits for himself. For example, civil servants often set up businesses that allowed them to seek and secure government contracts, with no intention of fulfilling the terms of the latter. Thus, such entrepreneurial activities became a framework for further plundering of the economy for additional benefits for the bureaucrat, with no benefits accruing to the society (LeVine, 1975, pp. 103–8).

Has corruption improved access to the bureaucracy for historically marginalized groups? The evidence from several developing countries does not point to improved access. In fact, the riots and demonstrations that engulfed many developing countries during the late 1980s and early 1990s (and were often called "people's revolutions") were the result of continued suffocation of civil society and the inability of many ordinary people in these societies to have access to their governments. Thus, despite the fact that corruption levels in these countries had increased significantly, access to the civil service for many people remained essentially nonexistent as it had been many years earlier. In 1998 and 1999, Nigeria and Cameroon were ranked by Transparency International (TI, the German nongovernmental organization that studies global corruption) as the two most corrupt countries in the world. Yet, bureaucracies in these countries remain as rigid as ever, civil servants as arrogant as they have ever been, and peasants and other historically marginalized people continue to find it relatively difficult to have access to their governments.

Throughout many developing countries, corruption has provided the ruling coalitions the resources that they need to bribe competitive elites, especially those who have the wherewithal to threaten regime security. Thus, in many developing countries in Africa, Asia, the Pacific, Latin America, the Caribbean, and the Middle East, military elites, who have a comparative advantage in the employment of violence, are favored in national resource allocations. In many African countries, the military has been the most favored department, after the presidency, in the allocation of the public budget (see, e.g., Mbaku, 1994; UNDP, 1990, 1995). Corruption has been very instrumental in helping incumbents maintain a monopoly on power and, consequently, on the allocation of resources.

Can corruption be used to remove bottlenecks in the bureaucracy and make it more efficient and responsive to the needs of the business class? In answering this question, one must recognize that many of the rigidities that exist in the bureaucracies of many developing countries are intentionally imposed by civil servants, with the expectation of extorting bribes from business owners when the latter want them removed. Bureaucratic roadblocks represent additional transaction costs to enterprise owners and make profitable operations more difficult. Thus, the entrepreneur is willing to pay bribes to the civil servant in order to minimize these costs on his business. Unless the regulatory system is reformed, bureaucrats are most likely to institutionalize these bottlenecks or rigidities and transform them into a permanent source of extralegal compensation for themselves. Where such institutionalization takes place, corruption will become a permanent obstacle to entrepreneurial activities and wealth creation and consequently will have a significantly negative impact on long-term economic growth and development. One must therefore emphasize that corruption is not an efficient and sustainable way to deal with bottlenecks in the bureaucracy. To remove these rigidities permanently and make the civil service more efficient and responsive to the business class, society should engage in institutional reconstruction through proper constitution making to develop and adopt institutions that are transparent, participatory, and accountable.

Granted, certain types of corruption may have nominal short-term economic and political benefits. However, corruption in general and in the long run has severe negative effects on sustainable economic growth and development. Through corruption, for example, poorly managed and inefficient firms can remain in business indefinitely, consuming scarce resources and generating meager or no returns at all. Most of the research conducted on corruption in the last several years in the developing countries has found that corruption has devastating effects on economic growth and development, as well as on political and social development. First, corruption can compromise the civil service and make it virtually impossible for civil servants to perform their jobs effectively. For example, civil servants who expect to derive a significant proportion of their yearly compensation from engagement in corrupt activities may intentionally distort public policies in order to create opportunities for the extraction of such income. There is a lot of evidence to show that civil servants in many developing countries during the last several decades have intentionally distorted public policies in order to secure additional (albeit illegal) compensation for themselves (see, e.g., Ihonvbere, 1994). In many African countries, as well as in other parts of the world, the transition to democratic governance is being intentionally mishandled by opportunistic politicians and civil servants seeking ways to enrich themselves (see, e.g., Mbaku, 1997; Takougang, 1996).

Second, in societies in which corruption is pervasive, the costs of public projects are usually inflated in an attempt to provide additional income for the civil servants and entrepreneurs engaged in these projects (see, e.g., Othman [1984] for an analysis of cost inflation on public projects in Nigeria).

Third, corruption raises the overall costs of financing the public sector, including the bureaucracy. In many Third World countries, taxpayers are forced to absorb the costs of supporting what is essentially a highly bloated, inefficient, and extremely wasteful bureaucracy. Perhaps more important is the fact that the taxpayers of these countries pay a lot of money to support an institution that provides them with inferior service. In general, public goods are supplied to society at a cost that is significantly higher than would have been the case in the absence of corruption and other forms of opportunism (e.g., rent-seeking). In public hospitals in Africa and many other developing societies, patients must often pay twice for what is relatively inferior service: first, as taxpayers to subsidize the hospital, and second, in the form of bribes to hospital staff who provide the service. In many instances, bribes demanded from prospective patients can be four times as much as the legal price for the procedure in question. Throughout the Third World, from Argentina to Zimbabwe, public goods and services are allocated in a selective and capricious manner, with most of them accruing to individuals who are able to pay the bribes demanded by the civil servants whose job it is to serve the public. In the process, the poor and highly deprived are cheated out of the opportunity to benefit from public services. Illegal levies designed to generate additional compensation for opportunistic civil servants prevent many historically marginalized and impoverished citizens from gaining access to free (public) goods in their own societies (see, e.g., Gould and Mukendi, 1989; Egunjobi, 1983).

Fourth, corruption can severely demoralize the bureaucracy. It generates distrust throughout the civil service and has a significant negative impact on the utilization of the society's human capital. For example, in assigning individuals to tasks within a given government department, a top civil servant may not place in a management position a person who is qualified to perform the task effectively and efficiently, but would instead prefer someone who can use the position to extort the most income from the private sector for himself and the boss. In fact, in countries where corruption is pervasive, recruitment into the civil service may not be based on merit as department heads seek ways to maximize their income from corruption. Senior civil servants, especially those with authority to hire, may use the process to generate additional income for themselves (e.g., through bribes extorted from prospective applicants).

Fifth, corruption can encourage the underutilization of a country's skilled and educated labor resources. For example, highly skilled individuals seeking work in the civil services may lie about their education and training in order to qualify for public-sector jobs for which they are overqualified but that significantly improve their chances of corrupt enrichment. A university graduate with a Ph.D. in engineering may seek employment as a clerk (a job that requires only a high school diploma) in the customs and excise department instead of teaching at the university because work in the customs department offers significantly more opportunities for extralegal enrichment. Evidence of this has been found in many developing countries. In fact, in Nigeria and Cameroon, many university students, regardless of their areas of expertise, prefer work in the customs department and other such public agencies (e.g., ministry of trade, where import and production licenses are issued; central bank, which regulates foreign exchange and issues permits for the acquisition of foreign currencies; immigration department, which issues passports; etc.) that offer significant opportunities for corrupt enrichment. While such an approach to public employment enhances the ability of the individual to engage in corrupt enrichment, it leads to severe underutilization of national labor resources and increases the level of venality in the public sector (see, e.g., Jua, 1998; Hogendorn, 1992).

Sixth, corruption can significantly distort international trade and the flow of investment. In fact, opportunistic civil servants can frustrate the efforts of foreign investors to penetrate the domestic economy, and thus cheat the people of the Third World of critical development resources. The tendency for civil servants to use their public positions to seek extralegal income for themselves is almost universal. However, this tendency is more widespread in the developing countries because existing institutional arrangements do not adequately constrain the ability of civil servants to engage in opportunism (McMullan, 1961; Jabbra, 1976).

Seventh, corruption can discourage investment and encourage the outward migration of capital (including skilled labor resources—i.e., brain drain) to less corrupt and more stable economies. In fact, during the last few decades, many highly educated and skilled individuals have migrated from the developing countries to the industrial economies of Western Europe and North America. In addition, significant levels of capital resources have also left the poor economies to the West. Although there are many reasons for such capital exodus, one of the most important is corruption, which significantly raises the opportunity costs of operating in such corruption-infested economies. Facing higher operating costs and significant levels of uncertainty and a high level of capriciousness on the part of regulators (i.e., civil servants), many entrepreneurs have opted to invest abroad and many highly educated individuals have decided in favor of self-exile to seek more stable opportunities for the utilization of their skills (see, e.g., Gordon, 1998; Bardhan, 1997).

Eighth, corruption can impose unexpected costs on already fragile and struggling economies. Many years ago, in Cameroon, the country's orange industry was effectively destroyed by a strange disease. The government never provided the people with an adequate and believable reason for the collapse of such an important sector of the economy. However, it was generally known among the country's agricultural experts that the disease that had destroyed the domestic orange crop was brought into the country by an individual who returned from overseas with oranges but had avoided the usual customs quarantine procedures by paying a bribe to border officers. Corruption allows individuals to subvert national rules and statutes and engage in behaviors that often have devastating long-term effects on society.

Finally, corruption can severely stunt innovation and subsequently prevent the introduction of new goods and technologies (see, e.g., Bardhan, 1997). In fact, today, many citizens of developing countries are having difficulties securing access to the Internet because of the impediments placed in the way of such technologies by civil servants, who expect to be bribed in order to remove the impediments. In many African countries, for example, high levels of corruption in the national telephone companies have delayed almost indefinitely the extension of service to many areas, making it difficult for people to gain access to the Internet. In addition, poor and unpredictable service by the national telephone company has meant that even those people who have a telephone may still not be able to benefit from the new trade-enhancing technology.

TRADITIONAL STRATEGIES FOR DEALING WITH CORRUPTION IN THE THIRD WORLD

During the last several decades, control of corruption in the developing countries has been limited to four main strategies. These are societal, legal, market, and political strategies (Gillespie and Okruhlik, 1991). According to the societal approach, each community defines a common standard of morality that can be used to determine corrupt behavior. Under this system, members of society are expected to remain vigilant and look out for individuals who stray from the generally accepted standard of morality. In addition, the state as well as civil society organizations are supposed to educate the general public about corruption and its negative consequences for the economy in particular and society in general. Such an educational process should make it easier for individuals within society to identify and report corrupt behaviors to the police and news media. Here, the news media is expected to have a significant part to play. They investigate and expose corruption, assisting the police in gathering the information needed to enhance the ability of the judiciary system to effectively prosecute offenders.

Legal strategies work through the police, the courts, and the news media. First, existing rules define and elaborate the responsibilities of bureaucrats and constrains them in the performance of their official functions. Second, the law defines corrupt behavior. Third, individuals within society are encouraged to look out for suspected corrupt activities and report them to the police, whose job it is to investigate such reports and present their findings to the courts. The latter are expected to prosecute the suspects and pass judgment according to existing laws. The press, as indicated earlier, plays an important part in this process. The media can investigate and expose incidents of corruption and serve as a check on the behavior of bureaucrats and other public employees who are most likely to engage in opportunism. The government can use special commissions of inquiry or special prosecutors to investigate incidents that point to large-scale corruption and public malfeasance, paving the way for prosecution by the courts.

As part of the legal strategies to control corruption, the government should be aware of the fact that the judiciary system itself might be corrupt. Thus, it is necessary to undertake reforms to improve the efficiency of the legal system in an effort to raise the opportunity cost of engaging in corrupt behaviors. Civil service pay scales should be made competitive with those in the private sector. Higher pay in the public sector, however, may simply force civil servants to demand bigger bribes to compensate for the risk of losing the now relatively more important and lucrative position. Some scholars have suggested that such reforms be supplemented with counteracting agencies such as an independent judiciary or some kind of independent review board, an ombudsman, or other investigative bodies (Rose-Ackerman, 1978, 1997; Elliott, 1997a, 1997b). However, it is important to note that such boards and institutions can become politicized and used by the incumbent leaders as instruments to punish their opponents and continue to monopolize power. In addition, these outside institutions can only be effective if they are free of corruption and can effectively resist pressure from the executive branch of government.

Market strategies for corruption cleanup are based on the belief that there is a relationship between the structure of the market and the incidence of corruption. Government regulatory programs create opportunities for individuals (especially civil servants) to engage in corrupt activities. Entrepreneurs are often forced to choose between paying a bribe to a bureaucrat and suffering significant costs associated with excessive government regulation. The traditional remedy prescribed is decreased government intervention in private exchange and greater reliance on the market for the allocation of resources. This advice has two major problems: (1) It emphases the manipulation of outcomes within a given set of rules and institutions instead of changing the latter to guarantee the outcomes desired by society. (2) The problem is not with the market, but with the incentive system that market participants (i.e., traders) face. Rules define the incentive structures faced by participants in markets and as a result, determine the outcomes that result from the interaction between traders. If a society reduces government intervention in markets and relies more on markets for the allocation of resources, but leaves the incentive structures the same, there will be little or no change in expected outcomes. To minimize opportunism, it is necessary to reform the rules that regulate sociopolitical interaction. The change of rules, as described here, does not imply deregulation. In the case of many developing countries, change implies reconstruction of the postcolonial state through proper constitution making (see, e.g., Mbaku, 1997; Brennan and Buchanan, 1985).

In applying political strategies to control corruption, emphasis is placed on governmental decentralization. It is argued that the concentration of political power in the hands of a few individuals at the center enhances their ability to engage in corrupt activities. Thus, a reform process that makes the political system more accessible to the people, especially those located in the rural areas (e.g., transparency in the public budgeting process), will significantly reduce corruption and other forms of opportunism in the country. Additionally, it is also recommended that civil service salaries be made more competitive with those of the private sector. A major problem with this approach to corruption control is that subsequent governments, in response to lobbying from special interest groups, can reverse reforms and reconcentrate power in the center.

In many developing countries, corruption control programs have often been motivated by political exigency and usually do not represent a genuine effort by the incumbent government to provide long-term solutions to widespread malfeasance and venality in the public sector. In countries such as Nigeria, Pakistan, Bangladesh, Ghana, Burkina Faso, Sierra Leone, Liberia, just to name a few, post-coup commissions of inquiry have usually worked to discredit the recently ousted regime in order to enhance the ability of the incoming government to legitimize its rule. Hardly any effort is made to undertake and sustain the kind of structural change that would minimize corruption and enhance wealth creation. An incoming government, faced with enormous economic problems and a challenge from competing elites may initiate a corruption control campaign in an effort to direct attention away from the country's impending problems and the state's inability or unwillingness to deal properly with these problems.

The corruption cleanup programs that we have briefly examined suffer from many problems. The most important of them is the fact that the success of each one of them depends on the effectiveness and professionalism of the country's existing counteracting agencies or institutions (e.g., the police, the judiciary, the press, etc.). It is also assumed that these institutions are well constrained by the law and, as a consequence, are relatively free of corruption. First, very few developing countries have independent media that can investigate and expose corruption without fear of severe censure by the government. Second, many developing countries currently do not have judiciary systems that are independent of the executive branch of government. Instead, in many of these countries, judiciary officers are appointed by the country's chief executive and serve at his pleasure. Because court officers owe their jobs to the head of state and not to the people they are supposed to serve, it is relatively difficult to punish recalcitrant and opportunistic judiciary officers. In most Third World countries, national judiciaries are regularly manipulated by the incumbent government, as those who serve in the latter seek ways to punish their enemies, generate extralegal benefits for themselves, and enhance their ability to monopolize power.

Third, many institutions in developing countries are pervaded by high levels of corruption. Thus, a corruption cleanup program backed by these agencies is not likely to function properly or achieve its objectives. On the other hand, an effective corruption control program calls for the selection of appropriate new rules (through proper constitution making) that (1) properly constrain the exercise of government agencies and (2) provide the foundation for the design and adoption of new and more effective counteracting institutions (e.g., an independent judiciary; a professional civil service; a well-constrained police force; a neutral and professional armed forces, etc.)—in other words, appropriate institutions to enforce compliance to the rules.

NEW STRATEGIES FOR CORRUPTION CONTROL IN DEVELOPING SOCIETIES: LESSONS FROM PUBLIC CHOICE

In a study published in 1985, Brennan and Buchanan argued that in market interaction, rules matter and usually determine the way individuals and organizations behave. What exactly do rules do? They determine the incentive structures faced by participants in both political and economic markets. As a result, the behavior of bureaucrats and the enterprise owners who bribe them can only be examined effectively within the context of the rules that exist in the society under study. Unless the analyst understands the laws and institutions of the society under study, any effort to analyze corruption and other forms of political opportunism would not produce policy-relevant results. To produce an effective corruption control program, it is necessary to first consider the impact of existing laws and institutions on the behavior of individuals participating in both political and economic markets (voters, politicians, civil servants, entrepreneurs, and special interest groups).

Brennan and Buchanan (1985) argue that rules perform several important and crucial functions. They (1) determine the nature of the interaction between individuals within a society; (2) provide a means for the peaceful resolution of conflict; (3) provide information, enhancing the ability of individuals to anticipate the behavior of other traders; and (4) impose constraints on the behavior of individuals, as well as on that of collectivities within society. For example, in performing their duties, police and judiciary officers are constrained by the law. Because laws and institutions determine the incentive structures in each society, any attempt to minimize corruption and other forms of opportunism (e.g., rent-seeking) must involve a negotiated change of the rules so that society can be provided with governance structures that effectively constrain the state (and make it much more difficult, for example, for civil servants to extort bribes from the private sector).

Rules can be implicit (e.g., custom and tradition) or explicit (e.g., a written constitution). Given a set of constitutional rules, corruption can be viewed as opportunistic behavior on the part of individuals or groups to extract extralegal benefits for themselves at the expense of greater society. This way, one can see corruption as part of the general problem of constitutional maintenance. The latter, of course, can only be handled effectively through a negotiated change of existing rules. Opportunism, as used here, is defined as behaviors designed to improve the welfare of an individual or group at the expense of other citizens and includes such activities as shirking, adverse selection, moral hazard, corruption, and free riding (Ostrom, Schroeder, and Wynne, 1993).

As has been seen in many developing countries (see, e.g., Mbaku, 1998, 2000), efforts to control corruption within rules that make opportunism quite lucrative usually yield very poor results. In fact, if as a result of rules adopted earlier, rent-seeking instead of managerial expertise and competition has emerged as the most important determinant of firm profitability, then business owners will devote most of their time and resources to rent-seeking instead of creating wealth—that is, producing and distributing goods and services. Employing the police force to stop business owners from taking advantage of highly rewarding rent-seeking opportunities would most likely not be successful, especially if the police force itself is pervaded by corruption. Here, the problem is not that the market has failed, thus requiring more government intervention. The problem is distorted or perverse market incentives made possible by existing rules. The appropriate way to deal with rent-seeking, corruption, and other forms of opportunism is to reform existing rules and alter the incentive structures. This approach has several advantages. First, reform can produce rules that adequately constrain the exercise of government agency, making it much more difficult for civil servants to extort bribes from individuals and businesses seeking access to government services. Second, proper reform can enhance economic freedom (the right of individuals to engage freely in exchange and contract) and significantly improve wealth creation. Finally, reform can provide more effective structures for the peaceful coexistence of groups, reducing communal instability, especially in developing countries, and providing a more enabling environment for the creation of wealth.

Unfortunately, in most developing countries today, third-party enforcement of constitutional rules is quite unreliable, inefficient, and not particularly viable. Traditionally, the police and the judiciary have been charged with the job of enforcing the rules. Unfortunately, in most countries (including the developed industrial countries), these institutions are susceptible to manipulation by interest or pressure groups. Additionally, in most developing countries, these institutions are not well constrained by the law, are pervaded by high levels of corruption, and usually do not enjoy any degree of independence. As a consequence, national judiciary systems and the police in the developing countries do not appear, at the present time, to be appropriate instruments for controlling corruption and effectively enforcing constitutional rules (Gwartney and Wagner, 1988).

Public choice scholars have developed a theory of constitutional maintenance whose main thesis is that one can eliminate opportunities for political opportunism from the postconstitutional society by making the constitution self-enforcing (see, e.g., Anderson and Hill, 1986; Congleton, 1994). One way to undertake this is to make certain that markets (economic and political) in the postconstitutional society are made competitive. First, there must be a devolution of power in favor of local, provincial, and/or regional political jurisdictions. In other words, power should not be concentrated in the center as is common in many developing countries today. In the system being advocated here, as many political functions as possible should be performed at the local level in order to bring government closer to the people. Decisions dealing with the production and distribution of public goods and services are more efficient and effective if the individuals and groups that actually consume these goods and services are provided the facilities and allowed to participate fully and effectively in the decision making. At the local level, individuals have more time-and-place information about conditions in their environment and are more familiar with their tastes and preferences than the civil servants in the center. It seems more sensible and economically more effective to allow production and distribution of public goods to be undertaken at the local level where demand and supply conditions can be determined with greater levels of accuracy. Second, the polity should be divided into as many political jurisdictions as possible. Third, citizens should be granted the right (by the constitution) to migrate freely between political units. This calls for the establishment of some form of constitutional federalism with a relatively large number of autonomous political units, minimizing the ability of the government (whether at the local or central level) to coerce citizens. A political arrangement of this kind enhances the ability of citizens to exit exploitative political jurisdictions. Under such a system, a local governmental unit would find it difficult to pursue perverse economic programs for fear of losing its taxable base through migration of citizens to jurisdictions with more investment-friendly tax policies (i.e., more attractive fiscal packages). Fourth, the power of the government to regulate economic activities should be constitutionally limited. As has been illustrated by many studies (e.g., Mbaku, 1997; Bardhan, 1997; Alam, 1989; Jabbra, 1976; Osterfeld, 1992), most opportunism (including corruption and rent-seeking) in the developing countries has been made possible by institutional arrangements, adopted at independence, that have failed to adequately and effectively constrain the exercise of government agency. In fact, throughout these countries, governments have been able to engage, almost indiscriminately, in the redistribution of income and wealth. Most of the political coalitions that captured governance structures at independence found out that under existing constitutional rules, they could easily manipulate the government's discretionary powers for their own interest instead of that of the nation. This approach to public policy has produced significant levels of social and economic inequality. Many of the deprived groups and individuals were forced to either turn to bribery or violence in order to gain access to markets or avert further marginalization. Throughout the Third World, the results have been a cycle of political violence and venality that have become endemic to these countries. If the constitution adequately restricts government redistribution powers, then interest groups would most likely not invest in rent-seeking, and the ability of civil servants to extort bribes from the entrepreneurial class will be severely constrained.

THE SELF-ENFORCING CONSTITUTION

As discussed earlier, the most effective way to make a country's constitution self-enforcing is to make the postconstitutional society's markets competitive. In addition, power should be devolved in favor of regional and local governmental jurisdictions. An effective way to introduce competition into the national political space is to divide the polity into as many autonomous political jurisdictions as possible and constitutionally grant citizens the right to migrate and settle in competitive jurisdictions. This implies the establishment of some form of constitutional federalism.

This constitutional arrangement is expected to enhance the ability of individuals living within the country to escape exploitation by their political jurisdiction through migration. If the citizen can migrate freely and at relatively low cost to competitive political jurisdictions, then the ability of the government to oppress its constituents would be severely diminished (Anderson and Hill, 1986; Congleton, 1994). The ability of the citizen to migrate freely is very important to the maintenance and proper functioning of voluntary agreements, such as those being proposed for developing societies. It is important to recognize, however, that internal migration can come with significant costs. Congleton (1994) argues that because most political jurisdictions are geographical, migration implies that the individual has abandoned his previous geographic habitat in favor of another one. Such a process can involve significant economic and social costs. For many people in the Third World, migration may not only involve the abandonment of one's geographic residence but may also include the loss of critical ethnic and family associations.

If exit costs are relatively high, then governments find it much easier to oppress citizens. Creating many political jurisdictions within the polity, however, should significantly reduce the physical distance associated with migration and hence the costs of exit. In addition, the presence of a large number of political jurisdictions within the polity should reduce the possibility that a citizen would actually have to change personal lifestyle. As has been argued by Congleton (1994), in the case where one can choose from several political jurisdictions, exit may be viewed as a change of neighborhood without radically altering one's lifestyle. In this case, the individual can actually retain his or her job and continue to enjoy relatively easy access to friends, family, and professional colleagues. In his conclusion, Congleton (1994, p. 18) states that "the smaller the governmental jurisdictions are, the *more* likely it is that affiliated individuals receive positive net benefits from local governments."

Wicksell (1967 [1896]) suggested that a more effective way to constrain legislators and minimize their ability to engage in opportunistic behaviors was to base membership in each legislative chamber on proportional representation and subject lawmakers to a rule of approximate unanimity instead of majoritarianism. According to him, if the legislature is constitutionally required to secure consensual or supramajority approval of all its members (e.g., 75 percent of its membership) before laws (especially those dealing with income redistribution) are passed, then interest or pressure groups will find it very difficult to subvert national rules for their own advantage. The supramajority rule is expected to minimize the passage of fiscally discriminatory laws, rent-seeking, corruption, and other opportunistic behaviors (Gwartney and Wagner, 1988).

The preceding discussion points to the adoption of highly decentralized federalist systems as a way to minimize corruption and other forms of opportunism in the developing countries. The actual mix of institutions would, however, have to be determined by the relevant stakeholder groups during proper constitution making because these groups and individuals have access to the required time-and-place information. Although a highly decentralized federalist system is more responsive to the values, interests, and objectives of both large (that is, dominant) and small ethnic groups, it is important to note that unless the right to migrate freely is constitutionally guaranteed, such a system could easily degenerate into a series of small unitary governments, with each monopolizing governance in its geographic region and burdened with the problems of centralized political systems.

THE CHALLENGE OF CONSTITUTION MAKING IN DEVELOPING COUNTRIES

One may argue that the type of constitution making and state reconstruction necessary to provide each society with accountable, transparent, and participatory governance structures—that is, laws and institutions that adequately constrain the government and enhance wealth creation—can only be successfully undertaken in countries with characteristics and traits that most developing countries do not now have. For example, it has been argued that presently in most of Africa, the ability of the ordinary citizen to make choices is significantly constrained by political and economic monopolies, limited information, and the distrust that many people have of their national institutions and leaders.

What is the constitutional situation in most developing countries today? First, many of the laws and institutions that exist in these countries are based on those imposed on these societies by European colonialists and managed by an alien class with values significantly different from those of the indigenous people. Colonial institutions, whether in Africa, Asia, or Latin America and the Caribbean, were despotic and exploitative and were not designed to enhance the ability of the indigenous people to maximize their values. These institutions, however, were designed to help the invading Europeans maximize their objectives. As a consequence, managers of these colonial institutions usually did not reveal to the indigenous people their true objectives, nor did they share with the local people enough information to help them properly understand the nature of these institutions. Second, at independence in many (but not all) of today's developing countries, there did not exist an indigenous managerial and entrepreneurial class capable of effectively managing postindependence markets because colonial authorities had purposefully stunted the development and growth of such a class. Third, many of these countries currently do not have properly functioning independent media. Finally, many of today's developing countries have significantly high rates of illiteracy. Some scholars have argued that "[n]either effective management nor democratic control is possible under such circumstances" (Brett, 1995, p. 204).

Granted, the absence of modern mass media structures have made it very difficult for the people of the Third World to remain informed about activities in their societies, especially in the operation of their governments. However, it is important for us to recognize that the absence of these so-called modern communications structures (e.g., television, radio, and newspapers and magazines) does not necessarily imply that many of the people in these societies are poorly informed about the goings-on in their political and economic systems. In many African countries, for example, despite the absence of modern communications structures, many people remain relatively well informed through the use of traditional and informal structures.

Fax machines, cell phones, and the Internet have a significant impact on the ability of the governments of the developing countries to control their domestic media. In several of these countries, journalists who have been forced underground by draconian laws are no longer able to publish and distribute their papers. However, they have not declared bankruptcy. Many of them now have Web sites from which they publish their papers, virtually without interference from their governments. Unfortunately, most of this Internet-based newsprint is read primarily by foreigners because most people in the Third World are still unable to gain access to the Internet.

One should note, however, that the availability of skilled and competent managers is a necessary but not sufficient condition for the efficient and effective management of political and economic markets. Unless each developing country provides its people with the appropriate incentive structures, through proper institutional reforms, individuals within the society are most likely to continue to engage in opportunism in an effort to generate extralegal income for themselves. Even if many of these countries are able to secure the required skilled personnel, human development and effective governance are not likely to be the outcome in the absence of the appropriate institutional arrangements. In addition, corruption and other forms of opportunism will remain pervasive.

CONCLUSION

In this chapter, we have examined corruption in developing countries and shown why traditional methods of corruption cleanup have not been successful in eradicating this scourge from these societies. Traditionally, societal, legal, market, and political strategies have been used to deal with corruption. We have shown that these strategies involve attempts to manipulate outcomes within a given set of rules and assume the existence of efficient counteracting agencies. If the laws of a country provide market participants with incentive structures that make opportunism highly profitable (that is, the laws encourage opportunistic behaviors), the only effective way to minimize these behaviors is to change the rules and by implication, the incentive structures. Any attempt to force different market outcomes (e.g., through policing) while leaving the existing rules unchanged will fail. If counteracting agencies (e.g., the police and the judiciary) are not properly constrained by the constitution (that is, the rules) and are pervaded by high levels of corruption, it is not likely that these institutions will serve as effective instruments for the control of corruption. Thus, a proper program to clean up corruption must begin with a negotiated change of the existing rules in order to provide an incentive structure that makes corruption the least likely outcome of market transitions.

A close look at the incentive structures present in many developing countries today shows that corruption is most likely to be an important market outcome. Using the traditional strategies to force a change in market outcomes is not likely to succeed, as evidence by more than fifty years of postindependence efforts to control corruption in former European colonies in Africa, Latin America, the Caribbean, and Asia has proven. The most effective way to control corruption is to undertake institutional reforms that seek to modify the incentive structures and force market participants to engage in behaviors that produce the outcomes favored by society. Thus, developing countries seeking ways to rid their societies of corruption, improve macroeconomic performance, and enhance development should engage their societies in the reconstruction of the postcolonial state through proper constitution making and provide themselves with transparent, accountable, and participatory governance structures.

REFERENCES

Alam, M.S. 1989. "Anatomy of Corruption: An Approach to the Political Economy of Underdevelopment." *The American Journal of Economics and Sociology* 48(4): 441–56.

Anderson, T.L., and P.J. Hill. 1986. "Constraining the Transfer Society: Constitutional and Moral Dimensions." *Cato Journal* 6(1): 317–39.

Bardhan, P. 1997. "Corruption and Development: A Review of the Issues." *Journal of Economic Literature* 35(3): 1320–46.

Bayley, D.H. 1966. "The Effects of Corruption in a Developing Nation." *The Western Political Quarterly* (Salt Lake City) 19(4): 719–32.

Becker, G.S. 1983. "A Theory of Competition among Interest Groups for Political Influence." *Quarterly Journal of Economics* 98:371–400.

Bentley, A.F. 1908. *The Process of Government*. Chicago: The University of Chicago Press.

Black, D. 1958. *The Theory of Committees and Elections*. Cambridge, UK: Cambridge University Press.

Brady, G.L., and G. Tullock. 1996. *Formal Contributions to the Theory of Public Choice: The Unpublished Works of Duncan Black*. Accord, MA: Kluwer Academic Publishers.

Brennan, G., and J.M. Buchanan. 1980. *The Power to Tax: Analytical Foundations of a Fiscal Constitution*. Cambridge, UK: Cambridge University Press.

———. 1985. *The Reason of Rules: Constitutional Political Economy*. Cambridge, UK: Cambridge University Press.

Brett, E.A. 1995. "Institutional Theory and Social Change in Uganda." In *The New Institutional Economics and Third World Development*, edited by J. Harriss, J. Hunter, and C.M. Lewis. London: Routledge.

Buchanan, J.M. 1972. "Toward an Analysis of Closed Behavioral Systems." In *Theory of Public Choice*, edited by J.M. Buchanan and R.D. Tollison. Ann Arbor, MI: University of Michigan Press.

Buchanan, J.M., and R.D. Tollison. 1972. *Theory of Public Choice*. Ann Arbor, MI: University of Michigan Press.

Buchanan, J.M., and G. Tullock. 1962. *The Calculus of Consent: Logical Foundations of Constitutional Democracy*. Ann Arbor: University of Michigan Press.

Congleton, R.D. 1994. "Constitutional Federalism and Decentralization: A Second Best Solution." *Economia Delle Scelte Pubbliche* (Italy) 11(1): 15–29.

Couch, J.F., K.E. Atkinson, and W.F. Shughart, II. 1992. "Ethics, Laws and the Outside Earnings and Politicians: The Case of Alabama's 'Legislators-Educator,'" *Public Choice*, 73(2): 135–145.

Downs, A. 1957. *An Economic Theory of Democracy*. New York: Harper & Row.

———. 1967. *Inside Bureaucracy*. Boston, MA: Little, Brown and Company.

Egunjobi, T.O. 1983. "Characteristics of Health Care Resource Problem in Nigeria." *Canadian Journal of African Studies* 17(2): 235–38.

Elliot, K.A. 1997a. *Corruption and the Global Economy*. Washington, DC: Institute for International Economics.

———. 1997b. "Preface." In *Corruption and the Global Economy*, edited by K.A. Elliot. Washington, DC: Institute for International Economics.

Gillespie, K., and G. Okruhlik. 1991. "The Political Dimensions of Corruption Cleanup: A Framework for Analysis." *Comparative Politics* 24(1): 77–97.

Gordon, A. 1998. "The New Diaspora—African Immigration to the United States." *Journal of Third World Studies* 15(1): 79–103.

Gould, D.J., and T.B. Mukendi. 1989. "Bureaucratic Corruption in Africa: Causes, Consequences and Remedies." *International Journal of Public Administration* 13(3): 427–57.

Gwartney, J.D., and R.E. Wagner. 1988. "Public Choice and the Conduct of Representative Government." In *Public Choice and Constitutional Economics*, edited by J.D. Gwartney and R.E. Wagner. Greenwich, CT: JAI Press.

Hogendorn, J.S. 1992. *Economic Development*. New York: HarperCollins.
Ihonvbere, J.O. 1994. *Nigeria: The Politics of Adjustment & Democracy*. New Brunswick, NJ: Transaction Publishers.
Jabbra, J.G. 1976. "Bureaucratic Corruption in the Third World: Causes and Remedies." *Indian Journal of Public Administration* 22: 673–91.
Jua, N. 1998. "Cameroon: Jump-starting an Economic Crisis." In *Corruption and the Crisis of Institutional Reforms in Africa*, edited by J.M. Mbaku. Lewiston, NY: The Edwin Mellen Press.
Kimenyi, M.S. 1987. "Bureaucratic Rents and Political Institutions." *Journal of Public Finance and Public Choice* 3: 189–99.
Leff, N.H. 1964. "Economic Development Through Bureaucratic Corruption." *American Behavioral Scientist* 8(3): 8–14.
LeVine, V.T. 1975. *Political Corruption: The Ghanaian Case*. Stanford, CA: The Hoover Institution.
Mbaku, J.M. 1991. "Military Expenditures and Bureaucratic Competition for Rents." *Public Choice* 71(1–2): 19–31.
———. 1992. "Bureaucratic Corruption as Rent-Seeking Behavior." *Konjunkturpolitik* (Berlin) 38(4): 247–65.
———. 1994. "Military Coups as Rent-Seeking Behavior." *Journal of Political and Military Sociology* 22 (Winter): 241–84.
———. 1997. *Institutions and Reform in Africa: The Public Choice Perspective*. Westport, CT: Praeger.
———. 1998. *Corruption and the Crisis of Institutional Reforms in Africa*. Lewiston, NY: The Edwin Mellen Press.
———. 1999. "Property Rights and the Exploitation of Africa's Environmental Resources: Preparing for the New Millennium." In *Preparing Africa for the Twenty-First Century: Strategies for Peaceful Coexistence and Sustainable Development*, edited by J.M. Mbaku. Aldershot, UK: Ashgate.
———. 2000. *Bureaucratic and Political Corruption in Africa: The Public Choice Perspective*. Malabar, FL: Krieger.
McMullan, M. 1961. "A Theory of Corruption." *Sociological Review* 9(6): 181–201.
Merton, R.K. 1976. *Sociological Ambivalence and Other Essays*. New York: Macmillan.
Mueller, D.C. 1989. *Public Choice II: A Revised Edition of Public Choice*. Cambridge, UK: Cambridge University Press.
Niskanen, W.A. 1971. *Bureaucracy and Representative Government*. Chicago, IL: Aldine-Atherton.
Nye, J.S. 1967. "Corruption and Political Development: A Cost-Benefit Analysis," *The American Political Science Review*, 61(2): 417–427.
Olson, M. 1965. *The Logic of Collective Action*. Cambridge, MA: Harvard University Press.
Osterfeld, D. 1992. *Prosperity versus Planning: How Government Stifles Economic Growth*. New York: Oxford University Press.
Ostrom, E., L. Schroeder, and S. Wynne. 1993. *Institutional Incentives and Sustainable Development: Infrastructure Policies in Perspective*. Boulder, CO: Westview.
Othman, S. 1984. "Class, Crises and Coup: The Demise of Shagari's Regime." *African Affairs* 83(333): 441–61.

Rose-Ackerman, S. 1978. *Corruption: A Study in Political Economy*. New York: Academic Press.

———. 1997. "The Political Economy of Corruption." In *Corruption and the Global Economy*, edited by K.A. Elliot. Washington, D.C.: Institute for International Economics.

Takougang, J. 1996. "The 1992 Multiparty Elections in Cameroon: Prospects for Democracy and Democratization." *Journal of Asian and African Studies* 31(1–2): 52–65.

Truman, D.B. 1951. *The Governmental Process: Political Interests and Public Opinion*. New York: Knopf.

Tullock, G. 1965. *The Politics of Bureaucracy*. Washington, DC: Public Affairs Press.

———. 1993. *Rent-seeking*. Aldershot, UK: Edward Elgar Publishing, Inc.

———. 1998. *On Voting: A Public Choice Approach*. Aldershot, UK: Edward Elgar Publishing, Inc.

UNDP (United Nations Development Program). 1990. *Human Development Report, 1990*. New York: Oxford University Press.

———. 1995. *Human Development Report, 1995*. New York: Oxford University Press.

Van Klaveren, J. 1990. "The Concept of Corruption." In *Political Corruption: A Handbook*, edited by A. Heidenheimer, M. Johnston, and V.T. LeVine. New Brunswick, NJ: Transaction Publishers.

Wicksell, K. 1967 [1896]. "A New Principle of Just Taxation." In *Classics in the Theory of Public Finance*, edited by R.A. Musgrave and A.T. Peacock. New York: St. Martin's Press.

Wiseman, J. 1990. "Principles of Political Economy: An Outline Proposal, Illustrated by Application to Fiscal Federalism." *Constitutional Political Economy* 1(1): 101–24.

World Bank. 1979. *Zaire: Current Economic Situation and Constraints*. Washington, DC: The World Bank.

9

Fiscal and Monetary Policies for Economic Development

James C.W. Ahiakpor

INTRODUCTION

Modern development economics provides no clear guidelines on the appropriate fiscal and monetary policies to promote economic development, as did the classical economists, most notably Adam Smith, David Hume, David Ricardo, and John Stuart Mill. According to the classical prescription, fiscal policy (or government taxation and spending) is to be limited to three principal "duties of the sovereign," namely national defense, administration of justice, and the creation of public works to assist the development of private enterprise (Smith, 1976 [1776]). Fulfillment of these duties requires no more than the barest of taxation to raise general revenue. Monetary policy, that is, variations in the quantity of money is even less the concern of government if money (specie) is privately created. Where paper money (currency) substitutes for specie, its creation is to be limited to the needs of trade in order to preserve the price level and the exchange rate (Hume, 1990 [1775]; Smith, 1976 [1776]; Ricardo, 1951, 1957; and Mill, 1965).

The Keynesian revolution, initiated through *The General Theory of Employment, Interest and Money* (1936), changed this consensus among economists on both fiscal and monetary policies. In modern macroeconomics, government spending is supposed to be a necessary factor in maintaining aggregate demand in order to sustain the level of production as well as to promote economic growth itself. Keynes also claimed to have turned monetary policy into a theory of production as a whole; the price level, according to Keynes, is determined by the supply and demand for goods and services, just as the prices of specific goods are determined in their own markets, whereas changes in the supply of money[1] determine the rate of interest and, along with other factors such as business confidence, determine the supply of output. The Keynesian revolution thus made activist fiscal and monetary policies prerequisites for economic development.

However, the frustration of not finding in extant macroeconomics readily applicable policy advice for the newly emerging nations of the 1950s and 1960s encouraged several prominent development economists simply to declare the whole discipline of neoclassical economics to be useless. Thus, Gunnar Myrdal (1957, 104, 106) called on students of the less developed countries to become "competent rebels" and throw away "large structures of meaningless, irrelevant and sometimes blatantly inadequate doctrines and theoretical approaches [of] Western liberal economics." Dudley Seers (1963) bemoaned the limitations of the "special case," which he regarded modern neoclassical economics to be, and Paul Streeten (1974, 83) declared that "the whole paraphernalia of contemporary neoclassical economics seems to have become suddenly obsolete."[2]

Such declarations offered little guidance for fiscal and monetary policy formulation to promote efficient economic development in the less developed countries (LDCs), but rather inspired several development approaches in the 1960s and 1970s, which mainly failed to promote their economic development. Out of such failures have emerged lessons such as the following: (a) The pursuit of manufacturing industry development over agriculture creates only a false start; (b) large-scale economic development plans mainly use up scarce human resources and other economic resources but hardly provide the development outcomes envisaged; (c) import-substitution industrialization strategies hardly promote efficient economic development; (d) overvalued fixed exchange rates create more problems for economic development than they are supposed to alleviate; (e) interest restrictions that create negative real interest rates do not promote adequate capital formation and economic growth; and (f) persistent government deficits harm the growth prospects of countries. These lessons have been incorporated in the structural adjustment prescriptions of the International Monetary Fund (IMF) and the World Bank since the early 1980s, but they hardly provide a consensus on the appropriate fiscal and monetary policies to facilitate economic development.

Since the 1970s, Milton Friedman's monetarism has been a major counter to the Keynesian monetary policy of expanding the money supply in order to lower interest rates and promote investment spending and growth, emphasizing the mostly inflationary consequences of monetary expansion around the world. But the record of monetary expansion in most less developed countries suggests that not much heed has been taken of Friedman's arguments, and in some respects with justification. A high growth rate of the monetary aggregate, *M2*, which Friedman holds up as the best measure of a country's money supply, does not consistently correlate with high rates of inflation in all countries, especially in high-income countries with highly developed financial sectors. The emergence of supply-side economics in the 1980s, emphasizing tax cuts, privatization, and limited government spending in order to encourage more efficient private sector savings and investment may have achieved some success in the more developed countries, but has yet to attain the same degree of acceptance among the less developed countries. Besides, attempts to provide an empirical basis for supply-side prescriptions of limited government spending as the key to efficient economic development have failed to yield consistent results: Countries in which the share of government spending, as a percentage of national income (GNP) or gross domestic product (GDP), is less than 20 percent have not always experienced the fastest growth among the less- or more-developed countries.[3] The lack of definitive empirical support for both monetarist and supply-side prescriptions that are in line with the classical tradition of fiscal and monetary policies therefore suggests the need for making the case for these policies afresh. That is the task of this chapter.

BACKGROUND TO CLASSICAL FISCAL POLICY

The classical prescription of limited government taxation and spending was founded on the recognition that government spending directly substitutes for private household and investment spending. The less a government spends, the less it takes from the private sector, hence the more spending done by households and firms. In general, households spend their income (Y) in three main categories: namely, consumption (C), savings or investment in financial assets ($S = FA^d$), and acquisition of cash balances (H_h), where H = high-powered money. Government taxation constitutes a fourth category of "spending" for households (tY), which withdraws funds from the other three; thus $Y = tY + C + FA^d + H_h$. In terms of the development process, it is the contraction of the rate of savings or capital accumulation by taxes that is most significant, $S = Y(1 - t) - C - H_h = FA^d$. Unless the productivity of government sector spending were greater than that of the private sector displaced by taxes, such reallocation of funds must retard the rate of economic growth.

Where government does not acquire its funds directly through taxation but from issuing bonds or treasury bills, the effect on the allocation of private sector savings is the same. Government securities (FA_g) and private sector IOUs (FA_p) constitute the total volume of financial assets (FA) purchased by households. Unless households increase their demand for financial assets when the government increases its supply of debt instruments or securities, there must be a direct substitution of government spending for private sector investment spending—complete crowding out. Again, the ultimate effect on the economy's growth path depends upon the relative productivities of the two expenditures.

Belief in the expansionary effect of fiscal policy in modern macroeconomics is founded mainly on two Keynesian principles: (a) Government spending is needed to make up for the community's savings, which is believed to be a withdrawal from the expenditure stream or the economy's aggregate demand, and

(b) government spending promotes economic growth from its presumed positive multiplier effect on the rest of the economy. But these two principles are seriously at odds with economic reality or sound reasoning. The first derives from Keynes's notion that saving is simply the nonspending of current (disposable) income on consumption goods and services (Keynes 1930, 1:172; 1936, 210); hence, for a closed economy, saving, $S = Y(1 - t) - C$. Businesses need spending by households on consumption goods and services both to sustain their current rate of production and to encourage increased investment spending. Thus, if saving is merely the failure of households to spend all of their income on goods and services, increased savings could only depress business profits and expectations by increasing inventory accumulation. Government spending directly on goods and services thus replaces the demand withheld from businesses by private savings.

The attribution of a positive multiplier effect on the economy from government spending derives from the fact that government spending creates income for those employed or from whom the purchases by government are made. From this fact is derived the extrapolation that the consumption spending of the new income recipients generates new incomes for others until, at the termination of the sequence of spending, a multiple (k) of the initial government spending is achieved; i.e., $Y = kG$, where $k = 1/(1 - MPC)$, where MPC = households' marginal propensity to consume. But the extrapolation is seriously misleading. It ignores the fact that it is from previously created income in the private sector that the government obtains its revenue to spend on those it hires or the goods it purchases. Thus, it is not the government spending that creates incomes but the prior private sector production that made the government revenue and spending possible. At best, the government spending only channels spending differently from where it might have gone in the absence of government taxation and spending. The notion of consumption spending driving production, without reference to prior production, is simply a myth (Ahiakpor, 2001, elaborates).

Moreover, the multiplier argument suggests that saving is not spending, which is correct only if saving meant the hoarding of income in money (cash), which it is not (Ahiakpor, 1995). People save by purchasing financial assets (FAs) such as bank deposits, mutual funds, bonds, and stocks; i.e., $S = Y(1 - t) - C - H_h = FA^d$. Thus, instead of being a withdrawal from the expenditure stream, as the Keynesian view presumes, saving rather transfers the nonconsumed purchasing power of households to borrowers or the issuers of financial assets. The recipients of the funds employ them on consumption as well as investment projects—purchasing machinery and equipment for production, renting the services of land and labor, and purchasing materials for further processing. Thus both households' consumption spending and savings drive the flow of spending in an economy, not just consumption. As Thomas Malthus, the classical economist Keynes most admired, points out, "No political economist of the present day can by saving mean mere hoarding" (quoted in Blaug, 1996, 161). J.S. Mill affirms the same point when he writes:

> The word saving does not imply that what is saved is not consumed, nor even necessarily that its consumption is deferred; but only that, if consumed immediately, it is not consumed by the person who saves it. If merely laid by for future use, it is said to be hoarded; and while hoarded, is not consumed at all. But if employed as capital, it is all consumed; though not by the capitalist. (*Works,* 2:70)

Thus, rather than being a requisite substitution for the spending withdrawn by private saving, government spending, other than that financed with funds borrowed from the central bank, is a forced substitution through taxation or the issuing of bonds to the public. This is why an expansionary fiscal policy may rather retard an economy's growth unless the productivity of such government spending were higher than would have resulted from the funds being spent by the private sector. That is, $Y/(G - Z) < 0$, where Z = private sector spending, is a distinct possibility rather than the positive number (multiplier) frequently derived in modern macroeconomics. In the long run, even a central-bank financing of government spending is at the expense of the private sector. The newly created money (credit) will raise the price level and reduce the real incomes of wage, interest, and rental earners as well as the purchasing power of cash balances to the extent of the increased government spending. Similarly, government spending financed by externally borrowed funds ultimately displaces private sector spending. Taxes have to be raised on the population to finance the government debt. Thus, the element of substitution between public (government) and private sector spending entailed in fiscal policy cannot be avoided.

BACKGROUND TO CLASSICAL MONETARY POLICY

The classical economists prescribed a steady growth in the supply of money (currency) to meet the needs of trade or the demand for money for transaction purposes as an economy grows. Were the demand for money to exceed its supply, the price level would fall, depressing economic activity at least in the short-run. The price level (P), being the inverse of the value of money ($V_m = 1/P$), is determined by the supply (H^s) and demand for money ($H^d = kPy$): $P = H/ky$ and $V_m = 1/P = ky/H$, where k = proportion of real income the public wishes to hold as cash balances (H/P), y = real income or output, and $H^d/P = ky$. Furthermore, growth of the price level will equal the difference between the growth in the supply of money (currency) and its demand, $P/P = H/H - k/k - y/y$. An increase in the price level due to an increase in the supply of money may increase real output and employment in the short run while nominal wages, interest rates, and rentals have yet to adjust fully to the monetary increase, but would only produce a higher price level or inflation in the long run. For real production to increase, it is not money that is needed but capital or savings—non-consumed income that is loaned out to investors or employed directly by savers to purchase producers' goods, and rent the services of land, labor, and equipment. J.S. Mill's advice on this point is worth quoting: "Capital by persons wholly unused to reflect on the subject, is supposed to be synonymous with money. ...

Money is no more synonymous with capital than it is with wealth. Money cannot itself perform any part of the office of capital, since it can afford no assistance to production. To do so, it must be exchanged for other things" (*Works*, 2:55). The short-run increase in output and employment that may result from the excessive creation of money (currency) is due only to the fact that fixed income (wages, rents, and interest) earners lose some part of their purchasing power to residual income (profit) earners when prices rise following the increase of money, a process the classics called "forced saving" and that modern economists describe as the positive effect of an unanticipated increase in the money supply. But the income redistribution is reversed when the contractual rates of wages, rents, and interest are revised to reflect the price-level increase.[4]

Increases in the money supply by a central bank also do not lower interest rates permanently, although they may temporarily depress them. The short-term effect arises from the fact that, to increase the quantity of money (H), the central bank either purchases financial assets and raises their prices ($P_{FA} = \$X/i$, where $\$X$ = dollar payments on a security or financial asset) or lowers its lending rate in order to induce more borrowing by financial institutions. But the subsequent spending of the newly supplied funds and the rise of commodity prices increase the demand for credit while reducing the rate of private sector savings, thus raising the equilibrium interest rates again. The classics well understood that the source of long-term interest rate reduction is increased savings relative to the demand for loanable funds or capital, not increases in the supply of central bank money. As David Ricardo, for example, explains:

> The interest for money ... is not regulated by the rate at which the Bank [of England] will lend ... but by the rate of profits which can be made by the employment of capital, and which is totally independent of the quantity, or of the value of money. Whether a Bank lent one million, ten millions, or a hundred millions, they would not permanently alter the market rate of interest; they would alter only the value of the money which they thus issued. (*Works*, 1: 363–64).[5]

The experience of currency values in several less developed countries (LDCs) being significantly depreciated, following periods of rapid currency creation by their central banks, is eloquent testimony to the validity of Ricardo's argument. The point has been recognized in modern macroeconomics by those who argue that current low interest rates may reflect past slower rates of monetary growth, and current high interest rates may reflect past higher rates of monetary growth.

In claiming to have turned monetary policy into a theory of production as a whole, Keynes was reasoning from the logic of his cash or liquidity-preference theory of interest rates. According to that theory, the rate of interest is determined by the supply and demand for liquidity or cash and has nothing to do with the supply and demand for savings, as the classical economists had explained. Thus, according to Keynes's perspective, increases in the quantity of money (currency) by a central bank, relative to its demand, lower interest rates and entice businesspeople to borrow more money for investment—purchase of materials, equipments, and machinery—and hire more workers for production, generating the following sequence: $M^s > 0\ i < 0\ I(i) > 0\ (E, GDP) > 0$, where E = employment and M^s = money supply, variously defined. As Keynes (1936, xxxv) explains the process, "The quantity of money determines the supply of liquid resources, and hence the rate of interest, and in conjunction with other factors (particularly that of confidence) the inducement to invest, which in turn fixes the equilibrium level of incomes, output and employment." The principal impediment to the working of this process, according to Keynes, is a sufficient disturbance of confidence as to create a situation of "liquidity trap," when increases in the quantity of money fail to depress interest rates because there is an infinite demand for money to hoard.

Keynes also firmly denied that increases in the supply of money directly affect the price level, as had been explained by the classical economists. Rather, Keynes (1936, xxxiv) declares, "I regard the price level as a whole as being determined in precisely the same way as individual prices; that is to say, under the influence of supply and demand." Even so, the price level is affected by increases in the quantity of money only under the condition of full employment of labor or productive capacity, depicted in modern macroeconomics as a vertical aggregate supply curve.

In contradiction, Friedman (1970, 1972) cites the record of Argentina, Brazil, Chile, and South Korea as countries that have experienced very high rates of inflation and high interest rates following their high rates of money creation to substantiate the point that increases in the quantity of money do not produce low interest rates but rather the opposite. Friedman also cites the record of Germany and Switzerland within the same time period to affirm the proposition that low rates of money creation keep interest rates low by keeping inflation low.

Indeed, the inflationary consequences of attempting to follow the Keynesian positive view of monetary expansion to promote economic growth in several LDCs has been partly responsible for the rejection of neoclassical economics as being irrelevant by the likes of Michael Todaro and Paul Streeten. However, international data do not consistently show that increases in the quantity of money, broadly defined such as $M2$, mainly cause high rates of inflation and high interest rates. In countries with highly developed financial and banking systems, most of $M2$ is composed of bank deposits, that is, forms in which the public holds its savings, such as savings and time deposits, and money market deposit accounts. Thus, the ratio of currency (H) or "reserve money" to $M2$ tends to be less than 10 percent in the high-income countries, and increases in $M2$ in these countries are not as closely associated with increases in inflation as with increases in H (see Table 9.1; note particularly the cases of Canada, New Zealand, United Kingdom, Switzerland, Singapore, Korea, Mexico, South Africa, Mali, Lesotho, India, and Pakistan).

Besides failing to provide a consistent relationship between increases in $M2$ and inflation across the world, the modern definition of money includes currency and bank deposits of various maturity periods ($M = C + D = C + R + BC = H + BC$, where C = currency in the hands of the public, R = bank reserves, BC = bank credit, and $C + R = H$). This renders the proper conduct of

Table 9.1
Average Annual Growth of *H*, *M2*, and Inflation: Selected Countries, 1990–1998/1999

Country	H	M2	Inflation	H/M2	GNP/Pop
HICs					
1. USA	6.90	4.43	1.8	9.96	30,600
2. Canada	3.82	7.08	1.3	7.21	19,320
3. Australia	9.17	7.99	1.6	9.07	20,050
4. Japan	4.26	3.12	0.1	9.78	32,230
5. New Zealand	3.31	6.98	1.5	2.80	13,780
6. United Kingdom	4.58	7.24	2.9	3.94	22,640
7. Switzerland	1.96	4.97	1.5	8.81	38,350
8. Sweden	2.76	2.88	2.1	17.10	25,040
9. Greece	17.23	11.76	10.1	28.68	11,770
10. Singapore	5.71	28.07	1.6	16.30	29,610
MICs					
1. Botswana	19.34	15.38	10.0	16.4	3,240
2. Ecuador	41.59	47.93	33.7	28.68	1,310
3. South Africa	11.71	14.60	10.2	7.81	3,160
4. Korea	6.33	17.98	5.8	16.71	8,490
5. Malaysia	17.28	17.61	5.06	26.77	3,400
6. Mexico	25.84	33.38	19.3	16.52	4,400
LICs					
1. Ghana	33.91	33.21	27.2	44.32	390
2. Mali	5.91	11.52	8.5	62.82	240
3. Nigeria	32.51	32.67	34.8	52.43	310
4. Lesotho	11.43	13.21	9.6	28.71	550
5. Zimbabwe	31.42	27.42	23.8	29.06	520
6. India	14.43	17.07	8.6	31.46	450
7. Pakistan	15.17	17.44	10.7	39.43	470
8. Honduras	33.94	27.34	19.8	31.17	760

Note: Average annual growth rates of base money (*H*), broad money (*M2*), and the average ratio of reserve money to broad money (*H*/*M2*) calculated from data in *International Financial Statistics Yearbook*, International Monetary Fund (2000), and inflation rates (implicit GDP deflators) and per capita GNP (GNP/Pop) for 1999 US dollars obtained from *World Development Report 2000/2001*, World Bank (2000). HICs = high income countries, MICs = middle income countries, and LICs = low income countries.

monetary policy as well as its instruments unclear. Must the monetary authorities focus on controlling broad money, such as *M2*, which includes mostly the public's savings, or only the central bank's own liabilities, *H*? Alternatively, must the monetary authorities attempt to control the rate of interest or the price level?

Recognizing that increases in the purchase of bank financial assets by households and other income earners increases the "money" supply, given the quantity of high-powered money, also leads to the recognition that a central bank may influence the growth of money (*M1* or *M2*) but cannot control precisely the rate of growth. For example, the simple money (*M1*) multiplier may be written as $m = (cu + 1)/(cu + r_d + r_e)$, where cu = the currency-deposit ratio, r_d = legal or reserves-deposit ratio, and r_e = excess or economic reserves-deposit ratio, and $M1 = m.H$. Thus, variations in cu and r_e affect the quantity of "money," $M1$, independently of a central bank's changes of H through open market operations or changes in the discount rate or the legal reserve requirement, r_d.

Moreover, the effort to control the growth of $M1$ or larger aggregates by increasing the legal reserves is misplaced. When the money supply other than the high-powered money increases, it represents an increase in financial investment by households, which facilitates increased investment by producers, and therefore income and employment growth without inflation. Inflation, the persistent increase in the price level, occurs when total spending exceeds the value of available goods and services. Production, and the subsequent increase in income, provides the means for spending. Thus saving merely transfers the purchasing power of income earners (directly or indirectly) into the hands of borrowers who issue the financial assets or IOUs purchased by the savers. The increased purchase of bank financial assets, reflected in increases of $M1$, $M2$, $M3$, and soon, at the expense of other financial assets such as bonds and equities, reallocates purchasing power among spenders but does not add to it. This is why such increases in "money" do not cause increases in the price level or inflation, but increases in high-powered money (H) do.

A clear understanding of the constituents of the modern "money supply" also helps to appreciate the futility of a central bank's efforts to control the level of interest rates as part of its monetary policy goals or targets. By lowering its discount rate, a central bank encourages financial institutions, mainly banks, to borrow from it. These institutions then are able to extend credit beyond the savings deposited with them and thus lower the overall level of interest rates. But as the additional purchasing power created by the credit extension increases total spending, the price level will rise, which will decrease private sector saving. The increase in prices may increase the expectation of profits while also raising the cost of materials required for processing in production. Firms are thus pushed to demand more credit as prices rise, which would tend to increase the level of interest rates in a cumulative process (Ricardo, *Works* 1 and 3; Wicksell, 1898; Fisher, 1912; Marshall 1923, 257).[6] This is why the attempt to lower interest rates by increasing the rate of money (currency) creation may succeed only in raising the level of market interest rates while the inflationary effects continue, $i = r + r^e + p^e$, where r = real rate of interest and p^e = expected rate of inflation. On the other hand, an increase in the rate of saving relative to the demand for loanable funds lowers the level of interest rates, the rate of interest being the price borrowers pay and at the same time the reward to savers for postponing their immediate consumption.

J.M. Keynes's (1936) redefinition of saving to mean simply nonspending or the hoarding of income in cash was greatly responsible for distorting the longstanding classical principle that the rate of interest is not governed by the rate of money (currency) creation but by the supply and demand for savings or capital (Ahiakpor, 1990). If saving were hoarding, then it would be correct to argue that the more saving occurred the fewer loanable funds would be available for borrowers, and would thus cause the equilibrium level of interest rates to rise. Contrary to Keynes, the correct meaning of saving is not hoarding but the purchase of financial assets or the supply of loanable funds.

The modern tendency to focus on *M2* rather than the central bank's own liabilities or high-powered money (*H*) as the target of monetary policy also carries some harmful consequences for the economy. The target leads a central bank to contract private sector credit by selling financial securities to the public (or raising the discount rate) when *M2* is expanding at a higher than some stipulated rate. But in the absence of a central bank's own expansion of high-powered money, an increase in the public's rate of savings in the form of bank financial assets expands the money supply ($M = m.H = H + BC$) through an increase in the money multiplier (m) or bank credit (BC). The central bank's credit contraction in such a situation merely reduces the economy's rate of capital formation and thus output and employment growth.

IMPLEMENTING FISCAL AND MONETARY POLICIES FOR DEVELOPMENT

The specifics of fiscal and monetary policies conducive to economic development in a particular country can be determined only in relation to the country's institutional details. Such details determine how much government spending is needed to provide the requisite national defense and administration of justice to ensure adequate protection of private property from external and internal violations as well as enforce commercial contracts. Civil strife is also an enemy of economic progress. The amount of government spending that may be required to preserve social peace needed to support economic activity also would have to be determined with regard to the specifics of a country. Where laws regarding the sale or transfer of property such as land and buildings are in need of development, it may well require more government spending to enhance such institutional development. As has been widely recognized, the system of land tenure in many less developed countries fails to provide clear, transferable titles to individuals and thus hinders commercial agricultural development. The extent of government expenditure required to provide adequate public health is also yet another variable that can only be determined by the particular circumstances of each country.

But the overall guideline for fiscal policy should be that governments engage in public spending bearing in mind that the funds involved are taken from individual income earners who would have spent them otherwise. Only in the specific instances that (a) the required expenditure would not have been forthcoming from private sources, as in the case of public goods like national defense and (b) public sector spending would yield a greater return than private sector spending would government spending be justified or conducive to economic development. Much of the modern concern has tended to focus on the design of tax regimes, considering whether value-added tax, excise tax, import and export taxes, or some combination of these would be the most appropriate for less developed countries (LDCs). Valuable though such examinations may be, they fall short of the requisite advice for LDCs unless they seek only to raise tax efficiency and not merely to facilitate increased overall government spending. The substitution of government spending for private sector spending constitutes a significant erosion of economic freedom for a country's citizens, and the recent finding of a strongly positive correlation between economic freedom and economic development across the world is worthy of note.[7]

In the area of monetary policy, the appropriate focus should be on varying the quantity of high-powered money (currency) to assure a stable price level or zero inflation. As in the case of fiscal policy, the specific growth rate required to achieve that goal depends on the particular circumstances of a country. An economy with an inadequately developed banking system in which a substantial amount of payments are made with cash instead of checks or electronic transfers requires a higher rate of currency creation as the economy grows. As David Hume (1752, 39–40) well recommends for a growing economy,

> [t]he good policy of the magistrate consists only in keeping [the quantity of money or currency], if possible, still increasing (*sic*); because, by that means, he keeps alive a spirit of industry in a nation, and increases (*sic*) the stock of labor, in which consists all real power and riches. A nation, whose money decreases, is actually, at that time, weaker and more miserable than another nation, which possesses no more money, but is on the increasing (*sic*) hand.

As the financial system develops and the need for cash for transactions purposes declines, the same rate of currency creation would lead to a greater rate of inflation, as some of the data in Table 9.1 appear to confirm. For example, Singapore has a slightly greater rate of currency creation than the United Kingdom (5.71 percent and 4.58 percent, respectively), but the rate of inflation is significantly lower in Singapore (1.6 percent) than in the United Kingdom (2.9 percent), which may partly be accounted for by the fact that the relative demand for cash is much higher in Singapore ($H/M2 = 16.30$) than in the United Kingdom ($H/M2 = 3.94$). Similarly, the relatively greater demand for cash in Japan ($H/M2 = 9.78$) may explain why the country experienced a significantly smaller rate of inflation (0.1 percent) for its currency growth of 4.26 percent than that of the United Kingdom as well as for New Zealand or Canada whose inflation rates were 1.5 percent and 1.3 percent, respectively, while their rates of currency creation were smaller than that of Japan, at 3.31 percent and 3.82 percent, respectively.

Of course, the data also pose some contradictions, as in the case of the United States with a relatively high currency ratio ($H/M2 = 9.96$), a high currency creation rate of 6.90 percent, but a rather small rate of inflation (1.8 percent) over the period. Such contradictions, however, require further explanation or examination of the data rather than constituting a definitive rejection of the classical principle that it is excessive currency creation that causes increases in the rate of inflation rather than currency plus savings, *M1*, *M2*, *M3*, and so on. The fact that U.S. currency is in relatively high demand around the world, both for illegal transactions and as a preferred store of value in countries with fast depreciating local currencies, may explain why its rate of inflation does not match its rate of currency creation, even controlling for its rate of real output or income growth.

Instead of attempting to control the growth of *M1* or *M2*, monetary policy rather should encourage the growth of these so-called monetary aggregates since, net of the currency issued by a central bank, these aggregates constitute the growth of savings channeled through a country's banking institutions. The growth of such savings or financial assets accumulation promotes real income and employment growth. This is the case being made by the proponents of "financial liberalization" in the LDCs, e.g., McKinnon (1986), who point out that the higher the ratio of *M2* to GDP (gross domestic product), the higher the growth of real GDP. Surely, the classical literature includes the association of bank credit creation with inflation, as in Thornton (1802), Ricardo (*Works*, 3: 52–99), and Mill (*Works*, 3: 538–55). But the classicals were describing a financial system in which bank credit was issued in the form of paper money (currency), which competed with money (specie) as a medium of exchange, and thus added to the total volume of currency when paper money was not readily convertible into specie. Fiat money (currency) replaces classical specie in the modern financial system, and thus private sector credit extension through banks is not the equivalent of classical paper money creation, hence not a source of inflation.

Finally, interest rates should be allowed to find their own levels in credit markets rather than be made a part of monetary policy. That way, interest rates will adjust to reflect expected rates of inflation in order to yield positive real rates to savers who purchase bank financial assets, bonds, and other securities. The notion that a central bank's money creation relative to the demand for cash is primarily responsible for determining the rate of interest arose from Keynes's failure to recognize that when the classical economists and Alfred Marshall (1920) explained that interest rates are determined by the supply and demand for capital, they meant by "capital" savings or loanable funds, not capital goods (Ahiakpor, 1990). Empirical evidence abundantly affirms the validity of the classical position, and policy makers need not continue to follow Keynes's misconceived recommendation of interest rate policy.

NOTES

1. See also Myrdal (1968), Streeten (1983), and Todaro (1982, 1985) for such sentiments.
2. Keynes (1936) uses the term "liquidity," but substituting cash for the term makes for a clearer meaning.
3. Landau (1983) finds support for the proposition that increased government spending out of national income hurts economic growth, but using a different specification, Ram (1986) reaches the opposite conclusion, including "the total effect of government

size on growth is positive" (196). However, Ram's conclusion seems evidently to be at odds with the common experience that government-operated enterprises in both the less- and more-developed countries tend to be less profitable than privately operated ones.

4. See also Hume (1752, 37–40), Ricardo (*Works*, 3:92–93, 318–19); Ahiakpor (1985, 1997) elaborates.

5. See also Ricardo (*Works*, 3: 92). Ricardo's argument is a reaffirmation of arguments by David Hume (1752, 49), endorsed by Adam Smith (*WN*, 1: 373, 376), and further reiterated by J.S. Mill (*Works*, 3: 508, 655).

6. Ahiakpor (1999) elaborates.

7. See O'Driscoll, Jr., Gerald P. Holmes, R. Kim, and Melanie Kirkpatrick (2001). *2001 Index of Economic Freedom.*

REFERENCES

Ahiakpor, J.C.W. 1985. "Ricardo on Money: The Operational Significance of the Non-Neutrality of Money in the Short-run." *History of Political Economy* 17 (Spring): 17–30.

———. 1990. "On Keynes's Misinterpretation of 'Capital' in the Classical Theory of Interest." *History of Political Economy* 22 (Fall): 507–28.

———. 1995. "A Paradox of Thrift or Keynes's Misrepresentation of Saving in the Classical Theory of Growth?" *Southern Economic Journal* 62 (July): 16–33.

———. 1997. "Full Employment: A Classical Assumption or Keynes's Rhetorical Device?" *Southern Economic Journal* 64 (July): 56–74.

———. 1999. "Wicksell on the Classical Theories of Money, Credit, Interest and the Price Level: Progress or Retrogression?" *American Journal of Economics and Sociology* 58 (July): 435–57.

———. 2001. "On the Mythology of the Keynesian Multiplier." *American Journal of Economics and Sociology* 60 (October).

Blaug, M. 1996. *Economic Theory in Retrospect*, 5th ed. Cambridge, UK: Cambridge University Press.

Fisher, I. 1912. *Elementary Principles of Economics*. New York: Macmillan.

Friedman, M. 1970. "The Counter Revolution in Monetary Theory." In *Monetarist Economics*, edited by M. Friedman. Oxford: Institute of Economic Affairs, 1991.

———. 1972. "The Factors Affecting the Level of Interest Rates." In *Money Supply, Money Demand, and Macroeconomic Models*, edited by J.T. Boorman and T.M. Havrilesky. Boston: Allyn and Bacon.

Hume, D. 1970 [1752]. *Writings on Economics*, edited with an introduction by E. Rotwein. Madison: University of Wisconsin Press.

International Monetary Fund. 2000. *International Financial Statistics Yearbook*. Washington, D.C.

Keynes, J.M. 1930. *A Treatise on Money*. 2 Vols. London: Macmillan.

———. 1976 [1936]. *The General Theory of Employment, Interest and Money* (paperbound edition). London and Basingstoke: Macmillan.

Landau, D. 1983. "Government Expenditure and Economic Growth: A Cross-Country Study." *Southern Economic Journal* 49 (January): 783–92.

———. 1991 [1920]. *Principles of Economics*, 8th ed. Reprinted. Philadelphia: Porcupine Press.

———. 1960 [1923]. *Money, Credit and Commerce*, New York: Augustus Kelley.

McKinnon, R.I. 1986. *Financial Liberalization in Retrospect: Interest Rate Policies in LDCs*. Center for Economic Policy Research Publication No. 74, Stanford University.

Mill, J.S. 1965. *Collected Works*, edited by J.M. Robson. London: University of Toronto Press.

Myrdal, G. 1957. *Economic Theory and Underdeveloped Regions*. New York: Harper.

———. 1968. *Asian Drama*. New York: Twentieth Century Fund.

O'Driscoll, Jr., G.P. Holmes, R. Kim, and M. Kirkpatrick. 2001. *2001 Index of Economic Freedom*. Washington, D.C. and New York: The Heritage Foundation and Dow Jones & Co.

Ram, R. 1986. "Government Size and Economic Growth: A New Framework and Some Evidence from Cross-Section and Time Series Data." *American Economic Review* 76: 191–203.

Ricardo, D. 1951, 1957 *Works and Correspondence*, Rd. Piero Sraffa. Cambridge, UK: Cambridge University Press.

Seers, D. 1963. "The Limitations of the Special Case." *Oxford Bulletin of Economics and Statistics* 25 (May): 77–98.

Smith, A. 1976 [1776]. *The Wealth of Nations*. edited by E. Cannan. 2 Vols. Chicago: University of Chicago Press.

Streeten, P. 1974. "Review of Anti-equilibrium: On Economic Systems Theory and the Tasks of Research." *World Development* 2 (April–May): 83–84.

———. 1983. "Development Dichotomies." *World Development* 11 (October): 875–89.

Thornton, H. 1965 [1802]. *Paper Credit in Great Britain*, edited by F.A. Hayek. New York: Augustus M. Kelley (Reprint).

Todaro, M. 1982. *Economics for a Developing World*, 2d ed. Essex: Longman.

———. 1985. *Economic Development in the Third World*, 3d ed. New York: Longman.

Wicksell, K. 1965 [1898]. *Interest and Prices*. Translated by R.F. Kahn. New York: Augustus Kelley (Reprint).

World Bank. 2000. *World Development Report 2000/2001*. Oxford: Oxford University Press.

10

Why Structural Adjustment Failed in Africa

George B.N. Ayittey

INTRODUCTION

Africa, consisting of fifty-four countries, is the least developed region of the Third World despite its immense wealth in mineral and natural resources. The statistics on Africa's postcolonial development record are horrifying. Indices of Africa's development performance have not only been dismal but have also lagged persistently behind those of other Third World regions. In 1997, for example, GDP per capita for Africa was $560, compared to $4,230 for Latin America and $730 for Asia. Economic growth rates in Africa in the 1970s averaged only 4 to 5 percent, whereas Latin America recorded a 6 to 7 percent growth rate. From 1986 to 1993 the continent's real GNP per capita declined 0.7 percent, whereas the average for the Third World increased by 2.7 percent. For all of Africa, real income per capita dropped by 14.6 percent from its level in 1965, which means that most Africans are now worse off than they were at independence.

In 1996, a ray of hope did appear on the horizon when Africa registered a respectable 5 percent rate of GDP growth. However in 1997, real GDP growth fell to 3.7 percent from 5 percent the previous year (*The Economist*, June 6, 1998, 44). In 1998, it dropped further to 3.3 percent, according to the U.N. Economic Commission for Africa (*The African Observer*, June 7–20, 1999, p. 23). Though they are all higher than the 2 percent growth rate of the early 1990s, subtract an average population growth rate of 3 percent and that leaves miserly rates of growth of less than 2 percent in GDP per capita. These rates were insufficient to reduce Africa's average poverty rates, which continue to be among the highest in the world. "Four out of 10 Africans live in absolute poverty and recent evidence suggests that poverty is on the increase. If Africa wants to reduce poverty by half over the next 15 years, it needs to attain and sustain an average annual growth rate of 7 percent—an enormous task" (*The African Observer*, June 7–20, 1999, p. 23).

Agriculture, which employs the bulk of Africa's population, has performed abysmally. Over the postcolonial period 1961 to 1995, "per capita food production in Africa dropped by 12 percent, whereas it advanced by leaps and bounds in developing countries in Asia" (*The Economist*, September 7, 1996). Zaire, now the Democratic Republic of the Congo, exported food when it was the Belgian Congo. Today, it cannot feed itself, nor can postcolonial Zambia, Sierra Leone, and Tanzania. In 1990, about 40 percent of sub-Saharan Africa's food was imported, despite the assertion by the Food and Agriculture Organization of the United Nations that the Congo Basin alone could produce enough food to feed all of sub-Saharan Africa. The situation has deteriorated so rapidly in Nigeria and the Democratic Republic of the Congo that many people eat once a day.

Various Western governments, development agencies, and multilateral development banks (MDBs) have been involved in Africa's postcolonial development and have provided generous assistance, pouring in more than $400 billion since 1960 to support Africa's development efforts. In the 1980s, Africans, who are about 12 percent of the developing world's population, were receiving about 22 percent of the total, and the share per person was higher than anywhere else in the Third World—amounting to about $20, versus about $7 for Latin America and $5 for Asia.

Total African foreign debt rose twenty-four-fold since 1970 to a staggering $350 billion in 1997, which was nearly 68 percent of its yearly GNP, making the region the most heavily indebted in the world. (Latin America's debt amounted to approximately 57 percent of its GNP [UNCTAD, 1998, p. 128]. Currently debt service obligations absorb about 30 percent of export revenue, leaving scant foreign exchange for the importation of capital goods, essential spare parts, and medical supplies. Only about half of the outstanding debts are actually being paid, whereas on the other half, arrearages are continually being rescheduled. A large chunk of Africa's foreign debt—about 80 percent—is owed to Western governments and multilateral financial and development institutions such as the World Bank, the IMF, and the UNDP.

The loans were extended to African governments under various foreign aid programs at concessional rates (below market interest rates with a grace period and a longer term to maturity) to finance development projects and to fund Structural Adjustment Programs (economic restructuring) and democratization programs in Africa. The general consensus among African development analysts is that multilateral lending to Africa has not been effective. It has failed to spur economic growth, arrest Africa's economic atrophy, or promote democracy. The continent is littered with a multitude of "black elephants" (basilicas, grandiose monuments, grand conference halls, and show airports) amid institutional decay, crumbling infrastructure, and environmental degradation. Even the donor community, which supplied much of the capital for development projects, now suffers "donor fatigue" after so many failures.

The situation is particularly precarious because Africa has remained unattractive to foreign investors. As a result, over the decades, ODA replaced private capital as the primary source of development funding. Net foreign direct investment in sub-Saharan Africa dropped dramatically from $1.22 billion in 1982 to $498 million in 1987. From 1989 to mid-1994, over half of British manufacturing companies with African subsidiaries disinvested from those operations. In mid-1989 there were ninety British companies with 336 equity stakes in Anglophone African manufacturing enterprises. By mid-1994 only sixty-five companies with 233 equity stakes remained (*African Business*, May 1995, 16). The French also have become disillusioned: "French direct investment in sub-Saharan Africa ran at $1 billion a year in 1981–1983; by 1988 that had translated into a net outflow of more than $800 million" (*The Economist*, July 21, 1990, 82).

ADJUSTMENT LENDING AND AFRICAN DEVELOPMENT

Africa's experience with development assistance can be divided into four phases. Phase I covers the period from independence in the 1960s to the beginning of the 1970s. During this period, bilateral aid was the main source of development finance in Africa. Private foreign investment was not significant, largely as a result of the socialist rhetoric and policies of African nationalist leaders. There was some recourse to private credit markets in the West, but this was modest and, where utilized, tended to be of very high cost, as in the case of supplier's credit. "Foreign direct investment was limited mainly to minerals and oil extraction, and in some cases to the production of wage goods such as beverages and textiles" (UNCTAD, 1998, p. 116). Although the former colonial powers (Britain, France, and Belgium) provided the bulk of bilateral assistance, other countries such as Canada, Norway, Sweden, the Soviet Union (mainly military aid), and the United States assumed an increasingly prominent role in aid disbursements to Africa.

Phase II began in the early 1970s when multilateral development banks (MDBs), such as the IMF, the World Bank, the European Development Bank, the OPEC Special Fund, the International Fund for Agricultural Development, the UNDP, the Arab Bank for Economic Development in Africa, the African Development Bank, and the Commonwealth Development Corporation, became increasingly important providers of development assistance. For example, in 1970, aid from multilateral sources accounted for only 13 percent of the total; by 1987, that figure had grown to 34 percent. Table 10.1 illustrates the phenomenal growth of multilateral aid in the 1970s, 1980s and 1990s.

By contrast, private commercial lending, including net foreign investment in Africa, has declined sharply, although it picked up in 1994. Between 1990 and 1995 the net yearly flow of foreign direct investment into developing countries quadrupled to over $90 billion, but Africa's share of this fell to only 2.4 percent.[1] According to the World Bank, in 1995 a record $231 billion in foreign investment flowed into the Third World. Singapore by itself attracted $5.8 billion, whereas Africa's share was a paltry 1 percent or $2 billion—less than the sum invested in Chile alone (*The Economist*, November 9, 1996, 95). "Even that meagre proportion has been disputed by some analysts who believe the true figure

Table 10.1
Gross Disbursements of External Loans to Sub-Saharan Africa ($ Millions)

Disbursements	*1970*	*1980*	*1987*	*1990*	*1994*	*1996*
Bilateral (concessional)	432	2,552	4,868	4,915	4,808	4,156
Multilateral	151	1,697	2,345	2,327	1,451	939
Private	593	6,330	3,346	2,533	4,636	4,426
TOTAL	1,176	10,579	10,559	9,775	10,895	9,521

Sources: World Bank, *Financing Adjustment in Sub-Saharan Africa, 1986–1990*; World Bank, *African Development Indicators, 1998–99*; UNCTAD, *Trade and Development Report*, 1998.

to be less than $1 billion, said *The African Observer* (11–24 April 1996, 20)." Although it increased dramatically to $4.7 billion in both 1996 and 1997, it dropped to $3 billion, leading the United Nations' Conference on Trade and Development (UNCTAD) to conclude that "Africa has lost attractiveness as market for Foreign Direct Investment as compared to other developing regions during the last two decades" (*The African Observer*, November 30, to December 13, 1998, 21).

Thus, the MDBs and bilateral donors have simply been filling the void vacated by private commercial lenders. Many of the loans extended by the MDBs during the second phase were project-specific: to fund infrastructural development (roads, dams, telecommunications, and schools)—public goods that were vital for an African country's development. A hydroelectric dam, such as the Akosombo Dam in Ghana financed by the World Bank, for example, generated not only electricity but also provided large "externalities": a low-cost power grid for an industrial base, a man-made lake that could provide income-earning opportunities from tourism and fishing. Road construction and telecommunications also fall in this category, because they facilitate movement of goods and commerce. Similarly, a steady supply of well-educated labor force aids industrial expansion. MDB loans were also used to finance agricultural and industrial projects in Africa, which were largely owned by the state. However, much of Africa's infrastructure has collapsed—for lack of maintenance or destroyed by civil wars for which the MDBs cannot be blamed. In addition, an overwhelming number of these African state-owned enterprises, the sectoral projects funded by the MDBs, were grossly inefficient and unproductive.

Phase III began in the early 1980s when it became apparent that most African economies were in crisis. Although the crises were triggered by the oil price shocks of 1979 and the Third World debt crisis of 1982, there was a general recognition that decades of misguided government policies had contributed immensely to Africa's economic morass. In fact, in May 1986, African leaders themselves collectively admitted on their own accord, in a rare moment of courage and forthrightness, before the United Nations Special Session on Africa that their own capricious and predatory management had contributed greatly to the continent's deepening economic crisis. In particular, they pointed to their own "past policy mistakes," especially the neglect of agriculture. A 1985 OAU Report, which served as the core of the African sermon at the United Nations, urged African nations "to take measures to strengthen incentive schemes, review public investment policies, improve economic management, including greater discipline and efficiency in the use of resources." Most notably, the report pledged that "the positive role of the private sector is to be encouraged."

Subsequently, African leaders agreed to the World Bank's structural adjustment programs (SAPs) in return for World Bank loans to ease balance-of-payment, debt-servicing, and budgetary difficulties. In June 1987, African leaders reaffirmed their determination to pursue the SAPs at a conference organized by the Economic Commission on Africa at Abuja, Nigeria. Under a structural adjustment program, an African country undertook to devalue its currency to bring its overvalued exchange rate in line with its true value. Supposedly a more realistic exchange rate would reduce imports and encourage exports, thereby alleviating the balance-of-trade deficit. The second major thrust of SAP was to reduce the size of the government by reining in soaring government expenditures, removing the plethora of state controls on prices, rents, interest, and the exchange rate, while eliminating subsidies, selling off unprofitable state-owned enterprises, and generally "rationalizing" the public sector to make it more efficient. By 1989, thirty-seven African nations had formally signed up with over $25 billion in Western donor support. It is important to note that SAP was not imposed on African leaders unilaterally without their consent. They willingly and freely consented to adopt SAP.

Phase IV began after the collapse of communism in the Eastern-bloc countries. Western donor governments and the MDBs added various "conditionalities" to aid disbursement: respect for human rights, establishment of multiparty democracy, and the like. For example, on May 13, 1992, the World Bank and Western donor nations suspended most aid to Malawi citing its poor human rights record, a history of repression under its nonagenarian "life-president" Hastings Banda (*Washington Post,* May 14, 1992; p. A16).

The record for both Phases III and IV has been dismal. The democratization process in Africa (the political conditionality) has stalled, and the list of African "economic success stories" touted by the World Bank and the IMF keeps changing and shrinking.

THE PAUCITY OF AFRICAN ECONOMIC SUCCESS STORIES

Adjustment lending has been a miserable fiasco in Africa. According to UNCTAD (1998),

> Despite many years of policy reform, barely any country in the region has successfully completed its adjustment program with a return to sustained growth. Indeed, the path from adjustment to improved performance is, at best, a rough one and, at worst, disappointing dead-end. Of the 15 countries identified as "core adjusters" by the World Bank in 1993, only three (Lesotho, Nigeria and Uganda) are now classified by the IMF as "strong performers." (p. xii)

The World Bank itself evaluated the performance of twenty-nine African countries it had provided more than $20 billion in funding to sponsor structural adjustment programs over a ten-year period, 1981–1991. Its report, *Adjustment Lending in Africa*, released in March 1994, concluded that only six African countries had performed well: The Gambia, Burkina Faso, Ghana, Nigeria, Tanzania, and Zimbabwe. Six out of twenty-nine gives a failure rate in excess of 80 percent. More distressing, the World Bank concluded, "no African country has achieved a sound macro-economic policy stance." A year later, however, this number had shrunk. In The Gambia, a military coup toppled Sir Dawda Jawara on July 24, 1994, quashing any hopes of economic recovery. Continuing political turmoil in Nigeria throttled economic reform, and difficulties became evident in Ghana by 1995 when the World Bank's Operations Evaluation Department noted in its December 1995 report that "although Ghana has been projected as a success story, prospects for satisfactory growth rates and poverty reduction are uncertain."

In 1998, four new countries (Guinea, Lesotho, Eritrea, and Uganda) were identified as the new "success stories." However, the Ethiopian-Eritrean war, the eruption of civil strife following an army takeover in 1998, and the eruption of civil wars in western and northern Uganda have eliminated most of the new "success stories." Table 10.2 provides the list of the African "success stories," whose economic performance can at best be characterized as "mediocre" to "abysmal."

Of the nine African "success stories" listed, six of them had income per capita in 1997 that was less than in 1980. Declining income per capita, used as an indicator of standard of living, can hardly be considered a "success." Prospects for the new millennium remain bleak (Schwab, 2001, p. 5).

WHY STRUCTURAL ADJUSTMENT PROGRAMS FAILED IN AFRICA

A huge emotional debate has erupted over the success or failure of structural adjustment in Africa. Much of the controversy derives from the involvement of

Table 10.2
The Success Stories—GNP per Capita (U.S. dollars)

	1980	1990	1991	1992	1993	1994	1995	1996	1997
Burkina Faso	260	290	310	280	230	200	210	230	240
The Gambia	430	320	330	350	350	340	340	340	350
Ghana	430	390	410	430	410	360	350	360	370
Guinea	...	460	470	480	500	520	540	560	570
Lesotho	440	540	530	590	590	620	660	690	670
Nigeria	710	270	270	280	250	230	220	260	260
Tanzania	...	190	180	160	170	160	170	180	210
Uganda	...	340	260	200	190	190	250	300	330
Zimbabwe	950	920	910	740	670	650	650	710	750

Source: African Development Indicators, 1998–99, p. 35.

the World Bank and International Monetary Fund in Africa's adjustment programs. These two institutions, deservedly or not, have a rather poor image in Africa, and their involvement in any program on the continent draws automatic flak. This is unfortunate because the efficacy of a program should be assessed objectively, regardless of its sponsor.

A program may fail for a variety of reasons. It may be poorly designed and poorly implemented, and this may have nothing to do with the Bretton Woods institutions or the SAP itself, just as Africa's problems with democratization have less to do with sponsoring Western agencies or "the inherent flaws in principle of democracy." In addition, the success or failure of a program depends upon the existence—or lack thereof—of supporting institutional infrastructure. For example, the removal of price controls alone does not automatically establish a free market. Such a market requires the existence of supporting infrastructure and institutions that establish civil society, fairness, due process, and rule of law. These supports include a private press (for the free flow of information), freedom of expression, an independent judiciary/legal system (to uphold the rule of law, enforce market contracts, and protect private property rights), and an independent central bank.

Meaningful market reform cannot endure if the legal system is not functioning and has been replaced with tribunals or kangaroo courts. In the absence of the rule of law, commercial properties can arbitrarily be seized by the state without due process. Where the central bank is under the thumb of the government, the state can gun down the money supply, wreaking disastrous inflationary havoc with fragile financial markets and business decision-making.

Because SAP is often referred to as "the bitter IMF pill," perhaps a more fruitful method of assessment is to use a patient-doctor analogy. A sick patient goes to see a doctor, who performs some tests. After determining the cause of the ailment and making a diagnosis, he prescribes a medicine. Whether the medicine cures the patient or not depends on a host of other variables that have nothing to do with the doctor. For example, to be effective, certain medications must be taken three times a day. It may not work if taken once a week. In addition, the medicine will only work under certain conditions. For example, it should be taken before meals, and the patient, while on the medication, may not consume alcohol or coffee, which may counteract the effectiveness of some drugs. Clearly, a patient who does not follow this regimen would not be cured.

By the late 1980s, it was clear that many African economies were "sick." Their governments saw the "doctor" (the World Bank/IMF), which prescribed SAP. Keep in mind that the World Bank was not the only "doctor" around. If an African government loathed the World Bank and its "fees," there were other "doctors" to consult. After years of "adjusting," however, Africa's economies were not "cured." The reason was simple: Although the pill was the right medicine, it was prescribed by the wrong doctor (World Bank), administered by the wrong nurse (a gangster African state), and implemented using the wrong tactics. Note only one "right" but three "wrongs."

THE RIGHT MEDICINE

In the postcolonial period, African governments, under various ideological guises, arrogated onto themselves the power to intervene in almost every conceivable aspect of their economies, ostensibly for "national development" and to protect the new African nation against "foreign exploitation." They were suspicious of "capitalism" and foreign exploitation, with most of them opting for socialism. Under socialism, a large role was envisaged for state participation in the economy through the operation of state-owned enterprises and the institution of a plethora of state controls.

Subsequently, state controls and state hegemony in the economy became pervasive. The bureaucracy swelled with payrolls padded with government/party supporters. The controls created shortages and opportunities for illicit enrichment by the elites and bred a culture of bribery and corruption. In addition, they killed off the incentive to produce. Inevitably, the state sector became grotesquely inefficient and wasteful. The rot at the government house propelled the military to intervene in politics. Notwithstanding the fact that the soldiers often made matters worse, their primary objective was explicit: to clean house. And most Africans would agree that the state sector had to be cleaned up and government operations rationalized.

The basic thrust of SAP—to grant greater economic freedom to the people—is unassailable. The pervasive control African governments wield over their economies needs to be rolled back. Peasants who produce foodstuffs and cash crops should be allowed to keep a larger portion of their proceeds. Countries that move away from a state-controlled economy toward greater reliance on the private sector generally do better economically. Innumerable examples, from Asia to Latin America and the former Soviet bloc, can be adduced for testimony.

In an effort to test this hypothesis empirically, the Heritage Foundation and the Fraser Institute attempted to find the correlation between economic freedom and wealth around the world over a twenty-year period. Essentially, economic freedom deals with property rights and choice. The two aforementioned organizations defined economic freedom as follows: "Individuals are economically free if property that they have legally acquired is protected from invasions or intrusions by others, and if they are free to use, exchange or give away their property so long as their actions do not violate other people's similar rights" (*The Economist*, January 13, 1996, 21). Thus, economic freedom does not exist when a government arbitrarily can confiscate private property (residential or commercial); conscript individuals for military service or forced labor; can dictate prices at which commodities may be sold and purchased; can restrict access into certain occupations, economic sectors, and markets; can prohibit the production and consumption of certain commodities and services; and even impose on its citizens the use of a currency rendered worthless by reckless monetary policies.

In terms of broad geographic regions, the study found that "apart from a handful of Middle Eastern countries, sub-Saharan Africa was the only area of the world that enjoyed no appreciable improvement in its level of economic freedom between 1975 and 1995"[2] (*The Economist*, January 13, 1996, p. 22). Where economic reform was implemented, the results were spectacular. A few African countries, such as Egypt, Ghana, Mozambique, Tanzania, and Zimbabwe, performed remarkably in the initial phases of reform. Once free of statist controls, Tanzania's agriculture expanded annually at 5 percent in the early 1990s. State-owned enterprises that Tanzania privatized also chalked up spectacular results.

The experience of the Ashanti Goldfields Corporation (AGC) of Ghana is illustrative of the impact of more economic freedom as this once state-owned corporation was privatized. The AGC, which accounts for 20 percent of Ghana's foreign exchange earnings, increased its output from 272,000 ounces in 1987 to 355,700 ounces by the end of 1989. "This represented an increase of 30.8 percent over the last 3 years" (*West Africa*, February 5–11, 1990, 190). Other state-owned enterprises chalked up impressive turnarounds after privatization:

> Most of the enterprises divested by the state have been modernized and brought back to life. The magnificent Golden Tulip Hotel, formerly Continental Hotel, at the time of its divestiture, had about 116 employees. Services at the then hotel were nothing to write home about. Today, the hotel under new management and new name now has 347 employees. The service of the hotel is rated number one in the hospitality industry.
>
> Tema Steel Works at the time also had about 130 employees with very poor production figures. After six years of operation under new management and injection of fresh capital coupled with the modernization of its production line, the company can now boast of about 584 employees.
>
> Alongside the government's stake of 25 percent, Swiss company *Industrie Bau Nord*, with more than 40 years experience in Africa has turned around Tema Food Complex—now Ghana Agro-Food (GAFCO), rehabilitating its plant and machinery, doubling output and increasing its workforce from 494 to 1,600.
>
> The Coca-Cola Company Limited which was formerly a subsidiary of the state-owned Ghana National Trading Corporation had a pre-divestiture employment of about 340. After just three years of operation, the company has increased its workforce to about 530, increased productivity, and added new product lines. The same pattern exists at the Ghana Rubber Estates Limited. Prior to divestiture in 1996, there were about 3,085 workers. Current statistics indicate that the company now has more than 3,833 employees.
>
> Another success story of the privatization program was the divestiture of Ghana Telecom. The company was privatized in December 1996, by selling a 30 percent stake to a consortium of strategic investors led by Telekom Malaysia. Since 1997, when the new managers of Ghana Telecom rehabilitated and installed new facilities, the services of the company have shown remarkable improvement. As at the end of February 1998, the company had delivered more than 27,000 lines and installed more than 1,000 pay phones in most urban cities. This exceeds the contractual agreement of the company to deliver 25,000 direct lines and 300 pay phones. (*Daily Graphic*, January 4, 1999, 23)

These few examples show that macroeconomic restructuring of an economy away from a state-controlled system does work, if pursued with dedication, seriousness, and honesty. As Stephen Buckley, a foreign correspondent, noted in the *Washington Post* (May 25, 1998), after the removal of price controls and providing better incentives to farmers:

Ghana doubled its corn production between 1986 and 1996. Nigeria's corn output leaped by 50 percent between 1990 and 1996. Mozambique, emerging from nearly two decades of civil conflict, has seen agricultural output grow by 50 percent. In the past decade, Ugandans have doubled or tripled production of several main crops. (p. A18)

WRONG DOCTOR

In Africa, the Bretton Woods institutions, deservedly or not, have a rather poor image and low credibility. As such, their involvement in any development program on the continent draws automatic flak and politicizes the issue. The late Julius Nyerere, for example, characterized the World Bank and the IMF as "imperialist institutions and devices by which powerful nations maintain their power over poor nations" (*Time*, January 16, 1984, p. 39). Marxists charge that the real objective of the IMF-sponsored liberalization measures in Africa is not domestic economic recovery but rather the "penetration of imperialist capital." Leftist radicals have denounced conditionality as unwarranted imperialist interference in their internal affairs. "The SAP as a strategy—a monetarist prescription of the supply-side economics variety—however, gave more power to donors in the planning and supervision of domestic African enterprises, and as a result most African countries who espoused SAP are poorer now than they were two decades ago" (*African Link*, First Quarter, 1998, 10). In Kenya, "the World Bank's policies are viewed as a monster that no one wants to hear about" (*The African Observer*, September 28–October 11, 1995, 21).

This kind of emotional rhetoric unnecessarily politicizes the debate and impedes the search for solutions. Additionally, it provides a convenient shield for incompetent African despots to conceal their own failures. They claim acceding to structural adjustment in this atmosphere amounts to succumbing to foreign dictates—a problem compounded by the fact that there is often no African input in the design of the programs—the very people who would be most affected by World Bank decisions.

The World Bank employs the services of management consultants. About 80,000 expatriate consultants work on Africa alone. Less than 0.1 percent are Africans. In 1988, the World Bank spent close to $1 billion on consultants. Most battered has been the World Bank's credibility in Africa. Back in the 1960s and 1970s, it funded disastrous statist policies in such African countries as Cameroon, Ghana, Ivory Coast, Kenya, Nigeria, and Zaire. Imagine the World Bank telling African governments to dismantle the very same statist structures it had helped them build! The World Bank's support for statism was reflected in its lending policies. Most of its loans focused on government-devised infrastructure projects. For example, throughout the 1980s, the Bank committed about 80 percent of its funds to government enterprises, or parastatals.

The IMF, on the other hand, provided less direct support for statism. Its focus was on balance-of-payment disequilibria, and its loans were subject to conditionalities such as devaluation, trimming budget deficits, and general macroeconomic management. However, IMF emphasis and insistence on conditionality and macromanagement had the effect of reinforcing the notion of state management and control. An African government that followed IMF prescriptions would solve its country's economic problems. Nothing could have played more into the hands of Africa's statist governments. "For 30 years, Zambia's statist policies of import-substitution, subsidized food prices and state enterprises were backed by western economic advisers including the World Bank. True, the IMF always disliked them, but then, as one IMF official says privately: 'Why did we lend $1.2 billion to a government whose policies we disapproved of?'" (*The Economist*, July 1, 1995, 34).

As Whitaker (1988) noted: "From the early 1960s on, the World Bank and the International Development Association supplied at least 25 percent of the loans to Africa. Indeed, the World Bank, the United States, and most Africans felt that development would occur by creating industries and services that would expand and diversify the economy. Governments themselves would move into areas that Europeans and Asians nearly monopolized. The United States and the World Bank actively supported national planning as the basis for government activity and their own projects."

WRONG NURSE

To compound the problem, the SAP medicine was administered by the wrong nurse. Too many African reformers lacked legitimacy, credibility, and trust. In fact, some "reformers" were the same incompetents who precipitated the economic crisis in the first place. In Burkina Faso, Ghana, Tanzania, and Zimbabwe, the "reformers" were avowed Marxists and socialists, whose conversion to free-market philosophy was at best dubious. Zimbabwe's president, Robert Mugabe, who in 1980 vowed to institute Marxist-Leninism, finally ditched socialism in 1990 and embraced the free market. Yet at ZANU-PF's preelection congress in Harare in September 1994, he declared ebulliently: "Socialism remains our sworn ideology" (*The African Observer*, January 12, 1995, 9).

In Ghana, the nurse was the Provisional National Defense Council (PNDC)—an unrepentant Marxist regime, heavily imbued with a "control mentality." The regime closely associated itself with Angola, Cuba, the former Soviet bloc, Libya, and Nicaragua's Sandinistas. It did not believe in the medicine, which entailed deregulation and loosening controls on the economy. Nor did it believe in private enterprise and free markets. Foreign investors that were assured that they were welcome in Ghana subsequently were lambasted for "exploiting Africa." The regime's lack of credibility did not arouse public confidence or support in the ERP, which jeopardized its success. More serious, perhaps, was the failure of the military regime to build a constituency for reform; that is, nurture a group or coalition of groups—in urban or rural areas—to support ERP, even among members of the regime itself. Said the Ghanaian newspaper, *The Guide*, in its September 10–16, 1996, editorial: "There was no attempt to convince anyone—not even members of the government—about the rationale for reform. For many Ghanaians, the tendency was to view ERP as a short-term government program that was a basic requirement for receiving aid" (p. 4).

WRONG TACTICS

Even worse was the manner in which the pill was administered. For example, the method chosen by Ghana's PNDC regime was brutal and savage. No attempt was made to cajole or persuade the public to accept belt-tightening. In fact, there was no public debate. Five years after the program started in 1983, the regime scheduled a public debate, that was canceled then finally held in 1997. The PNDC frequently lashed out at workers and threatened to withdraw their right to strike. Nor was any attempt made to associate the Trade Union Congress with the economic recovery program. As one senior TUC official complained: "Since 1983 the TUC has not been consulted. We are not in a position to participate" (Herbst, 1993, 34). In addition, Ghanaian industrialists did not openly embrace ERP because of stiff competition from imports, and market traders did not easily forget the brutal harassment by city officials and confiscation of their wares.

The PNDC made no effort to form peasant organizations. The People Defense Committees (PDCs), which were supposed to do that, proved to be ineffective and a failure. Through their terroristic activities in 1983, the PDCs quickly earned the scorn of the rural population and many chiefs condemned the activities of the PDCs in their areas.

Nor did the PNDC establish the environment conducive to investment. The PNDC made no progress whatsoever in instituting real legal reform. The absence of a well-functioning legal system and the PNDC's own policy blunders, reversals, and inconsistent rhetoric partly explain why the regime has had extreme difficulty in persuading foreigners to invest in Ghana.

Elsewhere in Africa, the commitment to reform has demonstrably been weak. Nigeria's privatization program was implemented halfheartedly with little conviction. The chairman of the Technical Committee on Privatization and Commerce (TCPC) excoriated many state governments for "not doing as much as they should to interest indigenes in the privatization program. He disclosed that some state governments were even refusing to air advertisements concerning the scheme unless they were paid in advance by the TCPC, adding that some state governments were reluctant to grant loans to their employees to enable them to participate in the program" (*West Africa*, February 19–25, 1990, 284). The TCPC was established in 1988 with a mandate to privatize 127 state enterprises. Two years later, only 17 had been privatized. In January 1997, privatization was nixed altogether when Nigeria's military rulers sought to defy what they perceived to be Western free-market orthodoxy.

Little progress was also made in Tanzania. In 1985, Tanzania was offering ideological asylum to 460 state enterprises—the largest collection of such "refugee" enterprises on the continent. Two years later, only 3 had been privatized in spite of the Structural Adjustment agreement signed with the IMF.

In July, 1988, the Tanzanian government under Mwinyi licensed six private companies to set up breweries. Private sector participation was to be allowed to break the decades-old state monopoly on breweries in a restructuring program. But after some of the companies had conducted feasibility studies and arranged financing, the industry and trade minister suddenly abrogated the licenses, claiming that the private breweries would falsify output data and evade taxes. In 1996 George Mbowe became the head of Tanzania's commission to dismantle government-owned entities. Ironically, he also played a key role in the nationalization drive launched by President Nyerere in the 1960s, under the failed socialist program of "*Ujamaa.*" Most industries were nationalized and agriculture collectivized. But within a decade, more than half of the 330 state-run enterprises were bankrupt. Was Mbowe now convinced that "*Ujamaa*" was a failure and privatization was the right policy? "I would not say *Ujamaa* was a failure," he offered. "It's just that the government spread itself too thin, building schools and roads" (*Wall Street Journal*, December 10, 1996, A6).

At the Pan-African Investment Summit on Privatization in Practice, Ishmael Yamson, chairman of Unilever Ghana, dismissed the government's privatization program as "being too slowly implemented. The divestment (privatization) program has already accrued some financial benefit to government, but where has the money gone?" (*The African Observer*, September 13–26, 1999, p. 18).

In many cases, public confidence in the program was shattered by government dishonesty and tomfoolery. For example, "land grabbing has become a common phenomenon in Kenya. Under the guise of privatization, people close to the president, often, like him from the Kalenjin ethnic group, are suddenly awarded title deeds to state land, a school soccer stadium or a site designated for a clinic (which happens to be a prime development plot)" (*The Economist*, April 18, 1998, 42). And believing that economic development occurs in a vacuum, the government of Angola drew up a grandiose Investment Code (Law 13/1988) to attract foreign investors. As *West Africa* magazine questioned: "Why should the foreign investor put money into agriculture, trade or manufacturing in war-torn Angola (or much less Ethiopia, Mozambique, Somalia, Sudan or Uganda) when a host of apparently stable, structurally-adjusting African countries (or better yet, Asian and now Eastern European countries) offer opportunities in the same sector and more?" (March 13–19, 1989, p. 407).

In Benin, reformist Nicephore Soglo railed against nepotism, lack of accountability, and transparency. Yet he was perpetrating the same malpractice: "His wife, a member of parliament, is accused of political tinkering. His brother-in-law is minister of state, the country's second-most powerful position. One of his sons is a special adviser. One of his brothers is an ambassador. Even his bodyguards are said to be relatives" (*Washington Post*, March 18, 1996, A11).

Hopeless inability of reforming African governments to control their own budgetary expenditures did not help matters. For ten years, there was no audit of public accounts in both The Gambia and Ghana. An audit in 1994 revealed an embezzlement of 535,940 *dalasis* at the Ministry of Agriculture and misuse of 60 million *dalasis* by the Gambian Farmers' Cooperative Union. In Ghana, the 1993 Auditor-General's Report detailed a catalog of corrupt practices, administrative ineptitude, and the squandering of over $200 million in public funds. A September 27, 1994, audit in Nigeria revealed that a total of $12.4 billion—more than one third of the country's foreign debt—was squandered by its military "coconutheads" between 1988 and 1994, and since 1994 the Lagos government account has not been audited (*P.M. News*, July 26, 1999).

Politically insecure reforming governments—even military ones—too easily capitulate to special elite interests. The Manufacturing Association of Nigeria opposed the closure of several inefficient industries and even demanded greater protection from the Babangida regime. Riots and demonstrations in 1988 prompted that regime to raise the minimum wage, unfreeze wages in the civil service, and remove the ban on civil service recruitment. The military was completely exempted from budgetary cuts; in fact, Babangida showered the officers of the armed forces with gifts of cars worth half a billion *naira*. His military successor, General Sani Abacha, maintained the controversial dual exchange rate system, which allowed the government to buy foreign exchange at a quarter of its market price, and suspended mass privatization of state-owned corporations.

Elsewhere, top African government officials also exempted themselves from cuts. In 1995 in Zimbabwe, barely a month after Mugabe's government stipulated a 10 percent annual salary increase ceiling, top government officials awarded themselves increases exceeding 50 percent. In Tanzania, senior government officials and major politicians exempted themselves from taxes to the extent that in 1993 there were over 2,000 such exemptions, costing the treasury $113 million.

THE RESISTANCE TO REFORM

For a variety of reasons, African despots are not willing to implement meaningful reform because they are loath to relinquish control or power. They would rather destroy their economies and countries than give up power.

Most African despots have built a cult of personality around themselves with an air of invincibility and infallibility. Their nation's fortunes and destiny are very much tied up with their personalities. Some of them behave as if the country belongs to them, and them alone. Witness their pictures on currencies and in every nook and cranny in the country. Every monument or building of some significance is named after them. They love the self-idolation. Because accepting reform of any kind is an admission of failure or fallibility, they put up all sorts of arcane reasons to block reform. Perhaps, the most famous was President

Daniel Moi's assertion that it took the United States 200 years after its independence in 1776 to establish genuine democracy. So Kenyans who just gained their independence in 1963 should not even dream of asking for it.

Even when African governments restructure, they often do so in a cyclical manner: aborted when the crisis abates and reinstated upon reemergence (Sudan, Equatorial Guinea, Zaire, Liberia). Even during restructuring, measures are often implemented perfunctorily without the conviction and the dedication needed to carry them through. Nigeria, which adopted SAP in 1986, suddenly abandoned its implementation in 1993. In Zambia, President Chiluba, who began "adjusting" the economy soon after his election in 1991, began to waver. In Sierra Leone, President Momoh declared to Parliament on June 2, 1989, that austerity and self-sacrifice must prevail—but not for his government. He explained that the government had continued to fund its activities by printing money, spending in excess of tax revenue, and borrowing from the Central Bank, while the nation's meagre resources were used for imports that were irrelevant to the needs of the economy (*West Africa*, June 12–18, 1989, p. 958).

In other instances, governments may accept reform but willfully sabotage or undermine it to prove that the plan advocated by the World Bank will not work. For instance, President Moi predicted that if Kenya establishes multiparty democracy, it would degenerate into tribal rivalry and strife. Indeed, since 1991, when Moi bowed to external donors and instituted multiparty "democracy," more than 1,500 Kenyans have been killed—mostly Kikuyus but also Luos and Luhyas—and 300,000 have been displaced in ethnic clashes. Said Nairobi lawyer Gitobu Imanyara, "We have a President who is determined to fulfill his prophecy that the country is not cohesive enough for multiparty democracy. His desire is to prove that he is right, even if it means destroying Kenya as a country" (*The Atlantic Monthly*, February 1996, 32).

Second, state controls allow African leaders to extract resources that are used to build personal fortunes and to dispense as patronage to buy political support. Occupying the presidency is a lucrative business. Abacha, Eyadema, Mobutu, Moi, and the other kleptocrats have amassed legendary personal fortunes. "Abacha, the late head of state of Nigeria, increasingly monopolized the oil trade himself," said John Bearman, a London-based oil industry analyst. "There's no deal that does not go through the presidential villa" (*Washington Post*, June 9, 1998, A19). Their business empires will collapse if economic reform strips them of state controls. Economic liberalization may also undermine their ability to maintain their political support base and, thus, prove suicidal. Thus, they profit from their own mismanagement of the economy. A case in point was that of the late General Sani Abacha of Nigeria.

In 1996 and 1997, more than $2 billion was diverted from the country's four state-owned oil refineries by corrupt Finance and Oil ministers, leading to the collapse of the refineries for lack of repairs. An artificial fuel shortage was thus created, forcing Nigeria to import refined fuels, such as gasoline. But almost immediately, the vampire elites saw a profitable opportunity and grabbed that trade too, skimming off a percentage. "The government subsidizes the sale price of gasoline and other fuels, but Abacha loyalists among the officer corps and civil service divert much of the available supply to sell on the black market or to neighboring countries" (*Washington Post*, June 9, 1998, A19).

The institution of "government" has now become so corrupted that what is now proven to exist in many African countries is a pirate or gangster state—a "government" hijacked by a phalanx of crooks who use the instruments of the state to "develop" their own pockets. Severin Tchonkeu, publisher of the independent French-language newspaper in Cameroon, described his government as "a giant organized-crime bazaar" (*Washington Times*, November 5, 1998, A19). When President José Eduardo dos Santos marked his fifty-eighth birthday on August 28, 1999, by raising his champagne glass to make a toast to "the fight against poverty and misery," the Roman Catholic Church in Angola reminded him that "to notch up foreign bank accounts at the cost of hunger, suffering, blood and death of others is a repugnant infamy" (*The Economist*, September 4, 1999, 48).

The third reason is fear. Many of Africa's heads of state have their hands so steeped in blood and their pockets so full of booty that they are afraid all their past gory misdeeds will be exposed if they step down. So they cling to power at all cost, regardless of the consequences.

Another source of resistance comes from the sycophants and supporters, often drawn from the leaders' own tribes. Ethnicity adds an even more dangerous element to the democratic reform issue. It casts the issue into tribal rivalry: One tribe, fearing that it may lose its dominant position in government, may oppose multiparty democracy, while the other excluded tribes may resort to violence to dislodge the ruling tribe from power. In Rwanda,

> Habyarimana's embrace of reform was conspicuously half-hearted, a capitulation to foreign coercion. It was universally understood that the north westerners, who depended on his power and on whom his power increasingly depended, would not readily surrender their percentage. While Habyarimana spoke publicly of a political opening, the *akazu* (the inner mafia-like core) tightened its grip on the machinery of the state. (Gourevitch, 1998, 82)

Other supporters are simply bought: soldiers, with fat paychecks and perks; urban workers with cheap rice and sardines; students with free tuition and hefty allowances; and intellectuals, opposition leaders, and lawyers, with big government posts and Mercedes-Benzes. In Nigeria, "defense and police budgets enjoy the largest slice of the national cake (and even so the figures are understated, since the military imports are paid for with dollars bought cheaply at the government exchange rates)" (*The Economist*, January 25, 1997, 41). Thus, even when the head of state does contemplate stepping down, his supporters and lackeys fiercely resist any cutbacks in government largesse or any attempt to open up the political system.

The final potent source of resistance may come from the elites: high government officials, intellectuals, lecturers, teachers, editors, and civil servants. "There have been numerous strikes against proposed sell-offs of state enterprises as unions fear loss of jobs or reduced benefits. Student activists, academics and others have condemned both the theory and practice of privatization" (*UN Recovery*, April 2000, p. 8). This class benefits immensely from government subsidies and controls. They may have access to free government housing and medical care and government loans for the purchase of cars, refrigerators, and even their own funerals. They too would resist any cutbacks of such government largesse. In Guinea, "progress [on reform] was slow because civil servants and others with a stake in the past sought to preserve it. Dissatisfaction produced a series of coups, the latest in February 1996, when a group of soldiers dissatisfied about going without pay joined forces with others in the military who sought General Conte's ouster" (*Washington Times*, October 17, 1996, A19).

In Zambia, resistance to reform is coming from within President Chiluba's own circle. Some clamor for the continued influence of state spending and patronage. For example, said Mundia Sikatana, a Chiluba adviser and a founder of the Movement for Multiparty Democracy, the government continues to provide vehicles and fuel to hundreds of civil servants. The government, he said, "cannot abandon the old habits. The structural adjustment program is not doing enough" (*Washington Post*, September 12, 1995, A12).

Other members of the elite class may oppose economic liberalization on purely ideological grounds. Africa's intellectual community has a deep-seated aversion to capitalism or free markets. This attitude is a throwback from colonial days, when capitalism and colonialism were confused. The involvement of the World Bank, generally castigated by African intellectuals as a "neocolonial institution" does not help matters.

More important, perhaps, is the fact that a shrinking state sector shatters the elites' dreams. Recall that the ambition of most educated Africans is to become the president or a minister. The state sector is where one makes his fortune. As far as the elites are concerned, there is no life outside the state sector.

To skirt elite opposition, African governments opted for politically safe budget cuts: education, health care, and road maintenance. Sub-Saharan African governments cut spending on education by more than 50 percent in the 1980s. Guinea, Malawi, Tanzania, Zambia, and Senegal slashed education budgets by 18 to 25 percent during the late 1980s. Real per capita spending on healthcare dropped below the 1980 level in over half of sub-Saharan African countries. Critics say those countries opted for politically safe budget cuts rather than slicing into their militaries or other bureaucracies. "They cut places like education because they knew the people wouldn't howl about that," said G.K. Ikiara, an economics professor at the University of Nairobi (*Washington Post*, July 23, 1995, A23). In Zimbabwe, for example, President Robert Mugabe slashed spending on health care and education, while spending $3 million a day on the 11,000 troops he had sent to the Congo" (*Washington Post*, May 5, 2000, p. A23). African governments constantly lament that SAP "hurts the poor." Of course, SAP will do so when these governments exempt the elites and shift the burden of adjustment disproportionately onto the rural poor, especially women and children.

Worse, the cuts on social services and infrastructure undermined the success of SAP. Roads, schools, and telecommunications systems fell apart. Rates of infant and child mortality, child malnutrition, primary school dropout rates, illiteracy, and nonimmunization have all increased. The number of teachers declined as salaries failed to keep pace with inflation. Zimbabwe experienced a mass exodus of doctors (estimated at about 1,400) to neighboring Botswana and South Africa. Communicable diseases such as yellow fever, malaria, and cholera reappeared with vengeance.

To compound the problem, the "politically safe" budget cuts were not enough to reduce budget deficits. With revenue collection systems in shambles, cash-strapped African governments resorted to printing money, which fueled inflation and provoked demands for wage increases. Between 1986 and 1991, Ghana's money supply increased at an astonishing average rate of 43 percent. That, in itself, created more problems as civil servants, teacher, doctors, and other governments, unable to cope with the rising cost of living, had to "invent" ways of living.

In Cameroon, the average civil servant's salary—with the exception of the military and police—was slashed by 70 percent. The wages of doctors, teachers, and engineers were cut to 100 francs ($1.33) a month. As a result,

> Teachers organized private classes. Doctors set up private clinics. In public hospitals, the health minister Lobe Monekosso concedes that only patients who pay "motivation fees" will be attended to quickly. Even journalists working for the state-owned *Cameroon Tribune* newspaper, as well as the electronic media, will refuse to cover an event unless they are offered kickbacks, known in media circles as "gombo." In return for huge sums of money, often as much as 800,000 Cameroon francs, school authorities now admit unqualified candidates from a vast army of the unemployed. The result has been a dramatic drop in the standard of education. The same story applies to Cameroon's medical school, the CUSS, where one million francs can now make you a medical doctor overnight. (*West Africa*, March 13–19, 2000, p. 17)

In sum, most African leaders lack the competence and credibility to institute real reform. Nor are they interested in it. They implement only the bare minimum cosmetic reforms that would ensure continued flow of Western aid.

Thus, the democratization process, which gained momentum after the collapse of communism in 1989, has been stalled by political chicanery and strong-arm tactics. In 1990, only four of the fifty-three African countries were democratic. This tiny number grew to fourteen in 1995 and remained stuck there: Botswana, Benin, Cape Verde Islands, Central African Republic, Madagascar, Malawi, Mali, Mauritius, Namibia, São Tomé & Principe, Senegal, Seychelles, South Africa, and Zambia. Since then, there have been some reversals in Congo (Brazzaville) and Sierra Leone, which saw their democratic experiment brutally terminated in 1997. Thus, political tyranny is still the order of the day.

Incumbent autocrats appoint their own electoral commissioners, empanel a fawning coterie of sycophants to write the constitution, massively pad the voter's register, and hold fraudulent elections to return themselves to power. For example, President Gnassingbe Eyadema of Togo, who has ruled for more than thirty-two years, stood for re-election on June 21, 1998. His Kabye tribesmen, who pack the army, the police, and the bureaucracy, fudged the electoral rolls, intimidated and denied opposition politicians access to the state-run media. Still, when it appeared that Eyadema was losing, paramilitary police halted the vote count, and burned the ballot boxes, as well as the offices of Togo's main opposition leader, Gilchrist Olympio. President Eyadema was then declared the winner. A few months later (September), Mathieu Kegbe Koffi, a member of an opposition party, was killed by an armed group in front of his own family.

CONCLUSION

In conclusion, structural adjustment or economic reform failed in Africa, not so much because it was sponsored by the World Bank. It failed because African despots have not been interested in reforming their abominable political and economic system because that would entail a diminution of their power and the erosion of the patronage system they employ to keep their political base. To them, economic reform is tantamount to suicide. Unfortunately, that is a myopic way of looking at the situation because, in the long run, failure to reform is far more costly and deadly.

Countries that do not reform eventually implode: Liberia (1990), Somalia (1993), Rwanda (1994), Burundi (1996), Zaire (1998), Sierra Leone (1998), Guinea (1999). Increasingly, more and more of their traditional allies are turning against them. At a press conference in London in April, U.N. Secretary-General Kofi Annan lambasted African leaders who, he says, have subverted democracy and lined their pockets with public funds, although he stopped short of naming names. "Billions of dollars of public funds continue to be stashed away by some African leaders—even while roads are crumbling, health systems have failed, school children have neither books nor desks nor teachers and phones do not work," he complained (*The African-American Observer*, April 25–May 1, 2000, p. 10).

The tragedy is, because African despots insist on repeating their own inane mistakes, more countries will explode, and the following are likely candidates: Burkina Faso, Cameroon, Kenya, Togo, Zimbabwe, among others.

NOTES

1. The percentages in the five previous years, beginning with 1990, were: 3.5, 5.2, 3.2, 2.6, and 3.7 percent.
2. This was also cited by Nicholas Eberstadt in the *Washington Times*, October, 1996, 19.

REFERENCES

Gourevitch, P. 1998. *Stories from Rwanda*. New York: Farrar, Straus and Giroux.
Herbst, J. 1993. *The Politics of Reform in Ghana*. Los Angeles, CA: University of California Press.

Schwab, P. 2001. *Africa: A Continent Self-Destructs*. New York: Palgrave.
United Nations, UNCTAD. 1998. *Trade and Development Report*. New York: United Nations Publications.
Whitaker, J. 1988. *How Can Africa Survive?* New York: Harper & Row.
———. 1994. *Adjustment Lending in Africa*. Washington, DC: World Bank Publications.
———. 2000. *African Development Indicators 2000*. Washington, DC: World Bank Publications.

11

Openness and Economic Performance of Developing Countries

Richard E. Mshomba

INTRODUCTION

Among the economic policies prescribed to, and by, developing countries to cure their economic ailments and strengthen their economies, none in the last two decades has been as widely prescribed as "economic openness." Since the early 1980s, the World Bank, the International Monetary Fund (IMF), and other international creditors have made economic openness an explicit precondition for loans and special assistance. Developing countries themselves are members of the World Trade Organization (WTO) and regional economic blocs because of the realized and perceived benefits of openness.

What role does openness (or protection) play in the economic performance of developing countries? This chapter considers the theoretical merits and shortcomings of openness on economic development.[1] It also presents a review and analysis of some empirical studies on openness and provides recommendations for researchers and policy makers.

The fundamental goal of economic policies is to achieve economic growth and economic development. Economic growth can be measured by the trend of the real GDP (or GNP) per capita. Economic development is a broader concept, incorporating not only economic growth but also such factors as income distribution, availability and accessibility of social services, and life expectancy.

Although many empirical studies suggest a positive relationship between economic openness and economic growth (Collier, 1999; Edwards, 1993; Eusufzai, 1998), whether it is openness that causes economic growth or vice versa or they simply sustain each other is still a wide-open empirical question (Esfahani, 1991; Harrison, 1996; Harrison and Hanson, 1999; Jung and Marshall, 1985). In fact, even economic openness itself is under scrutiny and criticism. There have been demonstrations against the policies of the WTO, the World Bank, the IMF, the

Group of Eight (G-8),[2] and overall increasing globalization, by various groups representing different interests.

This chapter is divided into four sections. The second section considers the distinction between economic openness and trade orientation. The third section reviews and analyzes some empirical studies on the impact of openness on economic growth and considers other implications of openness on economic performance more generally. The fourth section offers suggestions for researchers and policy makers. It also includes a table that provides a general idea of countries' openness to trade, their overall economic freedom, and their annual average GNP growth rates.

OPENNESS AND TRADE ORIENTATION

It is important to distinguish between openness (or "outward orientation") and trade orientation and examine methods of measuring a nation's level of openness. These terms, "openness" and "trade orientation," are not synonymous. Openness is the extent to which a country's policies allow the movement of goods, services, and capital between the country and the rest of the world. Trade orientation is the extent to which a country is integrated into the world economy, as measured by trade ratios. Trade ratios are a country's exports and imports as a percentage of gross domestic product (GDP).

Trade ratios are high for most small countries, as shown in Table 11.1. For developing countries, this is explained mainly by the fact that some of their major commodities, such as coffee, cocoa, rubber, and oil, are produced primarily for export. At the same time, these countries depend on the rest of the world for inputs, machinery, and other manufactured goods. The high trade ratios for some countries in Europe reflect the economic integration within the European Union.

Countries with high trade ratios, like most developing countries, do not necessarily have more open trade policies. (See Table 11.1.) Conversely, countries with low trade ratios may actually have more open trade policies. Though trade orientation is determined in part by a country's trade policies, it also depends on such factors as a country's size, the trade policies of trading partners, world prices of a country's major export goods, and the level of domestic vertical integration of economic activities. For example, the fewer forward and backward linkages in production (the lower the level of domestic vertical integration), the more integrated the country is likely to be in the world economy. Due to their relatively small industrial base, developing countries have limited vertical integration compared to developed countries.

EMPIRICAL STUDIES OF THE IMPACT OF OPENNESS ON ECONOMIC PERFORMANCE

In conducting empirical work on the impact of openness, two questions must be addressed at the outset: (a) which measure(s) of openness should be used and

Table 11.1
Economic Freedom and Other Economic Indicators

Rank/Country	Economic Freedom	Trade Policy	Exports/GDP Annual Average 1997-99	GNP Annual A Average Growth Rate 1996-97	1998-99
1 Hong Kong	1.25	1	132	5.2	2.9
2 Singapore	1.30	1	NA	8.8	5.6
3 Bahrain	1.60	2	73	NA	NA
4 New Zealand	1.75	2	30c	1.9	2.7
5 Switzerland	1.90	2	41	NA	1.4
5 United States	1.90	2	11	3.8	4.1
7 United Kingdom	1.95	2	30	3.4	1.7
7 Taiwan	1.95	2	NA	NA	NA
9 Bahamas	2.00	5	NA	NA	NA
9 Netherlands	2.00	2	57	3.2	3.0
11 Czech Republic	2.05	1	60	0.7	-0.5
11 Denmark	2.05	2	36	3.4	1.3
11 Japan	2.05	2	11	0.5	1.0
11 Luxembourg	2.05	2	112	NA	5.1
15 Canada	2.10	2	41	3.6	3.8
15 Belgium	2.10	2	76	NA	1.9
15 United Arab Emirates	2.10	2	72c	NA	NA
18 Australia	2.15	2	20	2.9	3.8
18 Austria	2.15	3	44	2.1	2.3
20 Ireland	2.20	2	84	7.5	8.6
20 Germany	2.20	2	29	NA	1.2
22 Chile	2.25	2	28	7.6	-1.4
23 Finland	2.30	2	38	4.6	3.7
23 Thailand	2.30	3	55	-0.4	4.9
25 Estonia	2.35	2	78	6.4	1.9
26 Kuwait	2.40	2	48	NA	NA
27 Norway	2.45	3	39	4.0	0.6
27 South Korea	2.45	3	42	4.8	11.0
27 Sri Lanka	2.45	3	36	6.9	3.8
27 Sweden	2.45	2	43	1.8	3.9
31 France	2.50	2	26	2.3	2.4
31 Iceland	2.50	2	35	NA	4.9
31 Panama	2.50	4	88	4.3	1.7
34 El Salvador	2.55	3	25	3.5	2.1
34 Trinidad and Tobago	2.55	5	NA	6.4	3.9
36 Cyprus	2.60	3	45	NA	3.3
36 Italy	2.60	3	26	1.3	1.0
36 Jamaica	2.60	2	42	1.9	0.1
36 Malaysia	2.60	5	110	7.5	4.3
36 Portugal	2.60	2	28	3.4	3.1
36 Spain	2.60	2	28	3.2	3.7
42 Argentina	2.65	4	10	6.1	-2.9

(continued)

(b) which measure(s) of economic performance should be used? The answers to these questions are determined, in part, by the availability of data, which is often limited and unreliable. Not surprisingly, even with sound model specifications and reasonable estimation techniques, any results are possible depending on the choice of variables and the choice of data.

Table 11.1 (continued)

Rank/Country	Economic Freedom	Trade Policy	Exports/GDP Annual Average 1997-99	GNP Annual Average Growth Rate 1996-97	1998-99
43 Belize	2.70	5	53	-1.0	4.7
43 Jordan	2.70	4	46	4.4	0.8
43 Uruguay	2.70	2	19	3.4	-3.4
46 Paraguay	2.75	2	26	14.5	-1.5
46 Morocco	2.75	4	23	-2.7	0.6
46 Oman	2.75	3	45	NA	NA
46 Tunisia	2.75	5	43	11.5	6.2
50 Costa Rica	2.80	4	48	2.6	1.5
50 Barbados	2.80	4	52	NA	NA
50 Guatemala	2.80	3	18	3.6	3.2
50 Israel	2.80	2	33	NA	NA
50 Philippines	2.80	5	51	5.8	3.6
50 Saudi Arabia	2.80	4	40	NA	NA
50 Swaziland	2.80	4	82[b]	-0.2	-0.9
50 Turkey	2.80	1	24	8.1	-6.4
50 Western Samoa	2.80	3	NA	NA	NA
59 Bolivia	2.85	2	20	NA	2.2
59 Botswana	2.85	5	52	5.7	4.7
59 Greece	2.85	2	20	3.4	3.3
59 Indonesia	2.85	2	39	4.4	1.9
59 Zambia	2.85	2	32[b]	7.9	2.6
64 Hungary	2.90	4	45[c]	3.9	5.3
64 Peru	2.90	3	14	1.7	3.4
64 Uganda	2.90	4	11[a]	5.3	7.7
67 Benin	2.95	4	27	5.3	5.1
67 Gabon	2.95	5	NA	6.4	-3.9
67 Latvia	2.95	4	49	NA	0.5
67 Lebanon	2.95	2	NA	NA	1.0
67 Malta	2.95	4	88	NA	2.9
67 Namibia	2.95	4	54[c]	3.8	3.0
73 Djibouti	3.00	4	NA	NA	NA
73 South Africa	3.00	5	25	1.3	0.8
75 Ecuador	3.05	3	29[c]	4.4	-12.5
75 Kenya	3.05	4	26	2.3	0.5
75 Slovak Republic	3.05	2	60	6.1	1.0
78 Colombia	3.10	4	16	NA	-1.9
78 Ghana	3.10	4	23[b]	3.1	4.8
78 Lithuania	3.10	2	47	2.7	-4.1
78 Mali	3.10	3	23[c]	6.6	5.8
78 Pakistan	3.10	5	16	2.8	3.6
78 Papua New Guinea	3.10	5	50[c]	-14.0	3.8
78 Slovenia	3.10	4	11[c]	NA	3.5
85 Honduras	3.15	4	45	7.6	-1.3

(continued)

MEASURES OF OPENNESS

Many studies have used in a misguided way, or have been constrained to use, trade ratios as a proxy for openness. In fact, openness can actually reduce trade ratios. For example, if a country that used to subsidize exports (a trade distorting policy) became more open and eliminated export subsidies, its exports/GDP ratio could actually decline. Recent studies have used better measures of open-

Table 11.1 (continued)

Rank/Country	Economic Freedom	Trade Policy	Exports/GDP Annual Average 1997-99	GNP Annual Average Growth Rate	
				1996-97	1998-99
85 Poland	3.15	4	27	6.8	3.4
87 Fiji	3.20	5	61	-0.5	7.8
87 Nigeria	3.20	5	NA	4.2	3.0
89 Algeria	3.25	5	28[c]	2.0	2.8
89 Madagascar	3.25	4	23	4.7	5.5
89 Senegal	3.25	5	32[c]	4.4	5.1
89 Tanzania	3.25	3	14	NA	5.6
93 Mongolia	3.30	3	NA	NA	2.7
94 Brazil	3.35	4	9	2.4	-2.0
94 Cô te d'Ivoire	3.35	5	42[b]	6.9	2.8
94 Mexico	3.35	3	31	8.0	4.1
94 Moldova	3.35	3	NA	NA	16.5
98 Romania	3.40	2	28	-6.6	-3.0
99 Cape Verde	3.44	5	NA	9.9	8.3
100 Armenia	3.45	2	20	5.6	2.7
100 Dominican Republic	3.45	5	47	11.7	8.1
100 Guinea	3.45	5	NA	7.2	3.2
100 Egypt	3.45	5	18	4.9	5.7
104 Burkina Faso	3.50	5	14	6.8	5.2
104 Guyana	3.50	4	81[b]	3.8	3.0
106 Cambodia	3.55	5	NA	NA	4.5
106 Malawi	3.55	5	27	3.1	6.9
108 Bulgaria	3.60	3	50	-6.8	3.0
108 Cameroon	3.60	5	25[b]	8.4	5.0
108 Ethiopia	3.60	4	14[c]	5.3	7.4
108 Gambia	3.60	4	NA	2.2	5.2
108 Nepal	3.60	4	24	2.7	4.6
108 Nicaragua	3.60	5	36	13.5	8.0
108 Venezuela	3.60	4	NA	7.4	-6.8
115 Albania	3.65	3	NA	NA	1.0
115 Lesotho	3.65	4	26	5.2	-0.8
115 Russia	3.65	5	33	NA	1.3
118 Bangladesh	3.70	5	17	5.4	5.0
118 Croatia	3.70	3	NA	NA	-0.3
118 Niger	3.70	5	20[c]	3.6	2.3
118 Zimbabwe	3.70	5	36[a]	2.1	0.0
123 Congo	3.75	5	72	0.5	7.7
123 Ukraine	3.75	4	45	-3.0	-1.2
125 Burundi	3.80	5	9	3.7	-0.5

(continued)

ness, such as deviation of actual from predicted trade flows under free trade, direct measures of trade barriers, the parallel market premium, and direct price comparisons (Harrison, 1996; Harrison and Hanson, 1999). Nonetheless, as Harrison (1996) points out, "no independent measure of so-called 'openness' is free of methodological problems" (425). Harrison and Hanson (1999) expose subtle,

Table 11.1 (continued)

Rank/Country	Economic Freedom	Trade Policy	Exports/GDP Annual Average 1997-99	GNP Annual Average Growth Rate 1996-97	1998-99
125 Chad	3.80	5	NA	6.8	-1.5
125 China	3.80	5	NA	8.9	7.2
125 Mauritania	3.80	5	46[b]	5.9	4.8
129 Belarus	3.85	5	61	11.1	3.4
129 Georgia	3.85	3	NA	NA	4.0
129 Sierra Leone	3.85	4	18	NA	-8.1
132 Yemen	3.90	5	35	NA	-1.3
133 Haiti	4.00	4	13	1.1	3.1
133 Mozambique	4.00	3	11	8.6	8.6
133 Suriname	4.00	5	74[b]	NA	NA
136 Rwanda	4.20	5	6	15.1	7.5
136 Sudan	4.20	5	NA	4.2	6.0
136 Syria	4.20	5	32[c]	2.0	-1.5
136 Dem. Republic of Congo	4.20	4	NA	NA	NA
140 Myanmar	4.30	5	1	NA	NA
141 Angola	4.35	5	NA	15.4	-35.5
142 Azerbaijan	4.60	5	NA	3.1	6.9
143 Iran	4.70	5	NA	1.2	2.1
143 Libya	4.80	5	24	NA	NA
143 Somalia	4.70	5	NA	NA	NA
143 Vietnam	4.70	5	NA	NA	4.2
147 Iraq	4.90	5	NA	NA	NA
148 Cuba	5.00	5	NA	NA	NA
148 Laos	5.00	5	NA	NA	4.0
148 North Korea	5.00	5	NA	NA	NA

Sources: Economic Freedom and Trade policy: Holmes, Kim, et al.(editors), *1997 Index of Economic Freedom,* The Heritage Foundation and Dow Jones Company, Inc., 1997, New York. Export/GDP Annual Average: The Exports/GDP ratios (the value of exports as a percent of GNP) were calculated using data from *International Financial Statistics Yearbook* 2000 and monthly issues, January–July 2001, International Monetary Fund, Washington, D.C. GNP Annual Average Growth Rate: *World Development Report* (1998/99 and 2000/2001), World Bank, Washington, D.C.

*Notes: Countries are ranked according to their economic freedom. The index of "economic freedom" is developed by The Heritage Foundation. According to The Heritage Foundation, "the index of economic freedom measures how well these countries score on a list of ten economic factors. The higher the score, the more government interference in the economy (hence, the less economic freedom there is). The factors are: trade policy, taxation policy, government intervention in the economy, monetary policy, capital flows and foreign investment, banking policy, wage and price controls, property rights, regulation, and black market." The index of "trade policy" (a factor in determining economic freedom) measures the degree to which governments allow or hinder the free flow of foreign commerce. The higher the score, the less open a country is. There are many challenges in measuring openness (let alone, overall economic freedom), as discussed in the chapter. The indices produced by The Heritage Foundation are not necessarily free of error or subjective interpretation. However, they still provide a useful overview of economic freedom.

yet result-inducing flaws in work by Sachs and Warner (1995) who used tariffs, quotas, the parallel market premium, state monopoly on exports, and the degree of socialism in a country to determine openness. For example, Sachs and Warner (1995) used end-of-period average tariffs to test average period growth rates. The critique by Harrison and Hanson (1999) can also be directed to another study by Sachs and Warner (1997) that focused on Africa.

Even where timely nominal tariffs are available, a better measure is the effective rate of protection (ERP). ERP measures actual protection on the domestic value added. The formula for calculating the effective rate of protection is given by:

$$g = \frac{t - \sum a_i t_i}{1 - \sum a_i}$$

where

g is the effective rate of protection;

t is the nominal tariff rate on the final product;

a_i is the ratio of the cost of input i to the price of the final product, at free trade prices; and

t_i is the nominal tariff on input i.

Here is a numerical example. Suppose one wants to determine the level of protection on cotton fabric in two countries, A and B. Suppose the situation in country A is as follows:

t is 40 percent—the nominal tariff rate on cotton fabric;

a_i is 75 percent—the ratio of the cost of cotton to the price of cotton fabric;

and

t_i is 20 percent—the nominal tariff on cotton.

The effective rate of protection on cotton fabric in country A would be:

$$g = \frac{.4 - (.75)\ (.2)}{1 - .75} = 100\%$$

Suppose the situation in country B is as follows:

t is 40 percent—the nominal tariff rate on cotton fabric

a_i is 75 percent—the ratio of the cost of cotton to the price of cotton fabric; and

t_i is 0 percent—no tariff on cotton.

The effective rate of protection on cotton fabric in country B would be:

$$g = \frac{.4 - (.75)\ (0)}{1 - .75} = 160\%$$

In this hypothetical example, if one were simply looking at the nominal tariff rates, both countries would be considered to have the same level of protection on cotton fabric. However, country B has a higher ERP and is, therefore, more protective.

The challenge in measuring openness extends beyond Harrison's methodological concerns to the broader issue of how openness should be defined. Even if data were available to allow various measurements of openness and their aggregation, that would still only provide a quantitative, and not qualitative, measure of openness. Qualitative considerations are ones that would temper the quantitative measures by taking into account reasons for trade policies, such as food and energy security, national security, health factors, equity, preservation of culture, revenue generation, and protection of infant industries. These qualitative considerations have been neglected in empirical studies, partly because there is no agreement on their relevance, and partly because they are difficult, if not impossible, to quantify. Nonetheless, it is hoped future studies will incorporate these qualitative considerations to the extent relevant and possible, especially in cross-sectional studies.

MEASURES OF ECONOMIC PERFORMANCE

The most common measure of economic performance in the context of openness is the growth rate of real gross domestic product (GDP) and/or the growth rate of per-capita real GDP. Economic theory and practice show that openness allows production on the basis of comparative advantage. Openness also has the potential to increase competitiveness, efficiency, the level and quality of investment, and opportunities for economies of scale. The compound benefit is that the real GDP of more open economies grows faster than the real GDP in less open economies, other things being equal.

Economic growth is certainly not the only barometer of performance. Some recent studies have looked at the role of openness on wage differentials, gender inequality, and overall income distribution within countries (Harrison and Hanson, 1999; Eusufzai, 1998; Seguino, 1997). The interest in other performance barometers is driven by economic theory and the need to see the impact of openness on actual development, as determined by the overall standard of living of the population. It also comes from concerns about the potential adverse effects of openness.

According to the basic Heckscher-Ohlin trade model, international trade increases demand for the abundant factor and decreases demand for the scarce factor of domestic production. Owners of the abundant factor gain, and owners of the scarce factor lose. Theoretically, one would expect that in developing countries openness would reduce the relative wage gap between unskilled labor and skilled labor and the income gap between the suppliers of labor and the suppliers of capital. However, the Heckscher-Ohlin model assumes complete mobility of labor and capital, which is hardly the case in developed countries, let alone developing countries. Moreover, openness in developing countries has the potential adverse effect of increasing gender inequality. Openness may shift production from nontradeables to male-dominated tradeables. Openness may also have adverse effects on the environment and may ease trafficking of illegal drugs and small arms.

As data become more available and more reliable, it is likely that there will be more studies using various measures of economic performance. Of course, openness has limited direct impact on real economic development. However, studies that investigate the impact of openness on development are important because they can shed more light on the kind of policies, programs, and regulations needed to complement openness.

With that preface, empirical studies on the impact of openness on economic growth will now be considered. For a survey of some of those studies, see Edwards (1993) and Medina-Smith (2001). In sum, these studies suggest a positive relationship between outward orientation and economic growth. A careful study of developing countries by Harrison (1996) estimates the impact of seven different measures of openness on economic growth and finds that "greater openness is associated with higher growth" (443).

Most studies that have compared and contrasted African countries with Asian countries have concluded that the apparent relative economic success of the latter is due to their relative outward orientation. Though this may prove to be correct and is increasingly accepted, it is important to remember that the studies to date have not conclusively settled the question of the causality between openness and economic growth (Jung and Marshall, 1985; Darrat, 1986; Esfahani, 1991; Harrison, 1996; Eusufzai, 1998; Harrison and Hanson, 1999). Many studies simply assume causality to be in one direction, from openness to economic growth.

Moreover, the conclusion that openness causes economic growth has often been reached on the basis of questionable assumptions. Consider Dollar's study (1992) of ninety-five developing countries for the period 1976–1985. Dollar uses price data estimated by Summers and Heston (1988) that assumes that countries consume the same basket of goods and services. In addition, Dollar makes the following assumptions: (a) Except for the existence of trade barriers and goods that are not traded internationally (nontradeables), the absolute purchasing power parity (PPP) holds;[3] (b) the relative price levels of nontradeables is determined only by relative differences in endowments that cannot be measured, and, therefore, the following assumption is made; (c) GDP per capita is a proxy of relative per capita factor availability; (d) relative price levels are only a function of GDP per capita and population density; and (e) GDP growth is a function only of real exchange rate distortion and variability (estimated under assumptions [b]–[d]), as well as investment. Based on these assumptions, Dollar estimates price distortion caused by trade policies, measured as a ratio of actual prices over some predicted prices. The higher the actual prices relative to predicted prices, the higher the distortion. African countries were found to distort prices the most.

There are significant problems with the assumptions made in Dollar's study. First, although the Penn World Tables estimated by Summers and Heston (1988) may cautiously be used for international comparisons, one must be sensitive to their pitfalls (Heston and Summers, 1996). For example, countries do not consume identical baskets of goods and services. In addition, some of the data used to construct the Penn World Tables is not reliable, particularly for low-income countries. Variables estimated on the basis of such data become even less reliable. In their assessment of the accuracy of the country estimates, Summers and Heston (1988) gave thirty-three out of forty-three African countries in the study a "D," the lowest grade. The rest got a "C" grade. High-income countries got an "A."

The assumption about the purchasing power parity is critical to Dollar's study. Because he assumes that only the existence of trade barriers and nontradeables causes deviation in the PPP, he tries to isolate the deviation caused by the existence of nontradeables. Thus, he regards whatever remains as a measure of price-distorting trade policies. However, deviations from the PPP may reflect other factors such as transportation and information costs, departures from free competition (in production), and different price elasticities of demand.

To the extent that purchasing power parity does not hold due to various factors, the choice of the goods and services for the identical baskets may have an upward bias in prices for countries that are net importers of those goods and services. They import them because they are cheaper where they come from. The relatively large difference between actual prices and predicted prices for African countries, for example, may also reflect the choice of goods and services—not just price distortion.

When one aggregates all these assumptions, it may not be possible to determine the exact nature of a systematic bias that may exist in the study. The main problem with Dollar's study, however, is not so much whether one can determine the exact nature of a systematic bias. Rather, the main problem is that given the bold assumptions, it is difficult to reach sound conclusions. Not surprisingly, Dollar found a number of anomalies and outliers. However, he considered the apparent anomalies to be outweighed by the advantage of applying his specification to a large number of countries.

It is interesting to note that Dollar, who started with 117 countries, omitted developed countries in his final empirical work. The justification for focusing on developing countries only (and omitting 22 developed countries) is that the effect of openness on growth is likely to be substantially different for backward and advanced economies (534). However, if the difference in economic development is so important, how could developing countries, with such a wide disparity in per capita incomes among them, be lumped together, dummy variables notwithstanding? According to the data used by Dollar, the per capita income disparity between two of the countries included in the study, Burundi and Hong

Kong, for example, was 1 to 16. The per capita income disparity between Hong Kong and all the omitted developed countries, except Canada and the United States, was less than 1 to 2.

Assumptions are a necessary evil in any empirical work. Nonetheless, when a study is compounded with a series of unrealistic assumptions and inconsistencies, how are the results to be interpreted?[4] Yet Dollar (1992) goes so far as to conclude:

> The results strongly imply that trade liberalization, devaluation of the real exchange rate, and maintenance of a stable real exchange rate could dramatically improve growth performance in many poor countries. The estimated gains of shifting to an Asian level of outward orientation and real exchange rate stability are increases of 1.5 percentage points in Latin America's per capita growth and 2.1 percentage points in Africa's. (p. 540)

The idea here is not to dismiss Dollar's study nor to suggest that his is the most extreme case. Moreover, economic theory suggests a positive relationship between openness and economic growth. Openness allows production on the basis of comparative advantage. It increases competition and efficiency. In addition to the benefits associated with production, openness provides benefits associated with consumption (exchange of goods). Nonetheless, Dollar's study illustrates conclusions reached by some empirical studies based on questionable assumptions. In addition, the "Dollar openness index" has been used by other studies (Matin, 1992; Merikas et al., 2000) as a measure of openness.

SUGGESTIONS FOR RESEARCHERS AND POLICY MAKERS

The preceding discussion suggests that empirical studies on the role of openness on economic performance still have a long way to go. As more data become available, more suitable measures of trade orientation and economic performance will undoubtedly be used. In addition, as discussed later, it is important for future studies to pay more attention to (a) the salient features of individual countries; (b) the qualitative considerations concerning openness; (c) the microeconomic impact of openness; and (d) the short-run and long-run impact of openness. It is important for both researchers and policy makers to understand these issues.

SALIENT FEATURES OF INDIVIDUAL COUNTRIES

Many empirical studies use groups of countries to compare their economic performance in relation to their degree of openness. There is an apparent economies-of-scale benefit associated with such studies. Moreover, when done carefully, they can provide some broad policy recommendations.

These studies, however, are quite susceptible to error. Developing countries are often lumped together as if they are homogenous. In reality, they can be quite different in terms of real GDP per capita, the stock of physical capital, the infrastructure base, the industrial and export base, trade barriers on their exports, the terms of trade, political systems, judicial systems, educational systems, weather conditions, and so on. Researchers usually try to capture these differences by using dummy variables, but the multitude of dummy variables tends to weaken the studies. Moreover, even when the dummy variables are statistically significant, they do not necessarily reveal the underlying differences. Individual country studies are, therefore, also important to capture the particulars of a given country. See, for example, Medina-Smith (2001), which uses Costa Rica as a case study.

QUALITATIVE CONSIDERATIONS CONCERNING OPENNESS

As described previously, qualitative considerations are ones that would temper the quantitative measures by taking into account reasons for trade policies. Consider, for example, health factors, revenue generation, and infant industries.

The World Heath Organization (WHO) estimates that tobacco-related diseases caused about 4 million deaths globally in 1998. It is further estimated that deaths attributed to tobacco will rise to 10 million annual deaths in about 2030, making tobacco the single greatest cause of death worldwide. This and other external costs (costs to third parties), such as the impact of secondhand smoke on nonsmokers, are instances of market failure. Market failure occurs whenever the price system does not reveal the full social costs. Where market failure occurs, government intervention can be appropriate. Trade barriers on tobacco products, therefore, can be part of a country's public health policy and should not be considered the same way one would consider trade barriers on textiles, for example.

Of course, it could be argued that even with products like tobacco, trade barriers are not the best policy. Other, more selective policies may be more optimal in addressing the market failures. While that may be true, trade barriers on products with external costs nonetheless correct some of the market failures, even though they create their own distortions. Establishing trade barriers on such products is better than doing nothing and just letting the free market reign. According to the theory of second best, if there are market failures in the economy, introducing a trade barrier, though suboptimal, may improve the situation. Thus, trade barriers that serve a public-health-related function should be viewed differently from trade barriers that do not serve such a function.

A lawsuit filed in 1998 by the Pharmaceutical Manufacturers Association in South Africa highlights how trade policy and public health policy can intertwine. The association, representing local subsidiaries of major pharmaceutical companies, challenged a South African law aimed at easing access of AIDS drugs. The South African law gave the Minister of Health the authority to produce or import, at much lower prices, generic versions of AIDS drugs (Cauvin, 2001,

2001a). Although the WHO did not want to be directly involved in the legal standoff, it supported the South African drugs legislation and the rationale of the law, which was to provide affordable medicines to its people, explaining that essential drugs were not ordinary commodities. After a three-year legal battle, in April 2001, the Pharmaceutical Manufacturers Association withdrew its court case against the South African government.

Another qualitative consideration concerning openness relates to the fact that some developing countries have very limited sources of government revenue. A relatively large proportion of output in these countries does not enter commercial channels. In addition, most transactions are not recorded. Therefore, governments have not been able to depend much on income taxes. For this reason, tariffs may be used not primarily as a trade barrier, as they are in developed countries, but rather to generate revenue. The share of revenue generated by import duties and export duties is above 20 percent for some developing countries. The simple average share of revenue generated by custom duties for developed countries in the 1990s was less than 1 percent (IMF, Government Finance Statistics).

Finally, temporary protection of or subsidies for infant industries that have the potential of gaining comparative advantage is not contrary to the principle of free trade. Comparative advantage is not static. Acquiring new skills, either through formal education, experience, or as a spillover from trading with other countries, changes opportunity costs and, thus, comparative advantage. In its purest form, therefore, the infant-industry argument for protection simply acknowledges the dynamic nature of comparative advantage (Fosu, 2000). The celebrated world role models for developing countries—South Korea, Singapore, and Taiwan—initially protected their infant manufacturing industries (under import substitution policies) to give them time to learn by doing (Helleiner, 1990; Edwards, 1993; Grabowski, 1994). East Asian countries pursued dynamic industrial policies marked by government intervention (Singh, 1994). As Helleiner (1990) observed: Virtually all successful exporters of manufactures except Hong Kong began their industrialization with import substitution under significant protection. Protection in support of import substitution may be usefully thought of as a temporary and obviously costly device to assist in the restructuring and development of an infant economy. Its costs are unfortunately, in practice, more certain than its ultimate benefits (888).

Asian countries successfully used the import substitution strategy to cushion their economies against external shocks and provide a stepping-stone toward outward orientation. They "pursued a combined strategy of export promotion in some sectors and import substitution in others" (Schmitz, 1984, 14).

In practice, the infant-industry argument faces several challenges. How is one to determine industries that have the potential for comparative advantage? What is the likelihood of removing protection if the industry remains infant, and therefore in continual need of protection, or if it matures to be a strong political constituency? There is also a question of the actual type of support to be given to the industry. Although a direct subsidy may not be politically popular or fiscally sustainable, it is superior to trade barriers, in terms of the overall costs to a nation. Notwithstanding these and other challenges, measuring openness without regard to policy objectives suggests that openness is a virtue in itself.

MICROECONOMIC IMPACT OF OPENNESS

Empirical studies on the impact of openness on economic growth are macroeconomic in nature. Their results can guide macroeconomic policy, such as exchange rate, interest rate, and overall trade policy. However, microeconomic studies that focus on specific industries or sectors are useful in guiding industrial policies, particularly considering the previous discussion. The point has already been made that economic theory strongly supports openness. History and evidence also tend to support the theory, overall. However, even when openness is (or should be) the ultimate policy goal, microeconomic studies are important to determine how to phase out the liberalization process and which complementary programs to establish. It is important to assess which industries should be liberalized first and at what pace. Consider, for example, Mauritius's successful gradual outward orientation that was borne out of a clear understanding of the individual key industries. The use of export processing zones (EPZs) in Mauritius in the 1970s was a way to liberalize the textile and apparel industry while still protecting other industries. Other industries were liberalized gradually beginning in the 1980s. According to Wellisz and Saw (1993) and Rodrik (1999), the gradual process made openness politically feasible, and it strategically reduced gender income inequality.

The creation of EPZs generated new opportunities for trade and employment (for women) without taking protection away from the import-substituting groups and from privileged male workers. The segmentation of labor markets was particularly crucial, as it prevented the expansion of the EPZ from driving wages up in the rest of the economy, and thereby disadvantaging import-substitution industries. New profit opportunities were created at the margin while old opportunities were left undisturbed. There were no identifiable losers (Rodrik, 1999, 46).

THE SHORT-RUN AND LONG-RUN IMPACT OF OPENNESS

Whatever one may think about openness or protection, it is important to go beyond the short-run impact and consider the long-run impact. Because long-term considerations involve more variables, and perhaps different variables for different countries, it is even more important to conduct empirical studies that explicitly incorporate key salient features of the countries and/or industries. Of course, such studies are limited by data constraints and the challenge of working with complex dynamic models.

In the short run, openness may increase the domestic unemployment rate as import goods displace domestic production. In the long run, as displaced resources have had time to relocate in other industries, the unemployment rate may decline. The same can be said about the short-run and long-run impacts of temporary protection on a potentially competitive industry. Such protection is costly in the beginning. However, in the long run, as the domestic industry matures and becomes competitive, it may not need further protection and the country may see the benefits of the initial protection.

Finally, policy makers must devise effective policies and programs to increase the mobility of resources. Gains from outward orientation accrue in two ways: from specialization in production and from the exchange of goods. They are, therefore, determined by the extent to which both producers and consumers are able to alter their production and consumption, respectively, in response to price signals. The mobility of resources is determined by several factors, including education and training opportunities, investment laws, labor laws, and rules and regulations on capital flows.

Though it is fair to say that openness is, overall, good, it is important to understand that openness is not always just a trade policy. In fact, if that were the case, empirical studies would be less important. We could just rely on trade theory, which is overwhelmingly supportive of openness. In practice, openness or protection may also be, explicitly or implicitly, public health policy, environmental policy, foreign policy, or industrial policy, to mention just a few possibilities.

Policy makers should implement openness guided by clear and sound objectives, while at the same time keeping in mind that trade barriers, even when justifiable, are often only "second best" policy. If the objective, for example, is to reduce consumption and production of tobacco products, a consumption tax and a production tax would be more successful than a tariff. A tariff acts as both a consumption tax and a production subsidy. Whereas the tariff would reduce the overall consumption (thus achieving some positive results in terms of public health), it would also encourage domestic production of tobacco, and thus stand in contradiction to the long-run objective.

In conclusion, policy makers will open their economies deliberately if they understand the advantages of outward orientation. At the same time, they must be cognizant of its limitations and the ways in which it may at times be inconsistent with other policy objectives. Openness, complemented by appropriate policies and programs, should contribute to economic growth and, ultimately, to overall economic development.

NOTES

1. Some of the discussion has been drawn from Mshomba (2000).

2. This group is traditionally called the Group of Seven (G-7), comprising Canada, France, Germany, Italy, Japan, the United Kingdom, and the United States. However, often Russia is invited to the meetings, thus making it the Group of Eight.

3. Absolute PPP implies that the equilibrium exchange rate between two or more countries is given by the price ratios in those countries. For example, if a basket of goods is $100 in the United States and 200,000 cedi in Ghana, the exchange rate should be 2000 cedi per dollar. Another way of explaining PPP is that goods in different countries tend to have the same price when measured in a single currency.

4. A lack of appropriate data, especially for developing countries, has often been used to justify using any other data available.

REFERENCES

Cauvin, H. 2001. "Access to AIDS Drugs at Issue in South African Trail This Week." *New York Times*, March 5.

———. 2001a. "Trial in AIDS Drug Lawsuit Opens in Pretoria." *New York Times*, March 6.

Collier, P. 1999. "Explaining African Economic Performance." *Journal of Economic Literature* 37(1): 64–111.

Darrat, A. 1986. "Trade and Development: The Asian Experience." *The Cato Journal* 6(2): 695–99.

Dollar, D. 1992. "Outward-oriented Developing Economies Really Do Grow More Rapidly: Evidence from 95 LDCs, 1976–1985." *Economic Development and Cultural Change* 40(3): 523–44.

Edwards, S. 1993. "Openness, Trade Liberalization, and Growth in Developing Countries." *Journal of Economic Literature* 31(3): 1358–93.

Esfahani, H. 1991. "Exports, Imports and Economic Growth in Semi-Industrialized Countries." *Journal of Development Economics* 35(1): 93–116.

Eusufzai, Z. 1998. "Do More Open Countries Have a Higher Growth Rate but More Inequality?" *Atlantic Economic Journal* 26(1): 32–43.

Fosu, Augustin, 2000. "Discussion" on "The Joys and Sorrows of Openness: A Review Essay." In *The Determinants of Economic Growth*, edited by M.S. Oosterbaan and N. Van der Windt. Boston: Kluwer Academic Publishers.

Grabowski, R. 1994. "Import Substitution, Export Promotion, and the State in Economic Development." *Journal of Developing Areas* 28(4): 535–54.

Harrison, A. 1996. "Openness and Growth: A Time-Series, Cross-Country Analysis for Developing Countries." *Journal of Development Economics* 48: 419–47.

Harrison, A., and G. Hanson. 1999. "Who Gains from Reform? Some Remaining Puzzles." *Journal of Development Economics* 59: 125–54.

Helleiner, G.K. 1990. "Trade Strategy in Medium-term Adjustments." *World Development* 18(6): 879–97.

Heston, A., and R. Summers. 1996. "International Price and Quantity Comparisons: Potentials and Pitfalls." *American Economic Review* 86(2): 20–24.

Jung, W.S., and P.J. Marshall. 1985. "Exports, Growth and Causality in Developing Countries." *Journal of Development Economics* 18(2): 1–12.

Matin, K. 1992. "Openness and Economic Performance in sub-Saharan Africa: Evidence from Time-Series Cross Country Analysis." *Policy Paper Working Paper No. 1025*, World Bank.

Medina-Smith, E. 2001. "Is the Export Trade-Led Growth Hypothesis Valid for Developing Countries? A Case Study of Costa Rica." *Policy Issues in International Trade and Commodities Study Series No. 7*, United Nations Conference on Trade and Development, Geneva.

Merikas, A. et al. 2000. "Trade Openness and Economic Growth Revisited." *Journal of Applied Business Research* 16(3): 75–85.

Mshomba, R. 2000. *Africa in the Global Economy*. Colorado: Lynne Rienner Publishers.

Rodrik, D. 1999. *The New Global Economy and Developing Countries: Making Openness Work*. Washington, D.C.: Overseas Development Council.

Sachs, J., and A. Warner. 1995. "Economic Reform and the Process of Global Integration." *Brookings Papers on Economic Activity* 1: 1–117.

———. 1997. "Sources of Slow Growth in Africa Economies." *Journal of African Economies* 6(3): 335–76.

Schmitz, H. 1984. "Industrialization Strategies in Less Developed Countries: Some Lessons of Historical Experience." *Journal of Development Studies* 21(1): 1–21.

Seguino, S. 1997. "Export-Led Growth and the Persistence of Gender Inequality in the Newly Industrialized Countries." In *Economic Dimensions of Gender Inequality*, edited by J. Rives and M. Yousefi. Westport, CT: Praeger.

Singh, A. 1994. "Openness and Market Friendly Approach to Development: Learning the Right Lessons from Development Experience." *World Development* 22(12): 1811–23.

Summers, R., and A. Heston. 1988. "A New Set of International Comparisons of Real Product and Price Levels Estimates for 130 Countries, 1950–1985." *Review of Income and Wealth* 34: 1–25.

Wellisz, S., and P. Saw. 1993. "Mauritius." In *The Political Economy of Poverty, Equity, and Growth: Five Open Economies*, edited by R. Findlay and S. Wellisz. New York: Oxford University Press.

12

Government Spending, Human Capital, and Endogenous Growth in Developing Countries

John Baffoe-Bonnie

INTRODUCTION

Recent years have witnessed a proliferation of research under the rubric of endogenous growth models. These models address the characterization of exogenous technological change or population in the Solow (1956) growth model. The argument is that empirical results based on the neoclassical growth models have failed to adequately explain the long-run growth. In fact, as Lucas (1988) and Romer (1989) pointed out, more than half of the growth in output cannot be accounted for using neoclassical growth models. Human capital accumulation and government activities have therefore been identified as alternative sources of sustained growth.

The new development in growth theory has been imbibed by many economic thinkers and has become the cornerstone of the World Bank and the International Monetary Fund's (IMF) economic advice and loan conditionality to its members. Two examples of such advice consistent with the endogenous growth model are government spending and investment in human capital, which have become yardsticks for assessing the impact of the new theory. This chapter is aimed at developing a closed economy endogenous growth model, which incorporates government spending and human capital and assesses their dynamic impacts on growth in some developing countries from 1960 to 1996.

The application of the model to developing countries is of interest for at least two reasons. First, most developing countries depend heavily on services provided by the public sector and less on the private sector. The dependency on and the growth of the public sector in developing countries have been cited as causes of the decline or the poor growth that face developing countries (Landau, 1983; Marsden, 1983; Diamond, 1989; Engen and Skinner, 1991; and Barro, 1991). Second, following the human capital revolution in the early 1960s, many governments in developing countries expanded their investment on human capital, such as education, to the detriment of other sectors. Empirical studies have consistently proven that improvement in human capital is an engine of growth. What this chapter seeks to demonstrate is that government spending that is human capital-intensive is likely to encourage growth. We deviate from the traditional neoclassical growth models in which technological progress is not explained by economic forces. We follow the recent endogenous growth models and assume that technological progress is positively related to the accumulation of human knowledge. That is, the higher the level of accumulated human capital, the faster is technological progress.

The effectiveness and direction of government spending on growth have been inconclusive in the empirical literature. Whereas some studies have found a positive and significant impact of government spending on economic growth (Ram, 1986, 1989), others have reported a negative and small impact of government spending on growth. The two divergent findings seem to suggest that we should examine the type of government spending and the interaction that such spending has with other sectors of the economy.[1] Several studies have provided evidence that an educated populace is an engine to economic growth (Barro, 1991; Mankiw et al., 1992; and Levine and Renelt, 1992). A larger educated workforce may increase growth either because of faster technological progress, as individuals build on the ideas of others, or by simply adding to productive capacity of a country.

Because human capital and government spending have been stressed as a prerequisite for economic growth, we concentrate on how these important determinants affect growth through time in developing countries. We begin by examining the relationships among the proportions of government spending on education, on goods and services, on physical capital, and the annual per capita growth rate of output in fourteen developing economies. Following the argument that growth rates may differ across countries for a long time due to differences in levels of human capital, we group the selected countries according to the level of human development using the human development index.[2]

THE MODEL

The model described here combines Barro (1990) government spending, Lucas (1988) human capital accumulation, King and Rebelo (1990) tax formulation, and the Barro (1990) utility function. We develop a model in which there are two production sectors, and both physical and human capital accumulation are endogenously determined. We also introduce direct government spending on schooling.

Consider an economy where an infinitely lived individual has an instantaneous utility function, u, which exhibits constant intertemporal elasticity of substitution of consumption, α, and is assumed to have a time-separable preference,

ρ. The production sector consists of physical output (y), human capital (h), and physical capital (k). Let θ denote a fraction of time used for the production of consumable and investment goods, and $(1 - \theta)$ the time allocated to the accumulation of human capital (i.e., schooling, on-the-job training).[3] The production of each firm is assumed to take the Cobb-Douglas form as in Lucas (1988):

$$y = Ak^{\beta}(\theta h)^{1-\beta} \tag{1}$$

where $A > 0$ is an exogenous technological factor capturing knowledge (which is not specific to an individual) and other omitted production function factors (such as land and energy inputs). If we consider public investment on human capital, the technology that describes the production of human capital in the economy is given by:[4]

$$h = \varphi g^{\gamma}[(1 - \theta)h]^{1-\gamma} \tag{2}$$

where φ is a productivity parameter as in Lucas (1988), g is government spending, γ is the share of public expenditures in the educational sector, and $(1 - \gamma)$ is the share of private investment in the human capital production. In this formulation, total human capital accumulation is determined by both government spending and private expenditures. Assuming that human capital depreciates at a rate δ, the evolution or the dynamic equation of human capital accumulation can be expressed as:

$$\dot{h} = \varphi g^{y}[(1 - \theta)h]^{1-y} - \delta h \tag{3}$$

Equation (3) demonstrates that the evolution of human capital depends upon the government expenditures on education, private acquisition of education, and depreciation of human capital through time. The physical capital accumulation is given by:

$$\dot{h} = y - g - c - \delta k \tag{4}$$

where c is per capita private consumption. In the absence of government debt, the government budget constraint is simply:

$$g = ty \tag{5}$$

where t is the average tax rate. Given all preferences and production parameters, the representative individual, and in the spirit of Barro's (1990) utility function, the individual maximizes an intertemporal utility function,

$$u = \int_0^{\infty} (c_t^{1-\alpha} - 1)\,(1 - \alpha)^{-1}\, e^{-\rho t}\, dt \tag{6}$$

subject to the human capital accumulation equation (3), physical capital accumulation equation (4), the government budget constraint equation (5), the production function equation (1), and the transversality conditions (i.e., $\lim_{t\to 0} \lambda(t)\, k(t) = 0$; $\lim_{t\to 0} m(t)\, h(t) = 0$).

The Hamiltonian of this dynamic optimization problem can be expressed as:

$$H = u(c)e^{-\rho t} + [v(\dot{h} + \dot{k}) + w(g + y)] \tag{7}$$

where v is the shadow price associated with $\dot{h}$ and $\dot{k}$ The growth rates of c, k, h, g, and y can be derived by solving the first-order conditions of equation (7). In the steady-state,

$$\lambda = \dot{c}/c = \dot{k}/k = \dot{h}/h = \dot{g}/g = \dot{y}/y.$$

It can be shown that the growth rate of output depends on the share of government spending on education (γ), the ratio of government spending on goods and services to output (g/y), and the share of physical capital in output (β).[5]

SPECIFICATION OF THE MODEL

We employ the vector autoregression (VAR) pioneered by Sims (1980) to examine the dynamic relationships among four of the variables in the proceding model. The use of VAR is appropriate because it traces how each endogenous variable in the model responds over time to a shock in that variable and in every other endogenous variable. The impulse response analysis (or synonymously, variance decomposition) traces the response of the endogenous variable to such shocks.

The VAR model to be estimated is represented by:

$$\begin{pmatrix} z_{1t} \\ z_{2t} \\ z_{3t} \\ z_{4t} \end{pmatrix} = \begin{pmatrix} b_{10} \\ b_{20} \\ b_{30} \\ b_{40} \end{pmatrix} + \begin{pmatrix} a_{11}(L) & a_{12}(L) & a_{13}(L) & a_{14}(L) \\ a_{21}(L) & a_{22}(L) & a_{23}(L) & a_{24}(L) \\ a_{31}(L) & a_{32}(L) & a_{33}(L) & a_{34}(L) \\ a_{41}(L) & a_{42}(L) & a_{43}(L) & a_{44}(L) \end{pmatrix} \begin{pmatrix} z_{1t-1} \\ z_{2t-1} \\ z_{3t-1} \\ z_{4t-1} \end{pmatrix} + \begin{pmatrix} V_{1t} \\ V_{2t} \\ V_{3t} \\ V_{4t} \end{pmatrix} \tag{8}$$

where

z_{it} = the variables in the system.
b_{i0} = the parameters representing the intercept terms
a_{ij} = the polynomials in lag operator L.
v_{it} = white-noise disturbances.

In a more compact form, equation (8) can be written as:

$$z_t = b_0 + a(L)z_{t-1} + v_t \tag{9}$$

where $z' = (z_1, z_2, z_3, z_4)$, is the vector of endogenous variables, b_0 is a 4×4 matrix, $a(\cdot)$ is a 4×4 matrix of polynomial in lag operator L, and v is a 4×1 vector of the unobservable disturbances. Since the right-hand sides of the equations in the system contain only the predetermined variables, the error terms are assumed to be serially uncorrelated with constant variance and zero mean. Hence, each equation in the system can be estimated using OLS. Moreover, OLS estimates are consistent and asymptotically efficient. Even though the error terms are correlated across equations, seemingly unrelated regression (SUR) does not add to the efficiency of the estimation procedure because all regressions have identical right-hand-side variables. The VAR model presented earlier indicates that the current innovations (v_t) are unanticipated but become part of the information set in the next period. The implication is that the anticipated impact of a variable is captured in the coefficients of lagged polynomials, whereas the residuals capture unforeseen contemporaneous events. A joint F-test on the lagged polynomials provides information regarding the impact of the anticipated portion of the right-hand-side variables. The impact of the unanticipated variable shocks (i.e., changes in government expenditures, education expenditures, and investment) on the growth rate of gross domestic product can be analyzed by employing the "impulse response functions" (IRF) and "variance decompositions" (VDCs) that are obtained from a moving average representation of the VAR model.

DATA ANALYSIS

The model is estimated using yearly data from 1960 to 1996. The variables included in the VAR model are the annual per capita growth rate of output (GDPR), the share of government expenditures on goods and services (GCON), total private investment as a percentage of gross domestic product (INV), and the total government expenditures on education as a percentage of gross domestic product (EDUX). We ignore taxes because of lack of data for many of the countries. We refer to GDPR as the target variable, and GCON, INV, and EDUX as the policy variables. Because our main interest is to investigate how changes in the policy variables affect the target variable (GDPR), the policy variables are expressed in changes. The data series are taken from the World Bank's World Development Indicators CD-ROM, 1998. All the variables are in real terms and expressed in logarithms. Yearly data are used instead of quarterly data because of the difficulty of obtaining quarterly data.

UNIT ROOT AND COINTEGRATION TESTS

Certain properties of the variables in the model must be checked in order to determine the appropriate specification for estimation purposes. First, it is necessary to determine whether the variables are difference stationary or trend stationary. This is done by testing the null hypothesis that each variable included in the model contains a unit root. If the variables are difference stationary, it is appropriate to estimate the VAR model by using the first difference of the variables. If the variables are trend stationary, the VAR model may be estimated by taking the residuals from a deterministic trend. Second, if the variables are difference stationary, it is necessary to establish whether the variables in the model share a common trend. If they do not, estimation of a VAR model in the first difference is appropriate. The unit root test involves testing whether the coefficient of the least square estimate, β_1, in the following equation,

$$\Delta y_t = \alpha_0 + \alpha_1 t + \beta_1 y_{t-1} + \sum_{i=2}^{n} \beta_i y_{t-i} \tag{10}$$

is equal to unity. The unit root test results should be interpreted with caution. Research has shown that the test for unit roots has a low ability to reject the null hypothesis of a unit root when it is false against plausible alternatives (Dejong and Whiteman, 1991). The unit roots are tested by using the Augmented Dickey-Fuller (1979) and Phillips-Perron (1988) tests. The results of these tests are reported in Table 12.1. Both test results suggest that all the variables are difference stationary.

Although these results indicate that the model variables are nonstationary when considered individually, it is possible that a stationary linear combination of the variables may be found, and the variables are then said to be cointegrated. When variables are cointegrated, estimating a VAR model where the variables are expressed in first differences would be inappropriate because first differencing would remove important information about the behavior of the variables contained in the common trend. Engle and Granger (1987) demonstrate that an error correction model is the appropriate model if the variables are cointegrated rather than a VAR in first differences. In the literature, a number of tests for cointegration have been developed. The cointegration test adopted is the Johansen and Juselius (1990) trace and maximum eigenvalue tests. The trace test is a test of the hypothesis that there are at most r cointegrating vectors or relations against the alternative hypothesis of full rank—that is, all series in the VAR are stationary. The maximum eigenvalue test is a test of the hypothesis that there are r cointegrating vectors (the number of cointegrating relations) against the alternative hypothesis that there are $r+1$ vectors.

Tables 12.2a and 12.2b indicate that the variables are not cointegrated and that the variables can be estimated by the VAR model because the moving-average coefficient matrix is nonsingular.

ESTIMATION AND EMPIRICAL RESULTS

Before estimating the model, the lag length must be chosen. The choice of the lag length was determined by using the Akaike Information Criterion (1973), which indicated a maximum lag length equal to 2. This was confirmed by employing the likelihood ratio test suggested by Sims (1980). I tested two lags versus a several lags specification and the results suggested that I could not reject the null hypothesis that two lags are sufficient.

Table 12.1
Test for Unit Roots Data in log levels [with constant and trend][1], and log difference [with constant]

	Augmented Dickey-Fuller Test				Phillips-Perron Test			
Variable	GDPR	GCON	INV	EDUX	GDPR	GCON	INV	EDUX
Low Human Development Countries								
Côte D'Ivoire	-2.81[c] (-3.13)	-4.01[a] (-0.82)	-3.02[b] (-1.96)	-6.80[a] (-1.47)	-6.48[a] (-2.06)	-4.73[a] (-0.74)	-5.37[a] (-2.03)	-8.57[a] (-2.23)
Ghana	-4.89[a] (-3.11)	-4.84[a] (-2.52)	-4.36[a] (-2.88)	-6.04[a] (-3.15)	-12.14[a] (5.93)[a]	-4.84[a] (-2.17)	-7.51[a] (-2.45)	-4.59[a] (-2.67)
India	-5.30[a] (-4.64)[a]	-4.70[a] (-2.55)	-5.10[a] (-2.70)	-6.33[a] (-2.36)	-11.75[a] (-5.53)	-7.70[a] (-3.00)	-6.88[a] (-3.05)	-17.58[a] (-2.36)
Kenya	-2.96[c] (-3.80)	-5.76[a] (-1.40)	-4.83[b] (-2.49)	-5.42[a] (-2.44)	-4.57[a] (-3.03)	-6.84[a] (-1.57)	-5.02[a] (-2.02)	-8.26[a] (-3.56)
Pakistan	-7.48[a] (-3.29)[c]	-4.04[a] (-2.19)	-3.80[b] (-2.76)	-7.58[a] (-1.44)	-16.61[a] (-7.46)[a]	-5.92[a] (-2.48)	-5.56[a] (-3.36)[b]	-7.58[a] (-3.90)[b]
Medium Human Development Countries								
Egypt	-5.29[a] (-2.11)	-4.93[a] (-2.19)	-4.12[a] (-1.75)	-4.37[a] (-2.33)	-10.36[a] (-3.50)[c]	-7.22[a] (-2.13)	-4.15[a] (-1.36)	-5.37[a] (-2.59)
Peru	-3.35[b] (-4.57)[a]	-5.02[a] (-2.23)	-3.91[a] (-3.13)	-5.24[a] (-2.14)	-4.91[a] (-3.61)	-7.49[a] (-2.83)	-3.91[a] (-2.16)	-8.46[a] (-2.80)
Philippines	-5.26[a] (-3.60)[b]	-3.90[a] (-1.30)	-4.70[a] (-2.27)	-4.49[a] (-2.68)	-6.26[a] (-4.15)[b]	-5.89[a] (-1.55)	-5.12[a] (-2.24)	-4.49[a] (-3.01)
South Africa	-6.31[a] (-3.59)[b]	-4.98[a] (-3.87)[b]	-4.48[a] (-2.24)	-4.32[a] (-3.11)	-8.00[a] (-3.88)[b]	-6.17[a] (-3.19)	-4.58[a] (-1.45)	-8.91[a] (-5.39)[a]
High Human Development Countries								
Argentina	-3.44[b] (-2.63)	-5.61[a] (-3.99)[b]	-4.37[a] (-3.39)	-5.48[a] (-2.08)	-6.77[a] (-3.64)[b]	-8.44[a] (-4.21)[b]	-6.70[a] (-3.10)	-7.12[a] (-2.40)
Chile	-5.48[a] (-3.94)[b]	-5.02[a] (-1.23)	-5.73[a] (-2.22)	-5.06[a] (-2.85)	-8.53[a] (-5.04)[a]	-7.09[a] (-1.23)	-5.98[a] (-1.99)	-7.44[a] (-2.93)
Jamaica	-3.35[b] (-1.01)	-2.66[c] (-1.36)	-4.28[a] (-1.46)	-7.76[a] (2.18)	-9.30[a] (-2.23)	-7.54[a] (-1.64)	-5.82[a] (-1.59)	-8.27[a] (-2.67)
Malaysia	-6.90[a] (-5.60)[a]	-5.12[a] (-1.97)	-4.03[a] (-3.12)	-4.22[a] (-1.25)	-11.06[a] (-7.93)[a]	-6.96[a] (-2.08)	-4.45[a] (-3.02)	-9.53[a] (-2.48)
Mexico	-5.36[a] (-3.91)[b]	-4.04[a] (-1.78)	-4.00[a] (-2.18)	-5.05[a] (-3.44)	-7.28[a] (-2.90)	-5.70[a] (-1.82)	-5.76[a] (-1.88)	-7.58[a] (-2.78)

[1]log levels in parentheses.

[a] Reject the null hypothesis (unit root) at 1% significance level.

[b] Reject the null hypothesis (unit root) at 5% significance level.

[c] Reject the null hypothesis (unit root) at 10% significance level. Critical values (levels in parentheses) are: 1% = −3.89 (−4.24); 5% = −3.05 (−3.54); 10% = −2.66 (−3.20).

Table 12.2a
Test for Cointegration (trace test)

r ≤	0	1	2	3
Low Human Development Countries				
Côte d'Ivoire	46.27	18.14	9.41	2.36
Ghana	68.97	26.00	11.90	3.06
India	57.17	17.01	3.13	0.0023
Kenya	46.76	25.11	8.99	2.72
Pakistan	55.49	33.81	16.49	4.13
Medium Human Development Countries				
Egypt	38.77	21.13	9.96	1.58
Peru	95.48	50.23	15.85	4.58
Philippines	37.84	17.10	7.15	0.29
South Africa	33.71	17.79	3.88	0.42
High Human Development Countries				
Argentina	69.12	27.09	6.37	0.85
Chile	51.47	19.06	5.32	0.29
Jamaica	38.77	12.53	4.49	0.10
Malaysia	71.54	34.27	9.46	1.16
Mexico	50.35	23.87	1.77	0.15

Table 12.2b
Test for Cointegration (maximum eigenvalue test)

r =	0	1	2	3
Low Human Development Countries				
Côte d'Ivoire	28.13	8.73	7.05	2.36
Ghana	42.97	14.10	8.84	3.06
India	40.16	13.88	3.13	0.0023
Kenya	21.65	16.12	6.27	2.72
Pakistan	22.13	17.32	12.36	4.13
Medium Human Development Countries				
Egypt	17.64	11.17	8.38	1.58
Peru	45.25	34.38	11.27	4.58
Philippines	20.74	9.95	6.86	0.29
South Africa	15.92	13.91	3.46	0.42
High Human Development Countries				
Argentina	42.03	20.72	5.52	0.85
Chile	32.41	13.74	5.03	0.29
Jamaica	26.24	8.04	4.39	0.10
Malaysia	37.27	24.81	8.30	1.16
Mexico	26.48	22.10	1.62	0.15

For trace test, 5% critical values are: r = 0(47.21), r ≤1(29.68), r ≤2(15.41), r ≤3(3.76). For maximum eigenvalue test, 5% critical values are: r = 0(45.4), r = 1(39.5), r = 2(33.6) r = 3(27.1). The critical values are from Osterwald-Lenum, 1992, page 468, Table 1.

F-TEST RESULTS

The estimation of the VAR model yields nine coefficients for each of the four equations in the system. As discussed earlier, the significance levels of the F-tests provide a summary for analyzing the impact of the input variables (*GCON*, *INV*, and *EDUX*) on the target variable (*GDPR*). The significance levels of the test, which is based on the hypothesis that all the lags of a given variable in a particular equation are zero, are reported in Table 12.3. For instance, the value of 0.13 (row 1 and column 5) in the Côte d'Ivoire results indicates that the hypothesis of two lagged coefficients of changes in educational expenditures in the annual per capita growth rate of GDP equation being equal to zero is accepted 13 times out of 100 and rejected as many as 87 times.[6] Table 12.3 also shows that fiscal policy (changes in government spending) is exogenous and is not influenced by other variables, except in Peru where fiscal policy is influenced by investment and the changes in educational expenditures. Also, except for Jamaica and Mexico, anticipated changes in private investment, government spending, and the annual per capita growth rate do not have much influence on changes in educational expenditures. For most of the countries, private investment is influenced by changes in government expenditures, the growth rate of GDP and changes in educational expenditures.

The results reveal that the main target variable, the annual per capita growth rate, is not influenced by anticipated fiscal policy in most of the developing economies. However, in the countries where anticipated fiscal policy influences *GDPR*, *INV*, and *EDUX*, the impact is strong. The growth rates of countries like Côte d'Ivoire, South Africa, Argentina, and Chile seem to respond to anticipated changes in government spending. Changes in private investment seem to be ineffective in influencing the annual per capita growth rate. The *GDPR* of a few countries such as Kenya, Egypt, Peru, and South Africa do mildly respond to anticipated changes in private investment. Human capital has the least impact on the annual per capita growth rate of the developing countries. The only countries whose annual per capita growth rates were influenced by changes in educational expenditures are India and Peru. In fact, the only country whose growth rate responds to changes in anticipated *GCON*, *INV*, and *EDUX* is Peru. The results seem to suggest that fiscal policy, investment in physical capital, and human capital may not be effective in changing the short-run growth rates of most of the developing countries.

DYNAMIC RESPONSES

The results in Table 12.3, so far, only enable us to analyze the impact of anticipated changes in government spending, private investment, and educational expenditures on the annual per capita growth rate. They do not give us a clear understanding of the dynamic behavior of the model. The impulse response coefficients provide information to analyze the dynamic behavior of a variable due to a random shock or innovation in other variables.

The impulse response traces the effect on current and future values of the endogenous variables of 1 standard deviation shock to the variables. To identify orthogonalized innovations in each of the variables and the dynamic responses to such innovations, we factor the variance-covariance matrix of the VAR using the Choleski decomposition method suggested by Doan (1989).[7] Sims (1980) has suggested that the graphs of the impulse response coefficients provide a better device to analyze the shocks. Figure 12.1 depicts the impulse response functions for annual per capita growth rates in response to changes in the government spending, private investment, and educational expenditures. In order to capture the dynamic effects, we consider responses over a ten-year period to a 1 standard deviation shock in these three policy variables. Only the impulse responses of the target variable (*GDPR*) to shocks in the policy variables (*GCON, INV,* and *EDUX*) have been presented because the main focus of the study is to analyze the dynamic impacts on the annual per capita growth rate from shocks in the policy variables. Figure 12.1 also illustrates the two standard error bands (two standard deviation confidence intervals) of the dynamics of the impulse responses. The error bands are obtained by using a Monte Carlo simulation procedure with 1,000 replications. There is no consensus on the explicit criteria for significance in VAR analysis. Runkle (1987) argues that a useful criterion for significance is to require that the posterior probability range be completely above 10 percent in variance decompositions. Sims (1987), on the other hand, refers to the impulse response functions and attributes significance to whether responses to a variable are large and bounded away from 0.[8] In Figure 12.1, the two standard error bands around the impulse responses generated from a shock in *GCON, INV,* and *EDUX,* in a number of cases, widen moderately for the entire period, and in a few cases the bands drift toward 0 in the long run, especially the responses in Pakistan and Jamaica.

The first row under each country in Figure 12.1 illustrates the dynamic response of *GDPR* to a 1 standard deviation shock in government spending, while rows two and three show the responses generated by a 1 standard deviation shock in the private investment and educational expenditures variables, respectively.

The impulse responses show that some countries, such as Ghana, India, Kenya, Egypt, Peru, Philippines, and Malaysia, experience a small increase in their *GDPR* due to a shock in *GCON*. For such countries, the positive impact occurs in the first two years and dies out after the third year. In countries whose *GCON* generates a negative shock to *GDPR*, the decline in *GDPR* lasts for about two years, and there is virtually no significant effect in the subsequent years. Countries like Côte d'Ivoire, South Africa, Argentina, and Chile that experience a relatively greater decline in their *GDPR* in the first two years of the *GCON* shock, have their *GDPR* converging to 0 in the tenth year of the shock. These dynamic

Table 12.3
Significance Level of F-test

	GDPR	GCON	INV	EDUX		GDPR	GCON	INV	EDUX
	CÔTE D'IVOIRE					**PHILIPPINES**			
GDPR	0.61	0.002[a]	0.66	0.13	GDPR	0.07[b]	0.003[b]	0.21	0.25
GCON	0.56	0.001[a]	0.39	0.68	GCON	0.12	0.001[a]	0.03[b]	0.11[b]
INV	0.03[b]	0.11[b]	0.001[a]	0.24	INV	0.59	0.17	0.001[a]	0.14[b]
EDUX	0.80	0.34	0.98	0.001[a]	EDUX	0.86	0.46	0.90	0.003[a]
	GHANA					**SOUTH AFRICA**			
GDPR	0.30	0.94	0.80	0.59	GDPR	0.04[b]	0.004[a]	0.002[a]	0.67
GCON	0.54	0.001[a]	0.48	0.88	GCON	0.83	0.005[a]	0.67	0.48
INV	0.07[b]	0.83	0.001[a]	0.20	INV	0.05b	0.39	0.001[a]	0.37
EDUX	0.83	0.28	0.93	0.12[b]	EDUX	0.22	0.03[b]	0.17	0.001[a]
	INDIA					**ARGENTINA**			
GDPR	0.72	0.52	0.78	0.002[b]	GDPR	0.34	0.004[a]	0.97	0.11
GCON	0.71	0.009[b]	0.25	0.95	GCON	0.65	0.64	0.74	0.12
INV	0.70	0.28	0.001[a]	0.97	INV	0.72	0.24	0.03[b]	0.70
EDUX	0.38	0.73	0.68	0.001[a]	EDUX	0.64	0.25	0.15	0.001[a]
	KENYA					**CHILE**			
GDPR	0.84	0.20	0.04[b]	0.61	GDPR	0.24	0.004[a]	0.24	0.82
GCON	0.65	0.02[b]	0.30	0.69	GCON	0.31	0.005[a]	0.67	0.20
INV	0.78	0.94	0.001[a]	0.61	INV	0.07[b]	0.05[b]	0.005[a]	0.98
EDUX	0.99	0.15	0.14	0.01[b]	EDUX	0.66	0.42	0.87	0.002[a]
	PAKISTAN					**JAMAICA**			
GDPR	0.47	0.57	0.30	0.84	GDPR	0.86	0.13	0.41	0.24
GCON	0.84	0.001[a]	0.33	0.45	GCON	0.89	0.04[b]	0.64	0.43
INV	0.12[b]	0.96	0.001[a]	0.56	INV	0.41	0.13	0.006[b]	0.63
EDUX	0.77	0.84	0.50	0.02[b]	EDUX	0.03b	0.50	0.004[b]	0.001[a]
	EGYPT					**MALAYSIA**			
GDPR	0.03[b]	0.68	0.02[b]	0.48	GDPR	0.44	0.41	0.52	0.53
GCON	0.85	0.002[a]	0.64	0.48	GCON	0.52	0.001[a]	0.30	0.84
INV	0.20[b]	0.07[b]	0.002[a]	0.15[b]	INV	0.004[a]	0.14	0.001[a]	0.09[b]
EDUX	0.38	0.86	0.97	0.002[a]	EDUX	0.36	0.29	0.33	0.003[b]
	PERU					**MEXICO**			
GDPR	0.56	0.12[b]	0.02[b]	0.01[b]	GDPR	0.23	0.50	0.13	0.20
GCON	0.12	0.001[a]	0.03[b]	0.11[b]	GCON	0.16	0.001[a]	0.28	0.79
INV	0.59	0.17	0.001[a]	0.14[b]	INV	0.001[a]	0.12	0.005[b]	0.39
EDUX	0.86	0.46	0.90	0.003[a]	EDUX	0.99	0.05[b]	0.61	0.001[a]

[a]Reject the null hypothesis at 1% level.

[b]Reject the null hypothesis at 5% level.

Figure 12.1
Impulse Responses of GDPR to Shocks

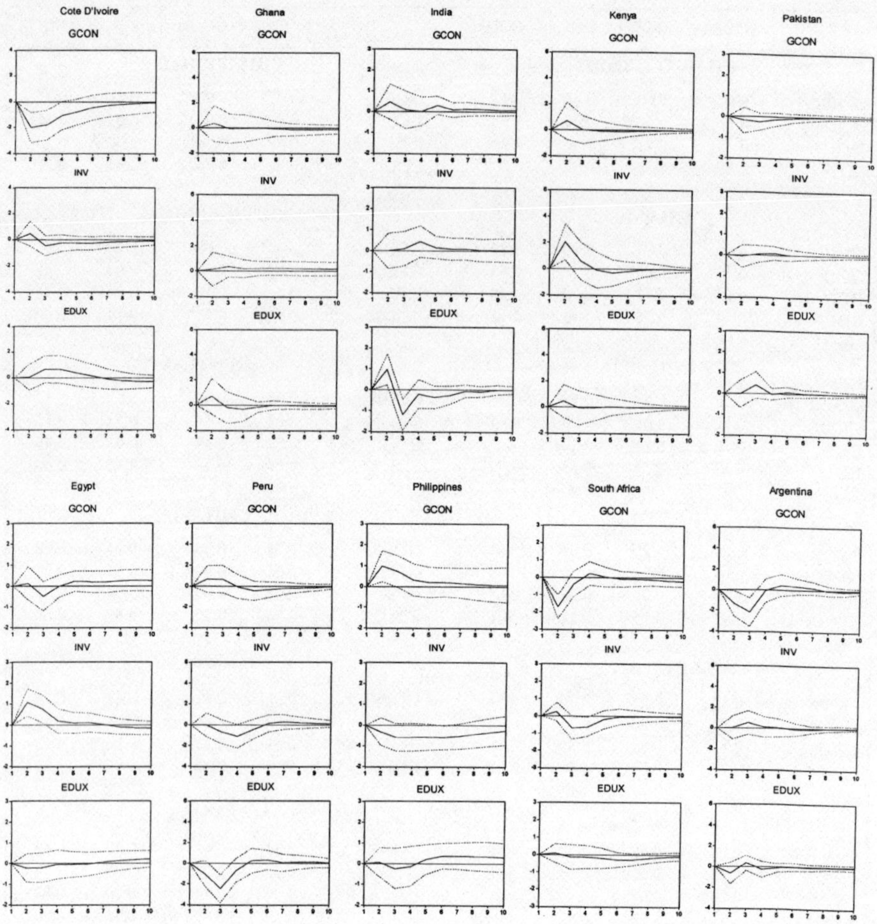

(continued)

results indicate that whereas the short-run impact of *GCON* may be indeterminate, the long-run impact is unambiguously negligible in developing countries.

Changes in private investment seem to have a mixed dynamic impact on the annual per capita growth rates of developing countries. Though some experience a positive but small increase in their *GDPR*, such increase is short-lived. The increase in *GDPR* of countries such as Côte d'Ivoire, India, Kenya, Egypt, and Malaysia occurs in the early part of the shock, and the impacts are felt for different time periods. The negative impact associated with *INV* in most countries is also small. With the exception of the Philippines, where *GDPR* consistently declines, the *GDPR* of countries such as Peru, South Africa, and Mexico approaches 0 in the long run.

Figure 12.1 (continued)
Impulse Responses of GDPR to Shocks

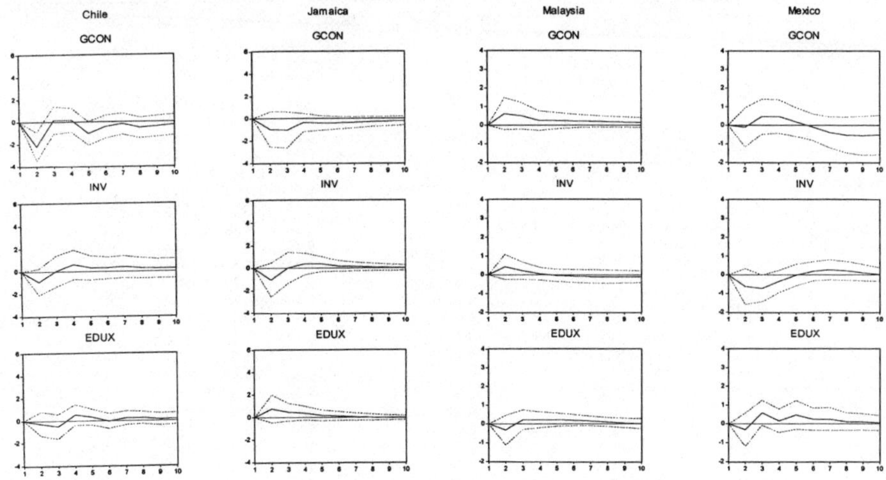

The dynamic behavior of the education variable does not provide any consistent impact on *GDPR*. Whereas the *GDPR* of some countries rises slightly in the short run, other countries experience a small decline in their *GDPR*. For countries such as Egypt, Kenya, Pakistan, and South Africa, the human capital variable is not a factor in the growth process. It is also noted that the level of human development is not related to the level of *GDPR*. In other words, countries that spend more on education do not necessarily experience higher growth rates. The dynamic impacts of *EDUX* on *GDPR* of countries in the High Human Development group are not significantly different from the impact of those in the Lower or Middle Human Development groups.

VARIANCE DECOMPOSITIONS

The impulse response functions illustrate the qualitative responses of *GDPR* to shocks in *GCON, INV*, and *EDUX*. To indicate the relative importance of these shocks requires a variance decomposition. In order to achieve this, consider the n-step ahead forecast of a variable based on information at time t. The variance of the error associated with such a forecast can be attributed to unforecastable shocks (or innovations) to each of the variables comprising the system that occur between $t+1$ and $t+n$. Given that the main focus of the study is to analyze the impact of the policy variables on the annual per capita growth of output, we discuss the variations of *GDPR*, which are explained by shocks in the three policy variables (*GCON, INV*, and *EDUX*) in the model. Table 12.4 reports the variance decompositions of the forecast errors for each variable in the model at horizons up to nine years.[9]

Table 12.4
Variance Decomposition—Proportion of Variance Explained by Shock

VAR.	PER.	S.E.	GDPR	GCON	INV	EDUX	VAR.	PER.	S.E.	GDPR	GCON	INV	EDUX
			CÔTE D'IVOIRE							**PHILIPPINES**			
GDPR	1	0.18	100.00	0.00	0.00	0.00	GDPR	1	0.10	100.00	0.00	0.00	0.00
	3	0.34	71.16	27.29	1.53	0.02		3	0.15	75.13	18.44	5.70	0.74
	5	0.63	52.10	41.30	2.41	4.18		5	0.22	69.73	16.99	12.01	1.27
	7	0.69	50.55	41.65	2.93	4.62		7	0.29	64.14	15.50	16.66	3.70
	9	0.78	50.90	40.97	3.02	5.10		9	0.42	61.63	14.57	18.18	5.62
			GHANA							**SOUTH AFRICA**			
GDPR	1	0.32	100.00	0.00	0.00	0.00	GDPR	1	0.07	100.00	0.00	0.00	0.00
	3	0.56	96.18	0.65	0.66	2.34		3	0.16	47.59	44.33	7.72	0.36
	5	0.59	95.23	0.65	1.00	3.11		5	0.27	44.46	41.54	12.86	1.14
	7	0.61	94.77	0.74	1.40	3.08		7	0.29	43.42	40.69	12.57	3.31
	9	0.62	94.31	0.88	1.69	3.11		9	0.30	42.90	40.62	12.42	4.05
			INDIA							**ARGENTINA**			
GDPR	1	0.29	100.00	0.00	0.00	0.00	GDPR	1	0.37	100.00	0.00	0.00	0.00
	3	0.42	67.09	2.97	0.12	29.82		3	0.45	63.12	32.74	1.46	2.69
	5	0.44	63.65	3.92	2.61	29.83		5	0.49	62.34	33.22	1.49	2.95
	7	0.45	62.92	4.17	2.73	30.18		7	0.52	61.80	33.72	1.60	2.96
	9	0.45	62.72	4.38	2.74	30.16		9	0.52	61.68	33.73	1.61	2.98
			KENYA							**CHILE**			
GDPR	1	0.54	100.00	0.00	0.00	0.00	GDPR	1	0.49	100.00	0.00	0.00	0.00
	3	0.58	75.74	2.28	21.04	0.94		3	0.51	73.21	21.50	3.78	1.51
	5	0.60	75.35	2.35	21.36	0.94		5	0.54	68.04	23.81	5.28	2.87
	7	0.61	75.14	2.40	21.52	0.94		7	0.55	66.79	24.08	6.11	3.02
	9	0.61	75.12	2.41	21.52	0.95		9	0.59	65.31	25.04	6.47	3.19
			PAKISTAN							**JAMAICA**			
GDPR	1	0.07	100.00	0.00	0.00	0.00	GDPR	1	0.48	100.00	0.00	0.00	0.00
	3	0.17	94.44	1.97	0.13	3.46		3	0.54	83.14	8.57	4.79	3.49
	5	0.19	93.71	2.37	0.34	3.58		5	0.56	80.57	9.50	5.81	4.12
	7	0.19	93.69	2.39	0.34	3.59		7	0.61	79.43	10.49	5.95	4.13
	9	0.19	93.68	2.39	0.35	3.59		9	0.62	78.93	11.00	5.96	4.11
			EGYPT							**MALAYSIA**			
GDPR	1	0.14	100.00	0.00	0.00	0.00	GDPR	1	0.29	100.00	0.00	0.00	0.00
	3	0.55	74.58	3.13	21.15	1.14		3	0.30	87.49	7.88	2.70	1.94
	5	0.59	75.01	3.53	20.32	1.13		5	0.32	85.19	9.13	2.67	3.02
	7	0.62	74.46	4.35	20.03	1.15		7	0.33	83.87	9.83	2.71	3.59
	9	0.63	72.70	5.82	19.82	1.66		9	0.34	83.30	10.20	2.88	3.62
			PERU							**MEXICO**			
GDPR	1	0.46	100.00	0.00	0.00	0.00	GDPR	1	0.31	100.00	0.00	0.00	0.00
	3	0.47	65.56	3.61	1.89	28.94		3	0.34	95.34	0.11	3.62	0.93
	5	0.53	60.92	4.00	6.93	28.15		5	0.37	83.77	3.44	7.74	5.05
	7	0.57	60.12	4.49	7.24	28.16		7	0.38	82.76	4.15	7.68	5.41
	9	0.58	59.82	4.59	7.45	28.13		9	0.41	79.44	7.63	7.63	5.30

The results of the variance decompositions seem to be consistent with the impulse responses. A very small portion of the variance in *GDPR* is explained by innovations to *GCON* for most of the countries. Fiscal policy seems to have a moderate effect on the long-run *GDPR* of Argentina, Chile, and the Philippines. The two countries whose long-run *GDPR* is largely influenced by fiscal policy are Côte d'Ivoire and South Africa. The variations in *GDPR* resulting from changes in government spending are 41 percent and 40.6 percent for Côte d'Ivoire and South Africa, respectively, and this occurs in the ninth year. It is important to note that, with the exception of Kenya and Egypt, the variations in *GDPR* of most developing countries are not due to changes in private investment. The implication is that private investment by itself may not have a substantial long-run effect on the annual per capita growth rate of most developing countries. Similarly, with the exception of India and Peru, investment in human capital alone may not be enough to influence the long-run *GDPR* of most developing counties. In fact, on the average, investment education explains about 3.6 percent of the variation in *GDPR* in the ninth year for all the developing countries excluding India and Peru. However, in India and Peru, about 30 percent and 28 percent of the variations in GDPR are explained by investment in education.

SUMMARY AND CONCLUSIONS

The main focus of this chapter has been to analyze the dynamic effects of three key production inputs on the growth rate in output of developing countries. A strong impression that emerges from the empirical analysis is that fiscal policy, private investment, and investment in human capital may not provide any significant positive effect on the annual per capita growth rate of many developing countries in the long run. Specifically the following can be deduced from the empirical results:

1. Fiscal policy may have a positive or negative effect on the growth rate of developing countries. In countries where the effect is positive, the effect is minimal and short-lived.
2. Changes in government spending do not account for any significant variation in the annual per capita growth rate for many countries.
3. Private investment does not seem to contribute much to the growth rate in output in the developing world, especially in the long run.
4. Surprisingly, education does not show any significant relationship with the annual per capita growth rate. In some countries, education expenditures tend to produce a negative impact on the short-run growth rate.
5. A close examination of the impulse response functions reveals that human capital intensity (more education expenditures) does not generate any marked differences in the dynamic response of *GDPR* among countries.

The implication of these dynamic results is that in developing countries, government spending, private investment, and investment in education by themselves may not be enough to stimulate growth. There may be other factors endemic in these economies that interact with these inputs to either promote or retard the growth process.

NOTES

This research was partially supported by a seed grant from the Penn State University Office of International Programs. I am specially indebted to Dr. Khalipha Bility, Head and Senior Program Officer, for his encouragement toward the Ghana project. I am grateful for the assistance given to me by the faculty and staff of the Economics Department of the University of Ghana.

1. Barro (1990) has summarized the empirical results of recent studies of government spending on growth (see pages S122–S124).

2. It must be noted that the construction of the human development index takes into account other factors such as life expectancy, GDP, and literacy. We assume that most of these factors depend on the level of education, and therefore countries with higher levels of education are likely to develop faster.

3. The assumption here is that individuals do not consume leisure.

4. See also Glomm and Ravikumar, 1992.

5. The derivation of the growth rates as well as the steady-state growth rate can be found in Barro and Sala-i-Martin (1999). See also, the appendix of Capolupo (2000). The growth rates also depend on other parameters but for lack of data, we concentrate on only four variables in the model.

6. If β_1 and β_2 are the coefficients of $EDUX_{t-1}$ and $EDUX_{t-2}$, respectively, in the *GDPR* equation. The null hypothesis is that $\beta_1 = \beta_2 = 0$ (based on F-distribution).

7. It must be noted that the Choleski decomposition depends on the ordering of the variables, and changing the order of the variables can change the impulse responses. Following Sims (1980), a lower triangular covariance matrix of the innovations with positive elements on the diagonal is adopted. Based on macroeconomic theories, we tried several orderings with variables that are not expected to have predictive value for other variables put last.

8. For a detailed discussion of error bands for impulse responses, see Sims and Zha (1995), and for variance decompositions, see Runkle (1987).

9. I estimated the forecast error for a longer period (twenty-five years) and found that the results were not significantly different from the first nine years.

REFERENCES

Akaike, H. 1973. "Information Theory and the Extension of Maximum Likelihood Principle." In *Second International Symposium on Information Theory*, edited by B.N. Petrov and F. Csaki. Budapest: Akademiai Kaido.

Barro, R. J. 1990. "Government Spending in a Simple Model of Endogenous Growth." *Journal of Political Economy* 98 (October, part 2).

———. 1991. "Economic Growth in a Cross Section of Countries." *Quarterly Journal of Economics* 106(2): 407–43.

Barro, R.J. and X. Sala-i-Martin, 1999. *Economic Growth*, Cambridge, MA: The MIT Press.

Capolupo, R. 2000, "Output Taxation, Human Capital and Growth," *The Manchester School*, 68(2): 166–183.

Dejong, D.N., and C.H. Whiteman. 1991. "Trends and Random Walks in Macroeconomic Times Series: A Reconsideration Based on the Likelihood Principle." *Journal of Monetary Economics* 28(2): 221–254.

Diamond, J. 1989. "Government Expenditure and Economic Growth: An Empirical Investigation." *IMF Working Paper*, WP/89/45.

Dickey, David A., and W.A. Fuller. 1979. "Distribution of the Estimators for Autoregressive Time Series with a Unit Root." *Journal of the American Statistical Association* (June): 427–31.

Doan, T. 1989. *Rats User's Manual*. Version 4.01. Evanston, IL.: Var Econometrics.

Engen, E., and J. Skinner. 1991. "Fiscal Policy and Economic Growth." Paper Presented at NBER Conference on Taxation, Cambridge, MA.

Engle, R.E., and C.W.J. Granger. 1987. "Cointegration and Error-Correction: Representation, Estimation, and Testing." *Econometrica* 55: 251–76.

Glomm, G., and B. Ravikumar. 1992. "Public versus Private Investment in Human Capital: Endogenous Growth and Income Inequality." *Journal of Political Economy* 100: 818–33.

Johansen, S., and Juselius, K. 1990. "Maximum Likelihood Estimation and Inferences on Cointegration—With Applications to the Demand for Money." *Oxford Bulletin of Economics and Statistics* 52: 169–209.

King, R.G., and S. Rebelo. 1990. "Public Policy and Endogenous Growth: Developing Neoclassical Implications." *Journal of Political Economy* 98: S126–S150.

Landau, D. 1983. "Government Expenditure and Economic Growth: A Cross-Country Study." *Southern Economic Journal* 49.

Levine, R., and D. Renelt. 1992. "A Sensitivity Analysis of Cross-Country Growth Regressions." *American Economic Review* 82: 942–63.

Lucas, R.E. 1988. "On the Mechanics of Economic Development." *Journal of Monetary Economics* 22: 3–42.

Mankiw, N.G., D. Romer, and D.N. Weil. 1992. "Contribution to the Empirics of Economic Growth." *Quarterly Journal of Economics* 107: 407–37.

Marsden, K. 1983. "Links between Taxes and Economic Growth: Some Empirical Evidence." *Staff Working Paper No. 605,* The World Bank.

Phillips, P., and P. Perron. 1988. "Testing for a Unit Root in Times Series Regression." *Biometrica* 75: 335–46.

Ram, R. 1986. "Government Size and Economic Growth: A New Framework and Some Evidence from Cross-Section and Time Series Data." *American Economic Review* 76: 191–203.

———. 1989. "Government Size and Economic Growth: A New Framework and Some Evidence from Cross-Section and Time Series Data: Reply." *American Economic Review* 79: 281–84.

Romer, P. 1989. "Capital Accumulation and Long-run Growth." In *Modern Business Cycles Theory,* edited by R.J. Barro. Cambridge MA, Harvard University Press.

Runkle, D.E. 1987. "Vector Autoregression and Reality." *Journal of Business and Economic Statistics* 5: 437–42.

Sims, C.A. 1980. "Macroeconomics and Reality." *Econometrica* 48: 1–48.

Sims, C.A. 1987. "Vector Autoregression and Reality: Comment," *Journal of Business and Economic Statistics* 5(4): 443–451.

Sims, C.A., and T. Zha. 1995. "Error Bands for Impulse Response." *Federal Reserve Bank of Atlanta Working Paper,* 95–6.

Solow, R.M. 1956. "A Contribution to the Theory of Economic Growth." *Quarterly Journal of Economics* 70: 65–94.

13

Life-Cycle Consumption, Economic Development, and Planning Horizon in Developing Countries

John Baffoe-Bonnie and Mohammed Khayum

INTRODUCTION

The time horizon of economic agents is an important element of dynamic economic analysis. The distinction between finite and infinite horizons, for example, has been shown to have important implications for the analysis of consumer and firm behavior (Blanchard and Fisher, 1989). This distinction has also received attention in discussions of the relevance of economic propositions and models across countries (Corden, 1985; Haque and Motiel, 1989). Empirical evidence on this issue across countries is limited, however, with much of the focus on testing conditions from which finite or infinite horizons can be inferred (Haque and Montiel, 1989). This chapter provides more direct estimates of the length of household planning horizons for different countries by employing the moving planning horizon (MPH) model of consumption developed by Winder (1988). The length of household planning horizons is compared for a sample of countries that have realized different levels of economic development.

The study tests the hypothesis of a direct relationship between the length of household planning horizons and the level of economic development. Although finite horizons have been inferred from the relationship between the discount rate for future income and borrowing costs (Hayashi, 1982; Blanchard, 1985), there are reasons to expect differences among economies based on the level of economic development. In many less developed economies, for instance, households may exhibit relatively shorter time horizons because of the prevalence of factors such as economic bottlenecks, a high degree of uncertainty about future income, limited safety nets, and inadequately developed credit markets. These factors may not only prevent many consumers from maintaining a relatively stable path of consumption but also limit their ability to engage in increased precautionary saving to cope with uncertainty about future consumption.

The testing procedure involves estimation of the length of consumers' planning horizon for a sample of countries exhibiting different levels of economic development. The analytical framework is an intertemporal optimization model of consumption that suggests that current income exerts considerable influence on current consumption. The current income classification of countries by the World Bank as high-income, middle-income, and low-income economies provides the basis for identifying countries at different levels of development.[1] The results provide empirical support for the hypothesis presented in this chapter, with middle-income economies having average household planning horizons in the range of 1.9 years whereas low-income economies exhibit an average horizon of about seven months.

The rest of the chapter is organized as follows. Section II discusses the recent literature on consumption modeling. Section III outlines the model used in the chapter. Section IV presents the data source and the results of unit root and cointegration tests of consumption and income. The empirical results and diagnostic tests of the consumption equation are discussed in section V, and the last section presents the summary and conclusions.

CONSUMPTION MODELING

For the past (two decades) fifteen years there have been two significant developments in modeling consumption behavior. These are the random walk (RW) model (Hall, 1978) and the error correction (EC) model based on the work of Davidson et al., (1978). Hall (1978) introduced the assumption of rational expectations in the evaluation of the consumer's intertemporal budget constraint. Within an intertemporal utility maximization framework, Hall predicted consumption to evolve as a first-order autoregression, where current events affect consumption through a disturbance term reflecting innovations due to new information on current and future real disposable income. From a research standpoint this consumption specification that focused attention on the serial correlation properties of time series data on consumption provided fruitful common ground with empirical developments such as the dynamic modeling approach in time series analysis. This section outlines the RW and the EC approaches and considers the most important attributes of these models and how they are related to the model to be used in this study.

THE RW APPROACH

The RW model is based on several key behavioral and institutional assumptions. First, consumers consider the future when they make their current spending decisions. Second, households prefer more to less and a smooth consumption stream rather than an uneven one. Third, the accumulation of wealth serves to maintain a smooth stream of spending. Fourth, financial markets are well organized and developed so that households do not face liquidity constraints and in periods of income declines can borrow against future income to maintain a stable path of consumption. Treating the consumer decision problem as one of intertemporal optimization under uncertainty, using a quadratic utility function and the evolution of consumer wealth in a rational expectations setting, Hall (1978) pointed out that consumption would follow a random walk. Consequently, only the surprise components of variables influencing the evolution of consumer wealth would affect consumption.

The basic framework involves specifying a representative consumer's utility function and the lifetime budget constraint under rational expectations. The preference assumptions include: homogenous utility, a subjective rate of time preference that is constant and reflects the consumer's degree of impatience, time separability, and a linear budget constraint. In general terms the maximization problem involves solving the following

$$\text{Max } E\left(\sum_{i=0}^{T} \beta^i U(c_{t+i})\right) \tag{1}$$

subject to the constraint

$$\sum_{i=0}^{T} (1 + r)^{-i} c_{t+i} = (1 + r)w_{t-1} + \sum_{i=0}^{T} (1 + r)^{-i} E(y_{t+i}|I_t) \tag{2}$$

with $U' > 0$, $U'' < 0$, where U' and U'' are the first and second derivatives with respect to c respectively. Real consumption and real disposable income are denoted by c_{t+i} and y_{t+i} respectively, w_{t-1} is accumulated real wealth, T denotes the consumer's lifetime, β is the time preference parameter, $0 < \beta < 1$, and r is the real interest rate that is assumed to be constant. E denotes the expectation operator and I_t is the information set available at time t used by the consumer. The first order conditions implied by (1) and (2) are

$$EU'(c_{t+1}) = [\beta(1 + r)]^{-i} EU'(c_t) \; i = 1, 2, \ldots, T \tag{3}$$

A specific solution for consumption from equation (3) requires the choice of a functional form for the utility function. In general, for a wide class of utility functions which satisfy the conditions of preference homogeneity and strict concavity, the implied solution of equation (3) is that consumption evolves as a random walk with drift.[2]

$$\ln(c_t) = a_0 + a_1 \ln(c_{t-1}) + \epsilon_t \tag{4}$$

Consumption regressions based on equation (4) have been used primarily in two ways to assess the empirical validity of the life-cycle/permanent-income theory of consumption.[3] One way is to view the regression as estimating a conditional expectation $E(c_t|c_{t-1}, I_{t-1})$, where I_{t-1} is a vector of information on variables known in period $t - 1$ (other than c_{t-1}, such as lagged real disposable income), and testing the hypothesis that this conditional expectation is not a function of I_{t-1}, which implies that the coefficients on the variables in I_{t-1} should be 0. This orthogonality or exclusion test is based on the argument that because all relevant information from the previous period was incorporated in the decision made about the previous level of consumption, then previous values of variables other than consumption lagged one-period should not improve the forecast of current consumption.

Hall's (1978) initial econometric test and subsequent exclusion test rejected the simple RW model. Indeed, a number of empirical findings pose major challenges for modern consumption theory, such as accounting for (1) the sensitivity of consumption to anticipated income, (2) the smoothness of consumption relative to unanticipated income, (3) instances of positive growth in aggregate consumption even when the rate of time preference exceeds the rate of interest, (4) the indications that at the later phase of the life cycle, dissaving does not occur in the predicted fashion among the elderly, and (5) the more favorable results to the life cycle model under uncertainty in panel data compared with time series data.

The evidence rejecting the simple RW model can be interpreted in a number of ways: (1) as a rejection of rational forward-looking behavior with the implication of suboptimal consumer planning, and (2) acceptance of rational forward-looking behavior, but within a framework of myopic consumer planning. Or, as has largely been the case, it can be interpreted as a measure of weakness in model specification or empirical methodology arising from the form of the utility function adopted (Winder, 1988; Rossi, 1988), the nature of constraint specification (Muellbauer, 1983; Wickens and Molana, 1984; Mankiw et al., 1985; Hubbard and Judd, 1986; King, 1986; Hall, 1988) or data-related issues (Haug, 1991).

THE EC APPROACH

The EC approach is a data-based approach to dynamic analysis of economic behavior in the tradition of the dynamic modeling framework developed by Sargan (1964). It is based on the notion that although economic theory often provides insights into long-run equilibrium relationships in an economy, there is always the likely possibility that at any point in time the economic system may be out of equilibrium for any number of reasons. This implies, for instance, that it takes time for changes in exogenous variables to have an impact on endogenous variables. The absence of such time allowance would imply that adjustment takes place immediately. Accordingly, this approach distinguishes between long-run influences and short-run adjustment to long-run equilibrium in economic behavior, with error correction referring to the adjustment process between short-run disequilibrium and a desired long-run position. Thus, we can represent the EC model with an equation given by:

$$F^Y_{t+1} = F^Y_t + \rho(Y_t - F^Y_t) \tag{5}$$

where F^Y_{t+1} represents the forecast for the period $t + 1$ of the variable Y, F^Y_t is the forecast for the period t, and $\rho(Y_t - F^Y_t)$ refers to the error correction process, with ρ measuring the speed at which the new forecast adjusts to the error. An important data-related issue underlying the EC approach is the fact that the data we work with often reflect realizations and not the intentions of economic agents that are usually presumed to underlie the theoretical relationships under investigation (see Spanos 1986). Thus, consumption in the context of a theoretical model is a concept that refers to the intentions of economic agents corresponding to the expected future values for the variables affecting their intentions. The observed data, however, refer to actual consumption expenditures that do not coincide necessarily with the theoretical concept all the time. Instead, the observed data refer to realizations of consumer spending and is in effect the actual adjustment process for consumption expenditures and not the original intentions of consumers. Hence, in the absence of additional information an estimated model reflects an adjustment equation (rather than a consumption function) that can be dominated by changes in constraints, institutional changes, or shifts in preference parameters. An important implication is that the consumption equation may not have any direct economic interpretation but should produce better short-run forecasts and will produce long-run forecasts that hold together in economically meaningful ways.

The seminal model of consumption within the EC framework was developed by Davidson et al. (1978) in their attempt to reconcile the disparate consumption specifications and results that existed for the United Kingdom. Their approach was to obtain an empirical relationship that could best track and forecast aggregate consumption behavior while conforming to a set of specification criteria that is at the core of data-based econometric modeling. These criteria (developed more fully in Hendry [1983]) include data coherency, parameter stability, consistency with steady-state (e.g., long-run proportionality between consumption and income) predictions of economic theory, and the ability to account for the range of previous findings. Ignoring the adjustments made by Davidson et al. to eliminate seasonality in unadjusted data and the term representing the rate of annual change in income, the empirical equation specified takes the form

$$\Delta \ln c_t = \theta_0 + \theta_1 \Delta \ln y_t + \theta_2(\ln y_{t-1} - \ln c_{t-1}) + v_{1t}; \quad 0 < \theta_1, \quad \theta_2 < 1 \tag{6}$$

which is a special case of a general first-order equation specifying the dynamic adjustment of consumption to income,

$$\ln c_t = \theta_0 + \theta_3 \ln c_{t-1} + \theta_1 \ln y_t + \theta_4 \ln y_{t-1}) + v_{2t} \tag{7}$$

Assuming long-run proportionality between consumption and income the "no change" (i.e., $\Delta c_t = \Delta y_t = 0$) steady-state equilibrium derived from equation (6) is

$$\ln c_t = \frac{\theta_0}{\theta_2} + \ln y_t \tag{8}$$

and the steady-state growth path, obtained when $\Delta c_t = \Delta y_t = g$, takes the form

$$\ln c_t = \frac{\theta_0 - g(1 - \theta_1)}{\theta_2} + \ln y_t \tag{9}$$

With an underlying steady-state such as

$$c_t = \alpha y_t; \quad \ln c_t = \ln \alpha + \ln y_t; \quad \Delta \ln c_t = \Delta \ln y_t \tag{10}$$

it is seen that long-run proportionality in levels holds when

$$\alpha = \exp\{[\theta_0 - g(1 - \theta_1)]/\theta_2\} \tag{11}$$

indicating that the specification in equation (6) can be derived from a nonstochastic steady-state theory, upon which a first-order stochastic disequilibrium relationship is imposed, the disequilibrium effect can be generated by ($\ln y_{t-1} - \ln c_{t-1}$). Because equation (6) illustrates that consumers can maintain long-run proportionality between consumption and income in a short-run stochastic environment along any given growth path, the EC specification combines the property of forward-looking behavior with adjustments to short-run fluctuations that form part of consumers' economic environment.

Early tests of EC models of consumption starting with Davidson et al. were favorable (see Davis, 1984). Overall, Patterson (1986), using a range of parameter stability tests for various EC specifications, found this approach to be the best-fitting nondurable consumption specification. The most striking feature of the empirical work on EC models of consumption is the growing diversity of specifications, which to a large extent has been in response to unfavorable results obtained with the favored specification in Davidson et al. (1978).

In fact, the empirical foundations underlying the EC approach have become much stronger with the development of cointegration methods by Granger (1986). Because two variables that are cointegrated would, on average, not drift apart over time, this concept provides insights into the long-run relationship between the two variables, and testing for the cointegration between two variables such as consumption and income would also be a test of the validity of an EC specification involving these variables.

Another significant issue raised from an empirical perspective has been the potential observational equivalance in the EC and RW approaches. The basic argument is that either feedback or expectational channels can be used to account for consumers maintaining a long-run proportional relationship between consumption and income. With regard to the modeling of consumption in general, the EC approach has also provided some useful insights. Firstly, it highlights the weaknesses of employing estimable specifications based solely on economic theory when dealing with available data that often do not coincide with theoretical concepts of interest. Second, it identifies an array of diagnostic tests that yield robust specifications for forecasting purposes, particularly in an uncertain environment. Third, it reflects an important fact of economic reality—that is, that even if there are desired equilibria, say, for example, by consumers with regard to asset-income and consumption-income ratios, it must be recognized that there are circumstances that may limit automatic or immediate realization because of the time dimension involved.

THE MOVING PLANNING HORIZON MODEL

Winder (1988) provides an approach that reconciles the intertemporal utility maximization process underlying the RW approach with the dynamic specification of the consumption obtained from EC approach when the planning time span falls short of the expected lifetime of the consumer. It is assumed that there are T time independent periods over the planning time span, which implies a shifting planning horizon as time goes on. The consumer is assumed to solve at each time period t the utility maximization problem outlined in equations (1) and (2). Given the following utility function[4]

$$U(c) = -\gamma^{-1} e^{(-\gamma c)}, \gamma > 0. \tag{12}$$

then the implied first-order conditions are:

$$c_{t+1}^{t} = i\gamma^{-1} \ln [\beta(1 + r)] + c_{t}^{t}, \quad i = 1, \ldots, T. \tag{13}$$

where c_{t+1}^{t} denotes the consumption plan for the period $t + i$ made at time t, and c_t^t is the realization c_t

$$\sum_{i=0}^{T} (1 + r)^{-i} c_t + \gamma^{-1} \ln[\beta(1 + r)] \sum_{i=1}^{T} i(1 + r)^{-i} = (1 + r)w_{t-1} + \sum_{i=0}^{T} (1 + r)^{-i} E(y_{t+i}|I_t) \tag{14}$$

For the next period, c_{t+1} is

$$\sum_{i=0}^{T} (1 + r)^{-i} c_{t+1} + \gamma^{-1} \ln[\beta(1 + r)] \sum_{i=1}^{T} i(1 + r)^{-i} = (1 + r)w_t + \sum_{i=0}^{T} (1 + r)^{-i} E(y_{t+1+i}|I_{t+1}) \tag{15}$$

Dividing equation (15) by $(1 + r)$, and substituting $w_t = (1 + r)w_{t-1} + y_t - c_t$, subtracting equation (14), using the transform of variables,[5] and rearranging we get

$$c_{t+1} - c_t = \gamma^{-1} \ln[\beta(1 + r)] - \mu_T^{-1}(1 + r)^{-T}\gamma^{-1}(T + 1)\ln[\beta(1 + r)] + \mu_T^{-1}(1 + r)^{-T}[E(y_{t+T+1}|I_t) - c_t] + \mu_T^{-1} \sum_{I=0}^{T} (1 + r)^{-i} [E(y_{t+i+1}|I_{t+1}) - E(y_{t+i+1}|I_t)] \tag{16}$$

where $\mu_T = (\Sigma_{i=0}^{t} (1 + r)^{-i})$. Equation (16) shows that from the optimization framework underlying the RW model, it is possible to derive a term, $\mu_T^{-1}(1 + r)^{-T} [E(y_{t+T+1}|I_t) - c_t$, that resembles the correction term in the EC approach. The model is completed by specifying the stochastic process for income. There are a variety of forms of stochastic processes (parametric and nonparametric) from which to choose as descriptions of observable phenomena. Here, we follow the general pattern in RW econometric modeling literature of treating income as a derived stochastic process. As Winder (1988) shows, if it is assumed that the change in income is generated by a moving average (MA) process of order 1,

$$\Delta y_t = \delta + v_t - \theta v_{t-1} \tag{17}$$

with the conditional expectations in equation (16) satisfying

$$y_{t+1} - E(y_{t+1}|I_t) = v_{t+1} \tag{18}$$

$$E(y_{t+i}|I_{t+1} - E(y_{t+1}|I_t) = (1 - \theta)v_{t+i}, \quad i \geq 2 \tag{19}$$

and

$$E(y_{t+T+1}|I_t) = y_t + (T + 1)\delta - \theta v_t \tag{20}$$

then substituting equations (18), (19), and (20) into equation (16) we get

$$\begin{aligned} \Delta c_{t+1} = {} & \gamma^{-1} \ln[\beta(1 + r)](1 - (T + 1)\mu_T^{-1}(1 + r)^{-T}) \\ & + \mu_T^{-1}(1 + r)^{-T} [(T + 1)\delta + y_t - c_t] \\ & - \mu_T^{-1}(1 + r)^{-T}\theta v_t + \mu_T^{-1}[(1 - \theta)\mu_T + \theta]v_{t+1}. \end{aligned} \tag{21}$$

Expressing the last term in equation (21) as

$$\begin{aligned} \mu_T^{-1}[(1 - \theta)\mu_T + \theta]v_{t+1} = {} & \mu_T^{-1}\mu_{T-1}[1 - \theta(1 + r)^{-1}] \\ & v_{t+1} + \mu_T^{-1}(1 + r)^{-T}[\Delta y_{t+1} - \delta] + \mu_T^{-1}(1 + r)^{-T}\theta v_t \end{aligned} \tag{22}$$

and substituting equation (22) into equation (21) yields

$$\begin{aligned} \Delta c_{t+1} = {} & \gamma^{-1} \ln[\beta(1 + r)](1 - (T + 1)\mu_T^{-1}(1 + r)^{-T}) \\ & + \mu_T^{-1}(1 + r)^{-T}\, T\delta + \mu_T^{-1}(1 + r)^{-T}\Delta y_{t+1} + \mu_T^{-1}(1 + \text{ı} \\ & (y_t - c_t) + \mu_T^{-1}\mu_{T-1}[1 - \theta(1 + r)^{-1}]v_{t+1}. \end{aligned} \tag{23}$$

Equation (23) may be rewritten as

$$\Delta c_t = \alpha + \alpha_1 \Delta y_t + \alpha_2(y_{t-1} - c_{t-1}) + \epsilon_t \tag{24}$$

where $\alpha_1 = \alpha_2 = \mu_T^{-1} (1 + r)^{-T}$ and equation (24) takes the form of a simple EC model. Following Engle and Granger (1987), if the error correction term in equation (24) is replaced with the residuals from the cointegration regression of c_t on y_t lagged one period, then the estimated model becomes

$$\Delta c_t = \alpha + \alpha_1 \Delta y_t + \alpha_2 EC_{t-1} + \epsilon_t \tag{25}$$

The combination of forward-looking behavior and a feedback process in the specifications obtained from the MPH approach is one of its strongest appeals. Additionally, the MPH approach allows for the calculation of the planning horizon of consumers and provides information on the speed of adjustment between the short-run and long-run consumption behavior. In particular, it can be shown that the length of the planning horizon (T) can be approximated by

$$T = \alpha_1^{-1} - 1 \tag{26}$$

where α_1 refers to the estimated coefficient of the change in income variable.

DATA ANALYSIS

The data used in this study comes from the International Monetary Fund (IMF) International Financial Statistics database and World Development Indicators, 1998 CD-Rom. The real private consumption expenditures, and real gross national product are annual data covering the period 1948 to 1996. Because private consumption is an aggregation of spending on durable and nondurable goods, it poses a problem because it combines durable and nondurable spending. It becomes necessary to use this aggregation because separate data on durable goods were not available for many of the countries in our study. Moreover, in the case of low- and middle-income economies, the problem may be insignificant because a relatively low share of aggregate consumption expenditures goes toward the purchase of durable goods. Also, unavailability of disposable income for many countries resulted in utilizing national income. As Zuehlke and Payne (1989) point out, there are a number of reasons that make the use of national income an adequate proxy for household income, especially for developing countries.

UNIT ROOT AND COINTEGRATION TESTS

Evidence from recent studies suggests that both consumption and income tend to be nonstationary series. In keeping with current practices, the consumption and income data are tested for unit roots. The results indicate that the consumption (c_t) and the income (y_t) series were nonstationary in levels, but stationary in the first differences for all the countries selected. Equation (25) is also valid empirically if the consumption and income series cointegrate. The test results reveal that the consumption and income series in most of the countries under study are cointegrated because the residual series from the cointegrating regression are stationary at the 10 percent level of significance.

EMPIRICAL RESULTS

Estimation results for equation (25) using ordinary least squares (OLS) are reported in Table 13.1. The error correction term (EC) represents the residuals obtained from regressing real consumption on real income. The consumption equation was tested for normality in the error term, heteroscedasticity, and residual autocorrelation. With regards to autocorrelation, the BP and LB test statistics are insignificant in the consumption equations of the countries selected. The null hypothesis of constant variance of the error term in the consumption equation is tested against the alternative hypothesis of an ARCH structure of 12 lags. The results indicate that an ARCH structure is nonexistent in the consumption equation residuals for all of the countries at acceptable levels of significance. The values of Jarque-Bera statistics (JB) also reveal that normality of the residuals obtained from the estimates for each country cannot be rejected at the acceptable levels of significance.

The results in Table 13.1 indicate that the change in real income and the error correction term variables are significant in the consumption equation for all countries at the 1 percent level of significance. The R^2 indicates a good fit with values ranging from 0.61 for Pakistan to 0.99 for Turkey and Mexico. A consistent result of the study is the direct relationship between a change in real consumption and a change in real income, and an inverse relationship between real consumption and the error correction term for all the countries.

The estimates of the length of the planning horizon (Table 13.2) show that consumers in the lower-income economies have the shortest planning horizon of about seven months. There was no significant difference between the length of the planning horizons for the lower-middle-income and upper-middle-income countries. The average planning horizons of the countries in the lower-middle-income and upper-middle-income economies are approximately 1.9 and 2.0 years, respectively. A plausible explanation for this variation is that, on the average, more of the countries in the middle-income group (lower-middle and upper-middle) may have better credit markets and more safety nets, which make it possible for consumers to plan longer than their counterparts in the lower-income countries. The results also indicate a variation in the speed of adjustment between the short-run and the long-run desired consumption behavior in different income groups. Although there is no consistent pattern in the speed of adjustment across the sample of countries, we find that on the average the speed of adjustment for consumers in the low-income economies is shorter than those in the lower-middle and upper-middle-income economies. This may be explained by the fact that many consumers in poor or less developed countries exist near

Table 13.1
Estimates of Consumption Equation (dependent variable is ΔC)

Country	Constant	EC(-1)	Δy_t	R^2	D.W.	S.E.R.
		Low-Income Countries				
Bangladesh	1.62	-0.72	0.68	0.82	2.02	34.76
	(2.89)	(-5.86) [a]	(3.99) [a]			
Côte D'Ivoire	15.04	-0.66	0.59	0.86	1.89	22.05
	(1.98)	(-3.32) [a]	(11.04) [a]			
Cameroon	3.26	-0.92	0.54	0.89	1.93	62.70
	(0.25)	(-6.05) [a]	(13.16) [a]			
India	30.57	-0.62	0.51	0.96	2.03	11.74
	(14.91)	(-2.23) [b]	(13.91) [a]			
Kenya	6.34	-0.75	0.71	0.93	2.07	67.85
	(1.61)	(-3.35) [a]	(5.21) [a]			
Nigeria	14.74	-0.36	0.54	0.78	1.84	49.26
	(1.73)	(-3.81)[a]	(3.51) [a]			
Pakistan	-0.01	-0.75	0.73	0.61	1.85	77.07
	(-0.51)	(-3.81) [a]	(5.83) [a]			
Sir Lanka	-0.08	-0.63	0.59	0.72	2.13	49.21
	(-1.16)	(-1.84)[c]	(2.03) [b]			
Tanzania	5.68	-0.91	0.51	0.87	1.81	72.35
	(1.21)	(-1.97) [b]	(3.16) [a]			
Uganda	12.09	-0.68	0.62	0.81	2.02	33.13
	(1.94)	(-2.97) [b]	(5.19) [a]			
		Lower-Middle-Income Countries				
Colombia	0.53	-0.72	0.25	0.89	1.75	56.10
	(4.99)	(-4.85) [a]	(5.18) [a]			
Costa Rica	-50.51	-0.33	0.31	0.74	1.83	20.48
	(-1.28)	(-4.36) [a]	(2.84) [b]			
Egypt	5.75	-0.46	0.42	0.89	1.97	15.58
	(3.66)	(-2.55) [b]	(5.31) [a]			
Indonesia	3.01	-0.61	0.47	0.89	2.09	15.61
	(4.11)	(-4.58) [a]	(3.23) [a]			
Korea	9.24	-0.55	0.29	0.75	1.76	6.34
	(3.96)	(-1.74) [c]	(6.42) [a]			
Peru	3.01	-0.46	0.41	0.94	1.87	24.89
	(0.70)	(-3.06) [a]	(24.16) [a]			
Philippines	18.22	-0.48	0.39	0.93	1.75	27.94
	(3.21)	(-2.97) [b]	(5.01) [a]			
Thailand	0.08	-0.38	0.42	0.79	2.13	35.50
	(2.62)	(-3.50) [a]	(6.44) [a]			
Turkey	-0.24	-0.53	0.38	0.99	2.33	72.37
	(-0.20)	(-3.41) [a]	(95.90) [a]			
Venezuela	-0.57	-0.58	0.28	0.65	2.03	21.56
	(-0.27)	(-3.08) [a]	(6.02) [a]			
		Upper-Middle-Income Countries				
Country	Constant	EC(-)	Δy_t	R^2	D.W.	S.E.R.
Argentina	3.14	-0.42	0.29	0.91	1.96	13.55
	(2.98)	(-7.51) [a]	(11.54) [a]			
Chile	-0.18	-0.54	0.38	0.96	2.15	13.18
	(-1.07)	(-4.68) [a]	(41.61) [a]			
Mexico	-2.73	-0.39	0.37	0.99	1.82	8.73
	(-1.14)	(-2.44)[b]	(78.81) [a]			
South Africa	5.38	-0.41	0.31	0.74	1.25	8.72
	(3.52)	(-4.22) [a]	(9.89) [a]			
Trinidad & Tobago	-9.76	-0.46	0.94	0.92	1.99	18.21
	(-0.53	(-3.20) [a]	(10.76) [a]			

Note: t-statistics are in parentheses.

[a]Significant at 1% level.

[b]Significant at 5% level.

[c]Significant at 10% level. S.E.R. = Standard error of regression.

Table 13.2
Length of Planning and Adjustment Periods

Income Group	Planning Period	Adjustment Period[1]
	Low-Income Countries	
Group Average[2]	0.60	0.7
Bangladesh	0.47	0.7
Côte D'Ivoire	0.69	0.7
Cameroon	0.85	0.9
India	0.96	0.6
Kenya	0.41	0.8
Nigeria	0.85	0.4
Pakistan	0.37	0.7
Sri Lanka	0.69	0.6
Tanzania	0.96	0.9
Uganda	0.61	0.7
	Lower-Middle-Income Countries	
Group Average[2]	1.88	0.5
Colombia	3.00	0.7
Costa Rica	2.22	0.3
Egypt	1.38	0.5
Indonesia	1.12	0.6
Korea	2.45	0.6
Peru	1.44	0.5
Philippines	1.56	0.5
Thailand	1.38	0.4
Turkey	1.63	0.5
Venezuela	2.57	0.6
	Upper-Middle-Income Countries	
Group Average[2]	2.00	0.4
Argentina	2.45	0.4
Chile	2.13	0.5
Mexico	1.70	0.4
South Africa	2.23	0.4
Trinidad and Tobago	1.50	0.5

[1]The coefficient on EC(−1) approximated to one decimal point.

[2]The average planning horizon and adjustment periods for all countries within that income group.

subsistence levels and face relatively greater uncertainty about future income prospects than their counterparts in the middle-income economies.[6]

SUMMARY AND CONCLUSIONS

Recent lifetime consumption models assert that consumers are forward looking and prefer a smooth consumption stream to an uneven one and that under certain conditions they are able to maintain a stable path of consumption throughout their lifetime. The model employed in this study does not dispute the idea that consumers exhibit forward-looking behavior, but incorporates the notion that consumers' planning horizons do not extend to their lifetime. That is, consumers are more likely to make consumption decisions for a much shorter time frame in the future than their expected lifetime. The empirical results suggest that the average length of the planning period for consumers in a sample of developing countries is about 1.4 years. The results also indicate that the length of the planning horizon is positively related to the level of economic development, increasing as the level of development measured by the real GNP increases. On average, consumers in low-income economies tend to be more myopic in their consumption decisions with their planning horizon averaging about seven months. This shortsightedness in consumption may be explained in terms of the high degree of uncertainty about income security and the limited opportunities for diversifiable income. Under these circumstances, consumption in low-income economies is more likely to track the path of current income than expected lifetime income as forward-looking consumers are forced to neglect periods far ahead in the future when making consumption decisions. An important implication of this myopic consumption behavior is that there can be some effectiveness to some policy measures that influence current income.

The planning horizon of consumers in the lower-middle-income economies is longer, averaging about 1.88 years. In the lower-middle and upper-middle economies, the better developed credit markets and the existence of some safety nets make it possible for consumers to plan longer than their counterparts in low-income economies. Thus, the planning horizon in the lower- and upper-middle-income economies ranges from about 1.12 to 3 years. It is noted that the adjustment process between actual consumer spending and a desired long-run position in the current period was shorter in low-income economies than both the lower-middle and upper-middle-income economies. This may be explained by the fact that many consumers in very poor countries exist near subsistence levels and face relatively greater uncertainty about future income prospects than their counterparts in middle-income economies.

NOTES

1. The classification used by the World Bank is based on per capita income figures, though there is a close correspondence with other characteristics that capture different stages of the development process. The average per capita GNP for the low-income, lower-middle-income, and the upper-middle-income economies are $255.00, $1,328.20 and $1,435.70, respectively. These figures are computed from the World Bank's World Development Indicators (1998 CD-Rom).

2. The process will be without trend in Hall's formulation if the real interest rate and discount rate coincide. Note that Hall (1978) originally derived the random walk in level and used logs in his 1988 paper.

3. This test is more sophisticated and has not been as widely used as the two other tests mentioned previously. The results from Hansen and Singleton (1982), Mankiw, Rotemberg, and Summers (1985), and Bean (1986) reject the restrictions implied by the RW model.

4. This exponential utility function, reflects the case of constant absolute risk aversion (CARA) and has the property that the marginal utility of consumption is finite at zero consumption, implying that consumption can be negative along the optimal path. This is in contrast to the quadratic utility function, which implies increasing absolute risk aversion, that is, a willingness to pay more to avoid a given bet as wealth increases. The case of the constant risk aversion (CRRA) utility function rules out negative consumption, but there is difficulty in obtaining a closed form solution.

5. For instance, $\Sigma_{i=1}^{T-t} (1 + r)^{-i} = \Sigma_{i=0}^{T-t-1} (1 + i)^{-i-1}$.

6. These results are consistent with Baffoe-Bonnie and Khayum (1997). That study indicated that consumption behavior is related to the level of development. In particular, the length of the planning horizon was found to be shorter for less developed countries (1.3 years for both lower-income and middle-income developing countries) than more developed countries. These results are reassuring and strengthen our previous results because this study employs a longer sample period, and more countries.

REFERENCES

Baffoe-Bonnie, J., and M. Khayum. 1997. "Economic Development, Life-Cycle Consumption, and Planning Horizon." *International Economic Journal* 11: 17–37.

Bean, C. R. 1986. "The Estimation of 'Surprise' Models and the 'Surprise' Consumption Function." *Review of Economic Studies* 53: 497–516.

Blanchard, O. 1985. "Debt, Deficits, and Finite Horizons." *Journal of Political Economy* 93: 223–47.

Blanchard, O., and S. Fisher. 1989. *Lectures on Macroeconomics*. Cambridge, MA: MIT Press.

Corden, M. 1985. *The Relevance for Developing Countries of Recent Development in Macroeconomic Theory*. Cambridge, MA: Harvard University Press.

Davidson, J.E.H., D.F. Hendry, F. Srba, and S. Yeo. 1978. "Econometric Modeling of the Aggregate Time Series Relation Between Consumption and Income in the U.K." *Economic Journal* 88: 661–92.

Davis, E.P. 1984. "The Consumption Function in Macroeconomic Models: A Comparative Study." *Applied Economics* 16: 799–838.

Engle, R.F. and C.W.J. Granger. 1987. "Co-integration and Error Correction: Representation, Estimation and Testing," *Econometrica* 55: 251–276.

Granger, C.W.J. 1986. "Developments in the Study of Cointegrated Economic Variables." *Oxford Bulletin of Economics and Statistics* 48: 213–28.

Hall, R.E. 1978. "Stochastic Implications of the Life Cycle-Permanent Income Hypothesis: Theory and Evidence." *Journal of Political Economy* 86: 971–87.

———. 1988. "Intertemporal Substitution in Consumption." *Journal of Political Economy* 96: 339–57.

Hansen, L.P., and Singleton, K.J. 1982. "Generalized Instrumental Variables Estimation of Non-Linear Rational Expectations Models." *Econometrica,* 50: 1269–1286.

Haque, N., and P. Montiel. 1989. "Consumption in Developing Countries: Test for Liquidity Constraints and Finite Horizons." *Review of Economics and Statistics* 71: 408–15.

Haug, A. 1991. "The Random Walk Hypothesis of Consumption and Time Aggregation." *Journal of Macroeconomics* 13: 691–700.

Hayashi, F. 1982. "The Permanent Income Hypothesis: Estimation and Testing by Instrumental Variables." *Journal of Political Economy* 86: 971–87.

Hendry, D.F. 1983. "Econometric Modeling: The 'Consumption Function' in Retrospect." *Scottish Journal of Political Economy* 30: 193–220.

Hubbard, R.G., and K.L. Judd. 1986. "Liquidity Constraints, Fiscal Policy, and Consumption." *Brookings Papers on Economic Activity*, 1–59.

I.M.F. International Financial Statistics. Various Issues.

King, M.A. 1986. "Capital Market 'Imperfections' and the Consumption Function." *Scandinavian Journal of Economics* 88: 59–80.

Mankiw, N.G., J.J. Rotemberg, and L.H. Summers. 1985. "Intertemporal Substitution in Macroeconomics." *Quarterly Journal of Economics* 100: 225–51.

Muellbauer, J. 1983. "Surprise in the Consumption Function." *Economic Journal* (Supplement) 93: 34–50.

Patterson, K.D. 1986. "The Stability of Some Annual Consumption Functions." *Oxford Economic Papers* 38: 1–30.

Rossi, N. 1988. "Government Spending, the Real Interest Rate, and the Behavior of Liquidity-Constrained Consumers in Developing Countries." *International Monetary Fund Staff Papers* 35: 104–40.

Sargan, J.D. 1964. "Wages and Prices in the United Kingdom: A Study in Economic Methodology." In: *Econometric Analysis for National Economic Planning*, edited by P.E. Hart, G. Mills, and J.N. Whittaker. London: Butterworth, 25–64.

Spanos, A. 1986. *Statistical Foundations of Econometric Modeling*. Cambridge, UK: Cambridge University Press.

Wickens, M.R., and H. Molana. 1984. "Stochastic Life-Cycle Models with Varying Interest Rates and Prices." *Economic Journal* (Supplement) 94: 133–47.

Winder, C.C.A. 1988. *Modeling Intertemporal Consumer Behavior, Theoretical Results and Empirical Evidence*. Amsterdam: Free University Press.

World Bank 1998. World Development Indicators, CD-Rom Version.

Zuehlke, T., and J. Payne. 1989. "Tests of the Rational Expectations-Permanent Income Hypothesis for Developing Economies." *Journal of Macroeconomics* 11: 423–33.

14

Defense Spending and Economic Growth

Wimal Rankaduwa

INTRODUCTION

A vast majority of recent research on the economic impact of military spending has been focused on the net growth effect of defense spending. Over the last three decades or so, the empirical research into the issue has produced at least three schools of thought.[1] The first school argues that defense spending leads to increases in purchasing power and aggregate demand, and improvements in infrastructure and human capital and thereby generates positive direct and indirect effects, which outweigh the negative effects. Therefore, the net effect on economic growth is positive. The second school maintains that the net effect is negative as the defense spending reduces savings and "crowds out" private investment. The third school argues that defense spending has no significant positive or negative net effect on economic growth. In view of these arguments, one cannot simply rule out the possibility of positive, negative, or zero net growth effect of defense spending in any given country without a thorough empirical investigation.

Sri Lanka provides an invaluable case for an empirical investigation into the role of defense spending in economic growth in the context of developing countries. Mainly due to an internal military and political turmoil, Sri Lanka experienced dramatic increases in its defense budget in the recent past. Table 14.1 presents some data about Sri Lanka's military spending and other important macroeconomic variables. In the 1960s Sri Lanka's average annual growth rate of defense spending was in fact negative. The entries in Table 14.1 clearly show that the defense spending decreased at an annual rate of 0.45 percent during the 1960s. During the period 1970–1976, defense spending grew only at a mean annual rate of 8.24 percent. The mean annual growth rate increased to 13.12 percent during the period 1977–1983. A more dramatic mean annual growth rate of 33.85 percent was recorded between 1984 and 1996 as a direct consequence of the "militarization of Sri Lanka's ethnic conflict." The government reaction

Table 14.1
Period Means of Some Important Variables (%)

	1961-69	1970-76	1977-83	1984-96	1961-83
y	4.759	5.741	5.562	4.831	5.302
gl	2.395	1.633	1.683	1.326	1.946
I/Y	15.046	16.365	25.930	24.080	18.760
M	-0.449	8.241	13.124	33.849	6.678
N	5.578	5.064	11.710	2.068	7.288
p	4.552	6.289	5.287	5.444	5.304
g	5.410	5.062	11.625	3.899	7.196
M/G	2.877	3.243	2.014	11.066	2.726
N/G	97.123	96.757	97.986	88.934	97.274
G/Y	28.567	26.414	33.717	29.712	29.479
M/Y	0.823	0.867	0.662	3.228	0.787
N/Y	27.745	25.547	33.055	26.484	28.692

Notes: Y = real GDP, I = real investment, M = defense spending, N = nondefense spending, G = total government spending, gl = growth rate of population, y, m, n are the growth rates of Y, M, and N.

to two violent upheavals by an extremist Marxist organization named Janatha Vimukthi Peramuna (JVP), once in the early 1970s and then in the late 1980s, and to the military threat of the Liberation Tigers of Tamil Ealam (LTTE), a separatist guerilla force that has been waging a fierce war with the government since 1983, have been directly responsible for the increase in the defense budget during the last three decades. Even though defense spending has been rising, the country achieved impressive economic growth rates relative to many other South Asian countries, except for a very few years in the late 1980s. Many policy makers have argued that, had there been no military conflict, the economic growth rate could have been even higher. The basis for this argument is the belief that the net effect of defense spending on economic growth has been negative and enormously high in magnitude.

The main purpose of this chapter is to assess the effect of defense spending on economic growth in Sri Lanka. To the best of our knowledge, there has not been any comprehensive empirical study of the role of defense spending in Sri Lanka's economic growth. The few studies that included Sri Lanka in their samples have produced conflicting results. For instance, the results of the Mintz and Stevenson (1995) study show that defense spending does not have a statistically significant effect, negative or positive, on Sri Lanka's economic growth. The results of the LaCivita and Frederiksen (1991) study indicated that defense spending does not affect the economic growth rate though the economic growth rate affects defense spending in Sri Lanka. The studies that include a large number of countries often fail to recognize the country-specific features of individual cases, and to incorporate them into their analysis. We observe that Mintz and Stevenson (1995) is no exception in this regard, as for instance, they did not account for possible structural breaks arising out of political regime changes, and other factors, in their model. Therefore, in the present study, particular attention is paid to the possible structural breaks in the model due to changes in the political regime. In particular, we examine possible changes in the parameter estimates in 1983 as the country entered into a period of persistent military conflict between the government and the LTTE.

The chapter is organized as follows. The next section presents a description of the models, methodology, and data used. Then comes a section containing a discussion of estimated results, followed by a final section presenting conclusions.

THE MODEL, METHODOLOGY, AND DATA

The model employed in this study has been derived within the neoclassical framework of an aggregate production function. Feder (1982) developed a two-sector production function model, which includes export and nonexport sectors. Ram (1986) adopted Feder's model to develop a two-sector production function model, which includes government and nongovernment sectors. Mintz and Huang (1990, 1991) extended the Ram (1986) model to develop a three-sector model by disaggregating the government sector into military and nonmilitary sectors. This extended model, which we also employ in the present study, has now become widely used in the studies of defense spending and economic growth (see for example DeRouen, 1995; Heo, 1997; Mintz and Stevenson, 1995).

The model assumes that the economy is composed of a government sector and a nongovernment sector. The government sector is divided into two subsectors, defense and nondefense sectors. Thus the total output is the sum of defense output (M), nondefense output (N), and nongovernment output (P). Each of the sectoral outputs depends on the levels of two primary resources, labor (L) and capital (K), allocated to each sector, and the intersectoral productivities of a given resource are different. In addition, the nongovernment sector's production function includes the outputs of defense and nondefense sectors as inputs because of the externality effects generated by the two subsectors on the nongovernment sector. Formally, the model is given by the following set of equations.

Sectoral production functions are:

$$M = f_m(L_m, K_m) \tag{1a}$$

$$N = f_n(L_n, K_n) \tag{1b}$$

$$P = f_p(L_p, K_p, N, M) \tag{1c}$$

where the subscripts m, n, and p refer to defense, nondefense, and nongovernment sectors of the economy. L_i and K_i, $i = m, n, p$, are labor and capital allocated to the sector i, respectively. Total labor, L, total capital, K, and total output, Y, are given by

$$L = L_m(L_n, L_p) \tag{2a}$$

$$K = K_m + K_n + K_p) \tag{2b}$$

$$Y = M + N + P) \tag{2c}$$

The ratios of sectoral marginal productivities of labor and capital are given by

$$(\delta N/\delta L)/(\delta P/\delta L) = (\delta N/\delta K)/(\delta P/\delta K) = 1 + \lambda_n \tag{3a}$$

$$(\delta M/\delta L)/(\delta P/\delta L) = (\delta M/\delta K)/(\delta P/\delta K) = 1 + \lambda_m \tag{3b}$$

where λ_n and λ_m account for the productivity differentials between each of the defense and nondefense sectors and the nongovernment sector. A negative λ_m indicates that marginal productivities in the defense sector are lower than those of the nongovernment sector.

The following growth equation can be derived from the production functions using equations (2) and (3):

$$y = a_1\, gl + a_2(I/Y) + [(\lambda_n/1 + \lambda_n) + \theta_n]n(N/Y) + [(\lambda_m/1 + \lambda_m) + \theta_m]m(M/Y) \tag{4}$$

where y is the growth rate of total output, gl is the growth rate of the labor force, I is the level of investment, n is the growth rate of nondefense output, and m is the growth rate of defense output. The terms θ_n and θ_m represent the externality effects generated by the defense and nondefense sectors on the nongovernment sector.

With the assumption that the output elasticity of the nongovernment sector with respect to each of the defense and nondefense sectors is constant, the following growth model can be derived from equation (4).

$$y = a_1\, gl + a_2(I/Y) + a_3\, n(N/Y) + a_4\, n(P/Y) + a_5\, m(M/Y) + a_6\, m(P/Y) \tag{5}$$

where the coefficients a_4 and a_6 are the elasticities of nongovernment output with respect to nondefense and defense outputs, respectively. They are the measures of indirect or externality effects of nondefense and defense outputs on the nongovernment sector respectively. The coefficients $a_3 = (\lambda_n/1 + \lambda_n)$ and $a_5 = (\lambda_m/1 + \lambda_m)$ are the direct effects of nondefense and defense spending on the economic growth rate, respectively. The coefficient a_1 is the elasticity of nongovernment output with respect to labor, and a_2 is the marginal productivity of capital in the nongovernment sector. Adding a constant term a_0 and a stochastic error term U to equation (5) results in the following econometric formulation of the model:

$$y = a_0 + a_1\, gl + a_2(I/Y) + a_3\, n(N/Y) + a_4\, n(P/Y) + a_5\, m(M/Y) + a_6\, m(P/Y) + U \tag{6}$$

The model has a broad theoretical basis unlike many other models used in similar studies. The model also takes into account both the direct and indirect effects of defense and nondefense spending on economic growth. The defense sector generates a direct effect on growth by absorbing productive resources. Whether the direct effect is positive or negative depends on the intersectoral relative factor productivities of the defense and other sectors of the economy. The defense sector also generates an indirect effect on growth via its externality effect on the other sectors of the economy. For instance, higher defense spending generates higher demand for the outputs of other sectors and thereby affects overall economic growth.[2]

APPLICABILITY OF THE MODEL

The preceding model is estimated using the Ordinary Least Squares (OLS) method and the annual time series data covering the period 1961–1996. The sources of data are the various issues of the IMF International Financial Statistics and Annual Report and Annual Review of the Economy published by the Central Bank of Sri Lanka. The values of GDP at 1980 constant prices, government defense spending, and government nondefense spending are used as the measures of total output, defense output and nondefense output, respectively. In the absence of reliable data on the labor force, the population growth rate, a popular proxy in the related literature, is used in place of *gl*.

One of the most important assumptions of this model is that both M and N affect P, but P does not affect either M or N. The model also assumes that M does not affect N, and N does not affect M. In order to verify the applicability of these assumptions, we tested for possible causal relationships between the growth rates of M, N, and P, using Hsiao's (1981) version of Granger (1969) causality tests. A brief description of the test procedure is presented.

In the Granger test of causality, a variable Y is said to Granger-cause X if the prediction of current values of X can be improved by using the past values of Y. The standard Granger causality test involves the estimation of the following two equations in detecting causality between the two variables

$$X_t = \alpha + \sum_{i=1}^{Q} \alpha_i X_{t-i} + \sum_{i=1}^{Q} \beta_i Y_{t-i} + u_t \tag{7}$$

$$Y_t = \gamma_0 + \sum_{i=1}^{Q} \gamma_i Y_{t-i} + \sum_{i=1}^{Q} \delta_i X_{t-i} + V_t \tag{8}$$

where, X and Y are two stationary series and u and v are error terms. Note that the equations have identical lags. Hsiao suggested a two-step procedure that does not require identical lags in estimating each of the two equations. The two steps involved in estimating equation (1) are given by equations (9) and (10).

$$X_t = \alpha_0 + \sum_{i=1}^{Q} \alpha_1 X_{t-i} + u_{1it} \tag{9}$$

$$X_t = \alpha_0 \sum_{i=1}^{Q=q^*} \alpha_i X_{t-i} + \sum_{j=1}^{R} \beta_j Y_{t-j} + u_{2it} \qquad (10)$$

Step 1 is to estimate the dependent variable as a one-dimensional autoregressive process, varying the lag order progressively from 1 to Q, and to compute the Final Prediction Error (FPE), equation (11), corresponding to each lag order. The lag order that yields the minimum FPE, q^*, is considered for the second step.

$$\text{FPE}(q) = (T + q + r + 1)\ \text{SSE}/(T - q - r - 1)\ T \qquad (11)$$

Where, T = Number of observations, q = the order of lags varying from 1 to Q, and SSE = residual sum of squares.

In Step 2, X_t, is treated as the controlled variable with the lag order set at m^* and Y_t is treated as the manipulated variable. Equation (10) is estimated varying the lag order progressively from 1 to R, and FPE is calculated at each lag order using equation (12).

$$\text{FPE}(q^*, r) = (T + q^* + r + 1)\ \text{SSE}/(T - q^* - r - 1)\ T \qquad (12)$$

The estimated equation with the lag order r^*, which yields the minimum FPE, FPE (q^*, r^*), in this stage is considered for making inferences about the causality running from Y to X. The existence of a causal relation from Y to X is indicated by an FPE (q^*, r^*) smaller than FPE (q^*). The same two-step procedure is applied to equation (8) in detecting the causality from Y to X.

The application of the causality tests requires that the data series be stationary. Therefore, the Phillips-Perron unit root tests were applied to each of the data series, prior to testing for relationships between growth rates of M and N. As assumed in the model, there is also no causality running from the growth rate of P to the growth rate of N, and there is no causality from the growth rate of N to the growth rate of P either. These results provide a sufficient level of support in favor of the applicability of the model to Sri Lanka (see Table 14.2, Table 14.3, and Table 14.4).

Table 14.2
Tests of Causality Between Defense Spending (*M*) and Nongovernment Output (*P*)

	Test of Causality from P to M		Test of Causality from M to P	
Lag Order	FPE(q)	FPE(q*,r)	FPE(q)	FPE(q*,r)
1	0.26800*	0.27408*	0.009594*	0.010108
2	0.27416	0.27473	0.010000	0.010643
3	0.27425	0.29068	0.010538	0.009659
4	0.26980	0.28781	0.010715	0.009339*
5	0.28548	0.30005	0.011050	0.009601

Note: *indicates a minimum.

Table 14.3
Tests of Causality Between Nondefense Spending (*N*) and Nongovernment Output (*P*)

	Test of Causality from P to N		Test of Causality from N to P	
Lag Order	FPE(q)	FPE(q*,r)	FPE(q)	FPE(q*,r)
1	0.028681*	0.028871*	0.009594*	0.009749*
2	0.030327	0.030492	0.010000	0.010195
3	0.031947	0.032263	0.010538	0.010756
4	0.033622	0.033470	0.010715	0.011386
5	0.033069	0.034356	0.011050	0.010966

Note: *indicates a minimum.

Table 14.4
Tests of Causality Between Defense Spending (*M*) and Nondefense Spending (*N*)

	Test of Causality from N to M		Test of Causality from M to N	
Lag Order	FPE(q)	FPE(q*,r)	FPE(q)	FPE(q*,r)
1	0.26800*	0.28304*	0.028681*	0.030307
2	0.27416	0.29772	0.030327	0.031369
3	0.27425	0.31066	0.031947	0.030257
4	0.26980	0.32789	0.033622	0.032025
5	0.28548	0.34713	0.033069	0.029636*

Note: *indicates a minimum.

VALIDITY OF THE SINGLE EQUATION MODEL

Economic theory provides a strong basis for including conventional inputs such as labor and capital in a model of a production function. However, the validity of a single equation model may be questionable when the nonconventional inputs such as defense and nondefense spending are introduced into the model, because of the possible interdependence between the value of the output and each of these inputs. Defense and nondefense spending are sectoral outputs, which are already included in the value of total output *Y*. While the growth of defense and nondefense sectors contributes to the growth of total output, the growth of total output may in turn contribute to the growth of these sectors in many ways. Some researchers who adopted the approach of causality tests in determining the link between defense spending and output have detected bidirectional causal relationships between the two variables (LaCivita and Frederiksen, 1991). These results clearly indicate the existence of mutual interdependence in some countries.

The single equation production function models are appropriate only when the level of output depends on the levels of inputs, and not vice versa. The presence of mutual interdependence between output and defense or nondefense spending invalidates the single equation models, and highlights the need for estimating simultaneous equation models. In order to determine whether the single equation model used in this study is appropriate for Sri Lanka, we tested for causal relations between the growth rate of output (*y*) and the growth rates of defense and nondefense spending (*m* and *n* respectively). The results of these tests are reported in Table 14.5 and Table 14.6. These results indicate that there is a strong unidirectional causality from the growth of defense spending to output growth, but no bidirectional causality between output growth and the growth rates of defense and nondefense spending. Therefore, the single equation model is appropriate for the case of Sri Lanka. It should be noted here that our results do not support the results of the LaCivita and Frederiksen (1991) study, which indicate that defense spending does not affect the economic growth rate though the economic growth rate affects the defense spending in Sri Lanka.

Table 14.5
Tests of Causality Between Defense Spending (*M*) and Output Level (*Y*)

	Test of Causality from Y to M		Test of Causality from M to Y	
Lag Order	FPE(q)	FPE(q*,r)	FPE(q)	FPE(q*,r)
1	0.26800*	0.27139*	0.004038	0.004074
2	0.27416	0.28694	0.004268	0.004314
3	0.27425	0.30323	0.004509	0.002846
4	0.26980	0.31584	0.003849*	0.002835*
5	0.28548	0.32991	0.004062	0.002984

Note: *indicates a minimum.

Table 14.6
Tests of Causality Between Nondefense Spending (*N*) and Output Level (*Y*)

	Test of Causality from Y to N		Test of Causality from N to Y	
Lag Order	FPE(q)	FPE(q*,r)	FPE(q)	FPE(q*,r)
1	0.028681*	0.030321*	0.004038	0.004040*
2	0.030327	0.031991	0.004268	0.004243
3	0.031947	0.033462	0.004509	0.004476
4	0.033622	0.034873	0.003849*	0.004739
5	0.033069	0.036933	0.004062	0.004942

Note: *indicates a minimum.

ESTIMATION OF THE MODEL

As stated earlier, the model is estimated using time series data, and it is therefore necessary to examine time series properties such as unit roots and cointegration among the variables included in the model. Following the standard procedure, we first tested for unit roots in each of the data series using Phillips-Perron (1988) unit root tests. All of the series except the investment variable (*I/Y*) are integrated of order 0, I (0), and satisfy the stationarity requirement. However, all of the series are integrated of order 1, I (1). Using the Phillips tests on the residuals of the cointegrating regression, we then tested for cointegration among the variables. The calculated *Z* and *t* statistics for these tests using the cointegrating regression with constant and without trend are −35.195 and −5.9169, respectively. The asymptotic critical values for the *Z* and *t* tests are −38.4 and −4.42, respectively. The *t* test indicates evidence for a cointegrating relationship among the variables. Moreover, the calculated *Z* and *t* statistics for these tests using the cointegrating regression with constant and trend are −31.240 and −5.9257 respectively. The asymptotic critical values for the *Z* and *t* tests are −43.5 and −4.70, respectively. In this case too, the *t* test indicates evidence for cointegration among the variables. Therefore, based on our unit root tests and the cointegration tests, we concluded that the model would not lead to spurious results.

In order to accommodate for possible structural breaks that may have resulted from the communal riots in 1983 and the political regime changes in 1970, 1973, and 1977, the standard intercept and interaction dummy variables are used. A sequential search procedure followed in search of structural breaks using the dummy variable techniques led us to the modified version of the model, the estimated results of which are presented in Table 14.7.

Table 14.7
Estimated Results of the Modified Version of the Model

Variable Name	Estimated Coefficient	Standard Error	t-Ratio 22df
gl	- 1.490	3.836	-0.389
(I/Y)	0.165**	0.091	1.824
n(N/Y)	- 0.009	0.401	-0.023
n(P/Y)	0.064	0.233	0.275
m(M/Y)	-45.580*	8.704	-5.237
m(P/Y)	0.503*	0.088	5.713
D70	0.091*	0.026	3.427
D73	- 0.107*	0.027	-4.007
D84	0.091	0.073	1.236
D84*gl	- 8.707**	4.794	-1.816
D84*n(N/Y)	-24.127*	4.409	-5.473
D84*n(P/Y)	11.096*	1.778	6.241
D84*m(M /Y)	34.497*	7.190	4.798
Constant	0.056	0.088	0.635

Notes: *Statistically significant at 1% level.

**Statistically significant at 10% level.

D70, D73, and D84 are simple intercept dummy variables $R2=0.87$, $adjR2 = 0.80$, $DW = 2.4400$.

ANALYSIS OF RESULTS

The estimated results of the modified version of the model, which accommodates for the structural breaks in 1970, 1973, and 1984, are presented in Table 14.7. The entries in Table 14.9 are the coefficients calculated for three subperiods, 1961–1969, 1970–1983, and 1984–1996, using the results in Table 14.7. The results reported in Table 14.7 show that the dummy variable D84, which accounts for a possible change in the intercept in 1984, is statistically insignificant. Therefore, the equation was estimated excluding D84 and yielded the results reported in Table 14.8. The estimated coefficients for the three subperiods in this exercise are reported in Table 14.10. On the basis of our results, the entire period under study can easily be divided in two subperiods, 1961–1983 and 1984–1996. The following analysis of results focuses mainly on the results reported in Tables 14.8 and 14.10.

1961–1983

The estimated coefficients of the defense variables *m* (*M*/*Y*) and *m* (*P*/*Y*) are statistically significant at the 1 percent level for this subperiod. The negative coefficient of *m* (*M*/*Y*) indicates that the factor productivities in the defense sector were substantially lower than those of the nongovernment sector and therefore the direct effect of defense spending on economic growth was negative. Nevertheless, defense spending has had a positive indirect effect on economic growth as indicated by the positive estimated coefficient of *m* (*P*/*Y*), which measures the externality effect or the output elasticity of the nongovernment

Table 14.8
Estimated Results of the Modified Version of the Model Excluding D84

Variable Name	Estimated Coefficient	Standard Error	t-Ratio 23df
gl	- 5.444*	2.141	-2.543
(I/Y)	0.196*	0.088	2.220
n(N/Y)	0.091	0.397	0.228
n(P/Y)	0.037	0.235	0.158
m(M/Y)	-51.164*	7.518	-6.806
m(P/Y)	0.534*	0.085	6.280
D70	0.091*	0.026	3.427
D73	- 0.074*	0.023	-5.035
D84*gl	- 2.864 *	0.082	-3.501
D84*n(N/Y)	-25.667*	4.271	-6.010
D84*n(P/Y)	11.715*	1.723	6.801
D84*m(M /Y)	39.364*	6.080	6.474
Constant	0.146*	0.051	2.882

Notes: *Statistically significant at 1% level. D70 and D73 are simple intercept dummy variables R2 = 0.86, adjR2 = 0.79, DW = 2.4994.

Table 14.9
Estimated Coefficients of the Model for Various Periods

Variable	Estimated Coefficient 1961-69	1970-83	1984-96
gl	- 1.490	- 1.490	- 10.197*
I/Y	0.165**	0.165**	0.165**
n(N/Y)	- 0.009	- 0.009	- 24.136*
n(P/Y)	0.064	0.064	11.160*
m(M/Y)	-45.580*	-45.580*	- 11.083*
m(P/Y)	0.503*	0.503*	0.503*
Constant	0.056	0.040 **(1973-83)*** 0.147 **(1970-72)***	0.131

Notes: *Statistically significant at 1% level.
**Statistically significant at 10% level.

Table 14.10
Estimated Results of the Modified Version of the Model Excluding D84

Variable	Estimated Coefficient 1961-69	1970-83	1984-96
gl	- 5.444*	- 5.444*	- 8.308*
I/Y	0.196*	0.196*	0.196*
n (N/Y)	0.091	0.091	- 25.576*
n (P/Y)	0.037	0.037	11.752*
m (M/Y)	-51.164*	-51.164*	- 11.800*
m (P/Y)	0.534*	0.534*	0.534*
Constant	0.146	0.163 **(1973-83)*** 0.237 **(1970-72)***	0.163

Note: *Statistically significant at 1% level.

sector with respect to defense output. The indirect effect shows that every 1 percent change in defense output led to 0.5 percent change in nongovernment output in the same direction during the 1960s and 1970s. However, the estimated coefficients of n (N/Y) and n (P/Y) are not statistically significant for the period 1961–1983. These two coefficients are the estimates of relative marginal productivities of the nondefense sector relative to the nongovernment sector and the elasticity of nongovernment output with respect to nondefense output, respectively. The estimated labor elasticity of output in the nongovernment sector during the period 1961–1983 suggests that the marginal productivity of labor in that sector was negative.

The estimated coefficient of n (N/Y), which measures the relative factor productivity of the nondefense sector relative to the nongovernment sector, indicates that the intersectoral productivity differential between the nondefense and nongovernment sectors is not significantly different from zero for the period 1961–1983. This implies that the direct effect of nondefense spending on economic growth was not a significant determinant of economic growth before

1983. The estimated coefficient of *n* (*P*/*Y*), which measures the elasticity of nongovernment output with respect to nondefense output, shows that the indirect effect of nondefense spending is also not significantly different from zero during this period. Based on these results, one can safely conclude that nondefense spending was not a significant determinant of Sri Lanka's economic growth during the 1960s and 1970s. This is not a surprising result in view of the fact that nondefense spending, a large portion of which has been rather welfare-oriented, could have made only a minimal contribution to short-term economic growth.

Sri Lanka has been well recognized in the development literature for its remarkable achievements in the field of social welfare despite relatively low economic growth rates realized since political independence in 1948. The positive role played by government welfare spending in these achievements has also been widely acknowledged both domestically and internationally. However, it has been argued that Sri Lanka's commitment to welfarism has severely constrained the government's ability to allocate resources for promoting economic growth. Our results clearly indicate that the direct effect of nondefense spending had not been a significant determinant of economic growth until 1983. The estimated coefficient, which accounts for the indirect effect of nondefense spending, is statistically significant only after 1984. For most of the period under this study, both the direct and indirect effects of nondefense spending were not statistically significant determinants of economic growth. We note that the direct effect had in fact been negative, though statistically insignificant, until 1983.

In an interesting article on Sri Lanka's welfarism, Osmani (1994) challenged the widely held view that in Sri Lanka there had been a trade-off between welfare spending and savings or investment during the 1970s. Instead, Osmani (1994) argued that the trade-off had in fact been between military (defense) and welfare spending. Our results show that, during the 1970s, defense spending had a substantially larger adverse net effect on growth than nondefense spending. Therefore, if one accepts Osmani's position, in light of our results, it can be argued that increasing welfare spending at the expense of defense spending in the 1970s would have been more favorable toward economic growth. However, as the marginal productivity of capital in the nongovernment sector was much higher than that of defense and nondefense sectors, diverting resources from defense to investment in the nongovernment sector would have been even more favorable in promoting economic growth.

1984–1996

Table 14.8 shows that all of the estimated coefficients are statistically significant at the 1 percent level for the subperiod 1984–1996. Our results show that there had been significant changes in both of the direct effects of defense and nondefense spending, the indirect effect of nondefense spending, and the labor elasticity of nongovernment output. The labor elasticity of nongovernment output and both of the direct and indirect effects of nondefense spending, which are not significant for the previous subperiod, are also statistically significant at the 1 percent level. The fact that the coefficient of *gl* is negative and significant at the 1 percent level indicates that the marginal productivity of labor and hence, the labor elasticity of output, both have been negative in the nongovernment sector during the post-1983 period.

During this period the direct effect of defense spending continued to be negative, but decreased from 51.164 to 11.8 in magnitude, indicating that the productivity differential between defense and nondefense sectors has decreased. The indirect effect of defense spending did not change significantly after 1983, and thus remained the same for the entire period. However, both the direct and indirect effects of nondefense spending recorded remarkable changes as the former changed from zero to −25.576 and the latter increased from zero to 11.752.

These changes indicate that the intersectoral productivity differential between the nondefense and nongovernment sectors has increased and the output elasticity of nongovernment sector with respect to nondefense spending has increased. The indirect effect of 11.752 shows that for every 1 percent change in nondefense spending, there is an 11.752 percent change in nongovernment output in the same direction. However, this positive indirect effect is much smaller than the estimated negative direct effect.

Based on the results discussed so far, we conclude that defense spending has an enormous negative impact on Sri Lanka's economic growth. Moreover, the fact that the direct effects of defense and nondefense spending are negative and larger than their respective indirect effects indicates that the net effect of total government spending on Sri Lanka's economic growth has been negative. These results seem to contradict the findings in Ram (1986) for Sri Lanka, which indicate that the net effect of total government spending has a positive net effect on economic growth.

CONCLUDING REMARKS

In this chapter, an empirical examination of the impact of defense spending on the economic growth of Sri Lanka has been undertaken using a model developed within the framework of an aggregate production function. The model incorporates both direct and indirect effects of defense and nondefense spending on economic growth along with possible structural breaks due to political regime changes and the "militarization of ethnic conflict." The time series properties of the data and the validity of the model estimated is verified using the standard tests of unit roots, cointegration, and causality.

In contrast to the findings for Sri Lanka in such studies as Mintz and Stevenson (1995) and LaCivita and Frederiksen (1991), this study finds that defense spending has been a statistically significant determinant of economic growth. Both the estimated direct and indirect effects of military spending are statistically significant at the 1 percent level for the entire period under this study. These results clearly indicate that both the direct and indirect effects of defense spending have been significant determinants of Sri Lanka's economic growth. We note that the estimated direct effect of defense spending is the highest of all the estimated parameters for the period 1961–1983 and was negative for the entire period. The indirect effect of defense spending has always been positive. Nevertheless, the net effect of defense spending has clearly been negative, as the positive indirect effect is far smaller than the negative direct effect. This result clearly supports the view that the net effect of defense spending is negative in many developing countries.

The nondefense spending was not a significant determinant of Sri Lanka's economic growth during the period 1961–1983 as both the direct and indirect effects of nondefense spending were not significantly different from zero. However, during the post-1983 period, nondefense spending became a significant determinant, as both the estimated direct and indirect effects are statistically significant at the 1 percent level. During this period, the negative direct effect of nondefense spending has been much larger than the negative direct effect of defense spending. Furthermore, the indirect effect of nondefense spending has also been much larger than that of defense spending.

As the net effect of defense spending is negative, it can easily be argued that the increasing defense spending has been significantly costly in terms of economic growth for Sri Lanka during the last four decades. Before 1983, this negative impact had been far greater than that of the period after 1983. During the period before 1983, diverting resources from defense spending to nondefense spending would have been more favorable toward economic growth. However, since 1984 the same practice is not as favorable as before, because the nondefense spending also generates a large net negative impact on economic growth. Therefore, unless the structure of nondefense spending has drastically changed so that growth-oriented spending has significantly increased, the increases in nondefense spending by reducing military spending would not promote economic growth. Of course, it is necessary to reduce defense spending in order to promote economic growth in the country, but it is also necessary to change the growth-oriented and welfare-oriented mix of the nondefense spending to ensure higher growth rates. In other words, a drastic restructuring of total government spending is necessary for faster economic growth in the future. Finding a political solution to the long-lasting military conflict would definitely be a major step toward such a structural change in government spending.

A comprehensive assessment of the economic impact of defense and nondefense spending requires further disaggregation of these two categories of spending and a detailed analysis of the multiplier effects of each of those disggregated components. Such an empirical analysis may be undertaken within the framework of an economy-wide macroeconometric model represented by a simultaneous system of equations. The methodology of this paper, which employs a single equation model of an aggregate production function for estimating overall direct and indirect effects of defense and nondefense spending, does not permit such a comprehensive analysis. However, the estimated model in the present study can be used to carry out simulation experiments to evaluate the net growth impact of changes in the defense and nondefense composition of government spending. For instance, a simulation experiment may be designed under a set of plausible assumptions, to evaluate the overall growth impact if the share of defense spending had in fact been growing at a moderate pre-1983 rate of growth during the post-1983 period.

NOTES

1. A good discussion of various theories of the growth effects of defense spending is found in Park (1993).
2. A complete description of the derivation of the model is available from the author.

REFERENCES

Central Bank of Sri Lanka. *Annual Report*. Various Issues.
Central Bank of Sri Lanka. *Annual Review of the Economy*. Various Issues.
DeRouen, Karl R., Jr. 1995. "Arab-Israeli Defence Spending and Economic Growth." *Conflict Management and Peace Science* 14(1): 25–47.
Feder, G. 1982. "On Exports and Economic Growth." *Journal of Development Economics* 12 (1): 59–73.
Granger, C.W.J. 1969. "Investigating Causal Relation by Econometric and Cross-sectional Method." *Econometrica* 37: 424–38.
Heo, U. 1997. "The Political Economy of Defence Spending in South Korea." *Journal of Peace Research* 34(1): 483–90.
Hsiao, C. 1981. "Autoregressive Modelling and Money Income Causality Detection." *Journal of Monetary Economics* 7: 85–106.
IMF, *International Financial Statistics*, Year Book 1994.
LaCivita, C.J, and P.C. Frederiksen. 1991. "Defence Spending and Economic Growth: An Alternative Approach to the Causality Issue." *Journal of Development Economics* 35: 117–26.
Mintz, A., and C. Huang. 1990. "Defense Expenditures, Economic Growth and the Peace Dividend." *American Political Science Review* 84(4): 1283–93.
Mintz, A., and C. Huang. 1991. "Guns Versus Butter: The Indirect Link," *American Journal of Political Science* 35(3):738–757.
Mintz, A., and R.T. Stevenson. 1995. "Defence Expenditures, Economic Growth, and the Peace Dividend." *Journal of Conflict Resolution* 39(2): 283–305.
Osmani, S.R.. 1994. "Is There a Conflict Between Growth and Welfarism? The Significance of the Sri Lanka Debate." *Development and Change* 25: 387–421.
Park, K.Y. 1993. "Pouring New Wine into Fresh Wineskins: Defence Spending and Economic Growth in LDCs with Application to South Korea." *Journal of Peace Research* 30(1): 79–93.
Phillips, P., and P. Perron. 1988. "Testing for a Unit Root in Times Series Regression." *Biometrica* 75: 333–46.
Ram, R. 1986. "Government Size and Economic Growth: A New Framework and Some Evidence from Cross-Section and Time-Series Data." *American Economic Review* 76: 191–203.

Index

About the Editors and Contributors

JAMES C.W. AHIAKPOR is a Professor of Economics at California State University, Hayward, where he also served as Department Chair from January 1994 to August 2000. He received his Ph.D. from the University of Toronto in 1981. Dr. Ahiakpor's main areas of research are economic development, history of economic thought, and monetary theory. His major publications have appeared in the *Journal of Development Economics, Economic Development and Cultural Change, Southern Economic Journal, History of Political Economy, Journal of the History of Economic Thought, American Journal of Economics and Sociology, International Organization*, and the *Journal of Modern African Studies*. He is the author of *Multinationals and Economic Development: An Integration of Competing Theories* (1990); *The Economic Consequences of Political Independence: The Case of Bermuda* (1989); and editor of *Keynes and the Classics Reconsidered* (1998). He is currently writing *Classical Macroeconomics: Some Modern Variations and Distortions*.

GEORGE B.N. AYITTEY is Associate Professor of Economics at the American University and President of the Free Africa Foundation. Dr. Ayittey is a former National Fellow at the Hoover Institution, Stanford University, and a Bradley Scholar at the Heritage Foundation, Washington, D.C. His publications include *Indigenous African Institutions* (1991); *Africa Betrayed* (1992); *The Blueprint for Ghana's Economic Recovery* (1997); and *Africa in Chaos* (1998). He has written numerous articles on Africa and the Third World, which have appeared in different reputable journals. He has appeared on several radio talk shows, and TV programs in North America. He has testified before U.S. congressional committees about the Third World Debt Crisis (February 1987), Foreign Aid to Africa (November 1991, February 23, 1993) and South Africa (March 1992) and served as a consultant to several organizations, including the World Bank, US AID, and International Council on Metals and the Environment (ICME).

JOHN BAFFOE-BONNIE is Associate Professor of Economics at Pennsylvania State University, Delaware County Campus. He received his Ph.D. from Dalhousie University, Canada, in 1985. Prior to joining Pennsylvania State University in 1988, he held faculty positions at the University of Manitoba and Drexel University in Philadelphia. His research interests have been in the areas of labor economics, applied macroeconomics, and development economics. Having specialized in labor economics and econometrics, he has geared much of his research toward an application of econometric techniques to analyze issues in the labor market, real estate market, and the economy as a whole. In the area of labor economics, his research has focused on labor market segmentation, efficiency wage models, transfer programs, and full-time/part-time issues, and topics on macroeconomics and development economics deal with issues of intertemporal consumption behavior in both developed and developing countries, and the dynamic effects of government policies. His research has yielded several publications in refereed journals. Dr. Baffoe-Bonnie is currently pursuing a collaborative research project with a faculty member in the Economics Department of the University of Ghana—a project sponsored by the University Office of International Programs of Pennsylvania State University.

FIDEL EZEALA-HARRISON is Professor of Economics at Jackson State University, and formerly Professor of Economics at the University of New Brunswick, Canada. With extensive research in applied microeconomic policy analysis, Dr. Ezeala-Harrison has published dozens of research papers in the fields of International Economic Development, Labor, and the environment; and is the author of *Theory and Policy of International Competitiveness* (Praeger, 1999), *Economic Development: Theory and Policy Applications* (Praeger, 1996), and co-editor of *Perspectives on Economic Development in Africa* (Praeger, 1994). During 1997, Dr. Ezeala-Harrison was a Visiting Research Associate on International Economic Growth and Development at the University of Newcastle, Australia, and a Visiting Professor at the Indonesian Institute of Management Studies, Jakarta, Indonesia. During 2000 he was Visiting Professor on International Competitiveness at Fujian Agricultural University, China.

JOHN GAFAR is Professor of Economics at Long Island University, a former Fulbright scholar and visiting scholar at Columbia University. Dr. Gafar has published extensively on the Caribbean region, in such academic journals as *Agricultural Economics, Applied Economics, Canadian Journal of Development Studies, Caribbean Studies, Journal of Latin American Studies, The Journal of Developing Areas, The Developing Economies, International Labor Review, Indian Economic Journal, Indian Journal of Agricultural Economics, The Indian*

Journal of Economics, International Journal of Development Planning Literature, and *Singapore Economic Review.*

KAZI NAZRUL ISLAM is a Ph.D. candidate in Economics at the University of Manitoba, Canada. He is currently a lecturer in the economics department of the University of New Brunswick, Saint John. His research is on financial development and the financial crisis of Thailand.

MOHAMMED KHAYUM is Professor of Economics at the School of Business, University of Southern Indiana. He is the chair of the Economics and Finance Department, and his principal areas of research and teaching include global economic issues, business cycles and economic growth, financial systems, risk behavior, and the role of the service sector. He has published on topics such as service sector growth, consumer planning horizons, exchange rate and inflation forecasts, purchasing power parity, and options pricing. He has published most recently in *Applied Economics, The Service Industries Journal, Journal of Economics and Finance, Multinational Business Review*, and the *International Economic Journal*. In other professional activities, Dr. Khayum conducts a quarterly regional business outlook survey and is a consultant on issues of regional economic development. Dr. Khayum received his Ph.D. from the Fox School of Business, Temple University.

MWANGI S. KIMENYI has been Associate Professor of Economics at the University of Connecticut since 1991. Between 1987 and 1991, he was Assistant Professor of Economics at the University of Mississippi. He received his Ph.D. in economics from George Mason University. He is Vice President and Chief Financial Controller of the African Educational Foundation for Public Policy and Market Process, Inc., and Managing Director of the African Institute for Public Policy and Market Process, Kenya. He is the author of *Economics of Poverty, Discrimination and Public Policy* (1995); *Ethnic Diversity, Liberty and the State: The African Dilemma* (1998); and co-editor of *Ethnicity and Governance in the Third World* (2001). He is the author of over sixty scholarly articles. His current research focuses on public choice and institutional reforms in developing countries.

JOHN LOXLEY is Professor of Economics at the University of Manitoba. Dr. Loxley's interests are in economic development, international finance, and community economic development. He has lived and worked in a number of developing countries and is currently the Chairman of the Board of Directors of the North-South Institute, Ottawa. His publications include *Debt and Disorder: Finance for External Development* (1986) and *Interdependence, Disequilibrium and Growth: Reflections on the Political Economy of North-South Relations at the Turn of the Century* (1999). He was a member of the Commonwealth Expert Group on protecting countries against the destabilizing effects of volatile capital flows in 1998. He is an advisor to the Minister of Finance, Province of Manitoba. He was the founding chair of CHOICES, a Winnipeg coalition for social justice and co-coordinated the Alternative Federal Budget exercise from 1995 to 2000.

JOHN MUKUM MBAKU is Willard L. Eccles Professor of Economics and John S. Hinckley Fellow at Weber State University, Ogden, Utah, and Associate Editor (Africa), *Journal of Third World Studies*. Dr. Mbaku is also President of the African Educational Foundation for Public Policy and Market Process, Inc. He was born in Cameroon and received the Ph.D. degree in economics from the University of Georgia in 1985. His present research interests are in public choice, constitutional political economy, trade integration, intergroup relations, and institutional reforms in Africa. He is the author of *Institutions and Reform in Africa: The Public Choice Perspective* (Praeger, 1997) and *Bureaucratic and Political Corruption in Africa: The Public Choice Perspective* (2000); editor of *Corruption and the Crisis of Institutional Reforms in Africa* (1998), and of *Preparing Africa for the Twenty-First Century: Strategies for Peaceful Coexistence and Sustainable Development* (1999). He is a co-editor of three books: *Multiparty Democracy and Political Change: Constraints to Democratization in Africa* (1998); *Institutions and Collective Choice in Developing Countries: Applications of the Theory of Public Choice* (1999); and *Ethnicity and Governance in the Third World* (2001).

RICHARD E. MSHOMBA is Associate Professor of Economics at La Salle University in Philadelphia, Pennsylvania. Dr. Mshomba was born and raised in rural Tanzania and worked for the government of Tanzania for nine years. His areas of research are international economics and development economics with a focus on sub-Saharan Africa. His book, *Africa in the Global Economy* (2000), was selected as a Choice Outstanding Academic Book. Many of his works have been published in journals and newspapers such as the *Eastern Africa Economic Review* and *The Arusha Times*. He has been a guest analyst on National Public Radio and Voice of America and has made numerous presentations at conferences, universities, community groups, and elementary and high schools.

WIMAL RANKADUWA is Associate Professor of Economics at the University of Prince Edward Island in Charlottetown, Prince Edward Island, Canada. Dr. Rankaduwa is also an Honorary Adjunct Professor of Economics in the Faculty of Graduate Studies at Dalhousie University in Halifax, Nova Scotia, Canada. Macroeconometric modelling of developing economies, and issues of economic development are his major areas of research. His current research focuses on the outcomes of economic liberalization in developing countries under globalization.

HENRY REMPEL is Professor of Economics at the University of Manitoba, Canada. His research on the dynamics of population growth, food supply, and environment in Africa was initiated in 1991–1993, when he served as Professor and Head of the Department of Economics at the University of Botswana. Dr. Rempel has published two books, and several articles in different refereed journals, including the *Journal of Development Economics, Oxford Bulletin of Economics and Statistics, World Development*, and *Journal of Development Studies*. He has also served as the editor of the *Canadian Journal of Economics*. Dr. Rempel was a senior policy analyst for the China Program sponsored by the Canadian International Development Agency. He was a visiting research scholar at the International Institute for Applied Systems Analysis in Laxenburg, Austria. He has been a consultant for many agencies, and a team leader of twenty-two development planning and project evaluation missions in eleven developing countries.

DAVID SHAPIRO is Professor of Economics, Demography, and Women's Studies at Pennsylvania State University. He received a Ph.D. in Economics from Princeton University in 1972, and following a stint at Ohio State University, he has been affiliated with Penn State since 1980. During his career, he has spent more than five years in sub-Saharan Africa, mostly in Kinshasa, capital of the Democratic Republic of the Congo, engaged in teaching, development work, and research. His research has been primarily in the areas of demography and labor economics. Dr. Shapiro has authored or coauthored two books and more than fifty journal articles and chapters in books. Since the late 1980s, he has worked with Basile Tambashe, and they have recently published *Women's Education, Employment, and Fertility: Kinshasa in Transition*. They are presently continuing their collaboration via ongoing research on the fertility transition in sub-Saharan Africa.

BASILE OLEKO TAMBASHE is Research Associate Professor in the Department of International Health and Development, School of Public Health and Tropical Medicine, and affiliate faculty at the Payson Center for International Development and Technology Transfer, Tulane University. He earned his Ph.D. in Demography in 1984 from the Vrije Universiteit Brussel in Belgium. Prior to joining Tulane in 1995, he served on the faculty of both the Department of Demography and the School of Public Health of the University of Kinshasa in the Democratic Republic of the Congo. From 1995 to 2001 in West Africa, he served as the Chief of Party and Director of the Operations Research component of the USAID-funded Family Health and AIDS in West and Central Africa Project. His research focus has been on the dynamics of reproductive behaviors in urban sub-Saharan Africa and on impact evaluation of HIV/AIDS and reproductive health programs. He counts, as author or coauthor, more than thirty journal articles, book chapters, and one monograph. His most recent publication, with Dr. David Shapiro, is *Women's Education, Employment, and Fertility: Kinshasa in Transition*.